Solicitors and their
Business Clients

Solicitors and their Business Clients

Fifth Edition

A. G. King MA, Solicitor (Hons)

Director of Education, Clifford Chance

Formerly Senior Lecturer, College of Law, Lancaster Gate, London W2

and

J. S. Barlow MA (Cantab), LLM (London), Solicitor

Principal Lecturer, College of Law, York

BLACKSTONE
PRESS LIMITED

This edition published in Great Britain 1990 by Blackstone Press Limited, 9–15 Aldine Street, London W12 8AW. Telephone: 081–740 1173

© Blackstone Press Limited, 1990
First edition 1982
Reprinted 1983
Reprinted 1984
Second edition 1985
Third edition 1986
Reprinted 1987
Fourth edition 1989
Fifth edition 1990
Reprinted 1992

ISBN: 1 85431 075 5

British Library Cataloguing in Publication Data
A CIP catalogue record for this book is available from the British Library

Typeset by Murdoch Evans Partnership, Tonbridge, Kent
Printed in Great Britain by Livesey Ltd, Shrewsbury

Contents

1 Introduction   2 Corporations   3 Sources of company law   4 Registration
5 Types of registered company   6 Public and private companies   7 Separate
legal personality   8 'Lifting the veil of incorporation'

1 Introduction   2 Steps leading to incorporation   3 The certificate of
incorporation   4 Steps necessary after incorporation 5 Methods of
incorporation   6 Pre-incorporation contracts

1 Division of powers within a company 2Appointment of directors
3 Removal of directors from office 4Alternate directors 5 Shadow
directors   6 Powers of directors   7 Directors' duties   8 Statutory provisions
concerning directors   9 Managing directors   10 Delegation by directors
11 The company secretary   12 Auditors

1 Membership of a company   2 The register of members   3 Powers and
duties of members   4 Meetings

1 Introduction   2 Issue of shares   3 Share capital   4 Financial assistance by
company for purchase of shares   5 Classes of shares   6 Profits   7 Procedure
for declaring and paying a dividend   8 Restrictions on sources of dividends
9 The power to borrow   10 Secured loans   11 Registration of charges   12
Priority of charges   13 Repayment of charges   14 Remedies of debenture-
holders   15 Receivers   16 Position of debenture-holders   17 Steps to be
taken by a lender to a company

Preface

The fifth edition of Solicitors and their Business Clients, like the first four, is intended principally for students of the Law Society's Final Examination. The book covers the whole of the syllabus for the Business Organisations and Insolvency paper in that examination.

Since the publication of the fourth edition, there have been a considerable number of developments in company law, in particular the Companies Act 1989. At the time of writing, that Act is only partly in force. This book is, however, written on the basis that the whole of the Act is in force. It is expected that this will be so by Spring 1991.

We would like to thank Mr & Mrs G. W. T. King whose combined efforts to convert many of the manuscript alterations into typescript are much appreciated.

We would also like to thank our colleagues Michael Petley, Lesley King, Lorraine Redman, Rachel Hawes, Nick Olley and Amanda Seager for a large number of helpful suggestions about the text (any errors are, of course, our own) and our publishers (especially Heather Saward and Alistair MacQueen) for again displaying their customary efficiency.

A. G. King
J. S. Barlow
August 1990

Table of Cases

Table of Statutes

Table of Statutory Instruments

List of Abbreviations

BNA 1985	Business Names Act 1985
CA 1985	Companies Act 1985
CA 1989	Companies Act 1989
CGTA 1979	Capital Gains Tax Act 1979
IA 1986	Insolvency Act 1986
IHTA 1984	Inheritance Tax Act 1984
EP(C) A 1978	Employment Protection (Consolidation) Act 1978
FA	Finance Act
ICTA 1988	Income and Corporation Taxes Act 1988
MHA 1983	Mental Health Act 1983
PA 1890	Partnership Act 1890
TMA 1970	Taxes Management Act 1970

Part I   Company Law

1   Introduction to Company Law

1   INTRODUCTION

This book is concerned almost exclusively with the formation and administration of private companies and partnerships which run businesses and with the question of whether a company is preferable to a partnership as a means of running a particular business.

The purpose of this chapter is to explain where a private company fits into the rather complex pattern of institutions which the law has created. A comparison will also be made between private and public companies (the latter are not dealt with elsewhere in the book) and the nature of the legal personality of a company will be considered.

2   CORPORATIONS

A 'company' is in law a corporation, that is, an artificial legal 'person' with rights and obligations distinct from those of its members. A corporation may be a corporation sole (which consists of one person acting in an official capacity — for example, a bishop) or a corporation aggregate (which consists of several natural persons). Companies are corporations aggregate. Business associations were occasionally made corporations by Royal Charter from about the sixteenth century (for example, the Honorable East India Company), but until the industrial revolution few businesses were incorporated. With the growth of the canal and railway systems incorporations were permitted in increasing numbers. Incorporation was appropriate for such businesses; first, because they needed to acquire investments from large numbers of people, and, second, because they required powers of compulsory purchase. In order to grant the company the compulsory purchase powers Acts of Parliament were passed. Since the passing of the Joint Stock Companies Act 1844 it has been possible to form a corporation to run a business without an Act of Parliament. The vast majority of corporations are now companies formed under the Companies Act 1985 or under earlier legislation superseded by that Act.

3   SOURCES OF COMPANY LAW

3.1   Company legislation

The Companies Act 1985 is the most important source of company law. The 1985 Act is a consolidating act which brings together legislation contained in a number of earlier Companies Acts and a few other pieces of legislation dealing with company law. The 1985 Act has been amended in significant respects by the Insolvency Act 1986 and by the Companies Act 1989.

The 1985 Act applies throughout Great Britain although a number of provisions apply only to Scotland or only to England and Wales. Northern Ireland has its own legislation which is substantially the same as the British legislation.

Some of the most basic rules concerning companies result from judicial decisions and do not appear in the Act. Of special importance are the rules of equity relating to fiduciary relationships (which play a major part in determining the legal position of company directors) and the rule in *Foss* v *Harbottle*. There are also hundreds of reported cases in which Companies Acts have been interpreted by the courts. Most of these cases were decided before the 1985 Act came into force but continue to be authoritative interpretations of the consolidated legislation.

3.2 Tax legislation

The taxation of companies is largely dealt with in the Income and Corporation Taxes Act 1988 as amended by the Finance Acts 1988 and 1989. Companies' capital gains are largely dealt with in accordance with the Capital Gains Tax Act 1979 as amended. Again, many decisions of the courts have interpreted the meaning of this legislation.

3.3 The company's own regulations

Despite the vast amount of law which applies to companies, a great deal of freedom of choice is given to each individual company as to how it will be administered. This is both desirable and inevitable because of the widely differing circumstances in which each company operates. To provide for its own internal administration each company must have a set of regulations known as articles of association (Chapter 2). These may be specially prepared for the company by the draftsman who assists with its formation; however, the Companies Act provides for a model form of articles (Table A) and most of the regulations adopted by a company will follow that model. The provisions of Table A are contained in a statutory instrument (SI 1985 No. 805) which came into force with the 1985 Act. Companies formed before the 1985 Act usually have regulations based on earlier versions of Table A.

3.4 The general law

Finally, it is worth pointing out that the general law applies to companies as it applies to individuals, except to the extent that it has been modified by specific rules of company law. The general law of contract, for example, applies to companies with very few modifications, as does the law of tort, conveyancing and so on. This is really just a consequence of the fact that a company is a corporation and, therefore, in law a 'person' with legal rights and obligations.

4 REGISTRATION

The process by which a company is formed under the Companies Act is called registration. The steps to be taken are considered in the next chapter. For the moment it is sufficient to point out that when the Registrar of Companies issues the certificate of incorporation, '. . . the subscribers of the memorandum, together with such other persons as may from time to time become members of the company, shall be a body corporate by the name contained in the memorandum.' (s. 13(3) CA 1985).

For the purpose of registering companies and keeping the various records which must be filed by a registered company, the Department of Trade maintains offices in Edinburgh (for companies registered in Scotland) and in Cardiff (for companies registered in England and Wales). The officials responsible for those offices are called Registrars of Companies (in this book references to 'the Registrar' are references to the Registrar of Companies for England and Wales).

Certain records concerning unregistered companies and companies registered overseas must also be filed with the Registrar if the company carries on a business in this country but a consideration of the rules relating to these matters is beyond the scope of this book.

5 TYPES OF REGISTERED COMPANY

5.1 Companies limited by shares

The vast majority of companies registered under the Companies Act are companies 'limited by shares'. This means that the members (or shareholders — the terms are almost interchangeable) have a limited liability to pay the debts of the company. When new shares are issued by a company the person who takes the shares must agree to pay for them. Usually payment will be made immediately but sometimes the shares will be issued 'unpaid' or 'partly-paid', in which case payment must be made later. If the company goes into liquidation and is insolvent the members are liable to pay for their shares in full if they have not already done so. This really means that a member who has paid for his shares stands to lose his shares *but nothing more* on the insolvency of the company; a member who has not paid for his shares in full stands to lose his shares and the unpaid amount but nothing more.

The position of a shareholder in a limited company is quite different from the position of a member of a partnership. If a partnership business fails each of the partners stands to lose not only what he has invested but also any private wealth which he may have. Limited liability can be an enormous advantage to a businessman, although creditors (particularly those who have lent money to the company) may require personal guarantees of the company's debts from shareholders, thus reducing the advantage (this topic is considered further in Chapters 12 and 20).

5.2 Companies limited by guarantee

A small number of companies are limited by guarantee rather than by shares. This means that each member undertakes to pay a specified amount if the company is wound up while he is a member or within a year after he ceases to be a member. The main difference between this type of company and a company limited by shares is that the guarantee does not become payable until the company is wound up, whereas shares must be paid for either immediately or when the company requires payment.

Most companies limited by guarantee are charities or other non-trading companies. One advantage of being limited by guarantee is that the company can apply for dispensation to drop the word 'limited' from the name of the company (s. 30 CA 1985) whereas a company limited by shares cannot.

5.3   Companies limited by guarantee with a share capital

Companies may be limited both by guarantee and by shares (so that the members are liable both to lose their investment and to pay money under the guarantee). However, the formation of new companies limited by guarantee with a share capital is prohibited by s. 1(4) CA 1985.

5.4   Unlimited companies

An unlimited company is one which is registered under the Companies Act but without any limit on the liability of the members. If an unlimited company goes into liquidation the members are liable to contribute the whole of their private wealth (if so much is needed) to the payment of the company's debts. The creditors cannot sue the members direct but must claim in the liquidation. The liquidator then calls for contributions from the members. The main advantage of an unlimited company is that it is exempted from the requirement of publishing its accounts (see Chapter 9).

6   PUBLIC AND PRIVATE COMPANIES

6.1   Classification

Nearly all company law rules apply equally to all companies. There are a small number of rules which distinguish between 'public companies' and 'private companies'. A public company is defined by s. 1 CA 1985 as 'a company limited by shares or limited by guarantee and having a share capital, being a company:

(a)   the memorandum of which states that the company is to be a public company; and
(b)   in relation to which the provisions of [the Companies Act] as to the registration or re-registration of a company as a public company have been complied with . . .'.

The same section defines a private company as any company which is not a public company. On incorporation the promoters (that is, the people who form the company) will decide whether it is to be a public company or a private company and will draft the memorandum accordingly.

6.2   Differences

The principal differences between public and private companies are as follows:

(a)   A public company cannot commence business until a certificate is issued by the Registrar showing that the authorised minimum share capital has been issued (s. 117 CA 1985). The authorised minimum is currently £50,000 but can be increased by statutory instrument. A private company can commence business as soon as it is incorporated.
(b)   A public company cannot issue shares unless they are immediately paid for at least to the extent of 25% of the nominal value and the whole of any premium

(s. 101 CA 1985) (for the definitions of nominal value and premium see ch. 5—2.1 and 2.3.3). Similar rules apply to a company which seeks to re-register as public. A private company can issue shares without requiring immediate payment for them.

(c)   A public company can issue shares or debentures to the public (hence the description 'public company'); a private company is prohibited from doing so by the Financial Services Act 1986.

(d)   The name of a public company must end with the words 'Public Limited Company' or its equivalent (equivalents include PLC and, for Welsh companies, Cwmni Cyfyngedig Cyhoeddus or CCC). The names of private companies cannot end with these words and must end with 'Limited' or its equivalent (e.g. Ltd, Cyfyngedig or Cyf), unless the company is unlimited or has obtained permission to dispense with the use of the word 'Limited' in its name.

(e)   A public company must have at least two directors, a private company need only have one (s. 282 CA 1985).

(f)   There are a large number of smaller differences between the two types of company — for example, the directors of a private company need not retire at 70, those of a public company must (s. 293 CA 1985: however, this section may be avoided even in the case of a public company); a proxy can speak only at a meeting of a private company; a single resolution at a meeting of a private company may validly elect two or more directors, in the case of a public company each appointment must be voted on separately.

6.3   Other definitions

All companies are public or private but there are a number of other categories of company to which special rules apply:

(a)   *Quoted company*   A company is in this category if its shares are quoted on a stock exchange. A quoted company must keep a special register of those shareholders with 5% or more of the shares. Because of Stock Exchange rules only public companies can obtain a quotation.

(b)   *Close company*   This category is relevant only for tax purposes; special tax rules apply to close companies (see ch. 15). Virtually all private companies are close and so are some public companies. A company which is not close is sometimes called an 'open company' but 'non-close company' is more correct.

(c)   *Small and medium-sized companies*   These are companies which because of their relatively small size (in financial terms) are exempt from providing certain information in their accounts.

(d)   *Partnership company*   This category will be introduced by regulations made under the Companies Act 1989. A partnership company will in most respects be an ordinary private company but with regulations suitable for a company which is owned by its own employees.

(e)   *Elective regime company*   This category is introduced by the Companies Act 1989. An 'elective regime company' is an ordinary private company which has opted out of certain provisions of the Companies Act. It will only be possible to opt out if the shareholders unanimously agree. Once they have done so the company need not hold an annual general meeting nor a shareholders' meeting to consider accounts. The procedure for calling meetings and issuing shares is also simpler than in the case of other companies.

6.4   Provision in articles

As was explained above, a company is now public if its memorandum says so and it complies with certain other requirements; otherwise it is private. Until the Companies Act 1980 came into force a company was public unless its *articles* made it private by including provisions which:

(a)   restricted the right to transfer shares;
(b)   restricted membership to 50;
(c)   prevented public issue of shares.

For a considerable time to come many private companies will have articles doing these three things because they were formed at a time when they could not be private companies unless their articles contained such restrictions. It should be noted that modern private companies need not include any of these provisions in their articles, although most do restrict the right to transfer shares and the restriction on public issue is imposed independently of the articles by the Financial Services Act 1986.

7   SEPARATE LEGAL PERSONALITY

As we have already seen, a company is a 'body corporate', that is, it is a legal person distinct from its members. A number of consequences flow from this so that, for example, a company is able to own property, it is liable for its own debts, it can sue its debtors and is liable to be sued by its creditors. A company is, in one important respect, quite different from a natural person since it has 'perpetual succession'. This means that the company does not cease to exist just because a member (however many shares he may own) dies or otherwise ceases to be a member.

The leading case of *Salomon* v *A. Salomon and Co Ltd* [1897] AC 22, illustrates the nature of a company's separate legal personality very clearly. Mr Salomon was a wholesale boot manufacturer with a fairly substantial business. He decided to form a company to buy the business which he valued at £40,000. £30,000 worth of shares were issued, fully paid, to Salomon over a period of time (of these, six were held by his relatives to satisfy the requirement that every company should have a minimum of seven members — two is now sufficient). The other £10,000 of the purchase price was left outstanding and was secured by a debenture (i.e., the assets of the company were mortgaged in favour of Salomon). Within a year the company became insolvent because the company lost its main source of income (which was supplying boots to the army). The liquidator of the company claimed that Salomon was liable to indemnify the company personally against the claims of the ordinary creditors because the company was 'a mere alias or agent of the vendor'. This argument was upheld in the High Court and in the Court of Appeal but the House of Lords reversed the decision. Lord Macnaghten explained the position of a registered company in the following way:

When the memorandum is duly signed and registered, though there be only seven shares taken, the subscribers are a body corporate 'capable forthwith', to use the words of the enactment, 'of exercising all the functions of an incorporated company' . . . I cannot understand how a body corporate thus made capable by statute can lose its individuality by issuing the bulk of its capital to one person, whether he be a subscriber to the memorandum or not. The company is at law a different person altogether from the subscribers to the memorandum; and though it may be that after incorporation the business is precisely the same as it was before, and the same persons are managers, and the same hands receive the profits, the company is not in law the agent of the subscribers or trustee for them. Nor are the subscribers as members liable, in any shape or form, except to the extent and in the manner provided by the Act. . . . Any member of a company, acting in good faith, is as much entitled to take and hold the company's debentures as any outside creditor . . .. It has become the fashion to call companies of this class 'one man companies'. That is a taking nickname, but it does not help one much in the way of argument. If it is intended to convey the meaning that a company which is under the absolute control of one person is not a company legally incorporated . . . it is inaccurate and misleading . . ..

Since Salomon had not acted fraudulently his security was valid even though his valuation of the business at £40,000 was probably excessive. In fact, Salomon assigned the debenture to a third party before the company collapsed so that he did not gain personally from the decision of the House of Lords.

Another good illustration of the nature of separate legal personality is given by *Macaura* v *Northern Assurance Co Ltd* [1925] AC 619. The appellant owned a timber business which he sold to a company in return for shares. Since the value of his shares depended entirely on the value of the timber owned by the company he took out an insurance policy in his own name with the respondent company. The timber was destroyed by fire and Macaura claimed on his policy. The insurance company refused to pay on the ground that he had no insurable interest in the property. The House of Lords held that the appellant was not entitled to claim on the policy because the property was owned by another (i.e., the company which he had set up and in which he owned practically all the shares).

Another rule which is at least in part a consequence of separate legal personality is the rule in *Foss* v *Harbottle* (1843) 2 Hare 461, which prevents a shareholder from suing when a wrong is done to his company. (This rule is considered in ch. 8.)

8 'LIFTING THE VEIL OF INCORPORATION'

There are a number of circumstances in which the court is willing to ignore the fact that a company is a separate legal person. Legislation also sometimes ignores the distinction between a company and its members. These circumstances are rather fancifully described as 'lifting the veil of incorporation' because the law looks behind the legal 'veil' which separates the company from its members.

The occasions when the veil of incorporation is lifted are hard to classify and it is probably open to the courts to extend the circumstances in the future. It is, of course, open to Parliament to do so by legislation.

8.1 Company legislation

The Companies Act 1985 and the Insolvency Act 1986 contain a number of rules which depart from the general principle of separate corporate personality:

(a)   The remaining member of a company becomes personally liable for its debts if the number of members falls to one and no new member is introduced to the company within six months. The personal liability only arises for debts incurred after the six months and then only if the remaining member is aware of the position (s. 24 CA 1985).

(b)   Section 213 of the Insolvency Act 1986 provides that any person who is or was knowingly a party to fraudulent trading by a company whose business is being carried on with intent to defraud creditors or other persons, may be liable to pay the debts of the company. This liability arises only if the company is being wound up (although criminal penalties may be imposed for fraudulent trading under s. 458 CA 1985 even if the company is not being wound up).

(c)   Section 214 of the Insolvency Act 1986 provides that directors of the company may be personally liable in cases of wrongful trading. This arises where a company becomes insolvent and the directors then fail to take steps to protect creditors. This type of liability only arises if the company is being wound up.

(d)   Personal liability is also imposed on any person acting on behalf of a company if he uses a seal purporting to be that of the company or issues or authorises the use of certain documents unless the company's name appears on the seal or document (see ch. 2—4.1 and 4.2).

(e)   Where companies are members of a group, group accounts must be produced to reflect that the financial transactions of the subsidiaries are in reality activities of the holding company.

8.2   Decisions of the courts

8.2.1   Attempts to avoid legal obligations

The courts have occasionally lifted the veil of incorporation by making orders against companies where the proprietors have used a company as a means of avoiding a personal legal obligation.

In *Gilford Motor Co Ltd* v *Horne* [1933] Ch 935, the defendant had been the managing director of the plaintiff company. One of the terms of his service contract was that he would not solicit the customers of the company after the end of his contract. In an attempt to avoid liability and after he left the plaintiff's employment he set up a company (J. M. Horne and Co Ltd), the shares in which were owned by his wife and a business associate and in which he was not a director. This company's business was in fact carried on by Horne and through it he solicited the plaintiff's customers. It was held that an injunction would be made against Horne *and* the company he had set up. Lord Hanworth MR said:

> Of course, in law the defendant company is a separate entity from the defendant Horne, but I cannot help feeling quite convinced that at any rate one of the reasons for the creation of that company was the fear of Mr Horne that he might commit breaches of the covenant in carrying on the business . . . I am quite satisfied that this company was formed as a device, a strategem, in order to mask the effective carrying on of a business of Mr E. B. Horne. The purpose of it was to try to enable him, under what is a cloak or sham, to engage in business which was a business in respect of which he had a fear that the plaintiffs might intervene and object. . . . Horne and the company as his agent and under his direction, have committed breaches of the covenant . . .

Similarly, in *Jones* v *Lipman* [1962] 1 WLR 832, the defendant had contracted to sell land to the plaintiff and later conveyed it to a company in an attempt to avoid the possibility of an order of specific performance (an order of specific performance cannot normally be made once a third party has acquired rights in the subject-matter of the contract). The company was owned and controlled by the defendant and so an order of specific performance was made against the company as well as the vendor.

8.2.2 Agency and trusts

In a few cases the court has held that a company is either an agent for its shareholders or their trustee. In *Smith, Stone and Knight Ltd* v *Birmingham Corporation* [1939] 4 All ER 116, the plaintiff company formed a subsidiary in which it owned all the shares and that subsidiary ran a business at certain premises which were compulsorily purchased by the Corporation. The profits of the subsidiary had always been treated as the profits of Smith, Stone and Knight Ltd and the two businesses had partly been run as one.

Atkinson J said that it was well settled that the mere fact of owning shares in a company does not entitle a shareholder to treat the business as his own nor does it make the company his agent for running the business. However, it is possible for a company to act as the shareholder's agent. Atkinson J listed the following six questions which may assist the court in deciding whether the company is acting as agent:

(a) Were the profits treated as profits of the shareholder?
(b) Were the persons conducting the business appointed by the shareholder?
(c) Was the shareholder the head and brains of the business?
(d) Did the shareholder govern the business and decide what capital should be embarked on the venture?
(e) Did the shareholder make the profits by his skill and direction?
(f) Was the shareholder in effectual and constant control?

Applying those tests to the present case the court concluded that the subsidiary was acting as the agent of Smith, Stone and Knight Ltd so that the latter was entitled to compensation.

The court has also held that a subsidiary company is the agent of its holding company in many cases where tax liability has depended on so finding.

In *Trebanog Working Men's Club Ltd* v *MacDonald* [1940] 1 KB 576, a company bought alcoholic drinks in its own name and sold them to members. It was convicted of selling liquor without a licence. However, the Divisional Court allowed the club's appeal on the ground that it held the liquor on trust for the members and, therefore, no true sale took place.

The exact scope of these decisions is rather unclear. A company will not generally be regarded as either an agent for or trustee of its members, so that the cases referred to above ought to be regarded as providing exceptions rather than general rules.

8.3 Tax legislation

Tax legislation often imposes tax liability on shareholders to reflect the fact that transactions of their company are in reality transactions conducted on their behalf. It is not proposed to deal with all the rules involved but the following examples should be sufficient to indicate their scope:

(a)   The companies in a 'group' of companies (i.e., broadly speaking, a holding company and its subsidiaries) are in many ways treated as one company for corporation tax purposes. Thus the rate of tax depends on the size of the group's profits rather than on the size of each company's profits, losses made by one member of a group can generally be set off against profits made by others, and dividend payments within the group may be ignored for tax purposes.

(b)   Gifts made by a close company are treated as made by its members for the purpose of inheritance tax.

(c)   The sale of a business to a company in return for shares can usually be ignored for capital gains tax purposes (see ch. 20).

2 Company Formation

1 INTRODUCTION

The solicitor who is asked to form a company on behalf of a trader must first discuss with him whether a company is, in fact, the appropriate medium through which to operate. If a limited company is appropriate to the trader's requirements, the solicitor must:

(a) Discuss with the client the effect of incorporation and the legal requirements of running a company.

(b) Discuss with the client whether the company should be formed by the solicitor or whether an existing company should be bought 'off-the-peg' from a firm of law stationers.

(c) Prepare the documents leading to incorporation (after taking the client's instructions as to their contents). If an 'off-the-peg' company is decided on, this step will be unnecessary.

(d) Inform the client as to the steps to be taken after incorporation, as required by the Companies Act 1985 (as amended).

(e) Advise the client as to the problems which may arise if contracts are made in the name of, or on behalf of, the company before incorporation.

This chapter considers each of these matters (though not in chronological order). It should be borne in mind that, especially in relation to the proposed company's constitution, the circumstances of each case will be different. This book is particularly concerned with the problems likely to be faced by a two- or three-man business.

2 STEPS LEADING TO INCORPORATION

For a company to be registered under the Companies Act, the 'promoters' (that is, the traders who wish to form the company) or their agents (for example, a solicitor or a law stationer) must deliver to the Registrar of Companies the following:

(a) a memorandum of association;

(b) articles of association (but see below, paragraph 2.2, for adoption of Table A by reference in the memorandum);

(c) Form G10, setting out details of the registered office, the directors and secretary of the company;

(d) Form G12 — a statutory declaration of compliance with the requirements of the Companies Act;

(e) the Registrar's fee (currently £50).

In this chapter we will consider the formation of private limited companies only. Of the documents that have to be submitted to the Registrar the most important are the company's memorandum and articles; great care must be taken to ensure that they are suitable for the particular circumstances.

2.1 Memorandum of association

Section 1 CA 1985 provides that every company must have a memorandum, which is sometimes described as the company's 'charter'. Its principal function is to set out the *raison d'être* of the company and to regulate its dealings with outsiders. The Companies (Tables A to F) Regulations 1985 set out model memoranda, the form of which must be followed when drafting this document. Table B is applicable to a private company limited by shares. Five compulsory clauses *must* be included in the memorandum. These relate to:

(a)   the name of the company;
(b)   the registered office;
(c)   the objects of the company;
(d)   the liability of the members;
(e)   the authorised capital of the company.

Further clauses may be included, covering anything which could be contained in the company's articles (see paragraph 2.2); however, this is rarely done in practice.

The memorandum must also contain the 'association' and 'subscription' clauses. The former states that the persons who subscribe (i.e., sign) the memorandum wish to be formed into a company and that they each agree to take a specified number of shares in the new company. The latter sets out the names, addresses and descriptions of the subscribers and the number of shares each agrees to take. The memorandum must be signed by a minimum of two subscribers, who sign in the presence of at least one witness, and each subscriber must agree to take at least one share.

We will now consider each of the clauses which must be included, in turn.

2.1.1   The name

Generally, the promoters have freedom of choice as far as the company's name is concerned. The purpose of a company's name is to differentiate the company from all other registered companies. Sections 25-26 CA 1985, therefore, prohibit the Registrar from registering a company with a name which:

(a)   does not end with the word 'limited' (or its Welsh equivalent 'cyfyngedig' if appropriate — see below) if the company is a private limited company; however, s. 30 provides that a company limited by guarantee may apply for dispensation from using the word 'limited'. The objects of a company applying for this exemption must be the promotion of commerce, art, science, education, religion, charity or a profession and its memorandum or articles must:
(i)   require any profits to be applied for promoting the objects;
(ii)   prohibit the payment of dividends;
(iii)   require the assets to be transferred to a similar body or institution on the company's liquidation. (The procedure for obtaining the exemption is beyond the scope of this book.)
(b)   is the same as that of an existing registered company; or

(c)   in the opinion of the Secretary of State constitutes a criminal offence, or is offensive;

(d)   includes the words limited, unlimited or public limited company (or the Welsh equivalents or abbreviations of these words) other than at the end of the name;

(e)   includes words suggesting a connection with the government or a local authority or particular words specified in regulations (made under s. 29 CA 1985). In such cases, however, the Registrar may give approval for registration of the name. In the case of words specified in the regulations, consultation with government departments or institutions specified in the regulations is sometimes required before the Registrar gives his approval.

If a name is rejected by the Registrar a certain amount of expense and delay is bound to occur, as the promoter will have to submit a further set of documents applying for formation with a new name. The new memorandum will have to be printed (although 'printing' in this context includes most types of photocopying) and so will the new articles (unless Table A is adopted by reference in the memorandum). To minimise the risk of a name being rejected the promoters should consult the index of company names kept by the Registrar of Companies shortly before the application for registration. If the name is already in use a new name should be chosen. If the name is not in use then the application should progress quickly as there is no procedure for reserving a name.

Registration of a company with a particular name does not give the company any protection against a passing-off action if an existing business trades under a similar name and its business is likely to be affected by the similarity. This potential problem can be partly avoided if the promoters inspect the trade marks register before applying for registration with any particular name.

Section 28, CA 1985 provides that, after a company is formed, it is free to change its name by passing a special resolution subject to the same restrictions as apply to choice of name by a new company. Section 28 also gives the Registrar the power to *direct* a change of name within 12 months of registration if it is the same as or too similar to a name which is, or should be, on the index (s. 28(2)). If the company provides misleading information when applying to use a name, by misrepresenting the size of its operation for example, or fails to fulfil undertakings or assurances given, a direction in writing to change the name within a specified period can be made within five years of registration. Furthermore, the Registrar has the power to direct a company to change its registered name if it gives so misleading an indication of the nature of its activities as to be likely to cause harm to the public (s. 32 CA 1985).

2.1.2   Registered office

The second compulsory clause in the memorandum sets out the situation of the company's registered office. It does not state the address of the company's registered office (this appears in Form G10 — see below), but only that the office is situated in England (which includes Wales for this purpose) or Wales (to the exclusion of England) or Scotland as appropriate. The function of this clause is to determine the company's domicile, and it can only be altered by Act of Parliament.

If the office is to be in Wales (to the exclusion of England), the company's name may end in the word 'cyfyngedig' rather than 'limited'. The memorandum and articles may, in such cases, be printed in Welsh but a certified translation into English is required.

2.1.3   The objects and the ultra vires doctrine

The third compulsory clause specifies the company's objects, or purposes, and the powers it is to have. Any contracts made, or acts done, by the company not within the objects clause or reasonably incidental thereto, used to be void as a result of the doctrine of 'ultra vires'. The doctrine became less important as objects clauses were more widely drafted and is now greatly affected by the new s. 35, CA 1985, as substituted by the Companies Act 1989.

A brief explanation will be given of how the ultra vires doctrine came about and its effects.

The doctrine was originally used to enable the courts to prevent public authorities from performing acts that were not authorised by the statutes which created those authorities and which specified their powers. Limited companies could not be created at common law and are therefore 'creatures of statute'; thus it was a natural progression to apply the doctrine to them as well. The doctrine was intended to protect the members and outsiders dealing with the company and limited the company's actions to those authorised by the objects clause. An ultra vires contract was void and incapable of subsequent ratification even if the members were unanimous in wishing to do so.

In order to avoid the consequences of a transaction being held to be ultra vires, objects clauses have traditionally been drafted at great length. In particular, it is usual to find many sub-clauses giving power to the company to run many types of business. In recent times it has also become usual to include a clause which gives the company power to 'carry on any other trade or business whatsoever which could in the opinion of the directors be advantageously carried on by the company in connection with or ancillary to any of the company's other businesses'. Such a clause was held to be a valid part of an objects clause in *Bell Houses Ltd* v *City Wall Properties Ltd* [1966] 2 QB 656, 694.

A typical objects clause would also contain a sub-clause stating that each part of the objects clause should be construed as independent of each other part. In *Cotman* v *Brougham* [1918] AC 514 the House of Lords held that such a clause was effective to allow the company to carry on any of the businesses stated in its objects clause even if they were in no way connected with the business referred to at the beginning of the clause as the company's main object.

2.1.4   The objects clause and the ultra vires doctrine after the Companies Act 1989

The Companies Act 1989 modifies the operation of the ultra vires rule by amending s. 35 CA 1985.

The new s. 35(1) provides that 'the validity of an act done by a company shall not be called into question on the ground of lack of capacity by reason of anything in the company's memorandum . . .'. This effectively abolishes the ultra vires rule as far as a person dealing with a company is concerned. However, there are three qualifications to be made:

(a)   Section 35(2) provides that a member may still seek an injunction to prevent an ultra vires act provided that he does so before the company enters into a legal obligation.

(b)   Section 35(3) provides that the directors remain liable to the company for any ultra vires act.

(c)   Section 322A (which is interpolated by the Companies Act 1989) provides that a transaction between the company and a director or a person connected with a director is voidable by the company if it is beyond the power of the board of directors. A transaction which is outside the scope of the objects of the company is beyond the power of the board and so is covered by this rule (for a fuller discussion of s. 332A see ch. 7 para. 2.2).

In addition to the virtual abolition of the ultra vires rule the Companies Act 1989 makes a further change in relation to objects clauses. Section 110 interpolates a new s. 3A into the Companies Act 1985 which provides:

Where the company's memorandum states that the object of the company is to carry on business as a general commercial company —

(a)   the object of the company is to carry on any trade or business whatsoever, and

(b)   the company has power to do all such things as are incidental or conducive to the carrying on of any trade or business by it.

Where a company adopts this simple form of objects clause the powers of the company will include power to carry on any trade or business. The possibility of a transction being prevented by injunction, of the directors being liable for entering into it or of its being avoided by the company will be very slight. However, a transction can still be challenged on the basis that it was not part of a trade or business nor is it incidental or conducive to caring on the trade or business. Certain gifts by a company could, for example, be challenged on this basis.

How many companies will choose to be incorporated with an objects clause in the new simple form remains to be seen. It is likely that many companies will still choose the traditional form and companies formed before the 1989 Act comes into force are unlikely to change their objects clauses.

2.1.5   The liability clause

This merely states whether the members' liability for the debts of the company is limited or unlimited but it does not specify the manner in which the member's liability is limited. The clause is unalterable but if a company wishes to change the nature of liability it may re-register under ss. 49-52 CA 1985. The detailed provisions are complex, and beyond the scope of this book; the main requirements are that the unanimous consent of all the members is needed to convert from limited to unlimited but only a special resolution — that is, a 75% majority — is necessary to change from unlimited to limited.

2.1.6   The capital clause

The final compulsory clause in the memorandum states the amount of the company's 'authorised share capital' and how it is divided into shares of a specified nominal value (sometimes called the 'par value'). It is possible to divide the shares into different classes enjoying different rights (such as a preferential dividend entitlement) but this is normally done, if at all, under provisions in the articles.

The company's authorised share capital sets an upper limit on the number of shares which it can issue but there are no legal rules to determine the maximum or minimum amount of a private company's authorised share capital (public companies must have a minimum of £50,000 authorised capital, of which at least one quarter must be paid up). Since the capital clause only deals with the nominal value of the share capital, it does not restrict the amount which can be invested in the company.

At this stage it may be useful to explain the different types of share capital:

(a)   *Authorised capital* limits the maximum number of shares which the company can issue. It can be increased or decreased (see ch. 6—6).

(b)   *Issued capital* is the part of the authorised share capital which has been issued to the members. The issued capital is calculated by multiplying the number of shares issued by their nominal value.

(c)   *Paid-up capital* is the amount received from the members to date, whether in cash or in the form of assets. Since the company may, if it wishes, call for only part payment at the time when shares are issued, the paid-up capital may be less than the issued capital.

2.2   The articles of association

The second document which must be considered before the company is incorporated is the articles of association (s. 7 CA 1985). These regulate the company's internal affairs and contain the regulations dealing with such matters as directors' powers, proceedings at members' meetings and so on. The promoters decide what form the articles take.

There are no compulsory clauses but the Companies (Tables A to F) Regulations 1985 contain a standard set of articles which contain regulations (called Table A) intended to be suitable for an 'average' company. The company may: have prepared specially drafted Articles; reprint Table A either with or without amendment; or adopt Table A by special reference in its memorandum (in which case it need not submit a printed copy of its articles when applying for registration). If this last procedure is followed the adopted Table A will be in the form laid down in the Regulations in force at the date of incorporation. While later Regulations and/or Acts may change Table A from time to time this will not affect companies already registered. Therefore, for the purpose of reference, copies of Table A in the appropriate form should be kept. It should be noted that the present Table A was introduced on 1 July 1985. It is substantially different from its predecessor (contained in the Companies Act 1948 and amended on a number of occasions) which will form the basis of the articles of most companies incorporated before July 1985 for many years to come.

Unless Table A is adopted by reference in the memorandum the articles submitted for registration must be 'printed' and must be signed by the subscribers to the memorandum in the presence of a witness. Photocopying is acceptable provided the print is permanent but typing is not, since this can be altered too easily.

When preparing to incorporate a company, one of the most important matters to discuss with the promoters is the contents of the articles and their effect. Because Table A is a standard form it may not be suitable for every company and should be altered to meet the circumstances. Additional articles that could be considered include those dealing with:

(a) giving authority under s. 80 CA 1985 to directors to issue shares;

(b) the exclusion, extension or variation of the pre-emption rights given by s. 89ff. CA 1985;

(c) the removal of directors:

(i) a *Bushell* v *Faith* clause (see ch. 8—2, whereby the director shareholder is given additional voting power on a resolution to remove him from office under s. 303 CA 1985) which has the effect of ensuring that he can only be removed with his consent:

(ii) a power to remove a director which dispenses with the necessity for special notice under s. 379 CA 1985.

Should the company be incorporated with unsuitable articles or should circumstances change, s. 9 CA 1985 allows amendments, provided a special resolution approving them is passed.

The Companies Act 1989 provides a further possibility as far as articles are concerned. This is the adoption of a new Table G which will contain articles for a 'partnership company'. Section 8A CA 1985 (interpolated by s. 128 CA 1989) defines a partnership company as 'a company limited by shares whose shares are intended to be held to a substantial extent by or on behalf of its employees'. At the time of writing, Table G has not been published.

2.3 Form G10

This is a statutory form required by s. 10(2) and sch. 1 CA 1985 which is a statement of the first directors and secretary and intended situation of the company's registered office. The form is supplied with notes explaining its completion. The following points should be noted:

(a) The address of the company's first registered office appears in this form, not in the memorandum; later it can be moved anywhere within the country specified in the 'office' clause in the memorandum. The registered office may be changed by giving notice to the Registrar. The change is effective in relation to service of documents when registered by the Registrar although service of documents at the old registered office remains valid for a further 14 days after registration.

A company is required to keep certain registers and documents at its registered office and to make them available for public inspection (see para. 4.3 below). A company is not liable for failing in this duty if it has to change its registered offices in circumstances where it is not practicable to notify the Registrar provided that it finds a new registered office as soon as practicable and informs the Registrar within 14 days (CA 1985 s. 287(6) as substituted by CA 1989).

(b)   The company must have at least one director and if only one is appointed he must not also be the company secretary. This ensures that every company has at least two separate officers.

(c)   The information required in relation to the directors includes details of other directorships.

(d)   The persons named as directors and secretary, and who sign the form to signify their consent, automatically become the first directors and secretary of the company even if the articles provide otherwise.

2.4   Form G12

This is a statutory declaration of compliance with the registration requirements of the Act. It must be completed by the solicitor engaged in forming the company or one of the company's directors or secretary named in Form G10.

2.5   The fee

The documents must be sent to the Registrar of Companies together with the fee of £50.

3   THE CERTIFICATE OF INCORPORATION

The Registrar will examine the documents and, provided they are in order and the chosen name is still available, he will sign a certificate of incorporation stating that the company was incorporated under the Companies Act 1985 and that the company is limited (if appropriate). The Registrar specifies the company's registered number on the certificate and this must be quoted on all official documents and business letters. Under s. 13(3), from the date of incorporation mentioned in the certificate, the subscribers of the memorandum, together with persons who subsequently become members of the company, become members of a body corporate by the name contained in the memorandum, capable of exercising all the functions of an incorporated company. The company, therefore, becomes a legal entity from the date of the certificate of incorporation. At the same time as the Registrar issues the certificate, he must (under s. 711 CA 1985) 'officially notify' the fact of issue. This means he must place a notice to this effect in the Government's official newspaper (in England and Wales, the *London Gazette*). From the date of incorporation the company is a legal entity separate from its members, who may deal with it in the same way as outsiders (as we have seen in *Salomon* v *A. Salomon and Co Ltd* [1897] AC 22). Furthermore, if the company is registered with limited liability, the members' liability is limited to the amount they have agreed to contribute to the company's share capital in exchange for receiving shares in the company. Section 13(7) CA 1985 provides that the certificate is conclusive evidence that the registration requirements have been complied with. This is because, once the company has been registered and commenced business, it would be disastrous if any person could allege that it was not duly registered.

4 STEPS NECESSARY AFTER INCORPORATION

Once the certificate of incorporation has been issued the company's existence begins. There are then certain procedural and statutory provisions to be complied with. In addition to matters such as the issue of shares and fixing the company's accounting reference date, which will be dealt with soon after incorporation, these steps relate to the following formal requirements:

(a) the company's seal (if there is to be one);
(b) the publication of the company's name;
(c) the keeping of certain statutory 'books'.

4.1 The seal

After the enactment of the Companies Act 1989, there is no longer any need for a company to have a seal. If the company does have one, the company's name must be engraved on it. Whether or not the company has a seal, documents signed by a director and the secretary and expressed (in whatever form of words) to be executed by the company will have the same effect as if they were under the company's seal.

4.2 Publication of the company's name

The Companies Act 1985 contains a number of provisions concerning publication of a company's name. A company is required to:

(a) display its registered name outside every office or place of business in which its business is carried on, in a conspicuous position and in letters which are easily legible (s. 348 CA 1985);
(b) ensure that its name appears on all business letters, notices, cheques, orders for money or goods, invoices, etc. (s. 349 CA 1985).

An officer of the company who uses an incorrectly engraved seal or issues a letter, invoice, etc. or signs a cheque, order for money, etc. on which the correct name does not appear is liable to a fine. However, where the document in question is a cheque, bill of exchange, promissory note, order for money or goods, there is additional, more serious, liability, in that the signer will be personally liable to the holder of the cheque, etc. This is a circumstance where the 'veil of incorporation' is lifted and is illustrated by the case of *Durham Fancy Goods Ltd* v *Michael Jackson (Fancy Goods) Ltd and Another* [1968] 2 QB 839. In this case the plaintiffs drew a bill of exchange on the defendants and wrote on it 'Accepted payable . . . for and on behalf of M. Jackson (Fancy Goods) Ltd'. On receiving the bill, a director of the defendant company signed his name and returned the bill. It was dishonoured by his company which then went into liquidation. The plaintiffs claimed against the director personally on the ground that he had contravened a provision of the Companies Act 1948 which was the same as s. 349 CA 1985. This was because the name included the word 'Michael' in full and not merely the initial 'M' as in the bill. It was held that this section had been contravened and that the director would have been personally liable but for the fact that it was the plaintiffs themselves who had written the incorrect name on the bill. It seems, however, that abbreviations may be used where they are in common usage as equivalents for the words for which they stand. Thus in *Banque de l'Indochine et de Suez SA* v *Euroseas Group Finance Co. Ltd* [1981] 3 All ER 198, an abbreviation of 'Company' to 'Co' was held not to be a breach of the section. Clearly these rules are important and should be drawn to the attention of the directors of a newly formed company.

A further practical point relating to the name and its publication is that the promoters will need to have stationery printed which complies with the statutory requirements. This cannot, however, be done until the certificate of incorporation has been issued, confirming that the chosen name was accepted and giving the company's number. Section 305 CA 1985 requires that if the name of *any* director appears on a business letter (other than in the text or as a signatory) on which the company's name appears, then the forenames (or initials) and surnames of *all* the directors who are individuals and the corporate names of all the corporate directors must appear in legible characters.

Finally, s. 351 CA 1985 requires the company's letters and order forms to specify:

(a)   the place of registration of the company and its registered number;

(b)   the address of its registered office;

(c)   that it is a limited company if it has been granted a licence to dispense with 'limited' as the last word of the name.

Failure to comply makes the company and every officer authorising the issue of a letter, etc. liable to a fine.

4.3   The statutory books

The Companies Act 1985 requires companies to keep certain books. The company can prepare its own books or buy them from law stationers. As far as a private limited company is concerned the most important books it must keep at its registered office are:

(a)   A register and index of members, containing each member's name, address, dates of entry on the register and cessation of membership together with details of the shares held.

(b)   A register of directors and a register of secretaries setting out their names, addresses, and, for directors only, details of any other directorships. It is advisable to include details of the period of holding office since problems may arise in the future as to whether a board decision was validly passed and enquiries of the directors holding office at the time may be necessary; similarly for secretaries.

(c)   A register of the interests of directors, their spouses and infant children in shares and debentures of the company, its holding and subsidiary companies as required by ss. 324-328 CA 1985. The purpose of this is to ensure that the extent of a director's direct or indirect control over the company is known.

(d)   A register of charges which must be kept even if the company has not yet charged any of its assets. It sets out details of the property charged and the terms of the charge.

(e)   Copies of the company's memorandum and articles.

All these books must be available for inspection by members, creditors and the general public for at least two hours daily during business hours. The Secretary of State has power, under CA 1989 to make regulations concerning the times when registers are to be available. Certain of the books may be kept at a place other than the registered office provided the Registrar is notified. Other documents which should be kept at the registered office include:

(a)   Copies of all instruments creating any charge over the company's property (whether or not registrable at the Companies Registry) and a register of brief particulars of the charges. The copies and register are available for inspection by members and creditors free of charge and by anyone else on payment of a fee to be prescribed by regulations.

(b)   The directors' service contracts, which can only be inspected by members.

(c)   The minute book of general meetings of the company, which can only be inspected by members.

5   METHODS OF INCORPORATION

The trader who wishes to trade using a limited company can have his company formed, following the procedure set out above, either by his professional advisers or by a firm of law stationers. Our aim is to make a comparison between a company which is 'tailor-made' to the trader's particular requirements in every way and one that is bought from the stock of 'shelf' or 'off-the-peg' companies maintained by law stationers.

5.1   The 'tailor-made' company

If the company's documentation is tailored to the promoters' requirements the memorandum will give express or implied authority for the company to do whatever its promoters desire (and the company will have the name the promoters have chosen), and the articles will include only those provisions appropriate to the particular circumstances of the case. Furthermore, the promoters may be the subscribers to the memorandum and articles and appear in Form G10, thus becoming the company's first members and officers.

The disadvantages are that there will be a delay between taking instructions and the company's incorporation and this method, at first sight, might appear more expensive.

5.2   The 'off-the-peg' or 'shelf' company

If this type of company is bought from a law stationers the only part of the documentation which is likely to be entirely suitable to the trader's needs will be the objects clause of the memorandum, since stocks of companies carrying on most types of business are maintained. Companies will also be available, stating that their object is to 'carry on business as a general commercial company'. However, while the objects clause will almost certainly be satisfactory, the name probably will not be and the articles may not be.

On incorporation the 'shelf' company will have been given a name which will have no connection with the company's future powers. If the name of their company is unimportant to the promoters this will cause no problems but if they wish their company to trade under their own names or a chosen name, the name will have to be changed. This is done by the members passing a special resolution. A fee of £40 is payable. A cheaper alternative is to use a business name, provided the promoters comply with the requirements of the Business Names Act 1985. This Act requires that where a company does not carry on its business under its corporate name, the corporate name must appear on all business letters, orders for goods or services to be supplied to the business, invoices and receipts issued in the course of the business as well as on written demands for payment of debts arising in the course of the business. In addition, an address in Great Britain at which service of any document relating to the business will be effective must be set out. Furthermore, in any premises where the business is carried on and to which the customers of the business or suppliers of any goods or services to the business have access, the company must display prominently a notice setting out this name and address. The Act requires the company to supply this information in writing to anyone dealing in the course of business with the company who asks for it. Failure to comply with any of these requirements may lead to a fine.

As regards the articles, the law stationers will have incorporated the company by using either Table A alone or as amended by their standard 'special' or additional articles. Great care must be taken to ensure that the articles are suitable. If they are not, they will have to be amended in accordance with s. 9 CA 1985, which requires the members to pass a special resolution approving the change. Having done so, a new print of all the articles will have to be delivered to the Registrar, which will take time and increase the expenses of formation.

Finally, as regards the documentation, employees of the law stationers will have signed the memorandum and the articles as well as being named in Form G10, with all the normal results this entails. Since they become the first members, their names should appear in the register of members and they would then have to transfer shares, incurring stamp duty payments. The law stationers have provided a solution to this problem by supplying a 'letter of renunciation' of rights as shareholders and company officers in favour of the company's shareholders. This means that the directors may allot the subscribers' shares to someone else.

Arguably the greatest advantage of this method is speed, since the trader can have his company immediately but this must be set against the corresponding disadvantage that although such companies are cheap initially, the changes necessary to make them comply with the trader's requirements can increase the cost considerably.

6 PRE-INCORPORATION CONTRACTS

A difficulty can arise in relation to contracts made by the promoters on behalf of a proposed company. They may wish to make contracts to acquire premises, machinery, stationery and so on, without incurring personal liability but, for some reason, may be unable to wait until the company is incorporated. This creates a problem as the company cannot enter into contracts until it has been registered as it is not yet a legal person.

Provided the promoters are aware of the difficulty, it can be minimised either by entering into a draft contract which the company will finalise on incorporation, or entering into a binding contract under which the promoters are personally liable until incorporation, at which time the company assumes responsibility usually under the terms of a new contract with the agreement of the other party.

Should the promoters enter into a contract *on behalf of* the unformed company, s. 36(4) CA 1985 will apply. This provides that 'where a contract purports to be made by a company, or by a person as agent for a company, at a time when the company has not been formed, then *subject to any agreement to the contrary* the contract has effect as one entered into by the person purporting to act for the company or as agent for it, and he is *personally liable* on the contract accordingly'.

The safest course would be to enter into contracts only after incorporation, but if this is impossible care must be taken to avoid the problems indicated.

3 Officials of a Company

1 DIVISION OF POWERS WITHIN A COMPANY

The power to take decisions on behalf of a company is divided between the directors and members. There are a number of powers which are exercisable only by the members under various provisions of the Companies Act — for example, the power to change the name, objects, articles and nominal capital (see ch. 6) and various powers in relation to the issue of shares (see ch. 5) and meetings (see ch. 4). The members' power to remove directors from office is considered in Chapter 8. As far as the vast majority of powers are concerned, the company is free to choose its own procedures, which will be laid down in the articles. Usually these give very wide powers to the directors.

2 APPOINTMENT OF DIRECTORS

2.1 Introduction

The first directors of a company are the people who have agreed to take office by filing Form G10 (see ch. 2—2.3); they automatically become directors as soon as the company is formed. From time to time it will be necessary to appoint further directors, either because one of the directors has ceased to hold office or because it is decided to increase the size of the board. Apart from a few statutory restrictions which will be dealt with shortly, the company is free to make whatever provision it wishes in its articles as to the appointment of directors. In particular, there is no general requirement that the directors should be shareholders, nor that they should be chosen by the shareholders. The provisions of Table A will be considered first and then some other possibilities.

2.2 Appointment of directors under Table A

Article 64 provides that the minimum number of directors is two and that there is no maximum number. However, the members can by ordinary resolution fix a different minimum number (including one) and/or fix a maximum number. The minimum and maximum can then be changed by further ordinary resolutions.

The main power to appoint directors is given to the members by art. 78. This provides for appointment by ordinary resolution (that is, by a simple majority at a meeting of the company or by unanimous written consent of the members). Article 76 requires notice to be given to the company at least 14 days before the meeting by a member who wishes to propose the appointment of a director unless the appointment is recommended by the directors. Article 77 requires notice to be given to the members by the company at least seven days before the meeting giving details of any person whose appointment is proposed, whether or not the appointment is recommended by the directors. This rule does not, however, apply to the re-appointment of a director who retires by rotation (see paragraph 3.1 below).

Appointments to fill vacancies on the board and appointments of additional directors (up to the maximum, if any, fixed by the members) may be made by the board itself. A person co-opted in this way holds office until the following annual general meeting (art. 79).

2.3 Other possibilities

In most cases the provisions of Table A as to the appointment of directors will be entirely satisfactory. However, in some cases it may be considered appropriate to make permanent appointments to the board; this can be achieved by removing the retirement provisions discussed below. It is also possible for the articles to name the first directors and to make them permanent or life directors without affecting the method of appointment of other directors. However, such appointments are ineffective unless the directors are also named as the first directors in Form G10.

It should be noted that Table A does not require a director to be a shareholder. If the company wants to restrict membership to the board to shareholders an article to that effect must be adopted on formation or by later amendment.

3 REMOVAL OF DIRECTORS FROM OFFICE

3.1 Retirement by rotation

If Table A or similar provisions apply, all the directors retire from office at the first annual general meeting and one third of them at each subsequent AGM (arts 73-74). The retiring directors are eligible for re-election and are automatically re-elected unless someone else is appointed, or the company resolves not to re-elect them, or the company resolves not to fill the vacancy (art. 75). If no AGM is held during a year (unless it is one of the first two years and the company is excused from holding a meeting in that year), there is authority for saying that all the directors who should have retired by rotation at the AGM cease to hold office on the last day on which the AGM could lawfully have been held (*Re Zinotty Properties Ltd* [1984] 1 WLR 1249; *Re Consolidated Nickel Mines Ltd* [1914] 1 Ch 883).

In the case of a private company provisions for retirement by rotation are unnecessarily cumbersome and are often removed so that, once appointed, directors hold office permanently until death, voluntary retirement, disqualification or removal from office under s. 303 CA 1985 (see ch. 8). If the directors are majority shareholders they will, of course, be able to ensure their own re-election in the face of opposition by the minority shareholders, even if the retirement by rotation provisions are included in the articles. If these provisions are excluded, there is no need to make reappointment at each AGM.

A company which has elected to dispense with the holding of an AGM (see ch. 4 para. 4.2) should amend its articles to remove the requirement of retirement at the AGM if it has not already done so.

3.2 Disqualification

Companies legislation contains the following provisions under which directors are disqualified either automatically or by court order:

(a)   Section 291 CA 1985 — provides for automatic vacation of office if qualification shares (when required) are not obtained within two months of appointment.

(b)   Section 293 CA 1985 — *does not apply to private companies* but provides for automatic retirement, subject to certain exceptions, of directors of public companies when they reach the age of 70.

(c)   The Company Directors Disqualification Act 1986 — provides for disqualification from acting as a director, liquidator, receiver or manager of a company and from being concerned with the management of a company for up to 15 years (five years if the order is made by a magistrates' court). Disqualification can be imposed following:

(i)   conviction for an indictable offence in connection with the management of a company;

(ii)   a finding that an offence involving fraud has been committed in the course of winding up a company;

(iii)   persistent default in filing returns with the Registrar (persistent default is conclusively presumed following three convictions for failure to file returns within five years); the maximum period of disqualification in this case is five years even if the penalty is imposed by a court other than a magistrates' court;

(iv)   a finding that a person is 'unfit' to be concerned in the management of a company. The order may only be made against a person who is or has been a director of a company which has become insolvent while or after he was a director. For these purposes a company is insolvent if it goes into insolvent liquidation, an administration order is made against it or an administrative receiver is appointed (these procedures are dealt with in Chapter 21). Where an order is made on the ground of unfitness, the disqualification period must be for a minimum of two years and a maximum of 15.

Section 11 of the Company Directors Disqualification Act 1986 makes it an offence for an undischarged bankrupt to act as a director or liquidator or otherwise manage a company.

The articles of a company may, of course, make provision for disqualification or automatic retirement in circumstances other than those specified in the Act. Table A art. 81 states that the office of director is to be vacated:

(a)   if a director becomes bankrupt (or makes a composition with creditors); this adds to s. 11 which stops the bankrupt *acting* as a director but curiously does not prevent him *being* a director;

(b)   if a director is or may be suffering from mental disorder and is admitted to hospital under the Mental Health Act or a court order is made against him on matters concerning mental disorder;

(c)   if a director is absent from directors' meetings (without the board's permission) for at least six months and the directors resolve that the office be vacated.

Article 81 also provides for the resignation of directors by giving written notice to the company. No particular period of notice is required. If the director has a service contract, as, for example, in the case of most full-time directors, there is an implied obligation to give reasonable notice but for the sake of certainty it is better to include a specific period in the contract.

3.3 Removal of directors (s. 303 CA 1985)

As has already been seen, shareholders appoint directors in most cases and, unless Table A has been altered, have an opportunity to get rid of them every three years when they retire by rotation. To give the shareholders a greater measure of control, s. 303 CA 1985 provides for removal of directors at any time by ordinary resolution (i.e., by a majority vote of the shareholders in general meeting). The power given by the section overrides anything in the company's articles (even, for example, an article naming a life director) or in an agreement with the director. This very important topic is dealt with in Chapter 8.

4 ALTERNATE DIRECTORS

Table A art. 65 gives a director power to appoint (subject to the approval of the board) an alternate director. Once appointed the alternate director has all the powers of the appointing director until he is removed by the appointing director or the appointing director ceases to be a director.

The provisions as to alternate directors were included in Table A for the first time on 1 July 1985. Therefore, in the case of companies formed before that date alternate directors cannot be appointed until special articles to that effect have been included in the articles of the company.

5 SHADOW DIRECTORS

A 'shadow director' is defined by s. 741(2) CA 1985 as 'any person in accordance with whose directions or instructions the directors of a company are accustomed to act'. However, a person who simply gives professional advice to the directors is not to be taken to be a shadow director.

Shadow directors are deemed to be directors of the company under some provisions of the Companies Acts. Their names should be included in the register of directors under s. 288 CA 1985. Most significantly, shadow directors are deemed to be directors for the purpose of s. 214 Insolvency Act 1986 and so may be held liable for wrongful trading. They may also be disqualified from holding office or being concerned in the management of any company (under the Company Directors Disqualification Act 1986) as if they were directors.

6 POWERS OF DIRECTORS

The powers of the directors are laid down in the articles. Table A art. 70 gives the directors wide powers, including in particular power to manage the business of the company. Article 70 is in the following terms:

Subject to the provisions of the Act, the memorandum and the articles and to any directions given by special resolution the business of the company shall be managed by the directors who may exercise all the powers of the company. No alteration of the memorandum or articles and no such direction shall invalidate any prior act of the directors which would have been valid if that alteration had not been made or that direction had not been given. The powers given by this regulation shall not be limited by any special power given to the directors by the articles and a meeting of directors at which a quorum is present may exercise all powers exercisable by the directors.

It should be noted that under the general law and under art. 70, decisions of the directors must be taken either at a board meeting at which a quorum is present or by unanimous agreement. This is, however, subject to the directors' power to delegate which is referred to in paragraphs 9 and 10 below.

Power given to the directors cannot be exercised by the members. However, if the directors are unwilling or unable to act (for example, because a quorum cannot be present at directors' meetings or the board is deadlocked), the members have the power to act to remedy the situation. The members also have power to sue in the name of the company and (under art. 70) to give directions by special resolution.

The powers of the directors must be exercised in accordance with the articles. Article 88, Table A allows the directors to decide how to regulate their own meetings and provides that any director may call a meeting or require the company secretary to do so at any time. No particular period of notice is required, so that a meeting will be validly held if reasonable notice is given. Notice need not be given to a director or alternate director who is absent from the UK.

Decisions at board meetings are taken by majority vote; if there is an equality of votes, art. 88 gives the chairman a casting vote. The chairman is chosen by the directors from among themselves (art. 91). The chairman's casting vote prevents deadlock (without it a resolution fails if there is an equality of votes), but it also means that the director who is the chairman has considerably more power than the others. In a company with only two directors he is, in effect, able to take decisions alone (provided that he calls a board meeting and outvotes his colleague). When a company is being formed the promoters should therefore consider very carefully whether arts. 88 and 91 need to be amended so as to remove the casting vote. Another matter that ought to be considered is the quorum. Article 89 allows the directors to decide on their own quorum but until they do so it is fixed at two. This may be entirely satisfactory but if the company represents several different interests, such as several different families, then a higher number may be appropriate.

Article 94 prohibits a director from voting or being counted towards the quorum on any resolution concerning a matter in which he has an interest or duty which is material and conflicts or may conflict with the interests of the company. However, this prohibition does not apply to:

(a)   a resolution concerning any guarantee, security or indemnity in respect of money lent to, or an obligation for the benefit of the company;

(b)   an arrangement whereby the company gives a guarantee, security or indemnity to a third party in respect of an obligation of the company guaranteed or indemnified by the director;

(c)   an interest arising from his buying any shares or other securities from the company; or

(d)   a resolution relating to a retirement benefits scheme.

Article 94 should be borne in mind when the quorum is fixed, so as to prevent problems, for example, when directors' service contracts are being discussed. Either the quorum can be reduced (to one if necessary) so that business can still be conducted when a director is interested in a contract, or art. 94 can be amended to allow the directors to count towards a quorum even if interested in a contract.

Article 93 allows the directors to pass valid resolutions without holding a board meeting provided *all* the directors entitled to receive notice of meetings (including alternate directors) sign a written resolution.

7 DIRECTORS' DUTIES

7.1 Fiduciary duties

Directors do not hold the property of their company on trust since the company is a separate legal entity and therefore is able to own property directly. However, directors do owe fiduciary duties to their company, that is, they are in the same position in respect of their powers as trustees or agents with respect to the company. Because of their fiduciary duties directors must not make any secret profit out of their position and they must exercise the powers given to them bona fide for the benefit of the company.

The concept of secret profit is a rather intangible one; it does not, of course, prevent directors from receiving remuneration for their services. A profit is a secret profit if it comes to the director because of his position as a director. Thus in *Cook* v *Deeks* [1916] 1 AC 554, two directors of a company negotiated a construction contract with the Canadian Pacific Railroad on behalf of their company. At a late stage in the negotiations they decided to take the contract in their own names. The Privy Council held that they were accountable to their company for the profit; it was only because they were directors of the company (which had previously contracted with the Canadian Pacific) that they were able to make the profit.

A secret profit must be paid over to the company even if the company itself could not have made the profit. This is well illustrated by *Boston Deep Sea Fishing Company* v *Ansell* (1888) 39 ChD 339. The defendant was a director of the plaintiff company and negotiated a contract on its behalf for the supply of ice to a fleet of fishing smacks owned by the company. The defendant was a shareholder in the ice-making company which had a policy of paying 'bonuses' to any of its shareholders who introduced work to it. The court held that the defendant was liable to the company for the bonuses even though the company itself could not have obtained them since it was not a shareholder in the ice-making company.

Although the fiduciary duty is to hand over what are described as secret profits, it seems that secrecy in this context means failure to obtain permission rather than actual secrecy. This is illustrated by the rather hard case of *Regal (Hastings) Ltd* v *Gulliver* [1967] 2 AC 134 (note), in which the plaintiff company owned a cinema and wished to buy two others in the same town with a view to selling all three together. The company could not raise sufficient money to buy the other cinemas and so another company was set up partly owned by Regal (Hastings) Ltd and partly by some of the directors of Regal (Hastings) Ltd who had money of their own to invest. The new company then purchased the other two cinemas. The purchasers who wished to acquire all three cinemas then purchased all the shares in Regal (Hastings)

Ltd and in the new company, thus acquiring control of the companies. The new board of directors then instituted proceedings on behalf of Regal (Hastings) Ltd against its former directors. It was held by the House of Lords that a secret profit had been made since the opportunity to invest in the new company only came to the defendants because they were directors of Regal (Hastings) Ltd. This profit was ordered to be paid to Regal (Hastings) Ltd even though that company had been unable to raise all the money needed for the purchase itself and even though, realistically, the consequence of the order was that the purchasers who had negotiated the purchase of the shares at a fair price got some of the purchase price repaid to their own company.

The second requirement of directors' fiduciary duties is that the directors must exercise their powers bona fide in the interests of the company as a whole. This involves two separate restrictions on directors' powers: first, that powers are given to directors for a particular reason or group of reasons and so their decisions can be challenged if they exercise powers for some other reason; and second, directors must not exercise their powers for motives of personal gain (this second reason will often overlap with the rule against secret profits). Many of the cases on this type of breach of duty have been concerned with the issue of shares by directors (a power which is in any case now much restricted by legislation — see ch. 5—2.2).

An illustration of the types of case where directors exercise power for motives of personal gain is given by *Piercy* v *S. Mills & Co Ltd* [1920] 1 Ch 77. In that case shares were issued, at a time when capital was not needed, purely for the purpose of strengthening and maintaining the directors' control of the company. The issue of shares was held to be invalid.

The fact that there is a breach of fiduciary duty where the directors exercise powers for reasons other than those for which they were granted even in the absence of personal gain, is illustrated by *Hogg* v *Cramphorn Ltd* [1967] Ch 254 and *Howard Smith Ltd* v *Ampol Petroleum Ltd* [1974] AC 821. In *Hogg* v *Cramphorn* directors issued shares to trustees for the benefit of the employees. The object of the directors in issuing the shares was to prevent the takeover of the company. It was held that the issue could be challenged even though the directors believed it to be in the interests of the company as a whole, since the power to issue shares is given to the directors so that they can raise capital. In *Howard Smith Ltd* v *Ampol* the Privy Council reached the same conclusion in a case where the shares were issued at a time when capital was needed by the company but the directors' real motive was to remove control from existing majority shareholders. Again, there was no suggestion of personal gain to the directors who thought the issue was in the interests of the company as a whole.

A breach of fiduciary duty may be ratified by the members and the directors themselves may vote in favour of the resolution. However, ratification is not possible where there has been a 'fraud on the minority'. It is not easy to draw a distinction between cases where ratification is possible and those where it is not, but it seems that breach of fiduciary duty without personal gain to the directors is ratifiable, breach of fiduciary duty coupled with personal gain by the directors and actual loss to the company is not. Thus in *Hogg* v *Cramphorn* the court adjourned before entering judgment so that a general meeting (at which the new 'shareholders' could not vote) could be called to consider ratification. A majority of the votes at that meeting was in favour of ratification so the issue of shares was validated. In *Regal (Hastings) Ltd* v *Gulliver* the court indicated that ratification would have been possible since the company had not been in a position to make the profit itself. The new shareholders were not, of course, willing to ratify the profit. The directors could have kept their secret profit if they had called a meeting of the company before selling their shares. In *Cook* v *Deeks*, on the other hand, ratification of the secret profit had been attempted but was declared invalid because a profit which could have been made by the company was diverted to the directors.

By analogy with the case of *Clemens* v *Clemens Brothers Ltd* [1976] 2 All ER 268 (which was not a case concerned with breach of directors' duties) there are probably circumstances in which ratification of a breach of directors' duties is not possible even though the company has not lost by the breach. In that case a majority shareholder (who owned 55% of the shares) and the directors (who were not then shareholders) wished to increase capital and issue shares to the directors. A general meeting was held at which a resolution was passed increasing capital and authorising the issue of shares to the directors. Although the directors have power to issue shares only so as to raise capital there is no doubt that the members may authorise or retrospectively ratify an issue of shares for other purposes (*Hogg* v *Cramphorn*) but nevertheless the court held that the right of members to vote at meetings of the company was subject to 'equitable considerations of fairness'. The object of the resolution for the issue of shares was to reduce the minority shareholders' interest in the company and so it was declared invalid.

7.2 Duties of care and skill

Directors may be liable to their companies for their negligence as well as for breach of fiduciary duty. The courts are always reluctant to interfere with business decisions, however foolish they may seem with the benefit of hindsight. The duty of care and skill required from a director is, therefore, a low one. In particular, the test applied is a subjective one, that is, a director need not exhibit in the performance of his duties a greater degree of skill than may reasonably be expected from a person of his knowledge and experience. Furthermore, directors are not liable because they have failed to attend board meetings at which they might have discovered that something was wrong, and are entitled to rely on officials (particularly a managing director) to whom the running of the business has been properly delegated (*Re City Equitable Fire Insurance Co Ltd* [1925] Ch 407). It is generally assumed (although without much authority from decided cases) that a full-time director will be held to a much higher standard of care than a part-time director, particularly if, as is very common, he has a service contract.

Where a company becomes insolvent a director may be held liable to contribute to the funds of the company on the basis that he has been guilty of 'wrongful trading'. Wrongful trading is an insolvency law concept and is dealt with in ch. 21 para. 7.3. For present purposes it is sufficient to note that the possiblity of such a finding should encourage a director not to act negligently in his business dealings despite the fact that a common law action by the company is unlikely to succeed.

7.3 Statutory duties

The duty to make returns to the Registrar of Companies will normally be performed on behalf of a company by its secretary, but directors are in some circumstances also liable to a fine if returns are not made (s. 730(5) CA 1985) and persistent default can lead to disqualification. The directors are also under a duty to keep minutes of their own meetings and to deliver accounts (for more details, see ch. 9).

Section 309 CA 1985 provides that directors shall have regard to the interests of the company's employees in general as well as the interests of its members. However, this duty is only enforceable by the shareholders, not by the employees.

7.4   Relief from liability

We have already seen that a breach of fiduciary duty may be excused by the members in certain circumstances. In the case of negligence a resolution not to sue the director has the same effect. Section 310, CA 1985 provides: 'any provision, whether contained in a company's articles or in any contract with the company or otherwise, for exempting any officer of the company . . . from, or indemnifying him against, any liability which by virtue of any rule of law would otherwise attach to him . . . is void'. Thus it is impossible to grant general exemption in advance to directors in respect of liability to the company. However, s. 310 (as amended by CA 1989) does specifically permit a company to take out insurance on behalf of a director against liability. A company may also indemnify a director against costs incurred in successfully defending any proceedings in which judgment is given in his favour or in which he is acquitted.

Section 727 CA 1985 gives the court power to relieve a director or other officer from liability for 'negligence, default, breach of duty or breach of trust' provided that he has 'acted honestly and reasonably and that having regard to all the circumstances of the case . . . he ought fairly to be excused . . .'. The director does not have to wait to be sued but can bring an application to seek relief if he 'apprehend[s] that any claim will or might be made against him . . .'.

7.5   Directors' duties to shareholders

Directors' duties are owed to the company and not to the shareholders. However, they may make themselves liable to individual shareholders by becoming their agents. For example, in *Allen* v *Hyatt* (1914) 30 TLR 444, directors who obtained options to purchase shares from other shareholders so as to facilitate the takeover of a company were held accountable to the shareholders for the personal profits which they made by taking the shares themselves.

7.6   Directors' duties to third parties

A director does not generally owe any duty to a person dealing with his company. However, a director makes himself liable to such a person in a particular case if he claims an authority to bind his company which he does not have. The action resulting from such a liability is called an action for breach of warranty of authority.

Similarly, a director may be liable to third parties under statutory provisions. For example, any person (including a director) who is knowingly a party to fraudulent trading by a company which goes into liquidation may be declared liable for the debts of the company by the court. A director may also be made liable for the debts of an insolvent company following a finding of wrongful trading. Directors are also liable to the DHSS for social security contributions not paid by the company and for unpaid tax in certain circumstances.

In *C. Evans & Sons Ltd* v *Spritebrand Ltd and another* [1985] 2 All ER 415, the Court of Appeal held that a director may be personally liable for torts committed by his company as a result of his decisions. This point was decided as a preliminary issue without a hearing on the facts, so that the scope of the decision remains unclear.

Finally, a director may make himself personally liable for the debts of his company by giving a personal guarantee for the company's liability. In practice such guarantees are frequently required by banks and others who lend to private companies. The giving of a personal guarantee may, in some cases, amount almost to the abandonment of limited liability by the person who gives it.

8 STATUTORY PROVISIONS CONCERNING DIRECTORS

Because of the very high degree of control which directors are able to exercise over their companies a number of statutory provisions have been enacted for the protection of shareholders and the public generally.

8.1 Disclosure of information

8.1.1 Register of directors
Section 288 CA 1985 requires every company to keep at its registered office a register of directors. In respect of each director (including any shareholder director) the following information must be given:

(a)   present Christian or other forename(s) and surname;
(b)   any former names (there are limited exceptions, the most important being that married women need not state their maiden names or other names by which they were known before marriage);
(c)   residential address;
(d)   business occupation;
(e)   other directorships held or which, during the last five years have been held by the director other than directorships in dormant companies or in companies wholly owned by or wholly owning the company.
(It is also advisable to include dates of appointment and removal from office.)

The same information must also be sent to the Registrar of Companies. Form G10 is used for notification of particulars of the first directors and Form G288 must be sent to the Registrar within 14 days of any change in the particulars (whether because a director is appointed or ceases to hold office, or because of changes in the particulars of the continuing directors). When he receives notice of a change in the particulars of directors the Registrar must officially notify (i.e., advertise in the *London Gazette*) the fact of receipt and until he has done so the company cannot rely on the change against any other person unless that person actually knew of the change (s. 42 CA 1985). As stated earlier, the register of directors kept by the company must be available for inspection by the members and the public at the registered office and, of course, the particulars may also be obtained by searching at the Companies' Registry.

8.1.2   Register of directors' interests

A director is under an obligation to give to the company certain information about his interests in the company's shares and debentures (s. 324 CA 1985) and the company must keep a register of such interests. Any type of interest in shares or debentures must be reported, including, for example, outright ownership, options to purchase and charges — the register, therefore, includes information which cannot be obtained from the register of members which deals only with legal ownership. Notification and registration are also required of interests of the spouse and infant children (including step-children) of the director. Any change in the particulars of directors' interests must be reported to the company within five days of the change or, if later, within five days of the director becoming aware of the change. The company must amend the register (which is open to inspection by the members and the public) within three days of receiving notice from the director. The register of directors' interests is *not* submitted to the Registrar of Companies.

8.1.3   Service contracts

Copies of directors' service contracts must be available for inspection by the members (s. 318 CA 1985). If a director does not have a written service contract then a written memorandum of his terms of service must be kept instead.

8.1.4   Publicity as to names of directors

Section 305 CA 1985 prevents a company from giving publicity to the names of directors in business letters unless the names (including forenames or initials) of all the directors are given.

8.1.5   Disclosure of interests in contracts

Section 317, CA 1985 requires a director who is directly or indirectly interested in a contract or proposed contract with his company to declare the nature of his interest at a board meeting. Notice must be given at the first meeting at which the contract is discussed or at the first meeting after the director becomes interested in the contract. Where the director is a member of another company or firm he may give general notice stating that he is interested in any contract with the company, and then he need not disclose his interest each time such a contract is discussed.

8.2   Restrictions on freedom of contract

8.2.1   Loans to directors

The latest of the successively more stringent provisions preventing loans to directors is contained in ss. 330-347 CA 1985. A private company may not make a loan or loans of more than £5,000 in aggregate to a director of the company or a director of its holding company nor may it guarantee or provide security in connection with a loan made by any person to such a director. However, a loan of any amount may be made if its purpose is 'to provide a director with funds to meet expenditure incurred or to be incurred by him for the purposes of the company or for the purpose of enabling him properly to perform his duties', provided that the members in general meeting give approval in advance or the loan is repayable within six months of the next annual general meeting (s. 337).

8.2.2 *Directors' service contracts*

The terms of directors' service contracts will usually be determined by the board although members are entitled to information about the terms of such contracts and a director may not usually vote on his own service contract (Table A art. 94). Section 319 requires the approval of the members in general meeting of a term in the service contract of a director under which he cannot be removed by notice for a period exceeding five years. Approval is also required where an existing contract is extended if the aggregate term exceeds five years. Although only the service contracts of directors require approval of the members in this way, it is not possible to circumvent the section by providing for employment in a capacity other than as a director (for example, as a consultant) after the directorship ceases.

8.2.3 *Property transactions*

A third restriction on the freedom of directors to contract with their companies is provided by s. 320 CA 1985. This requires the approval of the members in general meeting for the contracts to which it applies. Section 320 applies to any arrangement whereby a director or a person connected with a director is to acquire from the company one or more non-cash assets of the 'requisite value' or whereby the company is to acquire such assets from such a person. The 'requisite value' depends on the net assets of the company as shown in the company's most recent balance sheet. A non-cash asset is of the requisite value 'if at the time the arrangement in question is entered into its value is not less than £1,000 but, subject to that, exceeds £50,000 or 10% of the amount of the company's relevant assets'. Thus if the company's net assets are £500,000 or more the requisite value is £50,000. If the net assets are less than £500,000 but more than £10,000 the requisite value is 10% of such assets. If the net assets are £10,000 or less the requisite value is £1,000.

If a contract is made in contravention of the section it is voidable by the company unless: (a) restitution is no longer possible; (b) third party rights (acquired for value without notice) would be affected by avoidance; or (c) the contract has been affirmed by the members in general meeting. Furthermore, the directors who authorised the arrangement (not just the one who is a party to the contract) are liable to indemnify the company against any loss. The director or connected person who is a party to the contract is liable to account for any profit made, although a connected person is excused from liability if he did not know the circumstances. For the purposes of s. 320 a connected person includes (among others) a director's spouse, child or step-child.

The main purpose of s. 320 is to prevent directors from making substantial profits in transactions with their companies and so reinforces the rules of equity concerning secret profits. One fairly common type of contract which is subject to its provisions is a contract under which a director receives shares in return for assets, so that if a director who owns business premises (of the requisite value) wishes to transfer them to the company in return for shares, the approval of the members in general meeting must first be obtained.

9   MANAGING DIRECTORS

It is very common for one of the directors of a company to be appointed managing director. The functions actually performed by the managing director vary from company to company, but in practice he will usually be either the most senior director in the company's hierarchy or second in command to the chairman. A managing director cannot be appointed unless the articles (or, rarely, the memorandum) so provide. Table A, art. 84 does so provide and art. 72 provides that: '[the directors] may . . . delegate to any managing director . . . such of their powers as they consider desirable to be exercised by him'.

The board are also given the power to specify what his powers are to be and to impose conditions. The powers granted may even be to the exclusion of the powers of the board but can be revoked or altered at any time by the board.

In practice, the managing director will usually have a service contract even if the other directors do not. The terms of the contract will be negotiated by the managing director and the board; the members' approval will be required if he is given security of tenure for longer than five years (s. 319 CA 1985 — see above). The managing director is both a director and an employee of the company; like other employees he has certain statutory rights against the company if he is unfairly dismissed or made redundant. Since he automatically ceases to be managing director if he ceases to be a director, the members can remove him from both offices by passing an ordinary resolution (s. 303 CA 1985) but this may result in heavy damages being payable by the company for breach of the service contract.

10 DELEGATION BY DIRECTORS

The model form of articles in Table A appears to be drafted on the assumption that the directors will take most of the major decisions and may delegate their powers to a managing director. Table A is, however, sufficiently flexible to be used by companies with other corporate structures. For example, if the intention is that the company is to be run as if it were a partnership, equality of power can be achieved by not appointing a chairman or managing director. If, on the other hand, one person has built up the business of the company and intends to keep control of it, he can ensure that he retains control by keeping a majority of the votes; any other directors are then subject to removal under s. 303 and are often in commercial terms, no more than senior employees.

In the case of a company which has a substantial business it would not be possible for the board to take all the decisions collectively nor for the managing director to take them all personally. Delegation by the board is, therefore, necessary. Table A art. 72 (in addition to allowing delegation to a managing director) gives the board power to delegate any powers to committees of one or more directors. Delegation to directors holding 'executive office' is also permitted. It is not clear what is meant by executive office but it would probably include directors with titles such as 'financial director' and 'director of personnel' and possibly any full-time directors. In any case, as delegation is permitted to committees of one director, doubts as to the meaning of the term 'executive office' should not lead to any practical problems. In each case of delegation the board may impose conditions and the delegation may create powers collateral with those of the board or to the exclusion of the board's power, but the board always retains power to revoke or alter the terms of the delegation.

It is also recognised that implementation of decisions may be left to employees of the company. The directors are not liable to the company if they rely on employees who in fact behave improperly. The degree to which decision making is delegated to non-directors varies enormously from company to company and is obviously most necessary in the case of large companies.

11 THE COMPANY SECRETARY

Section 283 CA 1985 requires every company to have a secretary. The secretary may also be a director but, to ensure there are always two officers of the company, a *sole* director cannot also be secretary. The first secretary of a newly formed company is the person named in Form G10; subsequently the secretary is appointed and removed by the board who also decide on the terms of appointment (Table A art. 99). The secretary is responsible for keeping the various records of the company, such as minutes of board and general meetings and the various records which must be kept at the registered office. He is also an officer of the company and so is liable to a fine if the company is in breach of the provisions of the Companies Act which require information to be filed with the Registrar of Companies.

Many company secretaries are given powers far in excess of those contemplated by the Companies Act. Often the secretary is responsible for the administration of the company and performs the functions of an office manager as well as of a record-keeper. The courts have, therefore, recognised that an outsider is entitled to rely on a decision taken by the secretary which relates to administration even if it turns out that the decision was not authorised by the board (i.e., the secretary has ostensible authority to make such contracts). Thus in *Panorama (Developments) Guildford Ltd v Fidelis Furnishing Fabrics Ltd* [1971] 2 QB 711, the Court of Appeal held that a company was bound to pay for the use of cars hired by the secretary purportedly on behalf of the company but in fact for his own use.

Every company must keep a register of directors and secretaries and notify the Registrar of Companies within 14 days of any change (s. 288 CA 1985). In the case of a secretary the particulars to be given are the present and past names of the secretary (subject to the same exceptions as apply in the case of a director) and his usual residential address.

12 AUDITORS

The function of auditors is to examine the company's accounts and to make a report on them to the members in general meeting. Section 237 CA 1985 gives the auditor a right of access at all times to the books and accounts of the company and also a right to require the officers of the company to provide him with 'such information and explanations as he thinks necessary for the performance of the auditor's duties'. It is an offence for an officer of the company knowingly or recklessly to give false or misleading information to the auditor.

The auditor's report must deal with the accounts which he has examined including the profit and loss account, balance sheet and, where relevant, group accounts laid before the members in general meeting (i.e., the accounts which will usually be open to public inspection and submitted to the Registrar). The auditor's report must state whether the accounts have been prepared in accordance with the provisions of the Companies Act and whether the accounts give a 'true and fair view' of the company's state of affairs at the end of the accounting period and of the profit or loss made during the accounting period. If the auditor is not satisfied that proper records have been kept or is of the opinion that the accounts are not in agreement with the records he must say so in his report.

The auditor must exercise reasonable care and skill otherwise he is liable to the company for breach of contract. In *Re Kingston Cotton Mill Company (No. 2)* [1896] 2 Ch 279, Lopes LJ described the auditor's duty as follows:

> He is a watchdog, but not a bloodhound. He is justified in believing tried servants of the company in whom confidence is placed by the company . . . If there is anything calculated to excite his suspicion he must probe it to the bottom; but in the absence of anything of that kind he is only bound to be reasonably cautious and careful.

The auditor may also make himself liable in tort if he reports to an individual member or investor but he is not liable to the world at large merely because his report is open to public inspection (*Caparo Industries plc* v *Dickman* (1990)).

The members in general meeting appoint the auditor (s. 384 CA 1985, as amended); the appointment is made at the meeting at which the accounts are laid before the members and is effective until the next meeting at which accounts are considered. In the vast majority of cases this means that the auditor is appointed at the annual general meeting each year. The directors may appoint the first auditor (to hold office until the first meeting at which accounts are considered) and may also fill casual vacancies. An auditor may be removed from office by the members at any time; special notice (i.e., 28 days' notice to the company) must be given by any member who proposes such a resolution. Special notice is also required of a resolution appointing anyone other than the retiring auditor.

Private companies are able to dispense with the holding of meetings to consider company accounts by passing an elective resolution. Where this has been done auditors must be appointed within 28 days of accounts being sent to the members. (CA 1985 s. 385A inserted by CA 1989 s. 119). A private company may also pass an elective resolution to dispense with the annual appointment of auditors. In such cases the auditors remain in office indefinitely but the shareholders retain the right to remove them.

The requirement that company accounts should be properly audited is a matter of public interest as well as a matter of interest to the shareholders since the information about the accounts is open to public inspection. An auditor, therefore, requires a professional qualification from a 'recognised professional body'. In effect, this means he must be a professionally qualified accountant.

A firm may be appointed (this is, in fact, very common), in which case the appointment extends to all the qualified members of the firm at the date of appointment.

The auditor must be independent of the company. It is not, therefore, possible to appoint an officer or servant of the company or a person who is a partner of or in the employment of an officer or servant of the company.

4 Members and Meetings

1 MEMBERSHIP OF A COMPANY

When a company is first incorporated the subscribers to the memorandum automatically become members. As we saw in Chapter 2, at least two people must subscribe to the memorandum and must agree to take at least one share each. Section 22(1) CA 1985 provides that: 'The subscribers of a company's memorandum are deemed to have agreed to become members of the company, and on its registration shall be entered as such in its register of members'. When a company is formed by law stationers with a view to its sale at a later date to someone who wants to buy a company 'off-the-peg', the subscribers will not wish to take part in management once the company is sold. In such cases it is common for the subscribers to renounce their right to allotment of shares by writing to the company saying that they no longer wish to take the shares. The subscribers' names are simply not entered in the register of members; strictly speaking this is a breach of s. 22 and the subscribers remain liable to pay for the shares they have agreed to take (usually only one £1 share each) until all the nominal capital has been issued. In practice, however, this method of dealing with subscribers' shares is simpler than issuing the shares to the subscribers followed by a transfer to the people who wish to be the members of the company.

Section 22(2) CA 1985 provides that: 'Every other person who agrees to become a member of a company, and whose name is entered in its register of members, is a member of the company.' This means that, except in the case of subscribers, membership begins with the entry of the member's name in the register of members (which is dealt with in paragraph 2 of this chapter). The *right* to become a member under s. 22(2) may result from a contract between the company and the purchaser for the allotment of new shares (see ch. 5). The right may also arise where an existing shareholder transfers shares or where shares pass to personal representatives or a trustee in bankruptcy (see ch. 17).

Generally speaking, any person has legal capacity to be a member of a company:

(a)   Infants may be members (although a contract to buy the shares is subject to the general rules of contract law relating to infants' contracts and so is usually voidable by the infant within a reasonable time of reaching majority).

(b)   Personal representatives and trustees in bankruptcy may also be members (see ch. 17).

(c)   A company may also own shares in another company provided that the owning company is given power in its memorandum to own shares (most memoranda do give this power).

2 THE REGISTER OF MEMBERS

2.1 Contents

As mentioned earlier, every company must keep a register of members and, as explained above, it is the entry of a name in the register which makes someone a member of the company. Section 352, CA 1985 requires that the following information should be recorded in the register:

(a)   the names and addresses of the members;
(b)   the number of shares held and, where the company has more than one class of issued shares, the number of each class held by each member;
(c)   the amount paid or agreed to be considered as paid on the shares of each member;
(d)   the date at which each member was entered in the register;
(e)   the date at which each member ceased to be a member.

No particular form of register is required (since 1967 it may even be kept by a computer), but under s. 354 CA 1985 an index is required if the register is not kept in the form of an index and there are more than 50 members (this provision is of little relevance to private companies since very few of them have more than 50 members). The register must normally be kept at the registered office of the company and if kept elsewhere the Registrar of Companies must be notified (s. 353 CA 1985). The register of members itself is not sent to the Registrar but the annual return made by the company after each AGM contains details of the membership.

As noted in Chapter 2, the register (and, where there is one, index) of members must be open to inspection (by members free of charge and by the public on payment of 5p) during business hours for at least two hours during every business day (s. 356 CA 1985).

2.2   Trusts

Section 360 CA 1985 provides that 'no notice of any trust . . . shall be entered on the register . . .'. This means that the company must treat the registered holder of shares as beneficially entitled to those shares even if it knows that they are held on trust. The company must, therefore, pay dividends to the trustee and allow the trustee to exercise any voting powers attached to the shares. The effect of this rule is well illustrated by the case of *Pender* v *Lushington* (1877) 6 ChD 70, where the chairman of the meeting refused to count votes attached to shares owned by the plaintiff's nominee because under the rather unusual articles of the company no member could have more than a certain number of votes and Pender had transferred shares so as to circumvent this rule. The Master of the Rolls held that the chairman must ignore the trust and count the votes of the nominee.

In *Simpson* v *Molson's Bank* [1895] AC 270, a shareholder died and the shares were registered in the name of his executors, one of whom was a director of the company. The executors transferred the shares in breach of the provisions of the will. A copy of the will had been sent to the company to prove the identity of the executors. The company was held not to be liable to the true beneficiary of the will since it was not entitled to take notice of any trusts over the shares. Once satisfied that the executors were entitled to be registered and once it had registered them the company was bound to allow them to transfer the shares.

Section 360 does not, of course, affect the position as between the registered owner and his beneficiary. The registered owner must, therefore, hand over to the beneficiary any dividend he receives and vote in accordance with the beneficiary's wishes.

2.3 Rectification of the register

Section 359, CA 1985 gives the court power to order rectification of the register of members if:

(a) the name of any person is, without sufficient cause, entered in or omitted from [the register]; . . . or

(b) default is made or unnecessary delay takes place in entering on the register the fact of any person having ceased to be a member.

Application may be made by the person aggrieved, any member, or the company. Damages may be awarded to the person aggrieved in addition to an order for rectification. When a person is entitled to be registered or removed from the register the court will generally order rectification if the company has not made the necessary changes within two months.

In addition to its powers under s. 359 the court may order rectification of the register in other circumstances where it is just and equitable. Thus in *Burns* v *Siemens Brothers Dynamo Works Ltd* [1919] 1 Ch 225, shares were registered in the name of two joint holders. The articles of the company provided that where there were joint holders only the first named could vote (cf. Table A art. 55, which in such a case allows the second joint holder to vote only if the first does not). The person whose name appeared second sought rectification and the court ordered that half the shares should be registered with his name appearing first in the register.

One of the circumstances in which rectification may be applied for is when the company *wrongly* refuses to register a transfer. However, a person to whom shares are transferred does not always have a right to be registered (see ch. 17).

3 POWERS AND DUTIES OF MEMBERS

The powers of the members of a company are not easy to define succinctly. As we saw in Chapter 3, most of the decisions of a company are taken by the board of directors (unless the articles are very unusual), but certain powers are specifically given to the members by the Companies Act and these cannot be taken away by the memorandum or articles (for example, the power to remove directors from office (see ch. 8), and the power to alter the articles (see ch. 6—4)). In addition to these powers which are guaranteed by law, certain powers are also given to members by the articles. Thus, if Table A applies, the members have power to elect new directors and to declare dividends. It should be noted that the powers given to members are given collectively; therefore, a shareholder (or group of shareholders) who controls the majority of the votes at a company meeting is obviously in a far stronger position than a 'minority' shareholder.

In practical terms, a majority shareholder has extensive powers of control, exercisable ultimately by removing or threatening to remove the directors from office. A minority shareholder often has no real power (unless he is a director and/or can persuade the majority to agree with him), but his position is protected by a number of rights, mostly statutory, some of the most important of which are discussed later in this chapter and in Chapter 8. It should also be noted that both the powers and rights given to members depend in many cases on the holding of a particular proportion of the company's shares (or votes). For example, many types of decision require a special resolution (75% majority) — a shareholder who controls 75% of the votes is, therefore, able to exercise powers which a shareholder with a simple majority could not exercise alone. Conversely, a shareholder with more than 25% of the votes can block a special resolution even though he may not have enough votes to be in control of the company (this is sometimes called negative control).

Just as the powers and rights of members largely depend on the proportion of votes that they control, so the duties of members differ depending on whether or not they are in control of the company. The basic rule is that members (whether or not in control) can exercise their right to vote as they wish, so that they can take account of their own interests to the exclusion of conflicting interest of other shareholders. This does not mean that shareholders are *entirely* free to vote as they please; thus certain breaches of duty by directors cannot be ratified by the members (see for example, *Cook* v *Deeks* ch. 3—7) while other breaches can be ratified (*Regal (Hastings) Ltd* v *Gulliver* ch. 3—7). Shareholders may not commit a 'fraud on the minority', so that an alteration to the articles is invalid if it discriminates against some of the shareholders (see ch. 6—4). Both these exceptions to the basic rule are well established, but the case of *Clemens* v *Clemens Brothers Ltd* [1976] 2 All ER 268, suggests that the duty of controlling shareholders may be much more extensive than was previously thought. The facts were as follows. The plaintiff owned 45% of the shares in the company and her aunt all the remainder. The directors were not shareholders. Under the articles a shareholder had a right of pre-emption if another shareholder wished to transfer shares so that one day the plaintiff hoped to obtain control of the company. The aunt passed a resolution for the issue of shares to the directors and to a trust for the employees of the company. The object of the resolution was apparently to deprive the plaintiff of her power to block special resolutions. The court set aside the resolution and declared it invalid. Foster J said:

> I think that one thing which emerges from the cases to which I have referred [which were concerned with the established categories of fraud on the minority] is that in such a case as the present [the aunt] is not entitled to exercise her majority vote in whatever way she pleases. The difficulty is in finding a principle, and obviously expressions such as 'bona fide for the benefit of the company as a whole', 'fraud on the minority' and 'oppressive' do not assist in formulating a principle.
>
> I have come to the conclusion that it would be unwise to try to produce a principle, since the circumstances of each case are infinitely varied. It would not, I think, assist to say more than that in my judgment [the aunt] is not entitled as of right to exercise her votes as an ordinary shareholder in any way she pleases . . . that right is subject to equitable considerations which will make it unjust to exercise it [in the way she has].

The exact scope of this decision (which was not appealed against) remains to be seen, but it may well make an important turning point in the court's attitude to minority shareholders. The powers given to the courts by ss. 459-461 CA 1985 strengthen the position of minorities considerably (see ch. 8).

The powers of shareholders to control their companies are normally exercised by passing a resolution by the required majority at a meeting called by the appropriate notice at which a quorum is present. Alternatively, a written resolution may be used (see para. 4.6). Members who are absent do not, of course, count in the voting unless they have validly appointed a proxy to represent them.

4 MEETINGS

4.1 Types of general meeting

The meetings of a private company are of two types: annual general meetings and extraordinary general meetings. The meetings are called 'general' meetings to distinguish them from board meetings (that is, meetings of the directors), and class meetings (that is, meetings of classes of shareholders called to discuss matters of interest to one class of shareholders only). An annual general meeting (AGM) must be held once in every calendar year and must be within 15 months of the last AGM. However, a company need not hold an AGM during the (calendar) year of incorporation or during the next calendar year provided the first AGM is held within 18 months of incorporation. For example, if a company is incorporated on 20 November 1985 its first AGM may be held at any time up to 19 May 1987 (which is, just, within 18 months); but if a company is incorporated on 20 April 1985 it may not wait until 1987 (since any date in 1987 is more than 18 months after incorporation) to hold the first AGM.

Private companies are able to dispense with the need to hold an annual general meeting. In order to do so they must first pass an elective resolution (see paragraph 4.2 below).

Any meeting which is not an AGM is an extraordinary general meeting (EGM). An EGM is held as and when necessary. The procedure for calling such a meeting will be considered shortly, but first it is necessary to consider the types of resolution needed to transact business at general meetings.

4.2 Resolutions

A company in general meeting can only transact business by passing the appropriate type of resolution. There are four types of resolution: ordinary, extraordinary, special and elective. An ordinary resolution is one which requires a simple majority of votes in favour if it is to be passed (a simple majority means more votes in favour than against — an equality of votes is not sufficient). Where there is an equality an ordinary resolution may, however, be passed on the chairman's casting vote if the articles so provide. Table A art. 50 gives the chairman a casting vote. In the case of a small company the decision as to whether to allow an article giving a casting vote may be crucial. The presence of a casting vote resolves the problem of deadlock but may in some cases be considered to give the chairman too much power.

An extraordinary resolution and a special resolution both require a three-quarters majority — that is, at least three votes must be cast in favour of the resolution for every one cast against it. The difference between an extraordinary resolution and a special resolution is that an extraordinary resolution (like an ordinary resolution) requires the same length of notice as the meeting at which it is to be considered (14 days at an EGM, 21 at an AGM), whereas a special resolution requires 21 days' notice even if it is to be considered at an EGM. An elective resolution depends on the unanimous approval of all the shareholders or their proxies (unanimous agreement by all who attend and vote is not sufficient) and 21 days notice is required.

The Companies Act lays down many circumstances in which a special resolution is required. Among the most important from the point of view of the shareholder are resolutions to alter the articles or objects, and resolutions to exclude pre-emption rights on the issue of shares. Any generalisation as to when a special resolution is required is perhaps a dangerous simplification, but if there is a factor common to all the circumstances it is probably that they are all circumstances where minority shareholders need protection. It is a common mistake to suppose that all alterations to the memorandum require a special resolution. This is not so since, for example, capital can be increased by ordinary resolution if the articles so provide. A special resolution may be required by the articles of the company in any other circumstances where the Act does not require some other kind of resolution (an ordinary resolution is required by s. 303 for the removal of a director from office and an extraordinary resolution in the circumstances referred to below). It is, in fact, very uncommon for the articles to require a special resolution where the Act does not do so. If the company wishes to give the minority shareholders the greater protection of a three-quarters majority, the articles will usually provide for an extraordinary resolution.

An extraordinary resolution and a special resolution both require a three-quarters majority — that is, at least three votes must be cast in favour of the resolution for every one cast against it. The difference between an extraordinary resolution and a special resolution is that an extraordinary resolution (like an ordinary resolution) requires the same length of notice as the meeting at which it is to be considered (14 days at an EGM, 21 at an AGM), whereas a special resolution requires 21 days' notice even if it is to be considered at an EGM. An elective resolution depends on the unanimous approval of all the shareholders or their proxies (unanimous agreement by all who attend and vote is not sufficient) and 21 days notice is required.

The Companies Act lays down many circumstances in which a special resolution is required. Among the most important from the point of view of the shareholder are resolutions to alter the articles or objects, and resolutions to exclude pre-emption rights on the issue of shares. Any generalisation as to when a special resolution is required is perhaps a dangerous simplification, but if there is a factor common to all the circumstances it is probably that they are all circumstances where minority shareholders need protection. It is a common mistake to suppose that all alterations to the memorandum require a special resolution. This is not so since, for example, capital can be increased by ordinary resolution if the articles so provide. A special resolution may be required by the articles of the company in any other circumstances where the Act does not require some other kind of resolution (an ordinary resolution is required by s. 303 for the removal of a director from office and an extraordinary resolution in the circumstances referred to below). It is, in fact, very uncommon for the articles to require a special resolution where the Act does not do so. If the company wishes to give the minority shareholders the greater protection of a three-quarters majority, the articles will usually provide for an extraordinary resolution.

An extraordinary resolution is provided for by the Companies Act in a small number of circumstances where it is considered that minority shareholders require protection but the matter is urgent. The most important of these circumstances is where a resolution is passed to commence a voluntary winding-up because of the company's liabilities (s. 572(1)(c) CA 1985). As with a special resolution, the articles can require an extraordinary resolution in any circumstances where the Act does not require some other sort of resolution.

The Companies Act 1985, s. 379A (interpolated by CA 1989) allows a private company to simplify its own internal management by passing elective resolutions. Such resolutions may:

(a)   authorise the directors to allot shares for an indefinite period (see ch. 5 para. 2.2);

(b)   dispense with the need to hold a shareholders meeting for the consideration of accounts (see ch. 9 para. 5.2);

(c)   dispense with the holding of an AGM (see para. 4.1 above);

(d)   permit the holding of a meeting with short notice with the approval of 90% of the members (see para. 4.4 below); and

(e)   dispense with the need to make annual appointment of auditors (see ch. 3 para. 12).

The Secretary of State is given power to extend or limit the purposes for which elective resolutions may be passed by regulations. Once passed, an elective resolution may be revoked by an ordinary resolution.

An ordinary resolution is sufficient to transact any business at a general meeting save in those cases where the Companies Acts requires special, extraordinary or elective resolutions or where the articles require special or extraordinary resolutions.

4.3   Calling a general meeting

As we saw in Chapter 3, directors' meetings can be called quite informally at the request of any one of the directors. The position in relation to general meetings is much more complicated. As with so many aspects of company law, the rules are partly statutory and partly depend on the provisions of the company's own articles. Most of the statutory rules are designed to protect the shareholders whose voting rights would be worthless if they were not backed up by rights to call meetings. The statutory rules will be considered first and then the provisions of Table A.

Section 367, CA 1985 provides that if default is made in holding an annual general meeting when required, the Department of Trade can call a meeting on the application of any member and can order that one person shall constitute a quorum at the meeting.

Section 368 is the most important statutory provision dealing with meetings as far as the shareholder is concerned. This section allows shareholders who are registered as owners of 'not less than one tenth of such of the paid-up capital of the company as . . . carries the right of voting at general meetings' to requisition a meeting. The requisition must be in writing and signed and must be deposited at the registered office. Once this has been done the directors *must* call a meeting for a date within 28 days of the issue of the notice. If within 21 days of the requisition, the directors have not taken the necessary steps to call the meeting, the requisitionists may call the meeting themselves at the company's expense. Section 368 does not say that the requisitionists have a right to specify what resolutions are to be discussed at the meeting but s. 368(3) clearly implies that they have such a right. Most private companies have only a very small number of members, so that wherever there is any real chance of success (i.e., of passing a resolution) there should be no difficulty in requisitioning a meeting. In fact, it should not be necessary in many cases to use s. 368, since the directors will usually be willing to call a meeting when required (for the directors' power to call general meetings, see below).

Section 370 provides a separate power for 'two or more members holding not less than one tenth of the issued share capital' to call a meeting. In the majority of circumstances this adds little to s. 368, but it should be noted that under s. 370 the shares need not represent one tenth of the *paid-up* capital but only of the *issued* capital, nor need the shares carry the right to vote. Section 370 has one substantial advantage over s. 368 — that is, the members can themselves call the meeting (although they must, of course, give proper notice), so that there will be less delay before the meeting is held than in the case of s. 368. Unlike s. 368, s. 370 only has effect 'in so far as the articles of the company do not make other provision in that behalf': that is, it can be excluded or varied by the articles. Table A does not exclude s. 370.

Section 371 gives the court power to order meetings 'if for any reason it is impracticable to call a meeting of a company in any manner in which meetings of that company may be called'. The section gives the court power to order that a single member may constitute a quorum at such a meeting. The most obvious case in which s. 371 might be resorted to is where it is impossible to call a meeting, but in *Re El Sombrero Ltd* [1958] Ch 900, the court ordered a meeting with a quorum of one when a majority shareholder found it impossible to remove the directors from office because they refused to attend meetings and thus made a quorum impossible.

Although it is not concerned with the calling of meetings, s. 376 should be considered by minority shareholders who wish to have items discussed by the company. This section enables members with 5% or more of the voting rights to insist that a resolution should be included in the agenda of the next AGM. Notice requesting such inclusion must be given at least six weeks before the meeting. (Note: this section does not apply to an EGM.)

Table A art. 37 gives the directors power to decide when to call the AGM and to call an EGM at any time. The vast majority of EGMs will be called in this way. Article 37 also provides that if there are not sufficient directors present in the UK to constitute a quorum at a board meeting, a single director or any member may convene a meeting.

4.4   Notice of meetings

Business at a meeting cannot be properly transacted or relied upon unless proper notice has been given of the meeting. Section 370(2) provides that 'notice of the meeting of a company shall be served on every member of it in the manner in which notices are required to be served by Table A (as for the time being, in force)'. The articles in Table A dealing with notices are numbers 38-39 and 111-116.

Article 38 requires notice of general meetings (of both types) to be given to all the members, persons entitled to a share in consequence of the death or bankruptcy of a member, the directors and auditors. Article 112 relieves the company from the duty to give notice to members who have no registered address in the UK, and art. 116 provides that notice need only be given to personal representatives and trustees in bankruptcy if they have supplied the company with an address to which notices are to be sent; if they have not done so, service on the dead or bankrupt member is deemed effective if sent to his registered address as if the death or bankruptcy had not occurred.

Article 112 provides for personal service or service by post. Where service is by post, it is presumed to have been served 48 hours after posting.

Article 39 provides that accidental omission to give notice to someone entitled to it, does not invalidate the meeting. Accidental omission would include clerical errors but not a failure to give notice resulting from a failure to apply the articles properly (*Young* v *Ladies Imperial Club Ltd* [1920] 2 KB 523).

The length of notice required depends on the nature of the meeting and of the resolutions to be proposed at it. For an AGM, 21 days' notice is required. For an EGM, 14 days' notice is required, unless a special resolution (or, where Table A applies, a resolution appointing someone to be a director) or elective resolution is to be proposed, when the period is 21 days. Table A art. 38 provides that notice periods are to be 14 and 21 'clear days', that is, exclusive of the date of service and the date of the meeting. Thus, for example, if the directors wish to hold an EGM at which a special resolution is to be proposed and post the notices on Monday 1 March the meeting cannot be held before Thursday 25 March. (Notice deemed served on 3 March (art. 112), 4-24 March inclusive is the 21 clear days, so the meeting can be held on the next day.)

Section 369(3) and art. 38 provide that shorter notice than that normally required is valid if all the members attend the meeting and agree to short notice, in the case of an AGM, or a majority in number owning 95% (or such lesser percentage — but not less than 90% — as specified in an elective resolution) of the voting shares in the case of an EGM. For many private companies (especially family companies or companies where the members are all directors) this allows a meeting to be held at very short notice; it is not a practical alternative to the giving of proper notice for companies with large numbers of members.

The notice of a meeting must state the date, time, and place of meeting. It must also describe the business which is to be transacted sufficiently for members to be able to decide whether they wish to attend. It is a question of judgment in each case how much detail of the business needs to be stated, so that decided cases do not give much guidance to those drawing up the notice. One point that is clear, is that any personal interest of directors in the business of the meeting must be disclosed. In drawing up a notice it is better to err on the side of inclusion rather than exclusion.

If a special, elective or extraordinary resolution or a resolution which requires special notice (for example, a resolution to remove a director under s. 303 CA 1985) is to be proposed, it must be set out verbatim in the notice. Section 372 CA 1985 requires that the notice should tell the members that each of them is entitled to send a proxy (who need not be a member) to attend and vote on his behalf.

4.5 Proceedings at meetings

A meeting cannot consider business unless a quorum is present at the time when the meeting proceeds to business. Unless the articles otherwise provide, two members personally present are the quorum (s. 370(4)). In fact, Table A art. 40 provides that the quorum is two members present in person or by proxy. The company can alter the articles so as to require a larger quorum if this is thought desirable. The quorum cannot be reduced to one since one person (even if holding proxies for other members) cannot constitute a meeting (except by order of the Department of Trade or the court; see above, paragraph 4.3).

Discussion of resolutions is limited by requirements as to the notice of meetings, that is, sufficient notice and description of the business should be given to enable members to decide whether to attend. Amendments may be moved but only within the scope of the notice; therefore, no amendment of substance is permitted to a special, elective or extraordinary resolution and amendments to ordinary resolutions are limited. Proxies as well as members may speak at a meeting of a private company.

A vote on a resolution may be decided on a show of hands. On such a vote each member personally present has one vote (regardless of the number of shares owned), and a proxy cannot vote unless the articles provide to the contrary (Table A does not give a proxy a right to vote on a show of hands). Section 373 gives a right to demand a poll to: any five voting members; or any member or members with 10% of the voting rights; or any member or members with 10% of the paid-up capital with a right to vote. Table A art. 46 extends this by allowing any two members (instead of five) or the chairman to call for a poll. Proxies have the same right to call for a poll as the member or members they represent. When a poll is called, the votes are counted according to the voting rights of the members rather than according to the number of members. If necessary the meeting can be adjourned while the votes are counted but this is unlikely in the case of a private company.

4.6 Dispensing with meetings

A private company may, as an alternative to holding a meeting, pass resolutions in writing under CA 1985 s. 381A. For such a resolution to be valid it must be agreed and signed by or on behalf of all the members who would have been entitled to attend and vote if a meeting had been held. A written resolution is passed when the last member signs. By way of exception, a written resolution may not be used to remove a director from office under s. 303 nor to remove an auditor under s. 391. In certain cases, the Companies Acts require documents to be produced to members at a meeting before a resolution is passed. In such cases the documents must be sent to each member if a written resolution is to be passed. (For example, if a director's service contract is to exceed five years its terms must be sent to the members before the written resolution is passed.)

4.7 Minutes and returns

Minutes must be kept of all decisions taken at general meetings and must be available for inspection by the members at the registered office. Copies of certain resolutions must be sent to the Registrar of Companies within 15 days of being passed (s. 380 CA 1985). Included in this requirement are all special, elective and extraordinary resolutions.

5 Capital and Borrowing

1 INTRODUCTION

Once a company is formed it will need to spend money to get its business going. It may need to buy stock, buy or rent premises, pay wages, advertise and pay the general expenses involved in running a business. The money that the company needs to start its business is often called capital. Technically, however, 'capital' is the liability of the company to the people who have provided it with money on a long-term basis.

A company can raise money either in the form of a permanent investment by shareholders or in the form of loans. Once the business is established profits may be retained in the business thus producing a third source of finance.

2 ISSUE OF SHARES

2.1 Legal nature of shares

A share in a company is a chose in action. Its value to the shareholder depends on the particular contractual rights which he obtains from owning the share. These contractual rights are obtained when the shares are issued to him by the company if he is the original owner, or when they are transferred or transmitted to him. This section is concerned with the issue of shares; transfer and transmission are dealt with in Chapter 17. The rights attached to shares vary from company to company and a company may issue different classes of shares with different rights attached to them. It is, therefore, difficult to generalise about the exact nature of a share but the following general points may be of assistance:

(a) Nearly all shares give the shareholder a right to a dividend but a dividend is only payable if the company has made profits and it is decided to declare a dividend (see below, paragraph 7).

(b) Most, but not all, shares give the shareholder a right to vote at meetings of the company.

(c) If the company is wound up the shareholder will have a right to repayment of his investment (in the comparatively unlikely event that the company is then solvent) and in most cases a right to participate in any undistributed profit.

(d) The Stock Transfer Act 1982 lays down a procedure for the transfer of shares but does not guarantee the shareholder a right to transfer.

(e) Shareholders are given certain rights as a matter of law by the Companies Act. Many of these rights are, however, only given to shareholders who have a right to vote at company meetings (e.g. the rights to remove directors and to appoint and remove auditors referred to in Chapter 3).

In the case of a private company the voting rights will often be as important as the financial rights. This is especially so in the case of a shareholding which gives voting control, since it effectively carries with it the right to control the composition of the board of directors. The capital value of shares clearly depends to some extent on the rights attached to them but it also depends on other factors — particularly the profitability of the company.

All shares must have a 'nominal value' (also called 'par value') which is set out in the capital clause of the memorandum. This figure says little about the true value of the shares since, as we shall see shortly, shares can be issued for more (but not less) than nominal value and once issued their value will fluctuate either upwards or downwards as the company is more or less successful. The nominal value is really just a way of measuring one shareholder's interest against the interests of other shareholders.

2.2   The power to issue shares

When new shares are created by a company they are said to be 'issued' by the company to the people who have contracted to buy them. The articles of the company may give the directors the power to issue shares. Since 1 July 1985 Table A has not given the directors this power expressly. It is arguable that the directors have power to issue under art. 70. In the case of most companies formed before that date the power to issue shares will have been granted to the directors. Any power granted by the articles to issue shares is subject to the following restrictions:

(a)   The articles themselves may impose restrictions. For example, the power may extend only to issuing ordinary shares, the sanction of the members in general meeting being required for the issue of shares with special rights.

(b)   Shares may only be issued to the extent of the nominal capital of the company. If the articles give power to do so, the nominal capital may be increased under s. 121 CA 1985, but this requires the approval of the members in general meeting (see ch. 6—6.2).

(c)   As we saw in Chapter 3, the directors may not issue shares in breach of their fiduciary duty, so that the approval of the members is required if the motive behind the issue is anything other than the raising of further investment in the company.

(d)   The powers of the directors to issue shares (other than subscribers' shares and shares allotted under an employees' share scheme) is restricted by s. 80 CA 1985. This requires the directors to be authorised to issue shares either by the company in general meeting or by the articles. The authorisation may be given either for a particular exercise of the directors' power or generally and may be unconditional or subject to conditions. Whether the authorisation is given by resolution of the members in general meeting or by the articles, it must state the maximum amount of shares which the directors may issue and the date when the authority will expire. The authority cannot be given for more than five years from formation of the company or the passing of the resolution (as the case may be) and can be revoked or varied by the company in general meeting at any time. Once given, the authority can be extended by up to five years by the further resolution of the company. Resolutions under s. 80 may be passed as ordinary resolutions (so that a simple majority is sufficient), even though they alter the articles. The resolution must, however, be registered with the Registrar of Companies as if it were a special resolution. If the directors issue shares without authority they commit an offence and presumably would be liable to the company for breach of duty but the issue of shares remains valid (s. 80(10)). At first sight this section gives very considerable protection to the shareholders but in most private companies the directors and majority shareholders are the same people, so that all that will be required is an extra procedural step (the calling of a meeting of the company) at some time within five years before the issue. The section is, therefore, of most importance to the comparatively few private companies where the directors are not the controlling shareholders, and to public companies.

Following the enactment of the Companies Act 1989, in the case of private companies, it is possible to dispense with this five-year limitation if the authority is given by an elective resolution in accordance with the provisions of s. 80A CA 1985.

(e)   Under s. 89 CA 1985 if it is proposed to issue shares to any person they must first be offered to the existing shareholders, in proportion to their existing holdings, on terms at least as favourable as those proposed for the issue to that person. The members must be given 21 days to make up their minds. This right of pre-emption does not apply if the shares are to be issued for a non-cash consideration and can, in the case of a private company, be varied or removed by contrary provision in the articles. A special resolution can be passed, without altering the articles, to allow the directors to issue shares on a particular occasion as if s. 89 did not apply.

Section 89 gives shareholders a useful degree of protection in cases where the effect of issuing shares would be to water down their control of the company. A higher degree of protection will be given if the articles provide for pre-emption rights on *any* issue of shares, so that the company will not be able to offer shares for a non-cash consideration unless the members are willing to give up their rights. It should be noted that s. 89 is only concerned with the *issue* of shares. It is fairly common for articles to provide for pre-emption rights where an existing shareholder wants to transfer his shares (see ch. 17).

2.3   Payment for shares

2.3.1   Consideration

A contract for the issue of shares may provide for payment in cash or for some other consideration. If the agreement is for the payment of cash the full amount may be payable immediately or part of it may be left outstanding until the company makes a 'call' for the unpaid amount if the company goes into liquidation. Payment in full on issue of the shares is now usually required, so that partly paid shares are rather uncommon.

2.3.2   Discount

The amount to be paid for shares is a matter for negotiation between the company and the investor who wishes to become a shareholder. However, shares may not be issued at a discount, that is, for less than their nominal value (s. 100 CA 1985). If shares are issued at a discount the member is automatically liable to pay the difference between the nominal value and the agreed price with interest (s. 100(2)). In *Mosely* v *Koffyfontein Mines Ltd* [1904] 2 Ch 108 the Court of Appeal held that an issue of debentures at a discount which granted an immediate right to acquire fully paid shares for the full (non-discounted) amount of the debt was illegal as it amounted to an issue of shares at a discount.

When shares are issued for a non-cash consideration the court will not enquire into the adequacy of the consideration. This means that if a company issues shares in return for assets (e.g., on the transfer of a business to a company), the company may negotiate any price that it likes for those assets and the shares will not be regarded as issued at a discount even if, objectively, the assets are worth less than the nominal value of the shares. However, if the contract itself shows that the assets are worth less than the nominal value or if the contract is fraudulent the court will order the allottee to pay the nominal value of the shares.

2.3.3 Premium

Shares are quite commonly issued at a premium, that is, for more than their nominal value. The premium is treated as 'capital' of the company (for the consequences of this, see paragraph 3.2). When a company has already issued some shares and has made profits, an issue at a premium will usually be necessary to safeguard the interests of existing shareholders. For example, a company has net assets of £20,000 and has issued 1,000 £1 shares. It is decided to seek an investment of £10,000 by way of a further issue of shares. Clearly, the existing shareholders would be prejudiced by an issue of 10,000 £1 shares since the new investors would be entitled to ten times as much by way of dividends and ten times as many votes as the original shareholders. A substantial premium would, therefore, be required. On a simple mathematical calculation, 500 £1 shares should be issued at a premium of £19 per share, i.e., the new shareholders are contributing one third of the total value of the company's assets (which will now be £30,000) and so should get one third of the total number of shares (there will now be 1,500 shares). This calculation is, in practice, too simple — other factors must be taken into account, for example, the likely profitability of the company and the degree of control which the new shares will give.

2.4 'Return as to allotments'

Section 88 CA 1985 requires a return of allotment to be made to the Registrar of Companies within one month of the issue of shares. The form requires details as to the number and nominal amount of the shares, the names, addresses and descriptions of the shareholders, and the amount paid up on each share including any premium. Where there is a non-cash consideration, a written contract for the sale of the shares must also be sent to the registrar or, if the contract was oral, a memorandum as to the terms of the contract.

2.5 Issue of shares to the public

Section 81, CA 1985 makes it an offence for a private company to offer shares (or debentures) to the public or to issue them with a view to an offer for sale to the public. An offer is made to the public if it is made 'to any section of the public' (s. 59 CA 1985). The Act does not define what is meant by any section of the public but a private company would normally be in breach of s. 59 if it were to advertise for investment.

3 SHARE CAPITAL

3.1 Maintenance of capital

Once shares have been issued they are said to form part of the 'capital' of the company. Unfortunately, the term capital is somewhat ambiguous: it is often used to mean *assets* owned by somebody as opposed to his income. To an accountant, however, it means a liability owed to the proprietor of a business as a result of his investment in the business.

'Share capital' is really such a liability of a company, since the company will one day be liable to repay the shareholders' investment (usually, in fact, only when the company is wound up). For the protection of people dealing with the company, share capital has to be 'maintained' by the company. This does not mean that the money invested has to be deposited or set aside as a fund to guarantee the company's creditors; it only means that it must not, normally, be returned to the members in any way while the company is a going concern.

One consequence of this rule is that dividends may only be paid out of profits (see paragraph 8 below). Another is that capital invested cannot be returned to the members except: (a) with the approval of the court (s. 135 CA 1985 deals with the cases where capital can be returned or the liability to members cancelled with the approval of the court; this topic is dealt with briefly in ch. 6); or (b) where the company redeems or purchases its own shares (see below and ch. 17).

3.2 Share premium account

As has already been explained, it is common for shares to be issued for more than their nominal value. The excess is not strictly speaking share capital but is required by s. 130 CA 1985 to be credited to a 'share premium account' (i.e., an account showing the company to be liable to the members for the amount of the premium). The share premium account has to be maintained in the same way as share capital; thus assets representing it cannot be returned to members.

The share premium account may, however, be used for two purposes:

(a) To pay up bonus shares (i.e., shares for which no new payment is made) issued to the existing members. When this is done the liability shown in the share premium account is transferred to the share capital account so that the total liability of the company to its members is not changed and the creditors of the company are therefore not adversely affected.

(b) The preliminary expenses of the company may be written off against the share premium account. Preliminary expenses (e.g., the cost of formation) are shown in the balance sheet as an asset but since they are realistically of little value most accountants prefer to remove them as quickly as possible from the balance sheet and often the share premium account will be a suitable liablity to reduce.

3.3 Company as member of itself and purchase of own shares

A company may not be a member of itself, that is, it cannot be registered as its own shareholder. However, shares can be transferred to a trustee or nominee for the company. For example, in *Re Castiglione's Will Trusts* [1958] Ch 549, a shareholder left shares in a company to that company by will. The court held that the gift was valid provided that the company was not registered as the owner of the shares.

As long ago as 1887 the House of Lords held that it was illegal for a company to buy its own shares (*Trevor* v *Whitworth* (1887) 12 App Cas 409). This is because use of its money by a company to purchase its own shares is in effect a return to the shareholder of his investment and so is a reduction of capital.

Section 159, CA 1985 gives companies (if authorised by their articles) power to issue redeemable shares, that is shares which can be repaid at the option of the company or the shareholder. A company cannot, however, issue all its shares as redeemable shares. Table A art. 3 gives the company power to issue redeemable shares subject to this restriction. Following the enactment of CA 1989, it is now necessary for the articles to set out the terms on which shares may be redeemed. The articles must also fix the date or period of redemption or provide that the directors may do so before the shares are issued.

It was thought to be desirable for companies, particularly small family companies, to have the power to purchase their own shares as this would provide an additional market for the shares. Section 162 CA 1985 therefore gives companies power to purchase their own shares if authorised to do so by their articles (Table A art. 35 gives such authorisation). Examples of cases where the power will be useful include buying out dissident shareholders and the provision of funds to the estate of a deceased shareholder to assist in the payment of inheritance tax.

The contract for purchase must be approved by special resolution before the company enters into it. The members whose shares are to be purchased must not use the votes given to them by the shares which are to be purchased on that resolution. The resolution will be invalid unless a copy of the contract (or a memorandum of its terms) is made available for inspection by the members at the company's registered office for a period of at least 15 days ending with the date of the meeting and also at the meeting itself. Once the shares have been purchased by the company they are treated as cancelled.

Within 28 days after the shares have been purchased a return must be made to the Registrar of Companies stating the number and nominal value of the shares purchased and the date of purchase.

When shares are redeemed or purchased by the company the money used to pay for them must generally come out of profits or the proceeds of a fresh issue of shares. Where the shares are purchased or redeemed with assets representing profits the legislation requires the capital of the company to be maintained. Thus, s. 170 CA 1985 requires the company to open a 'capital redemption reserve' equal to the reduction in the share capital. This reserve is treated in the same way as share capital or the share premium account, that is, it is shown in the balance sheet as a liability due to shareholders which has to be maintained until the company goes into liquidation. In the case of a private company payment out of assets representing capital is permitted. The use of assets representing capital to redeem or purchase its own shares means that a private company can reduce its capital without seeking the sanction of the court. In order to protect the interests of members and creditors detailed procedural requirements must be satisfied. The articles must contain an express power to use capital assets for this purpose. The general power to purchase its own shares is not sufficient. (Article 35 of Table A does contain such a power.)

The directors must certify that the company will remain solvent and will, in their view, be able to carry on business as a going concern for at least a year. The directors' certificate must be supported by an auditors' report in which the auditors certify that they are not aware of anything which would indicate that the directors' view of the situation is unreasonable. Not later than one week after the date of the certificate a general meeting of the company must be held at which a special resolution approving the payment is passed. The members whose shares are to be purchased may not use the votes on those shares on this resolution. The payment for the shares must be made by the company not less than five nor more than seven weeks after the date on which the resolution is passed. This period is laid down so that members or creditors who object to the purchase have time to challenge the purchase in court. On such an application the court has power to confirm or cancel the purchase; it also has power to order the purchase of any shares in the company and to make various ancillary orders (ss. 176 and 177 CA 1985). An advertisement must be placed in the *London Gazette* and a national newspaper within one week of the company's resolution, giving the creditors notice of their right to apply to the court.

The tax consequences of redemption of shares and other purchases by the company of its own shares will be considered in Chapter 15. Prima facie, the payment by the company to the shareholder will be treated as a distribution of profits. However, if certain conditions are complied with the payment will be treated as a capital payment.

4 FINANCIAL ASSISTANCE BY COMPANY FOR PURCHASE OF SHARES

Section 151, CA 1985 makes it illegal for a company to give financial assistance directly or indirectly to assist someone to purchase shares in the company but there are important exceptions to this rule which will be considered in Chapter 17.

5 CLASSES OF SHARES

In most companies, all the shares issued have the same rights attached to them. It is possible, however, for a company to issue shares with different rights. The shares are then said to belong to different classes. For example, a company may issue preference shares, that is, shares which have a better right to receive a dividend than ordinary shares. It is also possible to give some shareholders a greater measure of control over the affairs of the company either by creating voting and non-voting shares or by providing that all shares are to carry a right to vote but that some will have more votes than others.

Table A art. 2 requires the approval of the members in general meeting for the creation of new classes of shares. Once class rights have been attached to shares they can be varied under the articles or in some cases under s. 125 CA 1985. The details of the variation procedure are beyond the scope of this book but normally require the consent of three quarters of the class affected.

6 PROFITS

Basically, there are four ways in which a company can deal with its profits:

(a)   retain them in the business;
(b)   pay them as dividends to the shareholders;
(c)   use them to pay interest on debentures;
(d)   pay directors' fees.

If profits are retained in the business the proprietors ought to benefit in the long run, since the capital value of the company (and thus of the shares in it) will increase. A payment of interest on debentures will often be a payment to an outsider, which reduces profits available to the proprietors of the business. However, a long-term loan to a company is really a method of investing in the company without buying shares, and so the payment of interest on such a loan may properly be regarded as a payment to an investor in the business. Directors' fees are expenses of the business which an accountant would regard as reducing the profit available to shareholders, but in the case of most small, private companies the directors and shareholders are the same people; thus a payment of directors' fees is really a payment of profit to the proprietors.

A company is not entirely free to choose between the four different uses of profits. Firstly, it will often be contractually bound to make payments of interest and directors' fees. Secondly, there are company law rules which prevent the company from paying dividends except to the extent of 'profits available for the purpose'. (The reason for this is that the original investment made in the company by shareholders may not be returned to them, except in limited circumstances, until the company is wound up — see above, paragraph 3.1). Thirdly, it will often be commercially unwise for the company to pay out all its profits, since some will be required to provide for future contingencies or for the expansion of the business.

The tax consequences of each method of using profits will be considered and a comparison will be made between them in Chapter 15.

7   PROCEDURE FOR DECLARING AND PAYING A DIVIDEND

A dividend is a payment to the shareholders of the company which provides them with a return on their investment. It is not a payment of interest on the money invested, since the shareholder does not have an automatic right to the dividend — as we shall see, it becomes payable only if 'declared' by the company (or otherwise authorised under the articles) and only if the Companies Act permits payment in the circumstances.

7.1   Table A

The provisions of Table A in respect of dividend payments provide for the following procedure:

(a)   During the course of an accounting period (i.e., a twelve-month period in respect of which the company's accounts are prepared), the directors may decide to pay an interim dividend (art. 103). However, the directors may only pay an interim dividend if it appears to them to be 'justified by the profits of the company available for distribution'.

(b)   After the accounts have been prepared the directors will consider what dividend, if any, ought to be declared, and will make a recommendation to the members in general meeting.

(c)   A meeting of the company will be held at which the question of declaring a dividend will be considered. In practice, this will be done at the AGM, although Table A does not prevent consideration of dividends at an EGM. The members may reject the directors' recommendation or declare a dividend smaller than that recommended, but Table A art. 102 prevents them exceeding the amount recommended by the directors. The reason why the members may not declare a dividend in excess of the directors' recommendation is that the directors are the managers of the company's business, and so are in a better position than the members to assess the economic ability of the company to pay dividends; it is therefore probably a sensible provision to include in the articles. If the members object to the dividend policy of the directors they can exercise their right to remove the directors from office under s. 303 CA 1985 (but not, of course, if the directors are in control of the general meetings, as they often will be).

(d)   Once the dividend has been declared, the members will be paid the dividend by the company. The amount of dividend paid to each member depends on the nominal value of the shares held, no account being taken of any premium paid on the shares. If there are different classes of shares they may have different rights to dividends. Thus, if there are preference shares, the ordinary shareholders will not be entitled to any dividend until the preference shareholders have received their dividend (which will be expressed as a fixed amount per share or a fixed percentage). For example, a company has 2,000 £1 shares of which 1,000 are ordinary shares and 1,000 are 10% preference shares; the company declares a dividend of £150. The preference shareholders are entitled to their 10% (i.e., £100) and the ordinary shareholders get the balance (i.e., £50 or 5p per share).

7.2   Other possible arrangements

The articles of the company may validly provide that directors are to declare dividends without holding a general meeting. It is also possible (although undesirable), for the articles to require payment of all the company's profits as dividends (subject to the legal restriction referred to below). If an elective resolution has dispensed with the need to hold an AGM a dividend could also be declared by a written resolution if the company does not choose to hold an EGM.

7.3   Legal entitlement to dividend

Once declared by the members in general meeting, a dividend is a debt due to the members from the company. The member is, therefore, entitled to sue the company if the dividend is not paid. (Since s. 14 CA 1985 provides that the articles form the basis of a contract under seal between the company and the members, it is a 'specialty' debt, so the limitation period is 12 years.) An interim dividend is not, however, a debt due from the company, so that the members have no right to it until it is actually paid.

Unless the articles provide to the contrary, all dividends must be paid in money. Table A art. 105 permits payment in the form of other assets but only if the members direct payment otherwise than in cash when they declare the dividend.

8   RESTRICTIONS ON SOURCES OF DIVIDENDS

8.1   The basic rule

So as to ensure that money invested by shareholders is not returned to them before the company is wound up, there have always been rules based on judicial decisions preventing the payment of dividends other than out of profits. The Companies Act 1985 now lays down clear rules as to what funds are available for the payment of dividends. These rules, which were first introduced in 1980, are designed to implement the European Communities' Second Directive on Company Law and differ somewhat from the rules previously established by the courts — the new rules are generally more restrictive.

Section 263(1) CA 1985 provides that: 'A company shall not make a distribution except out of profits available for the purpose.' The term 'distribution' is defined by s. 263(2) and includes all distributions of assets to members except: the issue of bonus shares; the redemption or purchase of its own shares by the company, reduction of capital (which requires the approval of the court — see ch. 6—6.4); or a distribution on winding-up.

Most dividends are paid in cash and are included in the definition of 'distributions', since cash is just as much an asset as other types of property.

8.2   'Profits available'

'Profits available for the purpose' of paying dividends are defined by s. 263(3) as 'accumulated, realised profits, so far as not previously utilised by distribution . . . less . . . accumulated, réalised losses . . .'. This means that each year it is necessary to calculate the company's trading profit and any capital profits that have been made on the disposal of fixed assets. These are the 'realised profits' from which must be deducted any realised losses, that is, any trading loss or loss made on the disposal of a fixed asset. However, a dividend is only payable if there are *accumulated* realised profits in excess of *accumulated* realised losses. This means that the balance of realised profits can be carried forward from year to year. It is not, therefore, necessary to make a profit every year in order to pay a dividend — all that is required is that there should be a balance of profits taking this year and previous years together.

For example:

	Realised Profit/(loss)	*Dividend*
Year 1	4,000	1,000
Year 2	2,000	1,000
Year 3	(3,000)	1,000

The dividend in year 3 is lawful because in year 1 the realised profits were £4,000 and the dividend only £1,000, so that £3,000 worth of profits could be carried forward. In year 2 the realised profits were £2,000 and the dividend £1,000, so that a further £1,000 could be carried forward. In year 3 there was a realised loss of £3,000 which had to be deducted from the accumulated profits of £4,000, thus leaving £1,000 for a dividend.

Just as realised profits not used to pay dividends may be carried forward to later years and used to pay dividends in those later years, so realised losses which are not balanced by realised profits accumulated from previous years must be carried forward to later years and set off against realised profits before a dividend can be paid. Thus (continuing the example above):

	Realised Profit/(loss)	*Dividend*
Year 4	(2,000)	nil
Year 5	1,000	nil
Year 6	2,000	1,000

In year 4 there was a loss, and since no accumulated profits were available from years 1-3, no dividend could be paid. In year 5 a profit of £1,000 was made but this could not be used to pay a dividend since the accumulated realised loss (£2,000 from year 4) was more than the realised profit. In year 6 the £1,000 dividend was the maximum which could be paid because £1,000 of the loss from year 4 had to be set off against the profit.

Section 263 CA 1985 does not lay down particular rules as to how profits and losses are to be calculated; normal accountancy practice must be applied in deciding whether a profit or loss has been realised. However, a few situations are specifically dealt with. Thus a profit which has been 'capitalised' (in this context a profit is capitalised only if it is used to pay up bonus shares or to replace capital repaid to members) cannot be treated as a realised profit. On the other hand, a loss which has been written off in a reduction of capital, is not treated as a realised loss. This is because when the capital is reduced the shareholders' investment is wiped out, with the approval of the court, to the extent of the reduction and so does not have to be maintained. If a 'provision' is made in the accounts of the company it must usually be treated as a realised loss (s. 275 CA 1985). A provision is an item shown in the accounts as an expense in respect of expected future expenses (e.g., it is usual practice to provide for depreciation of wasting assets — that is, to record the fact that they are declining in value). If the provision were not treated as a realised loss the company could write down the value of an asset in its accounts and then sell it for its written-down value thus (apparently) making neither a profit nor a loss, whereas in fact there was a substantial loss in value during the period of ownership of the asset.

The articles of a company may restrict the company's right to pay dividends further than is done by the Companies Act, for example, by preventing payment of a dividend out of a realised capital profit. Table A does not contain any such provisions. In most circumstances a company would be very unwise to distribute all the 'profits available' as defined by s. 263, since to do so would often create cash flow problems (a company always needs sufficient cash to buy stock, pay wages, etc.), and make expansion of the business more difficult.

It should be noted that, although realised losses must be made good out of realised profits before a dividend can be paid, there is no requirement that *unrealised* losses must be made good. For example, if a company owns land which it knows to be declining in value, it can still go on paying dividends out of realised profits, since the loss on the land is only realised when the land is sold. Similarly an unrealised profit cannot be used to pay a dividend. A company which is making small realised losses cannot, therefore, pay a dividend even if it knows its land is increasing in value by more than the losses.

8.3 The 'relevant accounts'

Whether a company has got any profits available for distribution can only be judged by reference to properly drawn up accounts. Section 270 CA 1985 lays down rules as to which accounts are to be used at any particular time for deciding whether there are profits available. Usually the company must rely on the last set of accounts prepared in accordance with s. 226 CA 1985 (substituted by s. 4 CA 1989 — as we shall see in Chapter 9, these are the accounts which must be audited, laid before the members in general meeting and sent to the Companies Registry where they are available for public inspection). However, if the company wants to pay a dividend which is not justified by those accounts it can prepare 'interim' accounts specially for the purpose of showing that profits are available for distribution. This might be done, for example, if the company had made a loss and so could not pay a dividend but has now started to make profits again and does not want to wait until the next full set of accounts are produced. Similarly, if a company wishes to pay a dividend before it has prepared *any* accounts under s. 226 CA 1985 (i.e., broadly speaking, during its first year after incorporation) it can prepare 'initial' accounts to justify the dividend payment.

Interim and initial accounts must be prepared and audited in much the same way as the normal final accounts of the company. Because of the expense involved in preparing such accounts it will usually be better to wait until accounts are produced in the normal way before paying the dividend.

8.4 Consequences of unlawful distributions

Section 277 CA 1985 requires any member to repay a distribution which he 'knows or has reasonable grounds for believing' to be illegal. If a dividend is paid illegally the directors will normally be personally liable to the company, since they will have recommended and paid (or permitted payment of) the dividend in breach of their duty.

9 THE POWER TO BORROW

9.1 Express and implied power

A trading company has an implied power to borrow for the purpose of its trade. This is because the trade will be authorised by its objects and the borrowing will be reasonably incidental to the power to carry on the trade (*General Auction Estate and Monetary Co* v *Smith* [1891] 3 Ch 432 and s. 3A CA 1985, as interpolated in the case of companies incorporated after the Companies Act 1989 comes into force and which have included the statement set out in that subsection as their objects).

A company with power to borrow also has an implied power to give security for the loan (*General Auction Estate and Monetary Co* v *Smith*). It is preferable to include express powers if a full objects clause is adopted rather than to rely on implied ones. In practice, banks (and other professional lenders) would probably continue to check the company's express powers despite the abolition of the consequences of the ultra vires rule referred to below.

9.2 Ultra vires borrowing

A lender to a company was formerly well advised to check the company's memorandum so as to ensure that the loan was within the powers of the company. However, the new s. 35 CA 1985 (as substituted by CA 1989) removes the need to do so by providing that 'the validity of an act done by a company shall not be called into question on the ground of lack of capacity by reason of anything in the company's memorandum'. (For the very limited exceptions to this, see ch. 2 para. 2.1.4.)

9.3 Exercise of borrowing powers

The power to borrow must be exercised in accordance with the company's articles of association. If the company has adopted Table A the directors will have power to borrow at least where the loan is to be used for the purposes of the business (art. 70).

The Table A in force before 1 July 1985 limited the powers of the directors to borrow on behalf of the company. Many companies formed before that date will therefore only be able to borrow substantial sums following approval of the loan by the members in general meeting. Restrictions on the power of the directors to borrow can now be imposed by the adoption of a special article to that effect.

10   SECURED LOANS

10.1   Types of security

A prudent lender will usually require security for a loan which he makes to a company. Any assets of the company may be charged by way of security.

Companies may give security for a loan in the form of a 'debenture'. Unfortunately, this is rather an ambiguous term. The legal definition seems to require only that there is:

(a)   a document, which
(b)   creates or acknowledges indebtedness by a company, and
(c)   the indebtedness arises from a loan.

It should be noted that a debenture does not necessarily require that any security be given in the form of a mortgage or other charge over assets. The term 'debenture' is often used in practice to mean a long-term loan to a company for the purpose of its business. Usually security will be required for such a loan in the form of a fixed charge, a floating charge or both.

In addition to a charge over the assets of the company a lender may frequently require personal guarantees from the directors. Where a personal guarantee is given the benefit of limited liablity is effectively lost to the extent of the guarantee.

10.2   Fixed charges

A fixed charge is a mortgage of a particular asset. The mortgage may be either legal
or equitable and the company, having created the charge, is not free to dispose of the
asset without the consent of the mortgagee. When a bank lends money to a company,
it will frequently require a fixed charge over any land owned by the company. Other
assets owned by the company, such as plant and machinery and book debts, may also
be available as security for a fixed charge.

10.3   Floating charges

A floating charge is an equitable charge over assets of a particular description owned
by the company from time to time. A floating charge can be given over assets which
are repeatedly dealt with by the company. Perhaps stock-in-trade is the clearest
example. A company cannot give a fixed charge over its stock since to do so would
prevent it from selling that stock. However, if it gives a floating charge over the
stock, the charge will 'float' over whatever stock the company owns from time to time
— it can therefore sell the stock free from the charge and buy new stock to which the
charge will automatically attach.

The nature of a floating charge was defined in *Re Yorkshire Woolcombers'
Association Ltd* [1903] 2 Ch 284, in the following way:

> . . . if a charge has the three characteristics I am about to mention it is a floating
> charge.
> (a)   if it is a charge on a class of assets of a company present and future;
> (b)   if that class is one which, in the ordinary course of business of the
> company, would be changing from time to time; and
> (c)   if you find that by the charge it is contemplated that, until some future
> step is taken by or on behalf of those interested in the charge, the company may
> carry on business in the usual way as far as concerns the particular class of asset I
> am dealing with.

At first sight a floating charge would seem to give no security at all to the lender since
the company can continue to deal with the assets which are charged. However, a
floating charge becomes a fixed charge on the charged assets owned by the company
at the time when the charge 'crystallises'. A floating charge crystallises when:

(a)   The winding-up of the company commences (in the case of a winding-up by
the court this is usually when the winding-up petition is presented (s. 524 CA 1985);
in the case of voluntary winding-up it is when the winding-up resolution is passed
(s. 574 CA 1985)).

(b)   A receiver is appointed by the court.

(c)   A receiver is appointed by the lender under a power given by the debenture.

(d)   Any other event occurs which the debenture specifies will cause
crystallisation.

When drafting a debenture secured by a floating charge the last of these occasions of
crystallisation should be carefully considered. It will usually be advisable to provide

for crystallisation if the company defaults in payment of interest due on the loan, or if it becomes insolvent or (in the case of loan by a bank) if the company takes its account elsewhere.

It should be noted that companies are the only type of business association which can create a floating charge. This is because the Bills of Sale Acts do not apply to them. A partnership or sole trader can, theoretically, create a floating charge. However, the security would be invalid except to the extent that a bill of sale had been registered at the High Court in respect of each separate asset subject to the charge from time to time. Clearly such registration would be impossible in practice.

10.4 Advantages and disadvantages of floating charges

As far as the borrowing company is concerned a floating charge has one great advantage over a fixed charge; that is, until crystallisation, it can deal freely with the charged assets without the permission of the lender. This means that the lender cannot be sure of the extent of his security until crystallisation. (He may, for example, lend £10,000 to a company on the security of its stock-in-trade which at the time of the loan is worth £20,000. The company may then run into cash flow problems and fail to replace its stock, so that by the time the charge crystallises the stock is only worth £5,000 and the security is, therefore, inadequate.) However, even from the lender's point of view a floating charge over assets which may fluctuate in value is better than no security at all.

From the lender's point of view a floating charge suffers from a number of disadvantages when compared with a fixed charge. In particular:

(a)   It is postponed to execution and distress for rent completed before crystallisation.

(b)   It is postponed to preferred creditors on a liquidation of the borrowing company. (Preferred creditors may include the Inland Revenue, Customs and Excise (for VAT), local authority (for rates) and employees (for wages).) In each case there is a limit to the extent of the preference.

(c)   It is postponed to later fixed charges in certain cases (see below, paragraph 12.1).

(d)   It may be invalid as a security if the company goes into liquidation within a year (see paragraph 12.3 below).

11   REGISTRATION OF CHARGES

11.1   Sections 395 ff CA 1985

The Companies Act 1989 introduced a new system of registration of charges. References to CA 1985 in this paragraph are references to the sections substituted by CA 1989. The system of registration previously in use is not referred to in this book but was described in earlier editions.

Section 396 CA 1985 lists the types of charge particulars of which a company must register. The list is quite extensive so that nearly all charges must be registered. In particular, registration is required of charges over land, goods (except where the chargee is entitled to possession of the goods or documents of title to them), goodwill, intellectual property and book debts owed to the company. Registration is also required where the charge is or includes a floating charge.

11.2 The registration process (s. 398 CA 1985)

Where a company creates a charge or acquires property which is already subject to a charge it must deliver (to the Registrar of Companies) 'prescribed particulars' within 21 days. At the time of writing, regulations prescribing the particulars which are to be registered have not been made. Although it is the duty of the company to register, any person with an interest in the charge has a power to register. Failure to register may lead to the charge being invalid (as to which see below) so that it is in the interests of the chargee to ensure registration. Once the charge has been registered the Registrar sends a copy of the registered particulars to the company and the chargee.

11.3 Consequences of failure to comply with registration requirements

11.3.1 Fine (s. 398(3))
If particulars of a charge are not registered within 21 days the company and every officer in default is liable to a fine.

11.3.2 No particulars delivered (s. 399)
If the particulars are not delivered within 21 days the charge is void against an administrator or liquidator of the company who is appointed after the creation of the charge. The appointment of an administrator or liquidator is a step in relation to the insolvency of a company (as to which see ch. 21). It follows, therefore, that if a charge is not registered the charge is void in the insolvency of the company. The chargee will rank as an ordinary creditor without security.

Similarly, if particulars are not delivered within 21 days the charge is void against any person who, after the creation of the charge and for value, acquires an interest in or right over property subject to the charge. The unregistered charge would therefore be void against a subsequent chargee or a purchaser.

It should be noticed that in both these circumstances a charge is only void if it is not registered within 21 days of its creation.

11.3.3 Effect of late registration (s. 400)
Particulars may now be registered outside the 21 day period (under previous legislation a restricted right to register out of time was permitted subject to the approval of the court). Where particulars are delivered late the charge is void against a liquidator or administrator appointed before delivery and against a person acquiring an interest in or right over the property before that time (see above). The charge is not, however, void against a liquidator or administrator appointed after the delivery unless the company is insolvent when the particulars are delivered (or becomes insolvent as a result of the charge) and insolvency proceedings begin within the 'relevant period'. The relevant period is six months from delivery of particulars (12 months in the case of a floating charge, two years in the case of a floating charge granted to a director or other connected person).

11.3.4   Examples of ss. 398-400

(a)   Charge created 1 March.
   Particulars registered 15 March.

The charge will be valid (unless there are other grounds for declaring it void e.g. as a preference — see ch. 21).

(b)   Charge created 1 March.
   Liquidator appointed 10 March.
   Particulars delivered 15 March.

The charge will be valid. (Where particulars are delivered within 21 days the charge is valid.).

(c)   Charge created 1 March.
   Liquidator appointed 10 March.
   Particulars never delivered.

The charge is void against the liquidator.

(d)   Charge created 1 March.
   Particulars delivered 25 March.
   Property sold 27 March.

The charge is not void against the purchaser. (Although particulars were delivered late they were deliverd before the sale to the purchaser.)

(e)   Charge created 1 March.
   Property sold 25 March.
   Particulars delivered 27 March.

The charge is void against the purchaser (opposite of last example).

(f)   Fixed charge created 1 March.
   Particulars delivered 25 March.
   Liquidator appointed 27 March.

Prima facie this is like (d) above. However, the charge will be void against the liquidator if the company was insolvent on 25 March (as it almost certainly was since the liquidator was appointed two days later).

(g)   Fixed charge created 1 March.
   Particulars delivered 25 March.
   Liquidator appointed 27 October.

The charge is not void. (Even if the company was insolvent on 25 March, the liquidator was not appointed within six months of the delivery of particulars.)

11.3.5   Errors and omissions (s. 402)

Provision is made for cases where particulars are delivered but the particulars are not complete and accurate. In such cases, the charge is void only in respect of rights not disclosed in the particulars and only to the extent that a person has been prejudiced by the error or omission.

11.3.6   Priorities between unregistered charges (s. 404)

Where a company creates two charges and particulars of neither are delivered the first is not void against the second under s. 399.

11.4   Crystallisation of floating charges (s. 410)

The Secretary of State is empowered to make regulations requiring registration of crystallisation of floating charges. This means that notice will have to be given to the

Registrar when the floating charge becomes a fixed charge (see para. 10.3 above). The regulations have not been made at the time of writing.

11.5 Discharge of charges (s. 403)
When a charge ceases to affect the company's property, the company may deliver a memorandum of discharge to the Registrar. This will be added to the company's file at the Companies Registry and so will be seen by anyone who searches the file.

11.6 Company's register of charges (s. 406-408 CA 1985)
Under s. 408 CA 1985, as substituted, the company is required to keep a register of its charges (which must be available for public inspection). It must keep copies of all charges whether or not the charges need to be registered under s. 398, as substituted. Furthermore, any person is able to require the company to send him within ten days of request (and on payment of the appropriate fee) a copy of any charge kept by the company or any entry in the company's register of charges. If the company refuses to allow inspection or fails to send a copy which has been requested the company and every officer who is in default are liable to a fine and the court may compel the company to comply with its duties.

11.7 Other types of registration

In addition to registration under the Companies Act, mortgages of land by a company may have to be registered at HM Land Registry or at the Land Charges Department (depending on whether the land is registered or unregistered respectively).

A fixed charge on registered land must be registered at the Land Registry or else it is void against a subsequent purchaser for value of a legal estate (including a later legal mortgagee). A fixed charge over unregistered land must be registered at the Land Charges Department if the mortgagee does not have the title deeds. However, registration at the Land Charges Department is not required if the mortgage was created before 1970 (when the Law of Property Act 1969 came into force). In such cases registration at the Companies' Registry is sufficient.

Floating charges over land are unusual but not impossible. A floating charge over registered land must be registered at the Land Registry against each piece of land from time to time subject to the charge. The mortgagee will not be in a position to know what land the company owns from time to time and so the instrument creating the floating charge should place the company under an obligation to notify the mortgagee of acquisitions and should provide for crystallisation on failure of the company to notify. (When the charge crystallises the fact that it is now a fixed charge must be registered.)

A floating charge over unregistered land apparently need not be registered at the Land Charges Department even if created after 1969, although the position is not entirely free from doubt.

12 PRIORITY OF CHARGES

12.1 Fixed charges

A company which creates a floating charge retains the right to deal with its assets. As we have already seen, this means that the value of the security may be reduced by the sale of the assets over which the charge floats. Furthermore, the company is free to deal with the assets by charging them. A floating charge, even though properly registered, is, therefore, normally postponed to a later fixed legal charge. This is because 'where the equities are equal the law prevails'. If the later fixed charge is equitable rather than legal the position is more complicated but the fixed charge will usually prevail since the fixed chargee will normally have a stronger claim to the security than the floating chargee.

The reason for the priority of later fixed charges is that the company is left free to deal with its property as it wishes. The floating charge will, therefore, have priority over later fixed charges if:

(a)   the instrument creating the charge prohibits the creation of later fixed charges ranking in priority to or *pari passu* (i.e., equal) with the floating charge; *and*

(b)   the later fixed chargee has *notice of this prohibition* at the time when he takes his charge.

Following the enactment of the Companies Act 1989, once a charge has been registered, s. 397(5) CA 1985 as substituted provides that any person acquiring a charge subsequently will be taken to have notice of matters disclosed on the register. Provided that a notice of prohibition is one of the prescribed particulars to be delivered to the Registrar, it should be included on the register and therefore any later chargee will have constructive notice of the prohibition. (The regulations have not, however, been made at the time of writing.)

12.2 Floating charges

As between several floating charges, the first in time will have priority provided that it is properly registered. However, a floating charge over some particular type of asset will probably take priority over an earlier floating charge over the whole of a company's property (*English and Scottish Mercantile Investment Co* v *Brunton* [1892] 2 QB 700).

12.3 Avoidance of charges

In certain circumstances charges may be avoided, other than for non-registration, if made within a short period before the commencement of insolvency proceedings. This topic is dealt with in ch. 21 paragraphs 7.4, 7.5 and 7.6.

13 REPAYMENT OF CHARGES

The company's obligation to repay a debt secured by a charge depends on the terms agreed with the lender. The date for repayment may be postponed indefinitely

(s. 193 CA 1985 permits this despite the rule of equity which prevents such a 'clog' on the equity of redemption in the case of borrowers other than companies). A debenture which the company need not repay at any particular time is called a 'perpetual debenture', but the company will almost always retain the right to redeem if it chooses, and the lender will be able to require repayment of the capital if the company defaults in interest payments.

14 REMEDIES OF DEBENTURE-HOLDERS

14.1 Express and implied powers

If the company fails to pay interest or principal money (i.e., the debt itself) the debenture-holder may sue as a creditor or petition for winding-up. In addition, the debenture may contain an express power of sale and a power to appoint a receiver (see below). The debenture will state the circumstances in which these powers are to arise. It may, for example, give such powers to the lender when his interest is in arrears for a specified period, when the company breaks any term of the debenture, when any other creditor of the company appoints a receiver and when the company suffers execution by a judgment creditor.

Section 101 of the Law of Property Act 1925 gives the lender implied power to sell and to appoint a receiver if the debenture is made under seal and interest is two months in arrears or principal money has not been paid three months after it becomes due. In drafting a debenture, express powers should be given since they can be made wider than the implied powers; if the debenture is not under seal, express powers are essential.

14.2 Application to the court

In the absence of express powers an application may be made to the court for sale or appointment of a receiver or manager if:

(a)   liquidation of the company has commenced; or
(b)   the company is in arrears with payment of principal or interest; or
(c)   the lender's security is in jeopardy.

If the court orders sale the chargee will be paid principal money and interest and any balance will be paid to the company. The assets will be treated as disposed of by the company so that a chargeable gain or allowable loss may result — thus affecting the company's corporation tax position (see ch. 15).

15 RECEIVERS

A receiver is appointed to realise the security of a debenture-holder. His position is, therefore, different from that of a liquidator, whose function is to wind up the company entirely. Once the receiver has paid the debenture-holder he will return any surplus to the company, which may then continue to trade. In fact, very often the appointment of a receiver by a debenture-holder will lead to the liquidation of the company, for example, because, after his appointment, the receiver finds that he can only obtain payment by winding up the company or because other creditors petition for winding-up.

For the effect of an appointment of an administrative receiver see ch. 21—4.

16 POSITION OF DEBENTURE-HOLDERS

Many debentures are short-term loans to a company (typically by a bank) on which interest will be paid by the company at a fixed or variable rate in accordance with the loan agreement. The lender who takes such a debenture will consider the interest part of his general profits rather than as a source of investment income — he may take an interest in the running of the business as a financial adviser but will not consider that he is an investor in the business.

Some types of debenture are issued to people who have lent money to the company on a long-term basis and who may, therefore, be regarded as investors in the business. The nature of their investment is quite different from the investment made by shareholders. As we shall see in Chapter 15, the tax treatment of debenture interest is usually different from the treatment of dividends paid to shareholders. There are a number of other important differences between the two types of investment, which may be summarised as follows:

(a)   Debenture-holders are not members and so do not have the right usually given to the members of voting at meetings.

(b)   Debenture interest is payable out of capital if the company fails to make profits, so that a debenture is a safer investment (although if the company makes large profits the debenture-holders will not usually benefit).

(c)   Debenture-holders are creditors on a winding-up and will usually have a charge over some or all of the company's assets, whereas shareholders are repaid their investment only if the company is solvent.

(d)   Debenture-holders, unlike shareholders, may be repaid while the company is a going concern (usually at a fixed date or at the option of the company). Shareholders may only be repaid where capital is reduced or where the company redeems or purchases its own shares.

17 STEPS TO BE TAKEN BY A LENDER TO A COMPANY

A person who wishes to lend money to a company should take the following steps either personally or through his advisers. Some of them are dictated by common sense, others by legal requirements:

(a)   Investigate the financial standing and management of the company.

(b)   Search at the Companies' Registry to see the company's last few sets of accounts and of what charge particulars have been registered.

(c)   Search at the company's registered office — inspect copies of charges and obtain evidence of discharge of any registered charges.

(d)   Search at the Land Registry or Land Charges Department (as appropriate) if a charge is to be taken over land.

(e)   If there are any floating charges, make sure that they have not crystallised (until regulations requiring registration of crystallisation are made there is no machinery for ensuring this, but the directors of the company should be asked to certify that no events leading to crystallisation have occurred and, if possible, confirmation should be obtained from the chargees).

(f)   Include in the debenture power to appoint a receiver and a power of sale. If the charge is a floating charge, provide for its crystallisation.

(g)   Ensure that the charge is registered within 21 days.

6 Altering the Constitution of a Company

1 INTRODUCTION

The 'constitution' of a company consists of the memorandum and articles of association. The contents of these documents were considered in Chapter 2 — this chapter deals with the steps which may be taken to amend them. Amendment will often be necessary (and should always be considered) when a company is bought 'off-the-peg' from law stationers. Amendment at other times may be necessary because of changed circumstances. Often amendment can be avoided by careful drafting and foresight at the time of formation. Some changes in the articles may be avoided by the use of a shareholders' agreement under which all the members mutually agree as to how the company should be run. Such an agreement cannot affect outsiders and so would not be suitable as a means of avoiding amendment to the memorandum.

Amendment to the registered office clause of the memorandum is not possible.

A limited company may re-register with unlimited liability and an unlimited company may re-register with limited liability, thus in effect amending the liability clause. Re-registration with unlimited liability requires, *inter alia*, unanimous approval of the shareholders and re-registration with limited liability requires *inter alia*, a special resolution. The procedures involved are not further considered in this book.

2 CHANGE OF NAME

Section 28 CA 1985 gives companies power to change their names by special resolution. A copy of the special resolution must be sent to the Registrar and within 15 days of the change a printed copy of the memorandum with the name changed should be delivered to the Registrar. The change becomes effective when the Registrar issues a certificate of incorporation 'altered to meet the circumstances' (that is, showing the new name of the company) under s. 28(6). Although a new certificate of incorporation is issued when the name is changed the company remains the same legal person so that its rights and obligations are not affected by the change (s. 28(7)). Once the name has been changed it must be used on the company's notepaper and other documents as required by ss. 348-9 CA 1985 (see ch. 2—4.2).

The issue of a certificate of incorporation by the Registrar must be officially notified (that is, advertised by the Registrar in the *London Gazette*) under s. 711 CA 1985. The company is not entitled to rely on the change as against any person until it has been officially notified unless that person actually knew of the change, nor may it rely on the change for the first 15 days after official notification against a person who was unavoidably prevented from knowing about the change (s. 42 CA 1985). It is, therefore, in the company's interests to ensure that the change is officially notified.

As on incorporation, a company has general freedom to choose whatever name it likes, but this is subject to restrictions contained in s. 26 CA 1985 preventing use of a name the same as that of an existing company, one which constitutes a criminal offence or is offensive. Approval of the use of certain words is required as on formation. The Secretary of State also has power to direct a change of name within 12 months if it is too like a name appearing in the index of names at the time of registration or the same as a name which should have been in that index. The Secretary of State may also direct a change of name within five years under s. 28(3) if misleading information was given at the time of registration (whether on first registration or on change of name). He may also so direct at any time under s. 32 CA 1985 if the name gives 'so misleading an indication of the nature of [the company's] activities as to be likely to cause harm to the public'.

3   CHANGE OF OBJECTS

3.1   Powers to change objects

As we have already seen (ch. 2—2.1.3) most companies, especially those formed in recent decades, have objects clauses so widely drawn that the company can lawfully undertake almost any type of business without any danger of transactions being held to be ultra vires. However, it may occasionally be considered desirable for the company to widen its objects clause. There may also be occasions when a company wishes to alter its objects clause so that it is more obviously appropriate to present circumstances. For example, a company with a 'main object' giving it power to carry on business in manufacturing may now largely be in the wholesale business and may, therefore, wish to change its objects to reflect that fact.

Power to alter the objects clause is given by s. 4 CA 1985 as amended. A special resolution is required.

A company which takes advantage of s. 3A CA 1985 as substituted and has incorporated a statement to the effect that its objects are to carry on business as a general commercial company is unlikely to need to change its objects clause.

3.2   Procedure for altering objects

A meeting of the company must first be held to pass the necessary special resolution. If the resolution is passed, then an application to the court may be made by 15% (by nominal value) of the shareholders, or of any class of shareholder (or of certain debenture-holders whose debentures were issued before 1 December 1947). The court to which the application is made is the High Court (Chancery Division) or, in certain cases, the county court for the area where the company has its registered office. The court has power to confirm the alteration in whole or in part or to refuse to confirm it. It may also impose terms, including terms requiring the company to purchase the shares of the shareholders who object to the alteration. An application under s. 5(2) must be made within 21 days of the passing of the special resolution.

A copy of the special resolution altering the objects must be sent to the Registrar (this requirement applies to all special resolutions). In addition a printed copy of the memorandum as altered must be sent to him. The amended memorandum must be delivered to the Registrar within 15 days of the last day on which an application to the court for cancellation of the amendment could have been made. However, if an application is made to the court for cancellation, the company must notify the Registrar of that fact 'forthwith' and send the amended memorandum (if any amendments remain) within 15 days of the court's decision.

The Registrar must officially notify his receipt of the altered memorandum. As with a change of name, the company cannot rely on the alteration against an outsider until it has been officially notified unless that person knows of the alteration, nor can it rely on the alteration for 15 days after official notification against a person who was unavoidably prevented from knowing that the alteration had taken place.

4 ALTERATION OF ARTICLES

4.1 Power to alter

Section 9, CA 1985 gives a company power to alter its articles by special resolution. The power of alteration is expressed to be 'subject to the provisions of this Act' — all this really means is that the altered articles may not conflict with other parts of the legislation (so that, for example, they cannot deprive the shareholders of a right to remove directors from office under s. 303 CA 1985). Anything which could have been included in the original articles may be included in the altered articles (s. 9(2)), so that the articles may not be made unalterable. However, an alteration requiring the members to buy more shares or otherwise invest more money is void as against persons who were members at the time of the alteration (s. 16 CA 1985).

The memorandum of association is regarded as being of greater authority than the articles, so that an article (whether included on incorporation or later) which contradicts the memorandum is invalid.

4.2 Registration

Once the special resolution altering the articles has been passed, the resolution and a printed copy of the amended articles must be sent to the Registrar within 15 days. The Registrar officially notifies his receipt of these documents and the company cannot rely on the changes until he has done so under the same rules as for change of name and alteration of objects. The company must ensure that copies of the altered articles are available, so that the directors and secretary may consult them and in case any member exercises his statutory right to a copy of the articles (s. 19 CA 1985).

4.3 Alteration to be for the benefit of the company

4.3.1 Shareholders may decide for themselves

There are no provisions in the Companies Act giving shareholders, or any particular proportion of the shareholders, power to challenge the validity of an alteration to the articles. However, the courts have held that an alteration is invalid if it is not 'bona fide in the interests of the company as a whole' (per Lord Lindley MR in *Allen* v *Gold Reefs of West Africa Ltd* [1900] 1 Ch 656). The test is very much easier to state than to apply to the facts of particular cases. As we shall see in relation to the rule in *Foss* v *Harbottle* (see ch. 8), the court is very reluctant to interfere with business decisions merely because some of the shareholders object to what has been decided.

The court will normally regard an alteration as being in the interests of the company if the majority of the shareholders are in favour of the alteration (as they must be since a special resolution will have been passed before any question as to the validity of the alteration can arise). Thus in *Allen* v *Gold Reefs of West Africa Ltd* the articles contained a provision imposing a lien on partly paid shares. One shareholder owed money to the company and the articles were altered to impose a lien on fully paid shares as well as on partly paid shares. The court regarded the fact that one (and only one) shareholder was indebted to the company at the time of alteration as something exciting suspicion as to the bona fides of the company, but nevertheless came to the conclusion that the alteration was in the interests of the company as a whole. Clearly it is in the interests of a company that it should have security for money due to it and no discrimination against particular members was expressed in the altered articles.

Shuttleworth v *Cox Brothers and Co (Maidenhead) Ltd* [1927] 2 KB 9, is perhaps a stronger illustration. The majority of the directors suspected that one of the board had been guilty of misconduct but they had insufficient proof of any grounds giving a right to dismiss him. They therefore altered the articles to say that any director would cease to hold office if requested to resign by the majority of the directors. The test applied by the court was whether any reasonable man could come to the conclusion that the alteration was in the interests of the company. If it was open to a reasonable man to come to that conclusion, the alteration would only be invalid on proof of actual bad faith. The court was satisfied that a reasonable man could come to the conclusion that the alteration was in the interests of the company and so, since the plaintiff could not prove actual bad faith, the alteration was held to be valid.

4.3.2 Discrimination

The courts have recognised that an alteration to the articles cannot be in the interests of the company as a whole if it discriminates against some members, however few. At first sight this seems strange in view of the two cases mentioned above, both of which involved actual discrimination against a particular shareholder. However, on closer analysis neither of those cases involved any discrimination. In *Allen* v *Gold Reefs of West Africa* the lien applied, potentially, to all the fully paid shares whoever owned them, so that it might apply to any shareholder at some time. Similarly in *Shuttleworth* v *Cox* the new article potentially applied to any shareholder who became a director and who fell into disfavour with the rest of the board. A good illustration of the type of case where an alteration *is* discriminatory and so void is given by the Australian case, *Australian Fixed Trust Proprietary Ltd* v *Clyde Industries Ltd* (1959) SR (NSW) 33. In that case the articles were altered so as to require shareholders who were unit trust managers to obtain the approval of the majority of their unit-holders before exercising the voting rights attached to their shares. This clearly discriminated against shareholders who happened to be unit trust managers and so was void.

The narrowness of the distinction between cases which are, and cases which are not, discriminatory is well illustrated by the cases of *Sidebottom* v *Kershaw, Leese and Co Ltd* [1920] 1 Ch 154, and *Brown* v *Abrasive Wheel Company* [1919] 1 Ch 290. In *Sidebottom* v *Kershaw, Leese* the articles were altered so as to give the directors power to direct a shareholder who was concerned with a competing business to transfer his shares. This was held to be a valid alteration. The company could properly come to the conclusion that it was in its interests that competitors be excluded from membership and there was no discrimination based on the number of shares owned. In *Brown* v *Abrasive Wheel Co* the articles were altered to give 90% of the shareholders power to require the minority shareholders to sell their shares. In fact, the majority shareholders (who owned 98% of the shares) had good commercial reasons for wanting the alteration, but nevertheless the court held that the alteration was invalid. Although it was bona fide in the interests of 98% of the present shareholders it was not in the interests of the other 2%, nor necessarily was it in the interests of future shareholders and so it was discriminatory.

4.3.3 The hypothetical member

It is sometimes suggested that whether an alteration is bona fide in the interests of the company as a whole can be tested by reference to the interests of a 'hypothetical member'. This was first suggested in *Greenhalgh* v *Arderne Cinemas Ltd* [1951] Ch 286, where, during the course of a long and frequently litigated dispute within a company, the articles were altered to allow a member to transfer shares to any person with the sanction of an ordinary resolution. (The articles as originally drafted contained pre-emption rights in favour of the remaining shareholders.) The real purpose of the alteration was to allow the majority shareholders to sell out. The alteration was held to be valid on the rather casuistic argument that every shareholder who wished to transfer shares was given the same right to ask for an ordinary resolution allowing transfer free of the existing pre-emption rights. The fact that a majority shareholder was certain of success whilst a minority shareholder had practically no chance, did not reduce the legal value of the rights given to the latter when compared with those given to the former. During the course of his judgment Sir Raymond Evershed MR said '. . . "the company as a whole" . . . means the corporators as a general body. That is to say, the case may be taken of an individual hypothetical member . . .'.

It can be seen from the facts of *Greenhalgh* v *Arderne Cinemas* that the hypothetical member is neither specifically a majority shareholder nor a minority shareholder since both those groups must be treated equally. It is doubtful how useful the hypothetical member test is in deciding the validity of alterations in other circumstances. Is he, for example, to be assumed to be neither specifically a unit trust manager nor a non-unit trust manager, so as to explain the *Australian Fixed Trust Pty Ltd* v *Clyde Industries* case? Is he to be assumed not to be in competition with the company so as to explain the *Sidebottom* v *Kershaw, Leese* case?

Probably it is safer to ignore the hypothetical member and to concentrate on the two basic rules which seem to have evolved from the cases:

(a) The members may generally decide themselves whether an alteration is bona fide in the interests of the company as a whole.

(b) The court will interfere with their decision where the members could not properly come to that decision because it discriminates between groups of members.

4.3.4 Clemens v Clemens

Although the case of *Clemens* v *Clemens Brothers Ltd* [1976] 2 All ER 268, was not concerned with alteration of the articles (see ch. 4—3), the general principles stated there are especially appropriate to alteration of the articles. Discrimination is not, therefore, the only ground on which an alteration may be held to be invalid. It is too early to speculate whether *Clemens* v *Clemens* marks a watershed or whether it will be limited 'to its own particular facts', but any move away from the rigidity and narrowness of the decision on alteration of articles is to be welcomed.

5   ALTERATION TO THE ADDITIONAL CLAUSES IN THE MEMORANDUM

As we saw in Chapter 2, five clauses must be included in the memorandum of association. The draftsman may also include in the memorandum anything which could have been in the articles. If this has been done the provisions included in the memorandum can be altered by special resolution (s. 17 CA 1985). (Both the special resolution and a printed copy of the amended memorandum need to be filed with the Registrar.) However, 15% of the shareholders of any class are given the right to apply to the court for cancellation of the alteration (this right does *not* apply to an alteration to the articles). Furthermore, the memorandum itself may specify that these additional clauses are unalterable, in which case no amendment can be made (s. 17(2) CA 1985). This is perhaps the only significant reason for including in the memorandum a term which could have been in the articles.

6   ALTERATION TO THE CAPITAL CLAUSE

6.1   The capital clause

As stated earlier, the capital clause merely states the company's authorised capital and how it is divided into shares of particular nominal value (also, very rarely, classes of shares may be distinguished in the capital clause) (ch. 2—2.1.6). In Chapter 5 we saw how shares are issued. The capital clause may be altered in a number of ways, the most important of which is by increasing the authorised capital. It should be noted that an issue of shares even long after incorporation does not always require an alteration to the capital clause. For example, the capital clause may say: 'The share capital of the company is £5,000 divided into 5,000 shares of £1 each.' Shortly after incorporation 1,000 of these shares may have been issued but this still leaves 4,000 unissued shares, so that an increase of capital will only be required if it is decided to issue more than 4,000 shares. If a further issue of shares is being considered, it is necessary to find out what the authorised capital is (by looking at the capital clause) and how much of it has been issued (by looking at the returns as to allotments). Once the company has held an AGM it is possible to find details of both authorised and issued capital by looking at its last annual return and then all that needs to be done is to check whether any shares have been issued since then.

6.2   The power to alter capital

6.2.1   Increase
Section 121, CA 1985 gives a limited company power to alter its capital in a number of ways provided that the articles authorise the alteration. The most important alteration permitted by s. 121 is the power for a company to 'increase its share capital by new shares of such amount as it thinks expedient'. If Table A applies, then the authorisation for an increase is given by art. 32, which says: 'The company may by ordinary resolution increase its share capital by new shares of such amount as the resolution prescribes'. Section 121(4) requires that the decision to alter capital must be taken by the company in general meeting. The aricles of the company could, therefore, provide for a special or extraordinary resolution for increase of capital but could not give the power to the directors.

6.2.2 Other alterations

Most alterations of capital under s. 121 will be increases of nominal capital but it is also possible under that section to consolidate or subdivide shares, convert shares into stock or cancel unissued shares. Shares are consolidated if shares of a smaller amount are consolidated into a smaller number of shares of a larger amount (e.g., 1,000 £1 shares become 100 £10 shares); subdivision is the opposite (1,000 £1 shares become 10,000 10p shares). If Table A applies the company has power to consolidate or subdivide under art. 32. However, since the change is really only a nominal one, there will seldom be any advantage in making it unless the value of each share is either extremely large or extremely small, in which case subdivision or consolidation may be of some cosmetic value.

A power to cancel unissued shares is also given by Table A art. 32. If unissued shares are cancelled, the company loses the right to issue them in future without first increasing capital. When directors were free to issue shares as they wished, cancellation might sometimes have been desirable to prevent them from making an issue to which the shareholders objected, but now it will be simpler to refuse authority for an issue or to withdraw authority if it has been given (see ch. 5—2.2). Cancellation of unissued shares does not involve a reduction of capital since no liability arises until the shares are issued.

Converting shares into stock involves a technical change in the status of the investment — a share cannot be divided, by its owner, into fractional parts, whereas stock can (thus the owner of a £1 share can transfer all of it or none of it; the owner of stock with a nominal value of £1 could transfer stock with a nominal value of 40p and retain the other 60p). Such a technical change is really of no practical significance.

6.3 Steps to be taken on increase of capital

The directors will normally propose the increase and so will summon a general meeting to consider an increase. The ordinary resolution will then be considered at the meeting. In the extremely unlikely event that the articles do not give the company power to increase capital, the articles will have to be changed first. In *MacConnell* v *E. Prill and Co Ltd* [1916] 2 Ch 57, it was held that the same special resolution could be used both to alter the articles and to exercise the power to increase capital.

After the meeting, if the alteration has been approved by the members, s. 123 CA 1985 requires that notice must be given to the Registrar of the increase, together (on Form G123) with a copy of the resolution and (within 15 days of the change) a printed copy of the amended memorandum. (This is one of the comparatively few circumstances in which an ordinary resolution requires registration.) Following the increase of capital steps will, of course, usually be taken to issue further shares (usually an increase will only be considered when such an issue is intended).

6.4 Reduction of capital

A reduction of capital is not generally permitted since capital must be maintained (see ch. 5—3.1). However, a reduction of capital is permitted in the following circumstances:

(a)   by court order under s. 459 CA 1985 (unfair prejudice; see ch. 8);
(b)   by court order when objection is taken to alteration of objects under s. 4 CA 1985 (see paragraph 3 above).

We have also seen that shares may be repaid on redemption or when the company purchases its own shares, but that in both cases capital must be maintained by the opening of a 'capital redemption reserve' (see ch. 5—3.3).

Section 135, CA 1985 provides a general power to reduce capital provided that the articles authorised this. A special resolution is required, as is 'confirmation by the court'. Table A art. 34 gives authority for reduction. The power to reduce capital given by s. 135 applies to anything which is a reduction but three types of reduction are specifically mentioned. They empower the company to:

(a)   extinguish or reduce the liability on any of its shares in respect of share capital not paid up; or
(b)   . . . cancel any paid-up share capital which is lost or unrepresented by available assets; or
(c)   . . . pay off any paid-up share capital which is in excess of the company's wants.

Section 135 is expressed in very wide terms, but because of the requirement of confirmation by the court reduction is very unusual. If the reduction involves a cancellation of liability to pay the unpaid part of share capital or involves a repayment to the shareholder, creditors have a right to object and the reduction will only be permitted if they are paid off or given security.

In all cases the court must have regard to the interests of creditors, potential investors in the company, and rights of the existing shareholders. As far as shareholders are concerned, the court will not normally object to an alteration provided they are all treated equally. However, with different classes of shares the problem is more complex. The court will only sanction a reduction if each class is treated according to the rights it would have if the company were wound up. For example, normally preference shareholders will be paid off first in a winding-up. They should, therefore, be paid off in full before ordinary shareholders on a reduction of capital. However, if capital is being reduced by cancellation of the company's liability without repayment, the ordinary capital would be cancelled first since the ordinary shareholders would be the ones who would lose their capital if the company were wound up.

7 Protection of Outsiders

1 INTRODUCTION

A company is not a natural person and so can only exercise its powers through agents. Usually contracts will be made on behalf of the company either by the directors or by more junior officials acting on the directors' authority. If a contract is made in accordance with the articles of the company it will be binding on the company, so that the 'outsider' with whom the company is dealing can sue the company if it fails to perform the contract. Where, however, a contract is made by the wrong people (e.g., the directors exercise a power which is vested in the shareholders, or an employee acts without the authority of the directors), or in the wrong way (e.g., a meeting is held but it has not been properly convened), the whole transaction is, prima facie, void. Contracts and other transactions decided upon without proper authority (or without a proper exercise of authority) are described as 'irregular'.

In dealing with irregular contracts the law is faced with a dilemma. If the contract is declared irregular and void the outsider will not be able to enforce it against the company even though he may be unaware of the irregularity. On the other hand, if the company is held to be bound by irregular contracts the directors will, in effect, be able to ignore the requirements of the company's articles to the possible detriment of the shareholders. The law deals with this dilemma by providing that irregular contracts, though prima facie void, are binding on the company in certain circumstances only. These circumstances result partly from statute, partly from decisions of the court concerned exclusively with company law rules, and partly from the general law of agency. The Companies Act 1989 has further extended the circumstances in which an irregular contract is valid.

2 STATUTORY PROTECTION

2.1 Sections 35A and 35B (as interpolated)

Statutory rules about the extent to which directors could bind their company despite irregularity were first included in the European Communities Act 1972. Similar provisions were included in s. 35 CA 1985. This section has now been significantly amended by CA 1989. The new provisions are contained in new sections 35A and 35B CA 1985. Section 35A(1) provides:

> In favour of a person dealing with a company in good faith, the power of the board of directors to bind the company, or to authorise others to do so, shall be deemed free of any limitation under the company's constitution.

The reference to the company's constitution (for this purpose) includes a resolution of the company and agreements between the company and its members as well as the memorandum and articles.

It should be noted that a person dealing with the company is entitled to assume that the directors have unlimited power to bind it. A similar assumption may also be made where the directors have purported to authorise 'others' to do so. Presumably, a person dealing with a single director who acts without any purported authorisation from the board would not be protected. However, there is authority (*International Sales and Agencies Limited* v *Marcus* [1982] 3 All ER 551) under the previous legislation which holds that a single director can bind the company where he is the sole effective director.

If a shareholder believes that the directors are about to exceed their powers by entering into an irregular contract he may be able to obtain an injunction to restrain them. However, this right is lost once the company incurs any legal obligation to a third party (s. 35A(4)). If directors enter into an irregular contract they may be liable to the company for any loss. (Section 35 gives them no protection personally (s. 35A(5).)

The protection of s. 35A is given only to persons who act in good faith. However, good faith is presumed unless the contrary is proved (s. 35A(2)(c)) and knowledge that the directors are acting beyond their powers is not of itself sufficient proof of bad faith (s. 35A(2)(a)). Section 35B provides that a person dealing with a company is not under any obligation to enquire into the powers of its directors.

Section 322A CA 1985 (as interpolated by CA 1989) makes a limited exception to s. 35A. This applies where the board of a company exceed their powers in a transaction with a director or a person connected with a director. In such cases the transaction is voidable by the company. Whether or not it is avoided, the director or connected person and any director who authorised the transaction is liable to account to the company for any gain he makes and to indemnify the company against any loss. Where a transaction is irregular and is made between the company, a director and one or more third parties the court has a wide discretion which enables it to protect any innocent third party.

The company's right to avoid a contract under s. 322A is lost if restitution becomes impossible (i.e., if a third party who has acquired rights bona fide for value would be affected), if the transaction is ratified or if the company has been fully compensated by indemnity from the director.

2.2   Section 285 CA 1985

Section 285 provides that, 'the acts of a director or manager are valid notwithstanding any defect that may afterwards be discovered in his appointment or qualification'. This section protects the company, the outsider dealing with it, and the director, if there is some sort of procedural defect in the appointment (e.g., proper notice was not given of the meeting at which the appointment was made).

It does not give any protection where there is a substantial defect in the appointment. This is illustrated by the case of *Morris* v *Kanssen* [1946] AC 459. Kanssen and C were the directors of a company and there was a disagreement between them. C and S, who was not a director, decided to remove Kanssen from his position in the company. They therefore wrote in the minute book of the company an entry saying that S had been appointed a director. C and S then appointed Morris a director and C, S and Morris then issued shares to themselves (at the time and under the articles of the company, the directors were free to issue shares to themselves without holding a meeting of the company; for the present position, see ch. 5). Morris did not know that S's appointment was invalid. Kanssen eventually discovered what had happened and sought rectification of the register of members (i.e., he sought to have the issue of shares declared invalid). C, S and Morris defended the action on the basis that they were protected by s. 143 CA 1929 (which was identical with the present s. 285). The House of Lords held that the section gave protection only in limited circumstances. Lord Simmonds said: 'There is . . . a vital distinction between . . . a defective appointment and no appointment at all. In the first case, it is implied that some act is done which purports to be an appointment but is by reason of some defect inadequate . . . : in the second case . . . there is no act at all . . . it would, I think, be doing violence to plain language to construe the section as covering a case in which there had been no genuine attempt to appoint at all'. The House of Lords went on to decide that the appointments of S and Morris were, therefore, invalid.

2.3 Section 74 of the Law of Property Act 1925

This section gives protection to a purchaser (i.e., in this context a person acquiring property in good faith and for valuable consideration) under a deed if there is some defect in the sealing or attestation of the deed.

3 THE RULE IN *ROYAL BRITISH BANK* v *TURQUAND*

3.1 Directors exceeding powers

A number of common law decisions decided before the European Communities Act 1972 gave protection to outsiders where contracts were made without authority. In view of the enactment of s. 35A and 35B the significance of these decisions is likely to be very slight in future.

These decisions held that a person dealing with a company was entitled to assume the correct procedures had been followed (*Royal British Bank* v *Turquand* (1856) E and B 327, 119 ER 886), that persons appearing to be directors had been properly appointed (*Mahony* v *East Holyford Mining Co* (1875) LR 7 HL 869) and that a board meeting had been lawfully held (*Browne* v *La Trinidad* (1887) 37 Ch D 1).

4 AGENCY

4.1 General position

A company can only act through agents; the authority of agents to act for a company depends on the general law of agency. The actions of an agent are binding on a principal if the agent has actual authority or authority arising from estoppel. The agent may also be personally liable to the third party (i.e., to the outsider) if the principal (i.e., the company) is not liable.

4.2   Actual authority

The scope of the actual authority of a company's agents depends upon the memorandum and articles of the company. As we saw in Chapter 3, the board of directors, acting collectively, usually has very wide powers to act on behalf of the company. The articles will usually permit delegation to committees of directors and to a managing director (or to a number of joint managing directors). The implementation of decisions may also be delegated to more junior officials. In the vast majority of cases decisions are taken in the name of the company by a person with actual authority to bind the company. In such cases no question of irregularity arises. It should also be noted that actual authority may be implied as well as express, so that if a particular power is delegated to an agent, either generally or for a particular occasion, the agent will impliedly have power to do things reasonably incidental to the express authority which has been given.

4.3   Agency by estoppel

A company may be bound by the acts of a person acting on its behalf when it is estopped from denying that person's authority. Agency by estoppel may result either from 'holding out' (that is, an actual representation that the agent has authority) or from a representation that the agent is a member of a particular class of agent which is recognised to have certain powers to bind its principals. The estoppel may prevent the company from denying that the alleged agent is its agent or that he has power to bind the company in a particular way.

4.3.1   'Holding out'

If a company is to be liable because an agent has been held out as having authority, the holding out must be done by the person or persons with actual authority to bind the company. This will usually mean that the holding out must be done by the board. The company will, therefore, be bound if the board authorises a letter or other communication telling the third party that a particular person has authority to bind the company. It is also sufficient if the board knowingly acquiesces in the action of the alleged agent.

4.3.2   Usual or apparent authority

It is a well established rule of the law of agency that a principal is estopped from denying that an agent of certain recognised classes has the authority normally associated with that class (unless, of course, he tells the third party that there is a restriction on the power of the agent). In relation to companies, this rule has been applied to managing directors. If a company describes one of the directors as a managing director, it is estopped from denying that he is a managing director (even if he has not been appointed) and that he has the authority of a managing director (even if his appointment includes terms restricting his authority). This type of authority is sometimes called 'usual authority' or 'apparent authority'.

The usual authority of a person described as a managing director extends to contracts concerned with the running of the company's business, but not to such matters as issuing shares. Usual authority may be implied from the fact that a person is permitted by the board to act as a managing director. This is illustrated by *Freeman and Lockyer* v *Buckhurst Park Properties (Mangal) Ltd* [1964] 2 QB 480. A company was set up by two people, both of whom became directors along with two further directors. The articles contained a power to appoint a managing director and although none was appointed, one of the founders acted as managing director. He negotiated a contract with the plaintiffs and the company was held to be bound by the contract. Diplock LJ said that four conditions have to be satisfied if the company is to be bound by a contract made without actual authority:

It must be shown:

(a)   that a representation that the agent had authority to enter on behalf of the company into a contract of the kind sought to be enforced was made to the contractor;

(b)   that such representation was made by a person or persons who had 'actual' authority to manage the business of the company either generally or in respect of those matters to which the contract relates;

(c)   that he [the contractor] was induced by such representation to enter into the contract, that is, that he in fact relied upon it; and

(d)   that under its memorandum or articles of association the company was not deprived of the capacity either to enter into a contract of the kind sought to be enforced or to delegate authority to enter into a contract of that kind to the agent . . . the board knew that Kapoor had throughout been acting as managing director . . . They permitted him to do so, and by such conduct represented that he had authority to enter into contracts of a kind which a managing director . . . would in the normal course be authorised to enter into on behalf of the company.

Since directors other than managing directors do not generally have authority to act alone, a company is not bound by the action of a single director who is not a managing director unless either he has actual authority or the board have held him out as having authority in the particular transaction.

The company secretary has been held to have usual authority to bind the company to contracts concerning administration (see ch. 3—11).

4.4   Liability of the agent to the third party

A person purporting to act as agent for a company will be personally liable for breach of warranty of authority if it turns out that he had no authority to bind the company.

4.5   Ratification

If a contract is made by an agent without authority so that the company is not bound by the contract, the company can ratify, and thus retrospectively validate, the contract. Ratification may be effected by the people with actual authority to bind the company (i.e., normally the board, but in some cases the members in general meeting). Ratification will usually be implied where the company has accepted performance of the contract.

8 Internal Disputes

1 INTRODUCTION

The courts are very reluctant to get involved in disputes within a company. In particular they are not willing to do anything which might amount to interference with business decisions. Internal disputes must therefore usually be resolved under the terms of the company's articles. For example, if there are disputes about business policy the view of the majority of the board will prevail. In the case of an equal division on the board the dispute will be resolved by the chairman's casting vote if the articles so provide (as they usually will).

As we saw in Chapters 3 and 4 the power of the shareholders is rather limited. In this chapter we will look at five procedures which are, however, available to shareholders for their protection. The first of these (removal of directors) gives *majority* shareholders ultimate control of the company. The second (s. 14 CA 1985) provides any shareholder with a procedure for enforcing his personal rights in the company. The other three procedures are designed chiefly for the protection of minority shareholders when a dispute arises.

2 REMOVAL OF DIRECTORS (s. 303 CA 1985)

Shareholders appoint directors in most cases and, unless Table A has been altered, have an opportunity to get rid of them every three years when they retire by rotation. To give the shareholders a greater measure of control, s. 303 CA 1985 provides for removal of directors by ordinary resolution (i.e., by a majority vote of the shareholders in general meeting). The power given by the section overrides anything in the company's articles (even, for example, an article naming a life director) or in an agreement with the director. The importance of s. 303 can hardly be overstated; it is the most effective way in which majority shareholders who object to the way in which their company is being run can keep control of the company. Where the directors themselves are the majority shareholders, as they very frequently will be in the case of a private company, the other (minority) shareholders have limited rights to object to the way the board is running the company (see below).

A shareholder who wants to propose a resolution for the removal of a director under s. 303 must give 'special notice' of the resolution; this means that he must give notice to the company at least 28 days before the meeting at which the resolution is to be discussed (s. 379 CA 1985). However, this requirement is deemed to be complied with if a meeting is called *after* notice has been given for a date within the 28 days. It has been held (in *Pedley* v *Inland Waterways Association* [1977] 1 All ER 209) that the directors are not under an obligation to put the resolution for the removal of a director on the agenda of a meeting merely because they have received special notice. This detracts slightly from the effectiveness of s. 303 but, as we saw in Chapter 4, any shareholders (or group of shareholders) with a 10% shareholding (5% in the case of an annual general meeting) can insist on the inclusion of a resolution on the agenda. Once the company has received the special notice a copy must be sent to the director whose removal is proposed (s. 304); he is also given a right to speak at the meeting even if not a member, and to require the company to circulate representations in writing of reasonable length to the members.

There are two ways in which the effectiveness of s. 303 is reduced. First, although the right to remove a director is absolute, the director is not deprived of any right to compensation or damages which he may have (s. 303(5)). It may, therefore, be very expensive to remove a director, in which case the majority shareholders should consider other methods of control (e.g., by the appointment of additional directors).

Secondly, the articles may validly give special voting rights to some of the shareholders either generally or in particular circumstances. In the case of *Bushell* v *Faith* [1970] AC 1099, the articles provided that 'in the event of a resolution being proposed at any general meeting of the company for the removal from office of any director, any shares held by that director shall on a poll in respect of such resolution carry the right to three votes per share . . .'. The director whose removal was proposed owned one third of the shares and so could not be removed. Nevertheless, the article was held to be valid, since all that s. 303 lays down is that an ordinary resolution may be used to remove a director and an ordinary resolution is one requiring a simple majority of votes. A clause of this type does not, therefore, prevent a resolution from being an ordinary resolution but effectively makes it impossible to remove the director without his consent.

The decision in *Bushell* v *Faith* has been criticised, but there are some circumstances where it may be appropriate to include in the articles a regulation which makes it impossible for the majority shareholders to get rid of a director who owns a minority of the shares. Such a regulation should be considered, for example, where a small number of people wish to run a company as a 'quasi-partnership' — that is, where they all intend to have a continuing right to take part in management. In other circumstances it may be appropriate to give the shareholders wider powers to remove directors than are given by s. 303 so that, for example, removal by ordinary resolution *without* special notice may be considered appropriate.

3 SECTION 14 COMPANIES ACT 1985

3.1 Contract between members and company

This important section creates a contract between a company and each of its members (without such a provision only the original owner of shares would have a contract with the company). Section 14 says '. . . the memorandum and articles . . . bind the company and its members to the same extent as if they respectively had been signed and sealed by each member, and contained covenants on the part of each member to observe all the provisions of the memorandum and of the articles'. Read literally only the members are bound by this contract since only they are deemed to have sealed the memorandum and articles and to have entered into covenants. However, the company has been held to be bound by the contract as well (*Re Compañía de Electricidad de la Provincia de Buenos Aires Ltd* [1978] 3 All ER 668).

3.2   Contract between members

The contracts laid down in s. 14 have been held to bind the members contractually to each other. Thus in *Rayfield* v *Hands* [1960] Ch 1, the articles of the company required the directors to purchase the shares of any member who wished to sell his shares. This obligation was held to be enforceable against the directors since they were shareholders in the company and were, therefore, parties to a contract with each of its members. As we shall see shortly, s. 14 has often been held to apply only to obligations owed by or to members in their capacity as members, but the court was able to say (without giving any very persuasive reasons for doing so) that the obligation to buy shares was imposed on the directors in their capacity as members.

3.3   Membership rights

An obligation imposed by the memorandum or articles on a member or on the company for the benefit of a member is only enforceable under s. 14 if it relates to membership rights. The most obvious examples of membership rights which have been enforced as a result of actions based on the section include the right to a dividend once lawfully declared (*Wood* v *Odessa Waterworks Co* (1889) 42 ChD 636), the right to share in surplus capital on a winding-up (*Griffith* v *Paget* (1877) 5 ChD 894) and the right to vote at meetings (*Pender* v *Lushington* (1877) 6 ChD 70). The most obvious obligation of a member which may be enforced by s. 14 is the obligation to pay calls on partly paid shares.

3.4   Other rights

Obligations imposed by the memorandum or articles which do not relate to membership rights are not enforceable under s. 14. A member may, therefore, be left without any remedy even though the company has failed to observe an article which would have benefited him. This is illustrated by the case of *Eley* v *Positive Government Security Life Assurance Co* (1876) 1 ExD 88. When the company was formed a provision was included in the articles naming the plaintiff as solicitor of the company. He was never, in fact, appointed to the office but did become a member of the company. It was held that he could not sue the company under the provisions of earlier legislation corresponding with s. 14. It may seem harsh that a member cannot sue in such a case to enforce an article of the company, but the justification for the rule is that it would be wrong to allow someone to sue just because he was a member, and furthermore it would lead to great inconveniences if members could sue every time there was a breach of the articles.

Just as a member cannot enforce rights against the company which do not relate to his rights as a member, neither can the company enforce obligations imposed by the articles other than in connection with membership. For example, in *Beattie* v *E. and F. Beattie Ltd* [1938] Ch 708, a dispute arose between a company and one of its directors concerning the latter's right to inspect documents. The company wished to refer the matter to arbitration in accordance with an article requiring arbitration of disputes with members, but was held not entitled to insist on arbitration since the dispute was between the company and the plaintiff in his capacity as director not in his capacity as shareholder. This case may be contrasted with *Hickman* v *Kent or*

Romney Marsh Sheep-Breeders' Association [1915] 1 Ch 881, where a shareholder was expelled from the company and sued. The action was stayed because the articles required arbitration of disputes and clearly a dispute about expulsion relates to infringement of membership rights.

The case of *Salmon* v *Quin and Axtens Ltd* [1909] AC 442, has been put forward as authority for saying that members have a right to enforce all the terms of the memorandum and articles on the basis that every member has a right as a member to see the company properly administered. This argument would, however, seem to be untenable in view of the weight of authority against it.

3.5 Implied contracts and shareholders' agreements

The terms laid down in the memorandum or articles may be impliedly incorporated into a contract made with the company. This is most likely to occur in relation to directors' service contracts. Thus, in *Read* v *Astoria Garage (Streatham) Ltd* [1952] Ch 637, a managing director whose service contract did not specify how long he was to remain in office was held to have an implied contract allowing for his dismissal in accordance with certain provisions in the articles.

If the members of a company wish to be able to enforce all the terms of the articles against the company and/or each other they are free to enter into a separate contract to that effect. Such a contract is generally referred to as a 'shareholders' agreement'.

4 *FOSS* v *HARBOTTLE*

4.1 Majority rule

A shareholder is not usually permitted to sue where a wrong is done to a company of which he is a member. This rule is known as the rule in *Foss* v *Harbottle* (1843) 2 Hare 461, and there are two justifications for it. Firstly, since a company is a separate legal person distinct from its members the company is the proper plaintiff in an action where a wrong has been done to the company. Secondly, the decision whether or not to sue can be taken either by the directors or by the members in general meeting, and the court is unwilling to interfere with this decision by imposing its own views on the company. At the same time, the courts have recognised that in some circumstances it is appropriate to allow a shareholder to sue on behalf of the company since otherwise justice cannot be done. There are, therefore, a number of exceptions to the rule in *Foss* v *Harbottle*, under which a shareholder can bring an action if the company will not.

These exceptional cases should be contrasted with cases where the personal rights of a shareholder are affected. In such cases, as we saw in the last paragraph, the shareholder need not rely upon an exception to *Foss* v *Harbottle* at all, but may sue because of the contractual rights which he has under s. 14. It is not always easy to decide which actions are permitted by the exceptions to *Foss* v *Harbottle* and which by s. 14. Minority shareholders are also given a number of statutory rights which may be directly enforced against the company (for example, to have the register to members rectified under s. 359 CA 1985), and are given a right to sue where they are 'unfairly prejudiced' by the way in which the company's affairs are being conducted (s. 459 CA 1985) (see paragraph 6).

4.2   Exceptions to *Foss* v *Harbottle*

The following are the circumstances in which a member can sue to remedy a wrong
done to the company.

*4.2.1   Where the majority exercise their votes so as to 'defraud' the minority
shareholders*
'Fraud' in this context is quite a wide concept, covering forms of conduct which do
not amount to the commission of a tort. Thus in *Clemens* v *Clemens Brothers Ltd*
[1976] 2 All ER 268, a resolution was declared invalid, the effect of which was to
increase the degree of control which the majority shareholder and her associates
could exercise (see ch. 4—3).

*4.2.2   Where directors who are in control of a company have been guilty of a breach
of fiduciary duty*
This exception will often overlap with the first exception, since a breach of fiduciary
duty will often involve a fraud on the minority. The reason for this exception is that if
the directors are in control of the company they will use their voting power so as to
prevent action being brought against themselves. Therefore, unless a shareholder
can sue on behalf of the company, there is no real chance of a remedy for the breach
of fiduciary duty. Where a breach of fiduciary duty can be ratified by the members in
general meeting (see, for example, *Hogg* v *Cramphorn*, ch. 3—7.1), an action by a
shareholder may be stayed pending the holding of a meeting, but the court will not
permit ratification in every case (see, for example, *Cook* v *Deeks*, ch. 3— 7.1).
    Where the directors are not in control of a company, an action cannot be brought
by a shareholder based on breach of fiduciary duty, since the company in general
meeting is then in a position to decide to sue. However, *Clemens* v *Clemens* shows
that in such cases the way in which the majority shareholders vote may be subject to
control by the court.

*4.2.3   Where the company (usually as a result of a decision of the board) is proposing
to act ultra vires or illegally*
In such cases the action may result in an injunction against the directors or an order
for compensation against the directors. The right to sue in such cases will not be
affected by the Companies Bill 1989.

*4.2.4   Where the company has purported to pass an ordinary resolution in
circumstances where a special resolution or extraordinary resolution is required.*
Similarly, an action may be brought to restrain a threatened breach of the articles
(which can only validly be altered by special resolution), although the exact scope of
this exception is far from clear.

*4.2.5   Where the company proposes to act on the authority of a resolution which is
defective because inadequate notice was given*
The notice may be inadequate either because the time between service and the
holding of the meeting is too short or because the details given in the notice are
insufficient to enable a member to decide whether to attend. For example, in *Baillie* v
Oriental Telephone Co. Ltd [1915] 1 Ch 503, the notice referred to the fact that a

resolution was to be proposed authorising certain payments of commission by a subsidiary company to the directors. It did not say that the payments effectively amounted to all the subsidiary's profits. This was held to be inadequate notice and, therefore, the resolution was set aside in an action brought by a shareholder.

4.2.6 Where the court decides that an action by a shareholder is in the interests of justice

There is some authority for saying that the list of exceptions to *Foss* v *Harbottle* is not closed and that the courts may allow actions in any circumstances where it is in the interests of justice. This was suggested in *Heyting* v *Dupont* [1964] 2 All ER 273 (although on the facts of that case the minority shareholder was refused a remedy). However, this view was doubted in *Estmanco (Kilner House) Ltd* v *GLC* [1982] 1 All ER 437, and in *Prudential Assurance Co. Ltd* v *Newman Industries Ltd (No. 2)* [1982] 1 All ER 354, the court observed that this was 'not a practical test'.

5 ACTIONS BY SHAREHOLDERS — PROCEDURE

When a member is able to bring an action under one of the exceptions to *Foss* v *Harbottle*, he is really doing so on behalf of the company. The plaintiff's interests are, therefore, the same as those of the other shareholders (other than any wrongdoers, usually the directors, who are defendants in the action). When a member sues to enforce the memorandum or articles under s. 14 he may be seeking a remedy for himself or for himself and a large number of other members whose rights have also been infringed. Order 15 r. 12(1) of the Rules of the Supreme Court makes provision for a representative action where 'numerous persons have the same interest in any proceedings'. This type of action may be brought where the cause of action arises under one of the exceptions to *Foss* v *Harbottle* or under s. 14. The plaintiff shareholder then represents the interests of all the shareholders (except the wrongdoers) and the judgment is normally binding on, and enforceable by, them.

If action is brought under one of the exceptions to *Foss* v *Harbottle*, the company will be made a nominal defendant. This type of action is sometimes described as a 'derivative action' because the right of the member to sue is not personal to him but derives from the right to sue which the company has failed to exercise. It should be noted that if this type of action is successful, the judgment will give a remedy to the company (which has been wronged) rather than to the plaintiff.

If action is brought under s. 14 it may or may not be representative but it will certainly not be 'derivative'. The right to sue is the plaintiff's own cause of action and in appropriate cases damages, specific performance or other directly beneficial orders will be made in his favour.

6 SECTION 459 COMPANIES ACT 1985

6.1 Unfair prejudice

Section 459(1) provides that:

A member of a company may apply to the court by petition for an order . . . on the ground that the company's affairs are being or have been conducted in a manner which is unfairly prejudicial to the interests of some part of the members (including at least himself) or that any actual or proposed act or omission of the company (including an act or omission on its behalf) is or would be so prejudicial.

A shareholder may petition under s. 459 if he can show that he has suffered unfair prejudice. The prejudice must have arisen from the way in which the affairs of the company were being conducted or from an actual or proposed act or omission by the company. The prejudice must have affected the interests of at least some of the members of the company. If these things can be shown then the court will have to consider what remedy would be appropriate.

The test as to what amounts to unfair prejudice is objective. It is not, therefore, necessary for the petitioning shareholders to show that anyone acted in bad faith or with the intention of causing prejudice. In *Re R. A. Noble (Clothing) Ltd* [1983] BCLC 273 the judge suggested that the unfairness of the behaviour could be tested by the 'reasonable bystander test'; that is, prejudice will be regarded as unfair if a hypothetical reasonable bystander would believe it to be unfair.

If the petitioner is to succeed he must show that his rights as a shareholder have been prejudiced. In *Re Postgate and Denby* [1987] BCLC 8 it was held that such rights include all rights given under the company's memorandum and articles, statutory rights and also rights arising out of agreements and understandings between members. An important example of the last category is an understanding between members (often falling short of a contract) that the company will be run as if it were a partnership. In such cases of 'quasi-partnership' a member who is excluded from management of the company may claim unfair prejudice (*Re Cumana* [1986] BCLC 430). However, the mere fact that a member has been excluded from his share of management of a quasi-partnership does not guarantee that he will succeed in a claim for unfair prejudice. Thus, in *Re A Company (No. 004377 of 1986)* [1987] 1 WLR 102 the petition failed as the articles of the company laid down exactly what was to happen if the quasi-partnership ended for any reason. This included a right for a majority shareholder to buy the shares of the minority. The minority shareholder might indeed be prejudiced by such a provision but he could not claim that the prejudice was unfair as he had (by joining the company) agreed to this in advance.

6.2 Powers of court

If a petition under s. 459 is successful the court 'may make such order as it thinks fit for giving relief in respect of the matters complained of' (s. 461(1)). Subsection 461(2) lists particular types of order which may be made but is expressly stated to be without prejudice to the general power given by s. 461(1). The powers listed in s. 461(2) are:

(a)   to regulate the conduct of the company's affairs in the future;

(b)   to require the company to refrain from doing or continuing an act complained of by the petitioner or to do an act which the petitioner has complained it has omitted to do;

(c)   to authorise civil proceedings to be brought in the name and on behalf of the company by such person or persons and on such terms as the court may direct;

(d)   to provide for the purchase of the shares of any members of the company by other members or by the company itself and, in the case of a purchase by the company itself, the reduction of the company's capital accordingly.

The power to authorise civil proceedings subject to terms may prove particularly useful. A shareholder may be deterred from fighting a complicated action, based on an exception to *Foss* v *Harbottle,* by the prospect of heavy costs. It may, therefore, be attractive to petition under s. 459 in the hope of obtaining an order for the action to be pursued by the company. The court will ensure that such a petition can be dealt with (in suitable cases) without the substantive issue being tried in the s. 459 proceedings.

In practice the most common remedy awarded to a successful petitioner is that his shares should be purchased by the wrongdoers who have caused the unfair prejudice. The question of valuation causes considerable problems in such cases. The courts have held that the shares should be valued as at whatever date is fair to the petitioner. This usually means that the shares are valued at the date when the prejudice to the petitioner began. If a different date is chosen the court will usually order that the valuer should value the shares as if the prejudice had not taken place.

The order made by the court under s. 459 may require an alteration to the memorandum or articles. If this is done, an office copy of the court order must be delivered to the Registrar within (usually) 14 days.

7   JUST AND EQUITABLE WINDING-UP

Companies may be wound up on a number of grounds. Winding-up is the process by which a company's existence is brought to an end; it usually results from the insolvency of the company. However, one type of winding-up is available as a remedy to shareholders of solvent companies — this is winding-up under s. 122(1)(g) Insolvency Act 1986, which provides for winding-up where 'the court is of the opinion that it is just and equitable that the company should be wound up'. Winding-up is a rather drastic solution to problems arising within a company and is likely to decline in importance now that a remedy is available for cases of unfair prejudice.

The 'just and equitable' ground laid down in s. 122(1)(g) (replacing similar provisions in earlier legislation) is expressed in general terms and can be regarded as, in effect, a 'sweeping-up' provision. While the courts have decided that a number of circumstances justify winding up the company, the illustrations given below are not exhaustive. It will be seen that the petitioner is usually a minority shareholder, but the ground for the petition does not have to be based on some circumstance affecting him as a shareholder. Section 122(1)(g) has been the basis of a petition in the following circumstances:

(a)   Where the 'substratum' of the company has failed. This arises where the company can no longer, or never could, achieve its 'main object'. In *Re Blériot Manufacturing Aircraft Co* (1916) 32 TLR 253, a company was formed to acquire the English part of the business of Blériot, the famous pilot. Unfortunately for the promoters of the company, he refused to sell the business. Since the company's *raison d'être* could not be achieved this warranted a winding-up on the just and equitable ground.

Similarly, in *Re German Date Coffee Co* (1882) 20 ChD 169, a company was formed with a view to using a German patent for manufacturing 'coffee' from dates. Since the German authorities never granted the patent, the court felt justified in making an order to wind the company up on the basis that its substratum had failed even though the company did in fact make coffee from dates using a different process. From this last case it follows that an order can be made if the main object cannot be achieved even where the objects clause incudes a *Bell Houses* clause enabling the company to carry on other businesses. Even if the majority of members want the directors to use their powers under such a clause or want to keep the company going after its business has been sold by investing the sale proceeds in accordance with a subsidiary object, an objecting minority shareholder may still successfully petition for a winding-up order (*Re Red Rock Gold Mining Co Ltd* (1889) 61 LT 785).

(b)   Where the company was formed in such a way as to resemble a 'quasi-partnership' and there are grounds that would justify the dissolution of a true partnership. This situation most commonly arises where an existing partnership is incorporated and it is intended that the rights of the former partners shall continue even though they are running their business through the medium of a company, for example, by each 'partner' enjoying equal voting and management rights. Thus the company can be wound up if:

(i)   There is deadlock between the 'partners' even though the company may be highly profitable (*Re Yenidje Tobacco Co* [1916] 2 Ch 246). Or:

(ii)   The 'partners' lack confidence in each other. However, to be successful the petitioner must show that his lack of confidence in, for example, the directors of the company arises out of some wrongdoing by them, such as their management of the business leading to the shares losing value (*Loch* v *John Blackwood Ltd* [1924] AC 783). Or:

(iii)   One 'partner' is excluded from managing the business. In *Ebrahimi* v *Westbourne Galleries Ltd* [1973] AC 360, two equal partners decided to incorporate their business with them both acting as directors of the new company. Soon after the incorporation the son of one of them was made a director and both Ebrahimi and the other partner transferred shares to him. The effect of this was that Ebrahimi was the minority shareholder, in effect, and was eventually removed form office by the father and son using the s. 303 procedure. He was thus denied the right to participate in the management of the business and, since the company had only paid its profits out by way of directors' fees, was denied any income as well. Ebrahimi's petition for winding-up was successful on the basis that while a director can be removed from office, if he can prove some 'special underlying obligation' on the part of his fellow members that he will be entitled to participate in the company's management, removal from office will justify liquidating the company. In this case the court was satisfied that when the partners incorporated their partnership they intended that the character of their association would continue.

(c)   Where the conduct of the company's affairs is oppressive to some part of the membership. To come within this heading, the petitioner must show a continuous process of oppression, not merely an isolated act. It must be of a serious nature and probably must involve a breach of the articles or a fraud on the minority.

(d)   Where the company was formed, or is being run, for an illegal purpose.

As has already been said, the illustrations given above are not exhaustive and in *Ebrahimi* v *Westbourne Galleries Ltd* the way was left open for other situations to be the basis of successful petitions. Such petitions are likely to be rare in future as s. 459 will usually provide a better remedy.

9 Publication of Information

1 INTRODUCTION

A great deal of information about a company can be discovered from a search at the Companies' Registry. The Registrar of Companies keeps copies of the information supplied to him by the company and this is available for public inspection. Searches can be made at the Companies' Registry in Cardiff or at the 'branch' office in London. An index of company names is kept at the Registry from which the company number can be obtained. With this information and on payment of a fee of £2.75 it is possible to obtain a copy of the company's file in the form of a 'microfiche' (which is in effect a collection of photographic negatives). The information is presented in date order so that the number of pages may be considerable in the case of long-established companies. However, for most purposes the searcher can obtain the information required by starting with the last annual return (see below) and working forward from that.

2 RETURNS

The information available for inspection at the Companies' Registry includes the following:

(a)   memorandum and articles of association (changes to be registered within 15 days);
(b)   particulars of directors and secretary (particulars of first directors and secretary on Form G10, changes thereafter on Form G288 within 14 days);
(c)   particulars of issue of shares;
(d)   particulars of (most) charges (within 21 days);
(e)   particulars of all special, elective and extraordinary resolutions (no particular form is required — copy resolution to be delivered within 15 days);
(f)   notice of accounting reference date (Form G224 within six months of incorporation);
(g)   notice of increase of capital (Form G123 within 15 days);
(h)   resolutions under s. 80 CA 1985 (no particular form — copy resolution to be delivered within 15 days);
(i)   particulars of address of registered office (first address on Form G10, subsequent changes on Form G287);
(j)   the annual return (see below);
(k)   the accounts (see below).

There is, of course, an interval between the happening of the events and the filing of the return, so that the information is always potentially out of date. The company may have charged its property or a receiver or liquidator may have been appointed without these events being apparent from an inspection. There is no system of priorities to protect a person who makes a search, as there is with searches at the Land Registry and Land Charges Department.

3 OFFICIAL NOTIFICATION

Section 711, CA 1985 requires the Registrar of Companies to advertise the issue by him or receipt by him (as the case may be) of certain documents in the *London Gazette*. This is called official notification and applies to the following:

(a)   issue of any certificate of incorporation;
(b)   receipt of any document making or evidencing an alteration to the memorandum or articles;
(c)   receipt of notification of change of directors;
(d)   receipt of the accounts;
(e)   receipt of notification of change of address of registered office;
(f)   receipt of copy of a winding-up order;
(g)   receipt of copy of dissolution order after winding-up;
(h)   receipt of return by liquidator following final meeting;
(i)   receipt of certain other documents in relation to public companies only.

In the case of the making of the winding-up order, alteration to the memorandum and articles, or change in directors, the company cannot rely on the happening of the event against another person until the notice is put in the *Gazette* unless the other person actually knew about it. The company cannot rely on the event for 15 days after it is put in the *Gazette* if the other person was unavoidably prevented from knowing about the event. The same rule applies to a change in the address of the registered office as regards service of any document on the company (i.e., service is effective at the old registered office until the change is gazetted), and also to the appointment of a liquidator in a voluntary winding-up (in this case, the notice is put in the *Gazette* by the liquidator not by the Registrar).

In addition to the file kept by the Registrar certain information about a company is available for inspection at the company's registered office (see ch. 2).

4 THE ANNUAL RETURN

Section 363 CA 1985 requires every company to make an annual return to the Registrar on Form G363 once in every year (a fee of £25 is payable).

The company is required to file returns signed by a director or the secretary made up to the company's return date, i.e., the anniversary of its incorporation (unless the previous return was made up to a different date in which case the return will be made up to the anniversary of that date).

The return must be filed with the Registrar within 28 days of the return date. The return must set out details of:

(a)   the address of the registered office;
(b)   the company's principal business activities;
(c)   the name and address of the company secretary;

(d)   the name and address of every director plus nationality, date of birth, business occupation and the particulars required for the register of directors;

(e)   the address where the company's register of members and debenture-holders is kept, if different from the registered office;

(f)   a statement that the company has elected to dispense with the laying of accounts in general meeting, if it has;

(g)   details of issued share capital;

(h)   the names and addresses of the members of the company on the date to which the return is made up plus the persons who have ceased to be members since the last return;

(i)   details of the shares held by members.

5   ACCOUNTS

5.1   Accounting records

Every company must keep accounting records sufficient to show and explain its transactions (s. 221 CA 1985). There are detailed requirements as to what the accounting records must show and in particular they must be sufficient to enable the production of final accounts for publication. The records must be preserved for at least three years in the case of a private company.

5.2   Published accounts

Every company must prepare a profit and loss account for each of its accounting reference periods. An accounting reference period is a twelve-month period ending with the company's accounting reference date (i.e., any date chosen by the company for the purpose — the company must choose an accounting reference date within nine months of incorporation and once chosen the date remains the accounting reference date for each year unless the company choses a new date). In addition to the profit and loss account the company must prepare a balance sheet showing its assets and liabilities as at the accounting reference date in each year.

Once prepared, the profit and loss account and balance sheet must be audited by a properly qualified auditor (see ch. 3—1). The accounts, auditors' report and directors' report (see below) must be laid before the company in general meeting and copies sent to all members (even non-voting members who have no right to attend meetings). In practice, this is usually done at the annual general meeting but the law does not require that it should be done at that meeting. The accounts must be laid before the company in general meeting within 10 months after the accounting reference date. However, the members of a private company may elect to dispense with the laying of accounts before the company in general meeting (s. 235 CA 1985). (An elective resolution is required.) In such a case the copies of accounts and reports sent under s. 238 must be sent not less than 28 days before the end of the period allowed for laying and delivering accounts (i.e., 10 months after the end of the accounting reference period).

5.3   Publication of accounts

A limited company (but not an unlimited company) must send a copy of its profit and loss account, balance sheet, auditors' report and directors' report to the Registrar of Companies within 10 months of the end of its accounting reference period. The Registrar officially notifies his receipt of the accounts and they are available for public inspection. A business which does not wish to make its accounts public must, therefore, trade as a partnership or an unlimited company.

5.4   Contents of accounts

Schedule 4, CA 1985 lays down detailed rules as to the form and content of published accounts. The company may choose between various 'formats' laid down in the schedule. These list the various types of income and expenses of the year in a particular order, which must be used for the profit and loss account, and the various types of assets and liabilities which must be used for the balance sheet. The company can depart from the statutory rules as to presentation to a limited extent, providing it states that it has done so and the auditors certify that there is a good reason for doing so. The company is free to give more information than is required by sch. 4 if it wishes but cannot give less than the required amount.

Certain companies are classified as 'small' or 'medium-sized' companies for accounting purposes. These companies may submit 'modified accounts' which do not give as much information as the accounts of other companies (s. 247 CA 1985).

A small company is a company which, for the financial year (i.e., accounting reference period) in respect of which the modified accounts are submitted *and* for the previous financial year, satisfies *any two* of the following conditions:

(a)   turnover was £2,000,000 or less;
(b)   assets were £975,000 or less;
(c)   the weekly average number of employees was 50 or less.

The modified accounts of a small company need not include a profit and loss account and the balance sheet may give a summary of the assets and liabilities.

A medium-sized company is a company which, for the financial year and the previous financial year, satisfies *any two* of the following conditions:

(a)   turnover was £8,000,000 or less;
(b)   assets were £3,900,000 or less;
(c)   the weekly average number of employees was 250 or less.

Such a company must submit a full balance sheet but the profit and loss account may be in an abbreviated form.

The accounting exemptions applying to small and medium-sized companies apply only to the accounts submitted to the Registrar of Companies for publication. The members are entitled to full accounts as in the case of other companies.

5.5 Directors' emoluments

Section 231 CA 1985 requires certain information about directors' emoluments to be given in a note to the accounts. The information required is:

(a)   the aggregate amount of directors' emoluments;
(b)   the aggregate amount of pensions paid to directors and past directors;
(c)   the aggregate amount of compensation for loss of office paid to directors.

'Emoluments' includes sums paid to a director in some other capacity, e.g., as an employee of the company. In addition to the aggregate amounts paid to the directors, further particulars must be given if the aggregate emoluments exceed £40,000. The further particulars are the amount paid to the chairman, the amount paid to the highest paid director if he got more than the chairman, and the number of directors (without specifying which) who got between £0 and £5,000, £5,000 and £10,000 and so on in bands of £5,000.

Details of loans to directors and their associates must be included in notes to the accounts, whether or not the loan is prohibited by s. 330 CA 1985.

5.6 The directors' report

The directors' report attached to the accounts must contain 'a fair review of the development of the business of the company . . . during the financial year . . . and . . . the amount (if any) which they recommend should be paid as dividend, and the amount (if any) which they propose to carry to reserves' (s. 234 CA 1985). The amount carried to reserves is the amount of profit which is to be retained in the business. In addition to the general report on the business and financial position, the following particular items must be included in the report:

(a)   the names of the persons who have been directors during the year;
(b)   significant changes in fixed assets;
(c)   details of directors' interests in significant contracts with the company;
(d)   details of acquisitions by the company of its own shares;
(e)   where the company carries on two or more businesses, a statement as to the turnover and profitability of each business;
(f)   the average number of employees (if 100 or more);
(g)   details of contributions to charities and political parties.

6   PENALTIES FOR FAILURE TO MAKE RETURNS

Failure to comply with the requirements of the Companies Act relating to the preparation, production and delivery of accounts results in criminal liabilty being placed on the company and any officer in default (i.e., any director or secretary who was responsible for the failure). In the case of failure to deliver accounts to the Registrar or to lay them before the company in general meeting every director is guilty of an offence. The amount of the fine varies and in some cases (*inter alia* failure to deliver accounts to the Registrar or lay them before the company in general meeting) includes a default fine, which is so much for each day of delay in filing the return.

In addition to criminal penalties a director who is persistently in default can be disqualified from being a director or otherwise concerned in the management of a company (see ch. 3—3.2). Failure to file the annual return may render the company itself liable to be struck off the register of companies.

Part II   Partnership Law

10 Introduction to Partnership Law

1 DEFINITION OF PARTNERSHIP

Much of the law relating to partnership is to be found in the Partnership Act 1890. The Act was mainly declaratory of the law of partnership as it had developed up to 1890 so that cases decided before 1890 may still be used as an aid to interpretation of the Act. The Act does not provide a complete code of partnership law, and indeed s. 46 specifically provides that: 'The rules of equity and of common law applicable to partnership shall continue in force except so far as they are inconsistent with the express provisions of this Act.' A number (although a surprisingly small number) of cases since 1890 have added to the body of partnership law by interpreting the Act and by dealing with matters not covered by it.

The definition of partnership is to be found in s. 1(1) PA 1890 which states: 'Partnership is the relation which subsists between persons carrying on a business in common with a view to profit.' A registered company is specifically excluded from the definition by s. 1(2). To satisfy the definition two or more persons must be carrying on a business. It follows from this that an agreement to run a business in the future does not constitute an immediate partnership, nor does the taking of preliminary steps to enable a business to be run. 'Business' is defined by s. 45 PA 1890 as including 'every trade, occupation or profession'. This definition has given rise to some problems in marginal cases but in the vast majority of cases it will be clear whether or not a business is being carried on.

Section 2 PA 1890 lays down certain 'rules for determining the existence of a partnership'. These provide that:

(a) Joint or common ownership of property 'does not of itself create a partnership' even where profits from the property are shared (s. 2(1)).

(b) The sharing of *gross* returns does not of itself create a partnership (s. 2(2)). A person is not, therefore, a partner in a business merely because he receives commission on sales which he has introduced.

(c) The receipt of a share of *profits* is prima facie evidence of partnership (s. 2(3)). This topic is dealt with in Chapter 12 paragraph 2.

It should be noted that the presence or absence of a written partnership agreement is not conclusive as to whether or not there is a partnership. The existence of a partnership is always a question of fact.

2 NATURE OF PARTNERSHIP

A partnership is, in law, a very different type of institution from a company. In commercial terms the most significant difference is that partners have unlimited liability for the debts of the partnership. (The liability of partners to creditors is considered in Chapter 13 and the exception provided in the case of limited partnerships is dealt with in paragraph 8 below.) Partnerships are not required to be registered in the way that companies are, nor are they required to give publicity to their accounts.

A partnership is not a separate legal entity. The partnership consists of the individuals who together form the partnership. However, to a limited extent in relation to litigation (see ch. 13) and taxation (see ch. 14) the existence of the partnership is recognised as being independent of the individual members.

3 NUMBER OF PARTNERS

The maximum number of persons who may be members of a particular parnership is usually 20. This is because s. 716 CA 1985 prohibits the formation of business associations with more than 20 members unless they are registered as companies under the 1985 Act. However, under s. 716(2) certain professions, including those of solicitors and accountants, are exempt from this limit. Other professions may also be exempt by regulations made by statutory instrument (regulations giving this exemption have been made in relation to a few professions).

4 CAPACITY

Generally speaking any person is legally capable of forming a partnership with any other person. Companies as well as individuals can, provided their objects clause gives them the power to do so, enter into a partnership with other companies or with individuals.

Minors (persons under 18) are capable of entering into a partnership. However, the contract is voidable at the option of the minor partner during his minority or within a reasonable time of reaching 18. A partner is not liable for the debts of the partnership incurred during his minority although he cannot claim his share of any partnership property in priority to the firm's creditors.

5 DURATION OF PARTNERSHIP

Most partnerships are partnerships 'at will'. This means that no particular period is agreed upon as being the time during which the partnership is to last. A partnership at will can be dissolved by notice unless there is an agreement to the contrary. A partnership for a fixed term or for a term defined by reference to some event (e.g., the completion of some particular job) is also possible. Such a partnership cannot generally be dissolved by notice.

There may sometimes be difficulty in deciding when a partnership begins. Because of the way partnership is defined this is essentially a question of fact. The terms of a partnership agreement as to commencement may be evidence (though not conclusive evidence) of when a partnership begins.

6 PARTNERSHIP NAME AND PUBLICITY OF INFORMATION

A partnership is entitled (subject to what is said below) to choose any name which it wishes. There is nothing in partnership law corresponding with the requirement that a company should have a corporate name which is registered with the Registrar of Companies.

The law relating to partnership names is now contained in the Business Names Act 1985 (which consolidates certain earlier legislation to the same effect). The Act permits the free use of certain names and requires approval for others. In addition it contains rules requiring publicity as to the membership of partnerships in certain circumstances.

6.1 Automatically permitted names

If the business of a partnership is carried on under a name which consists of the surnames of all the partners no restrictions apply (s. 1 BNA 1985). This is also the case where the name consists of the partners' surnames together with 'permitted additions' and nothing else. The permitted additions are the forenames or initials of the partners, the addition of an 's' to a surname to signify that there is more than one partner with that name, and/or a statement that the business is being carried on in succession to the business of a former owner.

Where the name of the partnership does not consist solely of the surnames of the partners or of the surnames of the partners together with permitted additions then the disclosure requirements of s. 4 BNA 1985 will apply and in some cases approval of the name is required under ss. 2 and 3.

6.2 Approval under ss. 2 and 3 BNA 1985

Section 2 of BNA 1985 makes it an offence to carry on business (without the approval of the Secretary of State) under a name which suggests a connection with the government or a local authority or which includes a word specified in regulations made under the Act. Section 3 gives the Secretary of State power to make such regulations. The regulations may also specify a government department or other body which is to be consulted in relation to the giving of approval for a particular word. Regulations have been made under the Act which specify scores of words for which approval is required. (They include, for example, words connoting a connection with the various medical professions, words such as 'Building Society' and 'Sheffield' — this last presumably as in 'Sheffield Plate', as most other towns are not included.)

Partners who are starting a business and who wish to use a business name should consult the regulations. If they find that their name includes a word covered by the regulations they should first write to the government department or other body (if any) which is to be consulted in relation to that word asking it whether it objects. They should then apply to the Secretary of State for approval stating that they have made such a request and enclosing a copy of any reply that they have received from the government department or other body that they have consulted.

6.3 Disclosure requirements of s. 4 BNA 1985

Any partnership which uses a business name (other than one permitted under s. 1 BNA 1985) is required to state the name of each partner (together with an address for service in Great Britain) on every business letter, order for goods or services, invoice, receipt and written demand for payment of a debt (s. 4(1)(a) BNA 1985).

The same information must also be given by a notice in a prominent position at each place of business of the partnership (s. 4(1)(b) BNA 1985). The same information must also be given (in writing) to anyone with whom the partnership has had dealings or negotiations and who asks for the information (s. 4(2) BNA 1985).

The requirement of including names and addresses in letters, etc., does not apply to a partnership with more than 20 members provided that none of the partners' names appear (other than in the text or as signatories) and provided the letter includes a statement of the address of the principal place of business and a statement that the names and addresses of the partners can be inspected there.

7 THE PARTNERSHIP AGREEMENT

A written agreement is not required for the formation of a partnership. This contrasts with the position of a company where the memorandum and articles, which have contractual effect under s. 14 CA 1985, must not only be in writing but must also be registered with the Registrar of Companies.

In practice many partnerships decide that the agreement between the partners, as to how the business is to be regulated, should be in the form of a written agreement. Such an agreement is often called a partnership agreement, a partnership deed or articles of partnership.

The draftsman of a partnership agreement should bear in mind that many provisions of the Partnership Act 1890 apply to regulate the relationship of the partners except to the extent that there is contrary agreement. However well intentioned and however well drafted such legislation is, it is unlikely that it will entirely coincide with the wishes of a particular group of businessmen setting up a partnership.

The draftsman's task in drafting a partnership agreement is more onerous than his task in drafting articles of association for a company. In the case of a company a 'model' set of articles (Table A) is provided, which will suit the needs of most companies with comparatively minor alterations. The provisions of the Partnership Act are both more out of date and less comprehensive than those of Table A. The nature of a partnership agreement must, of course, depend upon the circumstances, but among the most important matters to be considered are the following:

(a) *The parties* The agreement will specify who are the partners and may also make provision for the admission of new partners. In the absence of agreement to the contrary new partners may only be admitted with the unanimous consent of the existing partners (s. 24(7) PA 1890).

(b) *Nature of business* The ultra vires rule does not apply to a partnership. The business should, however, be specified so that a partner who objects to what is being done by way of new types of business can insist on the agreement being followed. Unless the partnership agreement provides to the contrary the clause specifying what business is to be carried on can only be altered with the unanimous agreement of the partners (s. 24(8) PA 1985). This clause may also specify where the partnership is to carry on business.

(c)   *Name*   The business name of the partnership should be specified. The requirements as to approval for, and publicity of, business names have already been mentioned.

(d)   *Capital*   A clause, or group of clauses, should be included dealing with the financial relationships between the partners. This should state what investment each partner is to make in the business, what, if any, return he is to get on his investment in the form of interest on capital, whether he is to be entitled to a salary and how any profits (or losses) are to be ascertained and divided. The related questions of what is to happen to the partnership assets on dissolution may be dealt with here or in the part of the agreement dealing with the right to dissolve.

(e)   *Property*   Provision should be made specifying which property is to be regarded as partnership property (see ch. 12) and which is to remain the property of individual partners.

(f)   *Management*   Small partnerships of two or three people will usually be run by the partners (perhaps in conjunction with a small number of employees) and each partner will have an equal say in management. In a large partnership (especially a professional partnership where there may be dozens of partners), a more complex management structure may be considered desirable and the structure should be specified. In the absence of contrary agreement all partners have an equal say in management. Among the more mundane, but very vital, matters which should be considered under this heading are questions such as who should be entitled to sign cheques for the partnership, who will allocate work to the employees, what authority is each partner to have in relation to buying stock, paying bills and so on. In most cases the clause dealing with management of the partnership should be stated in general terms. It is better, for example, to say that junior partners are to have such functions as are assigned to them by the managing or senior partners than to list in minute detail what they are to be authorised to do.

(g)   *Dissolution, etc.*   The agreement should include terms dealing with the dissolution of the partnership and providing for the death or retirement of partners.

(h)   *Restrictions*   Terms may be included dealing with the partners' obligations to the firm. It is quite common, for example, to provide that the partners are to give their whole time to the business of the firm or to provide that they are only to take up other businesses with the approval of their partners. Consideration should also be given to the inclusion of a clause preventing competition with the firm during the continuance of the partnership (even if the partners are not full-time), although such competition would in any case normally be a breach of the partners' duty of good faith. Similarly, it is often desirable to include a restrictive covenant preventing competition with the firm by a partner after he has left the firm. Such a term must be reasonable otherwise it may be declared void as being a term in unreasonable restraint of trade.

8   LIMITED PARTNERSHIPS

'Limited partnership' is something of a misnomer. A limited partnership may be formed under the Limited Partnership Act 1907. The liability of the partnership to its creditors is unlimited but the liability of some (but not all) of the partners is limited. There must be at least one general partner who bears unlimited liability for the debts of the partnership in the same way as a partner in an ordinary partnership.

In order to obtain limited liability for some of its members the limited partnership must be registered (at the Companies' Registry). The registered particulars must, among other things, specify which partners are general and which are limited partners. They must also specify the amount of capital contributed by each limited partner.

One very important feature of a limited partnership is specified in s. 6(1) Limited Partnership Act 1907. This provides that the limited partners lose their limited liability if they take part in the management of the business. However, they are permitted to examine the books, examine the state and prospects of the business and give advice to the general partners without losing limited liability.

Limited partnerships are little used in practice. Registrations each year are only a tiny fraction of the number of new company registrations.

11 Partnership Management

1 MANAGEMENT OF THE BUSINESS

The business of a partnership will usually be controlled by all the partners, each of whom will take an active part in management. Section 24(5) PA 1890 provides that (in the absence of any express or implied agreement to the contrary): 'Every partner may take part in the management of the partnership business'. Partnership law is sufficiently flexible, however, to permit a wide variety of management structures. For example, in a large partnership there may be different grades of partners, major decisions being taken only by the senior grade. Similarly, some partners may be 'sleeping partners', that is partners who have contributed capital but who do not take an active part in management of the partnership business or in decision-making. These alternative structures may be achieved by express or implied agreement between the partners. If the management structure of a particular partnership is to be different from the equality of partners which is presumed by s. 24(5), then express agreement should be made when the partnership is formed so that there can be no doubt as to what the parties intend.

2 THE LEGAL RELATIONSHIP BETWEEN THE PARTNERS (s. 24)

Section 24 PA 1890 lays down a number of rules which regulate the relationship between partners. These rules '. . . may be varied by the consent of all the partners, and such consent may be express or inferred from a course of conduct'. Several of the subsections of s. 24 deal with the relationship of the partners in respect of the distribution of profits and losses made by the partnership; these subsections are dealt with in Chapter 12.

Among the subsections dealing with the management of the partnership, perhaps the most important is subsection 8 which says that (subject to contrary agreement, express or implied):

> Any differences arising as to ordinary matters connected with the partnership business may be decided by a majority of the partners, but no change may be made in the nature of the partnership business without the consent of all the partners.

In most circumstances, therefore, a simple majority of the partners is required to take a decision. If there is an equality of votes a decision has not been taken and the status quo is preserved.

There are a number of limitations imposed on the ability of the majority of the partners to bind the whole firm. First, partners are under a fiduciary duty to each other and so must exercise their powers for the benefit of the firm as a whole. For example, in *Blisset* v *Daniel* (1853) 10 Hare 493, a power was given (by the partnership agreement) to the majority of the partners permitting them to expel a partner. The majority exercised this power with a view to obtaining the expelled partner's shares in the partnership cheaply. This was held to be an illegal use of the power to expel as it amounted to a breach of the duty of good faith required of a fiduciary.

Secondly, the majority may not impose their views on the minority without first consulting them (*Const* v *Harris* (1824) T & R 496). This is in some respects similar to the rule which requires the holding of a board meeting before the directors of a company reach a decision. However, in the case of a partnership there is no requirement that consultation should take the form of a meeting (unless the partnership agreement so provides).

Thirdly, provisions of the Partnership Act limit majority rule. Thus s. 24(8) itself requires unanimity for a change in the partnership business. This is so that a partner who has decided to invest in one particular type of business will not be forced to invest in something else against his wishes. Section 24(7) provides that: 'No person may be introduced as a partner without the consent of all the existing partners.' Such a rule is vital to the running of a small partnership where each partner will wish to ensure that his fellow partners cannot force him to go into partnership with someone of whom he disapproves. In a large partnership it may be considered appropriate that s. 24(7) should not apply (so that, for example, the senior partners may be given power to decide who to take on as junior partners and who to promote to senior partnership), in which case the partnership agreement must exclude the requirement of unanimity in this respect. Unanimity is also required (by s. 19) for an alteration to the partnership agreement. The agreement of the partners to an alteration can be inferred from a course of dealings. Section 25 prevents expulsion of a partner by a majority of the partners unless all the partners have *expressly* agreed to this.

Other provisions of s. 24 which affect the management of the partnership business are subsections (2), (6) and (9). Section 24(2) gives a partner a right to be indemnified by the firm in respect of payments made and personal liabilities incurred 'in the ordinary and proper conduct of the business of the firm or in or about anything necessarily done for the preservation of the business or property of the firm'. Section 24(6) says that a partner is not entitled to remuneration for acting in the business. We will return to the question of division of profits between partners in the next chapter; however, it should be noted that s. 24(6) means that where there are some working and some sleeping partners it is necessary to make specific provision to compensate the former for the work they do. Finally, s. 24(9) gives all the partners a right to inspect and copy the partnership accounts.

3 THE DUTY OF GOOD FAITH

The contract of partnership is a contract *uberrimae fidei* (of the utmost good faith), so that a partner is required to disclose all relevant information in his possession to his partners. If he fails to do so his partners may set aside transactions which they have entered into with him as a result of the non-disclosure.

Similarly, a partner owes a fiduciary duty to his fellow partners; that is he owes the duties of good faith to his partners in his dealings with them which a trustee owes to a beneficiary. This duty continues even after the dissolution of the partnership. For example, in *Thompson's Trustee in Bankruptcy* v *Heaton* [1974] 1 WLR 605, a farming partnership was dissolved at a time when it owned a lease. One of the former partners (Heaton) was permitted by the other (Thompson) to continue in occupation of the leasehold property. Heaton then (through a company which he owned) purchased the freehold reversion and sold it for a profit. It was held that the profit belonged to the partners, as it arose out of the ownership of the lease by the partnership. Thompson's estate was, therefore, entitled to an equal share in the profit.

The requirement of good faith in dealings between partners is of general application but three particular aspects of the duty are dealt with in ss. 28-30 PA 1890. Section 28 provides that: 'Partners are bound to render true accounts and full information of all things affecting the partnership to any partner or his legal representative.' This is really just a formulation in statutory language of the duty of disclosure imposed by equity. A good illustration of the working of the rule is given by *Law* v *Law* [1905] 1 Ch 140. In that case one partner offered to buy the share of another at a price which seemed fair to the vendor who was not actively engaged in running the business. The purchaser, however, knew of facts which made the vendor's share more valuable than the vendor realised. When the vendor discovered this it was held that he was entitled to rescind the contract of sale on the ground of non-disclosure.

Section 29 is concerned with secret profits; it states that:

(1) Every partner must account to the firm for any benefit derived by him without the consent of the other partners from any transaction concerning the partnership, or from any use by him of the partnership property, name or business connection.

(2) This section applies also to transactions undertaken after a partnership has been dissolved by the death of a partner, and before the affairs thereof have been completely wound up, either by any surviving partner or by the representative of the deceased partner.

This section imposes the same restrictions and duties on partners as apply to company directors. Any profit made in breach of the section is held on trust for the benefit of the partnership as a whole. The rule applies to transactions entered into by a partner where the opportunity came to him as a result of the partnership, to commissions received on contracts introduced to the partnership, to sales of property to the partnership by a partner and to profits derived from sales of partnership property. A partner may retain any such profit if his partners consent following full disclosure of the circumstances.

Section 30 PA 1890 provides that: 'If a partner, without the consent of the other partners, carries on any business of the same nature as and competing with that of the firm, he must account for and pay over to the firm all profits made by him in that business.' The provisions of s. 30 are quite narrow. In order to succeed under this section the partners must show that the businesses are of the same nature and that they are in fact competing for the same customers. Thus in *Aas* v *Benham* [1891] 2 Ch 244, a partner in a firm of shipbrokers was held not to be accountable for profits he had made from shipbuilding. However, in *Glassington* v *Thwaites* (1823) 1 Sim & St 124, a partner in a morning newspaper who set up an evening newspaper was held to be accountable. It should be noted that there is overlap between s. 30 and s. 29(1) — a partner may be held accountable because he is competing with his partners or because he is using 'the partnership property name or business connection'; often a partner who sets up a new business will be doing both these things.

A partner who sets up a non-competing business and who does not use the partnership property, name or business connection is not liable to his partners in any way under the Act. Many partnership *agreements*, therefore, provide that the partners are to devote their whole time to the partnership and specify that the partners are not to start any other businesses. With such an agreement the partners may be able to obtain an injunction, damages or dissolution of the partnership against the partner who sets up a new business, even though it does not compete with the firm's business. They will not, however, have any right to make him contribute his profits in the other business to the partnership.

4 DISPUTES WITHIN A PARTNERSHIP

4.1 Introduction

As we have already seen a decision of the majority of the partners on an 'ordinary matter' is binding on the minority. The wishes of the majority prevail over those of the minority who object. However, just as company law provides remedies for a minority shareholder in limited circumstances, so partnership law provides some machinery for protecting the partner who is aggrieved by what the other partners have done. The powers of the court in relation to a partnership are fewer than in the case of a company (there is, for example, no equivalent of ss. 459-461 CA 1985 which give the court power to intervene in the affairs of a company on the ground of unfair prejudice). The remedies available to a partner include dissolution of the partnership, appointment of a receiver and remedies available under the terms of the partnership agreement itself.

4.2 Dissolution by the court

Dissolution of a partnership may occur automatically (e.g., on the death of a partner) by notice (e.g., any partner can give notice dissolving a partnership at will) or by court order (e.g., in the case of permanent incapacity of a partner). The various circumstances in which dissolution takes place will be considered in Chapter 18. In this chapter we intend to consider only those types of dissolution which provide a remedy to a partner against his co-partners under s. 35(c), (d) or (f).

Section 35(c) provides that a partner may apply to the court for dissolution 'when a partner, other than the partner suing, has been guilty of such conduct as, in the opinion of the court, regard being had to the nature of the business, is calculated to prejudicially affect the carrying on of the business'. This paragraph may be relied upon even though the prejudicial conduct has nothing directly to do with the partnership. A conviction for dishonesty, for example, would be likely to be regarded as prejudicial conduct in the case of many professional partnerships even though the dishonesty did not relate to the practice as such. The test is an objective one so that it need not be shown that the guilty partner *intended* to affect the business (this is so despite the use of the word 'calculated' in s. 35(c)).

Section 35(d) provides that a partner may apply to the court for dissolution 'when a partner, other than the partner suing, wilfully or persistently commits a breach of the partnership agreement, or otherwise so conducts himself in matters relating to the partnership business that it is not reasonably practicable for the other partner or partners to carry on business in partnership with him.' This paragraph contemplates that the trust between partners has broken down. If this breakdown results from persistent breaches of the partnership agreement or conduct in relation to the business (although not conduct in relation to other matters), then the court can order dissolution. Many of the cases under this paragraph have revolved around financial irregularities (such as failure to account for money received on behalf of the partnership or payment of private debts from partnership money). Persistent incompetence might also be brought under this paragraph (this is at least a possible interpretation of *Atwood* v *Maude* (1868) 3 Ch App 369). It is also sometimes suggested that animosity between the partners can lead to dissolution under paragraph (d). However, unless it can be shown that this animosity results from persistent breach or the conduct of the defendant partner, the action for dissolution cannot succeed under paragraph (d), although it might under paragraph (f).

Section 35(f) provides that a partner may apply to the court for dissolution 'whenever in any case circumstances have arisen which in the opinion of the court render it just and equitable that the partnership be dissolved'. This provision is the equivalent of s. 122(1)(g) IA 1986, which is in essentially similar terms but applies only to companies. The cases decided under s. 122(1)(g) (and its predecessors) are relevant also to s. 35(f), especially where the company which was the subject of the petition was intended to be run as if it were a partnership. Indeed, most of the authorities are company law cases as there seem to be very few cases decided under s. 35(f). The paragraph is not construed *ejusdem generis* with paragraphs (a)-(e) and so is given a wide (and perhaps sometimes an unpredictable) interpretation. Deadlock or other irreconcilable differences between partners are the most likely grounds on which a successful petition could be based. Exclusion of a partner from management (contrary to s. 24(5)) would also be grounds for petition, although this case would also probably be covered by s. 35(d).

4.3 Appointment of a receiver

The court has power to appoint a receiver to run the business of a partnership for the protection of the partners. The receiver's duty is to carry on the business of the partnership for the benefit of the partners generally, not to realise a security, so that his position is quite different from that of a company receiver appointed by a debenture-holder. There is comparatively little authority as to when a receiver will be appointed but it does seem to be an exceptional step and the court is particularly reluctant to make an appointment in the case of a professional partnership (*Floydd* v *Cheney* [1970] 2 WLR 314).

4.4 Arbitration

Disputes may be solved by arbitration if the partners agree to this. It is common to make provision for arbitration in the partnership agreement. As in other types of contract an arbitration clause cannot effectively oust the jurisdiction of the court altogether. If an action is commenced despite the presence of an arbitration clause the court has a discretion to stay the proceedings to enable the arbitration to take place. The plaintiff in the action must show why he has not submitted to arbitration and must show sufficient reason why the court should not stay the action. The attitude of the courts as to how this discretion should be exercised is somewhat variable but the cases seem to show that:

(a)   Arbitration will not be permitted where there is an allegation of fraud, impropriety or other allegations which would (if proved) discredit the professional standing of the partner (*Turner* v *Fenton* [1982] 1 WLR 52).

(b)   An arbitration clause can even extend to dissolution of partnership (*Phoenix* v *Pope* [1974] 1 WLR 719 — earlier cases had doubted this, at least in the cases where the court has a discretion whether or not to wind up the partnership on the just and equitable ground).

The court action can continue without there being any question of a stay when, as a matter of construction, the court decides that the dispute which has arisen is not covered by the arbitration clause in the partnership agreement. The clause should expressly say that disputes arising during dissolution may be referred to arbitration and that the clause is binding on assignees of partners. If the clause is so widely drawn as to be an attempt to oust the jurisdiction of the court entirely it will be held to be void.

5   THE EXPULSION OF A PARTNER

We have already seen that in certain circumstances a partnership can be dissolved by the court so as to give the plaintiff partner a remedy against his co-partners. In Chapter 18 we will see that a partnership is sometimes dissolved by notice given by a partner or by the death or bankruptcy of a partner. In many circumstances some partners may wish to get rid of one or more of their co-partners without fully dissolving the partnership.

Section 25 PA 1890 says: 'No majority of the partners can expel any partner unless a power to do so has been conferred by express agreement between the partners.' The question as to whether expulsion should be provided for and if so by what majority and on what terms must be considered when a partnership agreement is being drafted.

If an expulsion clause is included in a partnership agreement then the power must be exercised strictly in accordance with the agreement and in a bona fide manner (see, for example, *Blisset* v *Daniel* supra, paragraph 1).

12 Partnership Capital and Borrowing

1 INTRODUCTION

The sources of finance for a partnership are basically the same as those available to a company. A partnership will need assets and cash in order to run its business. Money (or in some cases assets) may be contributed in the form of a permanent investment by the partners or it may be borrowed either from the partners or from outside sources. Once the business of the partnership has started further finance may also be provided by retention of profits.

The permanent investment of a partner is described as his 'capital'. The capital of a partner may be contributed by him in the form of cash or property (including, for example, business premises or the goodwill of an existing business). Just as the term capital is somewhat ambiguous in the case of a company so it is in the case of a partnership. The term is often used to mean the actual cash or other assets contributed to the partnership by a partner but is also used to mean the indebtedness of the partnership as a whole to the partner resulting from the contribution which he has made by his investment. A partner's capital in this latter sense should be contrasted with other debts which the firm owes to the partner, as repayment of the capital cannot normally be claimed from the firm until dissolution. Other indebtedness to a partner may be repaid before dissolution. For example, indebtedness resulting from the making of profits can be cancelled by the partner withdrawing his entitlement in cash and a loan should be repaid when it falls due.

2 SHARING PROFITS

As we saw in Chapter 10 the essential nature of a partnership is that two or more people are sharing profits of a business. A person who merely lends to a partnership is not a partner. The distinction between a partner and a lender is extremely important as a partner bears unlimited liability for the debts of the partnership whereas the lender only stands to lose the money invested if the business fails (if he has taken security for his loan, his risk of losing even that much may be small). However, if a business is successful a partner stands to earn a great deal of profit whereas a lender will receive only interest on his loan.

Many investors would like to have the best of both words, i.e., limited liability and a share of profits. This can be achieved by investing in a company or by means of a limited partnership. However, in other cases s. 2(3) PA 1890 effectively restricts this type of investment. Section 2(3) provides that: 'The receipt by a person of a share of profits . . . is prima facie evidence that he is a partner . . . but does not of itself make him a partner . . .'. The subsection then sets out some particular rules which provide that:

(a) A person does not become a partner merely because a debt or other liquidated sum is paid to him by instalments out of profits.

(b)   A servant or agent does not become a partner merely because his remuneration varies with profits.

(c)   A widow or child of a partner is not a partner merely because a proportion of profits is paid to that person as an annuity.

(d)   A lender whose interest varies with profits is not automatically a partner if the contract is in writing and signed by all the parties.

(e)   A vendor who receives payment for his business in the form of an annuity varying with profits is not automatically a partner.

Sharing of profis is only prima facie evidence of partnership and particular types of contract are covered by the five rules mentioned above. However, anyone who receives a share of profits *may* be held to be a partner and therefore personally liable for debts. Anyone entering into such an arrangement who does not wish to take on the risk of unlimited liability should take steps to ensure that he or she does not become a partner, e.g., by avoiding any suggestion that he has a right to take part in management and by having a written agreement setting out the terms of his involvement with the firm.

3   DIVISION OF PROFITS BETWEEN PARTNERS

Section 24 PA 1890 lays down a number of rules as to division of profits. These rules may be varied by an express or implied agreement of the partners. Section 24 deals with the division of both income and capital profits.

3.1   Share of profits and losses (s. 24(1))

The first rule is contained in s. 24(1) which states:

> All the partners are entitled to share equally in the capital and profits of the business, and must contribute equally towards the losses whether of capital or otherwise sustained by the firm.

This rule may be broken down into three parts, the first of which says that 'all the partners are entitled to share equally in the capital'. On the face of it this means that when a partner leaves the firm or when the firm is dissolved he is entitled to take out a part of the capital corresponding with the total amount of capital divided by the number of partners. However, in practice this is unlikely to be so. All the rules in s. 24 are subject to contrary agreement express or implied. Where the partners have contributed unequally to the capital, there is an implied agreement that they are entitled to withdraw capital unequally. For example, if A contributes £10,000, B £20,000 and C £30,000 those are the sums which each can withdraw on leaving in the absence of any express agreement to the contrary.

The second part of the rule in s. 24(1) says that 'all the partners are entitled to share equally in the profits of the business'. The provisions of capital in unequal shares does not give rise to the implication that *this* rule has been displaced. Thus in the example given above if the profits of the firm were £9,000, A, B, and C would each be entitled to £3,000. If a partner is to receive more than an equal share of profits because of his capital contribution or the work he does, this must be specifically agreed to and should be expressly stated in the partnership agreement.

The rule as to share of profits applies to capital as well as income profits. Thus when the firm in our example is dissolved any capital profit will be shared equally even though the capital was not contributed equally. Thus after A has received £10,000, B £20,000 and C £30,000, any surplus will be divided equally. The partners are, of course, free to agree to the contrary. It may well be decided that capital profits should be divided in the same ratio as capital was provided. The ratio in which capital profits are divided (sometimes called the 'assets surplus ratio') is often different from the income profit sharing ratio.

The third part of the rule in s. 24(1) says that losses of capital and income are prima facie to be shared equally. However, if the partners share profits unequally (because of an express or implied agreement to do so), then s. 44 PA 1890 says that losses will also be shared unequally unless there is an agreement to the contrary. For the avoidance of doubt the partnership agreement should state how both profits and losses are to be shared even if in fact the agreement follows some or all of the statutory presumptions.

3.2   Interest on loans

Section 24(3) provides that: 'A partner making . . . any actual payment or advance beyond the amount of capital . . . is entitled to interest at the rate of five per cent.' In the absence of contrary agreement a loan by a partner to the partnership carries only 5% interest. It should be noted that even this parsimonious rate of interest is only paid on 'actual payments or advances'. Interest is not payable under s. 24(3) on a share of profits which is simply left in the business. The partners are, of course, free to agree that interest will be paid on undrawn profits if they wish.

3.3   Interest on capital

Section 24(4) provides that: 'A partner is not entitled . . . to interest on capital.' Where capital is contributed unequally it may be considered appropriate to make provision for interest on capital to compensate the partner who has contributed more. The agreement should specify the rate of interest or the method by which the rate is to be determined. Interest on capital is not a deductible expense of the business. It is merely a preferential appropriation of profits. This means that once the net profit of the partnership has been ascertained the partners' first entitlement will be to interest and then the remaining net profit will be allocated in accordance with the agreed profit-sharing ratio.

3.4   Remuneration of partners

Section 24(6) provides that: 'No partner shall be entitled to remuneration for acting in the partnership business.' This really follows from the idea that partners are to be equally concerned with the business, which is exemplified in a number of subsections of s. 24. In many partnerships the division of work between the partners is unequal, and therefore it will be agreed that some of the partners be paid a salary to compensate them for the work which they have done. As with interest on capital, a salary payable to a partner is not a deductible expense but is merely a preferential appropriation of profit.

Example   In a partnership with three members it might be agreed that: (i) the profit-sharing ratio will be D 20%, E 40%, F 40%; (ii) that interest on capital will be paid at the rate of 10% p.a. (D's capital is £10,000, E's £20,000 and F's £30,000); and (iii) that D is to have a salary of £20,000 p.a. If profits of £100,000 are made they will be divided as follows:

		£	£
Profit			100,000
Interest:	D	1,000	
	E	2,000	
	F	3,000	
			6,000
Salary:	D		20,000
Share of profits:	D(20%)	14,800	
	E(40%)	29,600	
	F(40%)	29,600	
			74,000
			100,000

In some partnerships (particularly professional partnerships) there may be relatively junior partners who are entitled to a salary to the exclusion of any other share of profits. At first sight it is hard to see how such 'salaried partners' can be regarded as partners at all, as partnership requires that the partners are 'carrying on business in common with a view of profit' (s. 1(1) PA 1890). Nevertheless, in *Stekel* v *Ellice* [1973] 1 WLR 191, it was held that a salaried partner could be, in law, a full partner with all the rights and duties which that entails.

3.5   Drawings

The amount to which a partner is entitled from the profits in a firm (as salary and interest, if agreed to, and share of profits) will not be known until the profit and loss account has been drawn up after the end of the partnership's financial year. The partnership agreement will, therefore, usually provide that a partner is to have the right to take a specified amount of money on account of his expected profits during the course of the year. Sums taken on account in this way are called 'drawings'. If at the end of the year the partner has taken less than he was entitled to he can draw the balance; if he has taken more than it turns out he was entitled to then the partnership agreement will probably require him to pay back the excess and/or pay interest on it. The partnership agreement may provide that each partner is to leave undrawn in the business a proportion of his entitlement to profit. This is because businesses normally need to retain funds to meet increased costs of trading and to fund any future expansion.

4 PAYMENT OF INTEREST

A payment of interest by a partnership will usually be a business expense. This is because the interest payment will satisfy the test for deduction of expenses, that is, that the payment is incurred 'wholly and exclusively for the purposes of the trade'. A payment of interest on capital to a partner is not a business expense, it is an allocation of profits to the partner who will, therefore, pay tax on it under Schedule D Case I or II, not under Case III.

A payment of interest by an individual partner, rather than by the partnership as a whole, in some cases qualifies as a charge on income (and is, therefore, deductible in calculating the partner's own tax liability). This applies to interest paid on a loan used to buy a share in the partnership, interest paid on a loan where the money borrowed is used wholly and exclusively for the purposes of the partnership, and interest paid on a loan used to buy machinery and plant which qualifies for a capital allowance and which is used by the partnership.

Where a partnership receives interest this is treated as Schedule D Case III income of the partners and is taxed accordingly.

5 PARTNERSHIP PROPERTY

Partnership property is partly defined by s. 20(1) PA 1890 as: 'All property and rights and interests in property originally brought into the partnership stock or acquired, whether by purchase or otherwise, on account of the firm, or for the purposes and in the course of the partnership business . . .'. Section 21 deals with a slightly different situation and states: 'Unless the contrary intention appears, property bought with money belonging to the firm is deemed to have been bought on account of the firm'.

Whether property is partnership property or remains the separate property of a partner depends on the intention of the partners, express or implied. Property is not partnership property merely because it is used by the firm. Use of property by the firm is consistent with its being a partner's property which is rented by the firm or which is used by the firm under licence (with or without payment). The court does not readily assume that property introduced by a partner thereby becomes partnership property. This is illustrated by the leading case of *Miles* v *Clarke* [1953] 1 All ER 779. Clarke carried on a photographic business in premises of which he owned the lease. He and Miles went into partnership and for a time the business was successful. However, eventually a petition for dissolution was presented as the partners were unable to agree. The question arose as to which assets were partnership property and which belonged to the partners individually. Harman J held that in the absence of express agreement he would hold property to be partnership property to the extent necessary to give business efficacy to the agreement. Therefore, the lease of the business premises belonged on dissolution to Clarke alone, each partner was entitled to his own business connection which he had brought into the firm and only the stock in trade (unused films, chemicals, etc.) could be regarded as partnership property.

A different result was reached in *Waterer* v *Waterer* (1873) LR 15 Eq 402. In that case land was used as a nursery by three brothers who were in partnership. Two of the brothers bought out the third, paying one price for both the land and the business together. When one of the remaining brothers died the question arose as to whether the land was partnership property. There was no express agreement but it was held that the land was partnership property. First, the land had been purchased from the retiring brother without distinguishing it from other assets of the business and, secondly, a nursery (unlike a photographic business) depends very directly on the use of the land without which the business could not continue.

There are a number of reasons why it may be important to decide what property is and what is not partnership property. When the firm is dissolved each partner is entitled to retain any property which is his own personal property; property which is partnership property is used first to pay creditors of the firm and then any surplus is distributed among the partners in accordance with the terms of the partnership agreement (equally in the absence of contrary agreement). This is so, once it is decided that an asset is partnership property, even though the asset was introduced by one particular partner and the asset has risen in value thus creating a capital profit for the partnership. In the case of land held as partnership property the partners are beneficial tenants in common (in the absence of contrary agreement), so that the right of survivorship does not apply.

13   Liability of Partners to Outsiders

1   NATURE OF LIABILITY

Partners are liable for the debts and obligations of the partnership without limit. Their liablity is joint in the case of contractual obligations and joint and several in the case of tortious obligations. The significance of this distinction was much reduced by the Civil Liability (Contribution) Act 1978 which allows proceedings to be brought successively against persons jointly liable despite an earlier judgment against others.

Where a partnership is unable to pay its debts out of partnership property, the plaintiff is entitled to obtain payment from the private estates of the partners. Special rules apply in such cases, so as to attempt to do justice both to the creditors of the firm and to the creditors of the individual partners. It is not our intention to deal with these rules in detail. They may be summarised by saying that, in the first instance, the partnership property is used to pay partnership creditors in priority to private creditors and the private property of each partner is used to pay his private creditors in priority to partnership creditors. If the private creditors of a particular partner are paid in full from private property then partnership creditors may resort to the balance of that partner's private property. If the partnership creditors are paid in full from partnership property then the private creditors of a partner may resort to the balance of his share of the partnership assets.

2   PARTNERSHIP AND AGENCY

2.1   Introduction

The relationship between partnership law and agency is very close. Indeed, most of the rules regulating the relationship between a partnership and the outside world can be explained purely in terms of particular applications of agency principles.

The partnership as a whole is bound by a contract entered into by, notice received by, or a tort committed by, a partner acting within the scope of his authority. The authority of a partner may arise in a number of ways. First, the authority of the partners (or of a particular partner) may be specifically agreed upon by the partners — authority of this type is called 'express actual' authority. Secondly, authority may be implied either from a course of dealings between the partners (which amounts to an actual agreement) or because the authority is a natural consequence of an authority actually given to the partner — this is sometimes called 'implied actual' authority. Thirdly, authority may arise from the fact that a person dealing with a partner is, in certain circumstances, entitled to assume that the partner has authority to bind the firm — this type of authority is generally called 'apparent' or 'ostensible' authority, although terminology in agency law is far from consistent.

The scope of express and implied authority depends on the agreement between the parties. The partnership agreement may specify what powers the partners individually are to have and may specify that some are to have greater powers than others. The extent of actual authority, whether express or implied, is not, in practical terms, of great significance to a person dealing with a partner. This is because, whether or not there is actual authority, he will be able to rely on apparent authority in most circumstances in relation to most normal types of transaction. The outsider need only rely on actual authority where the partner has done something which the law does not consider to be within the apparent authority of a partner.

A partnership is bound by decisions and actions of its employees acting within the scope of their authority. An outsider seeking to rely on a decision or action of an employee would have to show that the employee had actual authority, had been held out (by the partners) as having actual authority or had been held out (by the partners) to be a partner. An individual partner cannot delegate authority to the employees (this is an application of the well known maxim of agency law *delegatus non potest delegare*).

The Partnership Act has little to say about a partner's actual authority. However, s. 6 recognises that the firm is bound by 'the acts or instruments' entered into with the authority of the firm.

2.2   Apparent authority

The scope of apparent (or ostensible) authority is not always easy to establish or describe. Such authority is sometimes said to result from a type of estoppel whereby the principal (in this case the partnership as a whole) represents, by words or conduct, that the agent (that is the partner who is negotiating with the outsider) has authority to bind the firm. Once such a representation is made and acted upon by the outsider the partnership cannot deny the authority of the individual partner to bind the firm. Alternatively, apparent authority may be said to arise simply from the fact that the partner who is negotiating *appears* to have authority to bind the firm and it is, therefore, reasonable for the outsider to assume such authority. In fact nothing really turns on this distinction, application of either test is likely to produce the same result in most circumstances.

It is clear that the liability of the firm may result from the actual holding out of an agent (not necessarily a partner) as having a particular authority. However, in most cases the outsider seeks to rely on an apparent authority resulting from the fact that a person is known to be a partner in a firm. The outsider is then entitled to assume that the partner has the usual authority of a partner to bind his firm. This principle is laid down in s. 5 PA 1890 which says:

Every partner is an agent for the firm and his other partners for the purposes of the business of the partnership; and the acts of every partner who does any act for carrying on in the usual way the business of the kind carried on by the firm of which he is a member bind the firm and his partners, unless the partner so acting has in fact no authority to act for the firm in the particular matter, and the person with whom he is dealing either knows that he has no authority, or does not know or believe him to be a partner.

A number of points arising from this section require further consideration. It does not say that anything which a partner does binds the firm. The easiest way to understand the scope of the section (and thus of that part of the partner's authority which derives from the usual authority given to partners generally), is to examine each of the qualifications on a partner's authority which the section recognises.

The first qualification is that the partner can only bind the firm 'for the purposes of the business of the partnership'. The partnership agreement may be of some assistance in deciding what is the scope of the partnership business. However, it is not conclusive. Although no change may be made in the nature of the partnership business without unanimous approval (s. 24(8) PA 1890), it should be remembered that agreement to change may be inferred from a course of dealings or acquiescence by all the partners. Furthermore, in *Mercantile Credit Co Ltd* v *Garrod* [1962] 3 All ER 1103, Mocatta J held that the test as to whether a type of business is within the scope of the partnership depends on what is apparent to the outside world in general. Consequently a sleeping partner in a garage business whose agreement specifically excluded dealing in cars was held liable on a contract for the sale of a car as this was within the scope of what outsiders would expect the business to include.

The second qualification in s. 5 is that the partnership is only bound if a partner does an act 'for carrying on in the usual way the business of the firm'. This restriction excludes the liability of the firm where the transaction is for the purposes of the business but is itself of an unusual type. For example, in *Niemann* v *Niemann* (1890) 43 ChD 198, a debt was owed to a partnership; one of the partners intended to accept payment of the debt in the form of shares in a company. This was held not to be binding on the other partner in the absence of a specific agreement. Similarly, *Powell* v *Brodhurst* [1901] 2 Ch 160 decided that a partner does not have ostensible authority to accept payment of a debt due to another partner personally rather than to the firm.

The third qualification to s. 5 is that the firm is not bound if the partner has no actual authority and the outsider either knows this or does not know or believe the person with whom he is dealing to be a partner. Clearly in such cases the firm is not bound whether one takes the view that apparent authority depends on estoppel or on appearance of authority. The outsider cannot say that he has relied on any misrepresentation nor can he claim that there appeared to be authority when he knows this to be untrue or does not think he is dealing with an agent at all.

Where, in accordance with normal agency principles, a contract made without authority is ratified by the partnership, it becomes binding on them as well as on the outsider. A partner who makes a contract with an outsider without authority will be personally liable to the outsider for breach of warranty of authority where the partnership as a whole is not made liable on the contract.

Section 8 PA 1890 provides that an outsider is not prejudiced by any restriction placed on the powers of a partner unless he has notice of it.

2.3 Examples of apparent authority

The question of what apparent authority a partner has in a particular case is determined by the application of s. 5 to that particular case. This is at least in part a question of fact. However, over the years the courts have decided upon examples of powers which will be assumed to be covered by apparent authority in the case of all partners in the absence of some special circumstance. The court has also recognised certain powers which it will be assumed all partners in a trading partnership have in the absence of some special circumstance. The powers of partners in a trading partnership are more extensive than the powers of partners in general. This is because the court recognises the need of the partners and the persons dealing with them to rely on normal trading practices.

Examples of powers assumed to be available to partners generally include:

(a) power to buy and sell goods (not just stock) used in the business;
(b) power to hire employees;
(c) power to receive payment of debts due to the partnership;
(d) power to pay debts owed by the partnership including a power to draw cheques for this purpose;
(e) power to engage a solicitor to represent the firm.

A partner in a trading partnership will be assumed to have all the above powers and also:

(a) power to grant security for borrowings (this does not, however, include a power to create a legal mortgage);
(b) a wider power than is given to a non-trading partner to deal with cheques and bills of exchange.

3 PERSONS HELD OUT AS PARTNERS

So far we have only considered the liability of actual partners to outsiders. A person who holds himself out as a partner or who 'suffers himself to be represented as a partner' is liable to anyone who 'on the faith of such representation' gives credit to the firm as if he were a partner (s. 14 PA 1890). The commonest example of the application of this rule is where a person allows his name to be used by the partnership (e.g., on notepaper) after he has ceased to be a partner (as to which, see ch. 18—3).

A person cannot be held liable under s. 14 unless he has in some way contributed to the mistake made by the person giving credit to the firm, for example by allowing his name to be given as a partner. It is not, however, necessary that he himself should have done anything to inform the person giving credit. Furthermore, the person giving credit can sue the apparent partner even if he acquires knowledge of the alleged partnership through a third party, at least where it is obvious that the third party may pass on the information which he has acquired and which suggests that the apparent partner is a partner.

Section 14 only applies where credit is given to the firm. This is construed widely so that, for example, the apparent partner is liable where goods are delivered as well as where cash is lent to the firm.

4 LIABILITY OF NEW PARTNERS

Section 17(1) PA 1890 provides that 'a person who is admitted as a partner into an existing firm does not thereby become liable to the creditors of the firm for anything done before he became a partner'. This provision ensures that an incoming partner is not liable to the existing creditors of the firm merely because he has become a partner.

As between himself and the existing partners the incoming partner may agree to pay a share of debts owed to existing creditors. This does not make him liable to the existing creditors as they are not privy to the contract. The new partner may become liable to existing creditors by a novation (that is, a tripartite contract between the old partners, the new partner and an outsider whereby the existing contract between the old partners and the outsider is discharged and replaced by a contract between the new firm, including the new partner, and the outsider).

The case of *Dyke* v *Brewer* (1894) 2 Car & K 82 deals with another circumstance where the new partner becomes liable on an existing contract. In that case a partnership had a contract for a regular supply of goods to the firm. A new partner joined the firm and it was held that he was liable to the supplier for supplies delivered after he joined the firm even though the contract was entered into before he joined. This is, however, only so where the contract is divisible. A partner is not liable on an entire contract made before he joins even though it is performed after he joins (unless there is a novation).

5 PARTNERS' LIABILITY IN TORT

A partner who himself commits a tort is liable according to general principles of the law of tort. The liability of the firm as a whole is governed by s. 10 PA 1890:

> Where, by any wrongful act or omission of any partner acting in the ordinary course of the business of the firm, or with the authority of his co-partners, loss or injury is caused to any person . . . the firm is liable . . . to the same extent as the partner so acting or omitting to act.

It should be noted that the firm (as opposed to the actual tortfeasor) is only liable if either the commission of the tort was authorised by the partners or was committed 'in the ordinary course of business'. A partnership is also liable to the same extent as other employers (under common-law principles of vicarious liability) for torts committed by its employees.

6 SUING OR BEING SUED

A partnership is not a separate legal entity. Nevertheless, the partners may sue or be sued in the firm's name under Ord. 81 of the Rules of the Supreme Court. All the partners at the date when the cause of action accrued are then parties to the action. If one partner objects to another partner bringing an action in the firm's name he may seek an order indemnifying him against costs. Where an action is brought against a partnership in the firm's name the writ may be served on any partner, on any person having control or management of the business at the principal place of business or by post to the principal place of business.

A person who has a judgment against a partner for the partner's personal liability may enforce that judgment against the partner's share of partnership property by means of a charging order (s. 23(2) PA 1890). He may not enforce such a judgment against the partnership property by means of execution or garnishee proceedings (s. 23(1)). Where a charging order is made the other partners may discharge it by paying off the judgment debt; if a sale of the property is ordered, they may purchase it. A charging order gives the other partners a right to dissolve the partnership if they wish.

Part III   Taxation

14   Taxation of Sole Traders and Partnerships

1   INCOME PROFITS

1.1   The tax schedules

Sole traders pay income tax on income. For a receipt to be income it must usually be recurrent or capable of recurrence (but 'one-off' receipts can be income in some circumstances), and must be included in the definition of income under one of the five schedules of the Income and Corporation Taxes Act 1988 (commonly called 'the Taxes Act'). It is beyond the scope of this book to deal with the various definitions of income in the schedules but the following table will give an idea of what is covered:

Schedule A	Rents
Schedule C	Government securities
Schedule D Case I	Profits of a trade
Schedule D Case II	Profits of a profession or vocation
Schedule D Case III	'Pure income' (interest, annuities and annual payments)
Schedule D Cases IV & V	Foreign trading profits
Schedule D Case VI	Miscellaneous income (casual profits and certain items specifically allocated to this case)
Schedule E	Income from an office or employment
Schedule F	Dividends

Each schedule lays down rules for the deductibility of expenses in calculating income and for the allocation of receipts to a particular year of assessment (each year of assessment starts on 6 April and ends on the following 5 April and is commonly called a tax year).

For a sole trader Schedule D Case I (trade) or II (profession or vocation) is usually the most important case. The rules for these two cases are almost identical, and are in many respects quite different from the other cases of Schedule D and from the other schedules, both in respect of the definition of income and the time when it is taxed. To determine the amount of profits it is necessary to calculate the amount of income generated from trading activities and deduct from that the amount of deductible expenditure.

Once the income has been calculated the taxpayer is liable to income tax on the whole amount less certain payments known as charges on income and certain sums known as personal reliefs. Charges on income are defined by s. 8(8) Taxes Management Act 1970 as 'amounts which fall to be deducted in computing total income'. This somewhat unhelpful definition is not explained further. Charges on income include annuities and other annual payments and certain interest payments.

A personal relief is a sum deducted in computing the taxable part of income, the amount of which depends on the taxpayer's circumstances. The tax is progressive, that is, the rate increases as income increases.

1.2 Definition of income

Income must be distinguished from capital receipts. In most cases there is no problem in deciding which an item is. Thus profits received from the sale of stock-in-trade are income: profits made from the sale of fixed assets are capital. For example, if the business is a grocer's shop, the food which is sold is stock but the shop itself, its shelves and counters are fixed assets. The evidence of accountants as to general accountancy practice is valuable but not conclusive in deciding whether an item is income or capital.

Almost all businesses produce final accounts on an annual basis. These show the amount of profit made according to normal accountancy practice and how it is allocated to the proprietor(s). These accounts are not, however, necessarily suitable for tax purposes, as often there are special tax rules which define what is taxable as income and what is deductible as an expense.

1.3 Deductible expenditure

Deductible expenditure is not fully defined in the Taxes Act. Expenditure is deductible if it is of a revenue rather than a capital nature. This distinction is similar to the distinction between income and capital receipts, so that, again, evidence of accountancy practice is valuable. Section 74 ICTA 1988 prevents the deduction of expenses in 15 circumstances.

The first paragraph of s. 74 provides that, 'in computing the amount of the profits or gains to be charged under Case I or II of Schedule D, no sum shall be deducted in respect of any disbursements or expenses, not being money *wholly and exclusively* laid out or expended for the purposes of the trade, profession or vocation'. Expenditure, if it is to be deducted, must, therefore, be 'wholly' incurred for the purposes of the trade, so that if a sum of money represents partly a business expense but is excessively large so that it also partly represents a gift it is not deductible. Expenditure must also be 'exclusively' incurred for the purposes of the trade, so that if money is spent and the motive is partly connected with the trade and partly not so connected (e.g., there is an element of personal enjoyment), then the payment is not deductible.

Certain types of expenditure are not deductible because of the provisions of paras. (b)-(q) of s. 74. Many of these paragraphs refer to types of expenditure which would be non-deductible anyway because they are not revenue expenditure or not wholly and exclusively incurred for the purposes of the trade. The section, among other things, prohibits the deduction of provisions for bad debts (but not of actual bad debts); and most business entertainment expenses are non-deductible under the provisions of s. 577 ICTA 1988.

1.4 Accounting bases

When calculating profit, it is important for any business, whether run by a sole trader, by a partnership or through a limited company, to apply a consistent method to determine whether receipts and expenses relate to one accounting period or to a later period. If it fails to do so its accounts are useless to the business for the purposes of comparison; what is more, the business could manipulate its receipts and expenses so as to avoid tax.

For tax purposes accounts have to be agreed with the Inland Revenue and must be prepared on one of three bases: the earnings, the cash or the bills delivered bases.

(a) *The earnings basis* Accounts are prepared on the basis of income earned (even if not received) and expenses incurred (even if not paid) during the relevant accounting period.

The value of stock unsold at the end of an accounting period and/or the value of work-in-hand at the end of the accounting period must be included when calculating profit (see paragraph 1.5 below).

(b) *The cash basis* Accounts are prepared on the basis of sums actually received and paid. No account is taken of amounts owed or owing or of the value of unsold stock or work-in-hand. This basis may give a misleading picture of the true profit where credit is given and/or received.

(c) *The bills delivered basis* Accounts are prepared on the basis of bills delivered to customers and received from suppliers irrespective of whether the bills have been paid. No account is taken of amounts owed or owing but not billed or of the value of unsold stock and work-in-hand. The fact that work-in-hand need not be valued makes this basis particularly popular with professional partnerships.

Trading partnerships are assessed on the earnings basis. Professionals, such as solicitors and accountants, are usually assessed on this basis for the first three tax years during which the profession is carried on but in the fourth and subsequent years (provided an undertaking is given to deliver bills promptly), the Revenue will usually agree to the bills delivered basis. The Revenue is normally reluctant to allow the cash basis except in special cases.

1.5 The need to value stock and work-in-hand

As explained above, when a business is taxed on the earnings basis, it is necessary to value stock and work-in-hand at the end of an accounting period, otherwise the accounts are misleading. If a trading business which makes a profit by buying and selling goods or other property simply compared its receipts and expenses, the accounts would give no real idea of the amount of profit. For example, £1,000 worth of goods are bought during a particular period and half of them are sold for £1,200 — clearly the profit is more than £200 since half the goods remain. Ignoring other expenses (wages, rates, electricity bills, etc.) the profit could be said to be £700 since goods purchased for £500 have been sold for £1,200.

Clearly it would be impractical to record the sale price of each item and deduct from it the original purchase price. To calculate a trading profit, stock must be valued at the end of the period. If the closing stock figure (i.e., the value at the end of the year) is deducted from the total of the opening stock figure and the amount spent on stock during the year (which accountants call 'purchases') the cost of goods sold has been calculated. This figure can then be deducted from the receipts from the sale of stock (called 'sales') to calculate the gross profit.

Example

	£	£
Sales		50,000
Opening stock	10,000	
Add: Purchases	35,000	
	45,000	
Less: Closing stock	(12,000)	
		33,000
Gross profit		17,000

(Other deductible expenses such as wages are then deducted from the gross profit to arrive at the net profit which enters into the tax calculation.)

Clearly the amount of profit depends on the value placed on stock — the lower the closing stock figure the smaller is the profit (and, therefore, the tax on it). Stock is valued according to normal accountancy principles, which allow each item of stock to be valued at the lower of cost or market value. Thus where stock has risen in value an upward valuation is not required, but where it has fallen in value immediate relief is given by the revaluation. Once a closing stock figure has been arrived at for a period it becomes the opening stock figure for the next period.

A business which supplies services will not have trading stock left at the end of an accounting period. It will, however, have work-in-hand at that date (that is, work commenced but not yet billed). The same principles are applied as with trading stock. Thus, where the earnings basis applies, the work-in-hand at the end of the year will increase profits, whereas work-in-hand at the start of the year will reduce them.

2   INCOME TAX — THE BASIS OF ASSESSMENT

Almost all traders find that a suitable accounting period is twelve months. The period chosen need not correspond with the year of assessment (tax year). A trader pays tax on the income of the year of assessment according to the rates fixed for that year by the annual Finance Act (taking into account his tax-free personal reliefs for the year). Because the accounting period and year of assessment do not usually correspond, rules are needed for allocating the profits of accounting periods to years of assessment.

2.1   Preceding year basis

In most circumstances the 'preceding year basis' applies to business profits (whether of a trade, profession or vocation). The profits taxable in each year of assessment are deemed to equal the profits of the accounting period ending in the preceding year of assessment. For example, a trader makes up his accounts to 31 December each year. His profits for the tax year 1990-91 will therefore be the profits of the accounting period which ended in the year of assessment 1989-90, i.e., the profits earned between 1 January 1989 and 31 December 1989.

Since the tax on trading profits is payable in two instalments — on 1 January during the year of assessment and on 1 July after its end — this effectively means that there is a considerable time-lag between an increase in profits and an increase in tax; the extent of this time-lag will depend on the date chosen for the end of the accounting period. (For example, if the accounting period ends on 5 April, the first instalment of tax for that period will be payable nine months later; if on 7 April, 21 months later.)

2.2 Early years of trade

The preceding year basis cannot apply in the early years of trade because there is no preceding year with profits. The rules for the opening years of assesment are as follows:

Year of commencement	Profits from date of commencement to following 5 April
Second year	Profits of first 12 months of trade
Third and subsequent years	Preceding year basis

In the second and third years only, the *taxpayer* has a choice and can elect to be taxed on the actual profits of both those years (but not on only one of them) if he wishes. Such an election is advisable if profits are falling.

Where necessary, profits taxed on the actual basis are calculated by apportioning the profits of one or more accounting periods on a time basis. the following examples should make the rules clearer:

(a)   A trader starts business on 1 January 1987. Accounts are made up to the 31 December each year and profits are as follows:

1987	£5,000
1988	£6,000
1989	£7,000

The income for tax purposes is:

Year of assessment

1986-87	£1,250 approx.	(actual basis, i.e., £5,000 apportioned to the period of 3 months)
1987-88	£5,000	(first 12 months)
1988-89	£5,000	(preceding year basis)
1989-90	£6,000	(preceding year basis)
1990-91	£7,000	(preceding year basis)

An election for the actual basis for 1987-88 and 1988-89 would produce incomes of £5,250 and £6,250:

		£	£
1987-88:			
6 April 1987 to 31 December 1987		$^9/_{12} \times 5,000 =$	3,750
1 January 1988 to 5 April 1988		$^3/_{12} \times 6,000 =$	1,500
			5,250
1988-89:			
6 April 1988 to 31 December 1988		$^9/_{12} \times 6,000 =$	4,500
1 January 1989 to 5 April 1989		$^3/_{12} \times 7,000 =$	1,750
			6,250

Note: In doing this calculation we have worked in whole months for the sake of simplicity. In practice the calculation would be done on a daily basis.

The election for the actual basis should not be made.

(b)   A trader starts business on 1 January 1987. Accounts are made up to 31 December each year and profits are as follows:

1987	£8,000
1988	£6,000
1989	£4,000

Income for tax years:

1986-87	£2,000 approx	(actual basis, i.e., £8,000 apportioned to the period of 3 months)

		£	£
1987-88:			
6 April 1987 to 31 December 1987		$^9/_{12} \times 8,000 =$	6,000
1 January 1988 to 5 April 1988		$^3/_{12} \times 6,000 =$	1,500
			7,500
1988-89:			
6 April 1988 to 31 December 1988		$^9/_{12} \times 6,000 =$	4,500
1 January 1989 to 5 April 1989		$^3/_{12} \times 4,000 =$	1,000
			5,500

1989-90	6,000 (preceding year basis)
1990-91	4,000 (preceding year basis)

An election for the actual basis of assessment for the second and third years would be made. If it was not made the profits assessed to tax for 1987-88 would be the profits of the first 12 months, £8,000 and those for 1988-89 on the preceding year basis would be £8,000.

2.3   Closing years of trade

Special rules also apply to the closing years of a trade, since if the preceding year basis continued to apply a trade could be artificially closed down and a new trade started after a particularly good accounting period without the profits of that period ever being used as the basis of a tax assessment.

The closing year rules are:

Last year	Actual profits from 6 April to discontinuance
Penultimate year	Preceding year basis
Pre-penultimate year	Preceding year basis
Earlier years	Preceding year basis

In the penultimate and pre-penultimate years the Revenue can elect to tax the profits on the actual basis if this produces a larger amount of profit taking both years together (they will do so if profits are rising).

Where necessary, profits taxed on the actual basis are calculated by apportioning the profits of one or more accounting period on a time basis.

The following examples should make the closing year rules clearer:

(a)   A trader ends his business on 31 December 1991. His accounts are made up to 31 December each year and the profits are as follows:

1991	£10,000
1990	£12,000
1989	£14,000
1988	£16,000
1987	£20,000

The income for the tax years is as follows:

1991-92	£7,500 approx	(actual profits 6 April 1991 to 31 December 1991, i.e., £10,000 apportioned)
1990-91	£14,000	(preceding year basis)
1989-90	£16,000	(preceding year basis)
1988-89	£20,000	(preceding year basis)

The Revenue would not elect to make the assessment on the actual basis for 1990-91 and 1989-90 since the profits would then be £11,500 and £13,500 respectively:

	£	£
1990-91:		
6 April 1990 to 31 December 1990	$^9/_{12} \times 12,000 =$	9,000
1 January 1991 to 5 April 1991	$^3/_{12} \times 10,000 =$	2,500
		11,500

1989-90:

6 April 1989 to 31 December 1989	$^9/_{12} \times 14,000 = 10,500$
1 January 1990 to 5 April 1990	$^3/_{12} \times 12,000 = \underline{3,000}$
	$\underline{13,500}$

(b)   A trader ends his business on 31 December 1991. His accounts are made up to 31 December each year and the profits are as follows:

1991	£16,000
1990	£12,000
1989	£ 8,000
1988	£ 6,000
1987	£ 4,000

The income for the years is as follows:

		£	£
1991-92:			
6 April 1991 to 31 December 1991		$^9/_{12} \times 16,000 =$	12,000

1990-91:		
6 April 1990 to 31 December 1990	$^9/_{12} \times 12,000 =$	9,000
1 January 1991 to 5 April 1991	$^3/_{12} \times 16,000 =$	4,000
		13,000

1989-90:		
6 April 1989 to 31 December 1989	$^9/_{12} \times 8,000 =$	6,000
1 January 1990 to 5 April 1990	$^3/_{12} \times 12,000 =$	3,000
		9,000

1988-89	(preceding year basis) 4,000

The Revenue would make the assessment on the actual basis for 1990-91 and 1989-90 since the profits on the preceding year basis would be £8,000 and £6,000 respectively — in fact, assessments will already have been made on those figures because it is not known until the end of 1991 that they are penultimate and pre-penultimate years. The assessments will, therefore, have to be retrospectively adjusted.

2.4   Assessment — conclusions

The basis of assessment under Cases I and II is highly artificial. In practical terms some profits in the early years are taxed more than once and some near the end of the trade not at all. As long as the profits near the end of the trade are higher than those soon after the beginning the taxpayer may ultimately benefit, but even with inflation there is no guarantee that profits will be higher near the end of the trade.

   If a trade is short lived, the opening years and closing years may overlap, in which case the closing year rules take priority.

It should be noted that the amount of tax paid by a trader does not depend on what he does with his profits. Subject to the deduction of charges on income, they are fully taxed whether withdrawn or retained in the business (unless a capital allowance can be claimed).

3. CAPITAL ALLOWANCES

3.1 Machinery and plant

As was explained above, capital expenditure is not deductible in computing income profits (nor may depreciation on fixed assets be claimed as a deductible expense). However, a form of relief which ultimately operates as a depreciation allowance is given on certain types of capital expenditure under the Capital Allowances Act 1968 as amended.

If expenditure is incurred for the purposes of the trade on or after 1 April 1986, it will qualify for a writing-down allowance of up to 25% in the first and subsequent years. Different rules exist for assets purchased prior to 1 April 1986.

For example, machinery is purchased for £50,000 on 1 January 1987 and writing-down allowance of 25% (£12,500) is claimed:

	Written-down value	*Allowance*
2nd year	£50,000 − £12,500 = £37,500	£9,375
3rd year	£50,000 − £21,875 = £28,125	£7,031
4th year	£50,000 − £28,906 = £21,094	£5,273

When the asset is sold there is a balancing charge on the difference between the sale price and the written-down value. In the above example, the written-down value after the fourth year was £15,821, so if the machinery were sold for £17,821 there would be a charge to tax (under Schedule D Case VI) on £2,000. This means that, taking all the years together, the amount on which relief is finally given is equal to the amount of depreciation. A balancing charge can never be on more than the amount of allowance given — any actual profit made on the sale of the asset being liable to capital gains tax if taxable at all. The allowances are of up to 25% of the *unrelieved expenditure* (i.e., the purchase price less any allowances already taken). Thus, the annual allowance is a percentage of an ever-reducing balance so that it can take many years before the entire expenditure has been set against profits.

If more than one item of machinery and plant is owned by a business the allowances are given by reference to a 'pool' of expenditure, i.e., all the assets are treated as if they were one asset. The amount of the writing-down allowance is 25% of the total of expenditure on machinery and plant less all allowances so far claimed. Where an item is disposed of, the sale price is deducted from the written-down value of the pool, so that smaller allowances are available in later years — a balancing charge is therefore only made where items are sold for more than the written-down value of the whole pool. Motor cars which are used only for business purposes qualify for full writing-down allowances but motor cars which are used for private as well as business purposes qualify for a 25% writting-down allowance subject to a maximum allowance calculated on the basis that the original cost was £8,000. Motor cars which are not used solely for business purposes do not enter into the pool.

If an asset acquired after 31 March 1986 is expected to be disposed of at less than the purchase price less capital allowances within a period of five years from its acquisition, an election can be made (within two years of the year of acquisition) for the asset to be dealt with outside the pool of machinery and plant.

Allowances for such assets which have been removed from the pool continue to be on the 25% reducing balance basis. Provided that the asset is either disposed of or scrapped within the five-year period, the balancing allowance or charge will be calculated by reference to its own capital allowance history. If the asset is not, in fact, sold or scrapped within the five-year period, its written-down value will be added to the pool of machinery and plant and thereafter treated as if it had never been de-pooled.

3.2   Industrial buildings

Allowances are available for the construction of industrial buildings or structures (such as factories, but not offices), and for manufacturing (but not distributive) trades. In the case of expenditure incurred on or after 1 April 1986 a writing-down allowance of 4% of the original cost of construction can be claimed for every year when the building is in use (which can include the year an initial allowance is claimed, if an initial allowance is available). Since the writing-down allowance is a percentage of the *original* cost price, full relief will be obtained once 25 years have elapsed. Again, different rules exist for expenditure incurred prior to 1 April 1986.

4   LOSSES UNDER THE INCOME TAX SYSTEM

If a trader makes a trading loss (i.e., deductible expenses exceed income profits) during an accounting period, there will be a 'nil' assessment in the following tax year if the preceding year basis applies (as it will unless the trade is just beginning or is coming to an end). This does not give any relief for the loss, its effect being to reduce the income to nothing rather than to the negative figure which the loss represents. Loss relief is, however, given in a number of ways.

(a)   Under s. 380(1) ICTA 1988 the amount of the loss may, if the taxpayer so elects, be deducted from any income of the taxpayer taxable in the year of assessment during which the loss is made. Where, as is usual, the loss-making period is partly in one tax year and partly in another the Revenue will, in practice, allow the whole of the loss to be set off against the income of the tax year during which that period ends.

If a loss is not fully relieved under s. 380(1) either because the income of the year of the loss was insufficient or because the taxpayer did not elect to take the relief, a similar election may be made for the next year of assessment, provided that the trade is still being carried on by the taxpayer on a commercial basis (s. 380(2)).

It should be noted that under both subsections the loss may be set off against *any* of the taxpayer's income from whatever source: because of the preceding year basis this may (in the case of subsection (1)) include a profit from the same trade made in an earlier accounting period.

Special rules apply to prevent relief under s. 380 being given where the trade is not being carried on with a view to profit.

(b) Under s. 385 ICTA 1988 a loss may be set against income from the same trade (but not from any other source) in future years to the extent that it has not been completely relieved under s. 380, either because no relief was claimed or because the income was insufficient. Relief is given by means of a deduction from the income of the next tax year in which there are profits and then the year after that and so on until the loss is completely relieved.

The following example should make the operation of ss. 380 and 385 clear. The profits and loss of a trade made during accounting periods ending on 31 December each year are as follows:

1987	£ 5,000	profit
1988	£20,000	loss
1989	£ 6,000	profit
1990	£ 7,000	profit

In addition to his trade the taxpayer has a part-time employment producing an income of £2,000 per annum throughout the period. If claims for relief under ss. 380 and 385 are made the income tax position is as follows:

	1988-89	1989-90	1990-91	1991-92
DI income	5,000	nil	6,000	7,000
Schedule E income	2,000	2,000	2,000	2,000
	7,000	2,000	8,000	9,000
Loss relief	7,000*	2,000**	6,000***	5,000***
Final income	nil	nil	2,000	4,000

*s. 380(1)   **s. 380(2)   ***s. 385

Note:

(i) On these figures full relief is not given until 1991-92 even though the loss was made in 1988.

(ii) It would probably be better not to claim relief for 1989-90 since much of the income for that year would have been covered by personal reliefs which are tax-free anyway. The loss relief is therefore wasted.

(iii) The deduction in 1990-91 is only £6,000 because in that year no relief is given against income from other sources. After the deduction of £5,000 in 1991-92 full relief has been given for the loss.

(c) Under ss. 388 and 389 ICTA 1988 a loss made during the last year of a trade may be deducted from income from the same trade in the three years of assessment before the discontinuance (relief under s. 380 will be available for the year of discontinuance), taking later years before earlier years. This section is really s. 385 in reverse since it allows the loss to be carried back rather than forwards. It should be noted that the relief only applies where the loss is made in the last year of a trade. If a business makes losses for a number of years before discontinuance there will be no loss relief unless the trader has other sources of income — s. 385 cannot help since there will be no future profits, nor can ss. 388 and 389, since the loss can only be carried back three years and those years will have had nil assessments because of the earlier losses.

(d)   Under s. 381 ICTA 1988 losses made during the first four years of a trade may be set off against income of the three tax years before the loss, taking earlier years before later years. The loss can be deducted from all the income of those years from whatever source and the rules of s. 380 dealing with the order in which relief is given where there is more than one source of income apply to s. 381. The principal effect of s. 381 is to allow a person who starts a trade to set the loss off against income received before the business started.

As would be expected, all the sections giving relief prevent double relief being claimed in respect of the same sum (for example, if relief is claimed under s. 381 only the unrelieved balance, if any, may be carried forward under s. 385). In many cases relief is given by setting a loss off against income which has already been taxed; where this happens the relief is given by means of repayment of tax.

It should be noted that loss relief is not intended as a subsidy for unsuccessful business; there is no guarantee that just because a loss is made relief will one day be given. Where relief is given the saving is, of course, the amount of the tax on the amount of the relief, so that for the basic rate taxpayer a loss of £100 saves £25 in tax.

5   INCOME TAX LIABILITY OF PARTNERSHIPS

A partnership is not a separate legal person. It is a group of individuals each of whom is taxed on his own share of the partnership profits or losses in the light of his own personal reliefs, charges on income and other sources of income. However, for the purposes of *assessment* and *collection* of tax the Revenue does recognise the partnership as an entity (see below).

The income on which the partnership is assessed to tax in a particular tax year is calculated according to the preceding year basis, the opening year rules (subject to the provisions of ss. 61 and 62 ICTA 1988 — see ch. 18 paragraph 3.3.1.1) or the closing year rules as appropriate.

A trading partnership will be charged to tax under Schedule D Case I. It is normally assessed on the earnings basis. A professional partnership will be charged to tax under Schedule D Case II. It is also assessed on the earnings basis initially, although the Inland Revenue will normally agree to the bills delivered basis in the fourth and subsequent accounting periods, provided an undertaking to bill promptly is given (for a fuller discussion of the three bases see paragraph 1.4 above).

The taxable profit is calculated by applying normal income tax principles to ascertain taxable receipts and deductible expenses. However, in the case of a partnership, it is necessary to examine any payment made by the business to a partner to determine whether it is a deductible expense or merely an allocation of the taxable profit amongst the partners. A payment which falls into the latter category cannot reduce the taxable profit of the partnership.

The following items merit special attention:

(a)   *Salary*   The tax treatment of a 'salary' payable to a 'partner' depends on whether the Revenue regard the recipient as a true partner sharing in the profits in a particular, agreed way (the decision to allocate profits in this way is normally taken to ensure that one partner is entitled to an agreed portion of profit in priority to the other partners) or whether the recipient is merely an employee in receipt of a salary who is described as a 'partner'. In making their decision, the Revenue will consider all the facts and the terms of the partnership agreement entered into by the parties. The terms of the agreement are not conclusive (*Stekel* v *Ellice* [1973] 1 WLR 191). Where salary is treated as an allocation of profit, it is not deductible from the firm's taxable profits. Where it is a true salary, it is deductible and will be assessed under Schedule E with tax deducted at source under the PAYE procedure.

(b) *Interest* 'Interest' payable to a partner will not be a deductible expense if it is payable on a partner's contribution of capital to the firm. Such a payment is regarded as part of the agreed method of allocating profits. However, if a partner makes a loan to the partnership, interest payable on the loan will normally be a deductible expense.

(c) *Rent* Where a partnership pays rent to a partner for the use of assets owned by the partner the amount of the rent will be a deductible expense (unless it is excessive).

Once the taxable profit on which the partnership is to be assessed to tax in a particular year has been calculated, the 'precedent partner' must make a return of the partnership income to the Revenue. (The precedent partner is normally the partner whose name appears first in the partnership agreement.)

In addition, each partner submits a personal tax return to the Inland Revenue showing his share of the partnership profit (including any 'salary' and/or 'interest' on capital which falls to be treated as an allocation of profit, where appropriate), together with full details of other sources of income (if any) and his entitlement to personal reliefs and charges on income, if any. The Inland Revenue calculates how much tax is due from each partner on his partnership income and then, having added together all such amounts, issues a joint assessment in the partnership name for the total amount due (s. 111 ICTA 1988).

The Revenue provides the precedent partner with information as to how the bill was calculated so that the total tax bill can be apportioned amongst the partners. The tax is due in two equal instalments, on 1 January in the current tax year and 1 July in the following tax year.

The individual partners can remit their own share of the amount due to the Inland Revenue direct or the firm can pay the whole payment and charge the individual partners for their share.

Example A and B are in partnership sharing profits equally. A is a married man; he has charges on income of £2,000. B is an unmarried woman; she has charges on income of £5,000. The taxable profits of the partnership to be assessed in 1990-91 are £26,000.

	A	B
	£	£
Share of partnership profit	13,000	13,000
Income from other sources	—	—
Personal reliefs: Single person's	(3,005)	(3,005)
Married couple's:	(1,720)	—
Charge on income	(2,000)	(5,000)
	6,275	4,995
Tax at 25%	1,568.75	1,248.75

The partnership's tax liability is £2,817.50. A and B are jointly liable for the whole amount.

If there is a change in the profit-sharing ratio, the income is allocated to each partner for tax purposes according to the ratio in the year of assessment rather than that used in the accounting period to which the income relates.

For example, A and B are in partnership; they share profits equally until 6 April 1990 when A's share goes up to 75% and B's down to 25%. The profits for accounting periods ending on 31 December are:

1988	£10,000
1989	£10,000
1990	£20,000

The income for tax purposes will be:

	Partnership	A	B
1989-90	£10,000	£ 5,000	£5,000
1990-91	£10,000	£ 7,500	£2,500
1991-92	£20,000	£15,000	£5,000

Thus A pays tax on £27,500 during the three years of assessment even though during the corresponding three accounting periods his receipts from the partnership were:

1988	£ 5,000	
1989	£ 5,000	
1990	£13,750 approx	(½ share of profits 1 Jan-5 Apr i.e., 5,000 ÷ 2 = 2,500
		¾ share of profits 6 Apr-31 Dec i.e., 15,000 ÷ ¾ = 11,250)
	£23,750	

The rules applicable if a partner dies or retires or joins the firm are considered in Chapter 18.

When a partnership makes a loss, each partner can choose what type of relief to claim in respect of his share of the loss. For example, some of the partners may prefer to claim relief under s. 380 ICTA 1988 immediately; others may prefer to wait and claim relief under s. 385 ICTA 1988. The discontinuance caused by death, retirement or the admission of a new partner does not give the whole partnership a right to claim relief under ss. 388 and 389 ICTA 1988 (terminal loss relief) or under s. 381 ICTA 1988 (relief for losses of new trades): only the leaving or joining partners, respectively, may claim such reliefs.

Partners, being self-employed, are liable to make national insurance contributions at a rate lower than the rate applicable to employees (but the benefits are correspondingly lower), and they are entitled to deduct one half of their contributions when calculating their income tax liability.

6 CAPITAL GAINS TAX

6.1 General

Capital gains tax and income tax are mutually exclusive; any receipt which is liable to income tax is not liable to capital gains tax. Subject to that very important exception, nearly all disposals of assets (whether by sale or gift) may give rise to capital gains tax under the Capital Gains Tax Act 1979. The tax is payable on a current year basis on 'chargeable gains' (which are calculated by deducting certain specified expenditure from the sale price or, in the case of a gift, from the market value) realised during a year of assessment. The expenditure which may be deducted is broadly:

(a)   the acquisition value; this is the purchase price or if purchased prior to 31 March 1982, its value at the date of or, in the case of a gift, the market value at the time of acquisition;
(b)   incidental costs of acquisition;
(c)   money spent on enhancing the value of the asset;
(d)   incidental costs of disposal.

Thus the sum on which tax is paid is the profit made on the sale of the asset or, in the case of a gift, its increase in value since acquisition, less any expenditure incurred. Account is taken of inflation in calculating the gain, but only to the extent of inflation since April 1982 or the end of the month in which the asset was acquired, if later. The rules relating to this indexation allowance are considered in Chapter 17 paragraph 6.1. The first £5,000 of gains in each year of assessment are exempt. There are also rules to exempt from tax the part of any gain which arose before the tax was introduced in 1965. If a loss is made (calculated in the same way as a gain), it may be set off against the gains made in the same tax year and, to the extent that it is not relieved in that year, may be carried forward and set off against the first chargeable gains made thereafter.

Once the amount of the gain chargeable to capital gains tax has been ascertained it is taxed at the rate(s) which would be appropriate if it were the top slice of the taxpayer's income. There is no capital gains tax when a person dies (except in one rare type of case involving trusts). The beneficiaries of the will or intestacy are deemed to acquire the asset at market value at the time of death.

It is not intended to give more than the briefest outline of capital gains tax here, but three reliefs of particular relevance to the businessman will be referred to.

First, if a business asset is disposed of and the consideration is used to acquire a new business asset then 'roll-over relief' is available under s. 115 CGTA 1979. The trader may pay tax on the disposal of the asset if he wishes, but if he prefers he may claim relief, in which case here is no tax on the disposal but the gain reduces the consideration for the acquisition of the new asset. This means that when the new asset comes to be sold tax will be payable on both gains (although if the new asset is replaced the relief may be claimed again or some other relief may be available). The relief is only available if the replacement asset is purchased in the period twelve months before or three years after the disposal of the old asset. Roll-over relief is available only in respect of assets used wholly for the purposes of a trade and the assets must be in one or more of the following categories:

(a)   buildings occupied and used for the purposes of the trade;
(b)   land occupied and used for the purposes of the trade;
(c)   fixed plant and machinery;
(d)   ships, aircraft and hovercraft;
(e)   satellites, space sations and space craft (including launch vehicles);
(f)   goodwill;
(g)   milk quotas.

Secondly, relief is available on the disposal of a business or part of a business (which includes a share in a partnership) by a person at age 60 or by a person who has retired on the grounds of ill-health at an age below 60. This 'retirement relief' is considered in more detail in Chapter 17 paragraph 8 but, in brief, the relief is available by reason of the transferor's age or retirement due to ill-health and takes the form of a deduction from the amount of the chargeable gain realised on a disposal by the transferor. There is a full exemption for the first £125,000 of gains and thereafter a half exemption for the balance of gains up to a limit of £500,000. However, whether the full relief is available depends on the length of the transferor's ownership of the business or the interest in it. No relief is available if the business, or interest in the business, has been owned for less than one year, but 10% of the relief is available once it has been owned for exactly one year. The relief is then given on a sliding scale reaching 100% after 10 years of ownership. There is no limitation on the time which the transferor must devote to the business (which differs from the position applicable to a shareholder who must either be a full-time working director or devote at least 10 hours per week to the company while acting in an administrative or technical capacity).

Thirdly, hold-over relief is available to defer capital gains tax on a gift of business assets. A gift is a disposal; an asset which is given away is deemed to be disposed of at its market value at the date of the gift. Thus, capital gains tax may well be payable.

However, s. 126 CGTA 1979 (as amended) provides that where a person makes a gift of business assets the donor and donee may jointly elect to 'hold over' the gain. This means that no tax is payable at the time of the gift but the donee's acquisition value is reduced by the amount of the donor's gain. This prima facie means that the donee will face an increased tax charge when he disposes of the assets but it may be that other exemptions or reliefs such as retirement relief will be available to extinguish or reduce this liability.

'Business assets' are:

(a) assets used in a trade, profession or vocation by the donor or his 'family' company; or

(b) shares in a trading company which are not quoted on either a recognised stock exchange or the unlisted securities market; or

(c) shares in a trading company which is the donor's 'family' company.

'Family' company means that the donor holds at least 25% of the voting rights or has at least 5% of the voting rights and at least 50% are held by himself and his family.

6.2 Partnerships

When a firm disposes of an asset, normal CGT principles apply in determining what gains, if any, the firm has made. There are difficulties involved in applying the normal CGT principles in a partnership context. The problems are seen most clearly in connection with changes in the membership of the partnership (see ch. 18—4). The Revenue has published statements of practice (SP D/12 1975 and SP 1/79) which set out the way in which they regard the principles as applying in this context but it is obviously unsatisfactory to have to rely on statements of practice. What is needed is coherent and comprehensive legislation designed to deal with the particular problem of partnerships.

The premise on which the Inland Revenue Statement of Practice of 17 January 1975 is based is that each partner is to be treated as owning a fractional share of each of the chargeable assets of the partnership (including goodwill) and not, for this purpose, as owning an interest in the business as a whole. When the firm disposes of an asset to an outsider, each partner is treated as making a disposal of his fractional share in the asset.

The assessment and collection of CGT is treated differently from the assessment and collection of income tax. The precedent partner delivers a return to the Inland Revenue giving full details of disposals. The assessment is made on the individual partners (s. 60 CGTA 1979 and s. 12(4) TMA 1970). Each partner's share in the gain is calculated in accordance with his share in the asset disposed of.

In order to calculate the CGT liability of the individual partners in relation to the disposal of assets it is, therefore, necessary to know the proportions in which assets are owned. This is often referred to as the partners 'asset surplus share'.

The partnership deed may specify the proportions in which asset surpluses are to be shared. If it does, it is conclusive. If there is no express provision in the partnership deed, the assets surplus sharing ratio is deemed to be the ratio in which profits are shared. It is common for a partnership deed to provide an 'asset surplus sharing ratio' which is different from the profit sharing ratio. For example, the agreement may provide for an individual partner's right to share in an asset surplus to be greater than his right to share in income profits to reflect the fact that he has made a substantial capital contribution to the firm while contributing comparatively little to earning income profits.

When an asset is acquired by a partnership each partner's share in the acquisition value is determined by his share in the asset surplus *at that time*. Similarly, on a disposal, each partner's share in the proceeds of disposal is determined by his share in asset surpluses *at that time*.

Example   A and B are in partnership. They share profits equally and have made no special agreement as to sharing asset surpluses. They acquire an asset for £20,000.
The acquisition value for each partner is:

A   ½   £10,000
B   ½   £10,000

They sell the asset for £36,000. The share in the proceeds of disposal of each partner is:

A   ½   £18,000
B   ½   £18,000

The chargeable gain of each partner is (ignoring indexation):

A   £18,000 − 10,000 = £8,000
B   £18,000 − 10,000 = £8,000

Each partner is personally liable for his own chargeable gain and will be assessed to tax at the rates appropriate to his level of income.

Particular difficulties are involved in the application of the CGT rules to partnerships where the asset surplus sharing ratio is changed (whether or not there is also a change in the personnel of the partnership). The effects of such a change are considered in Chapter 18 paragraph 3.3.2.

If there is a gain realised on the disposal, the exemptions and reliefs referred to in paragraph 6.1 above may be available. To the extent that there is a gift element in a disposal, hold-over relief is available to postpone the payment of tax. This relief can be claimed not only in respect of partnership assets but also in respect of assets owned by an individual partner which are used by the firm. (However, in this case there may be a potential IHT liability to take into account as well.)

A disposal of partnership property in circumstances where the partners intend reinvesting the sale proceeds can attract 'roll-over' relief under s. 115 CGTA 1979. This option to postpone payment of tax is also available to a partner who owns an asset which is used by the partnership (irrespective of the terms on which the asset is used by the firm).

Where the disposal occurs at age 60 (or earlier on retirement due to ill-health) the partner disposing of his share can claim retirement relief provided he has owned his interest in the partnership for at least one year. (He will qualify for the full 100% relief if his ownership covers at least 10 years — see para. 6.1 above for the details of the relief.) The relief can be claimed irrespective of the size of the partner's share in the partnership. If the partner owns assets which are not partnership property, the relief is available if the disposal is associated with the disposal of the partner's share. If the partnership has been providing consideration for the use of the asset by paying a full market rent, the 'retiring' partner will not be able to claim a relief, save for a fraction of it which is in proportion to his share of the rent. A larger proportion of the relief will be available if the rent charged is less than a full market rent.

7 INHERITANCE TAX

7.1 General

It is not intended to deal with the general principles of inheritance tax in this book. The tax position on a gift of business assets is dealt with in Chapter 18 paragraph 3.3.3 and on a gift of shares in Chapter 17, paragraph 7.

7.2 Partnerships

The IHT legislation contains few provisions dealing specifically with partnerships. According to the general principle of IHT, any transfer of a partnership asset or of an interest in a partnership will be a transfer of value by the individual partners if the transfer is by way of gift or there is an element of gift in the disposition.

A transfer will be exempt if it is made between spouses. It will also be exempt if it was not intended to, and was not made in a transaction intended to, confer any gratuitous benefit and either it was an arm's-length transaction between unconnected persons or was such as might be expected to be made between unconnected persons (s. 10, Inheritance Tax Act 1984).

Many inter vivos transfers which might appear to be transfers of value will escape IHT as a result of s. 10. For example, when a new partner is admitted and is given a share in the assets without making a payment, there would be a transfer of value were it not for s. 10. This matter is considered further in Chapter 18.

On death, a deceased partner's interest in the partnership will be a part of his estate. The position is considered more fully in Chapter 18, but business property relief will normally be available.

15   Taxation of Companies

1   CALCULATION OF PROFITS — CORPORATION TAX

1.1   Income

Companies pay corporation tax on their profits. For the purposes of the tax, unincorporated associations (such as members' clubs), other than partnerships, local authorities and local authority associations, are taxed as companies (s. 832(1) ICTA 1988). 'Profits' means income and capital gains (s. 6(4)(a) ICTA 1988).

Income profits are calculated according to income tax principles (see ch. 14), so that the various schedules of income are as relevant for corporation tax as for income tax. Similarly, the rules for deduction of expenses which apply for income tax purposes also apply to corporation tax (s. 9 ICTA 1988). There are some exceptions to these rules, particularly in relation to dividends, losses, charges on income and capital allowances. Companies, unlike individuals, have no right to claim any personal allowances.

1.2   Charges on income

A charge on income is defined for corporation tax purposes as any yearly interest, annuity or other annual payment and any other interest (i.e., interest on a loan for a period which cannot exceed a year) paid to a bank. Sums which are deductible as business expenses are not within the definition. A charge on income payable out of profits may be deducted from profits liable to corporation tax. Deduction is not, however, permitted unless the charge was incurred for valuable and sufficient consideration. Individuals may also deduct certain items as charges on income in computing tax liability (see ch. 14—1), but the definition of charges on income is in some respects wider (for example, mortgage interest relief is available) and in others narrower (some covenanted payments are not deductible) than for corporation tax purposes. Charges should be distinguished from business expenses (which are deductible from receipts in calculating profits rather than from profits once calculated). A charge on income is deducted when paid, whereas a business expense is deducted when it accrues due.

1.3   Capital allowances

Companies are entitled to claim the allowances at the same rates as individuals (see ch. 14—3). Capital allowances of companies are treated as trading expenses of the accounting period in respect of which they are claimed, and balancing charges are treated as trading receipts of that period. For income tax purposes, capital allowances and balancing charges are technically not trading expenses and receipts, but the practical differences between the two systems are slight.

1.4 Capital gains

Capital gains of companies are calculated according to capital gains tax principles (s. 345(2) ICTA 1988).

Since companies are not individuals they are not entitled to annual exemptions. A company can, however, claim the relief for gains realised when replacing business assets set out in CGTA 1979, ss. 115-121 (see ch. 14—6.1).

Retaining appreciating assets in a company can lead to an element of double taxation since, on realisation of the asset, the company pays tax (subject to the relief for replacement assets). The company's gain after tax may be reflected in an increase in the value of the company's assets. This will cause the value of the shares in the company to increase which will result in a greater gain being realised (subject to exemptions and reliefs) on a subsequent disposal of shares by the shareholder.

2 ASSESSMENT — CORPORATION TAX

2.1 Basis of assessment

Although income tax and capital gains tax rules are used to calculate the amount of profit, the basis of assessment for corporation tax is quite different from either of those taxes. For income tax different bases apply for the various cases and schedules (for Schedule D Cases I and II see ch. 14), and capital gains tax is payable on the gains made in each tax year. For corporation tax purposes, tax is calculated by reference to each accounting period of the company (s. 12 ICTA 1988). An accounting period is normally twelve months ending with the company's accounting date, that is, the date to which its accounts are made up (see ch. 9—5.2). If the accounts are made up for a period of less than twelve months, then the accounting period is also less than twelve months; if for a longer period, special rules apply and the profits are divided on a time basis between two or more accounting periods, none of which may be longer than twelve months. Corporation tax is payable nine months after the end of the accounting period or, if later, one month after assessment (s. 10(1) ICTA 1988), so that the date chosen does not affect the length of time between the end of the period and the date of payment. Companies are generally liable to pay tax on trading profits considerably earlier than sole traders and partners, since the preceding year basis does not apply.

2.2 Rates of tax

Although companies pay tax on the profits of their own accounting periods, the rate of tax is fixed for financial years, that is, periods starting on 1 April and ending on the following 31 March. For the financial year 1990 (i.e., the period 1 April 1990 to 31 March 1991) the rate is 35%.

Unless the company happens to make up its accounts to 31 March the profits will have to be apportioned (on a time basis) between two financial years if the rate changes. For example, a company makes up its accounts to 31 December. Its profits for the accounting period ending on 31 December 1991 are £1,460,000 — the rate of corporation tax for the financial year 1990 (1 April 1990—31 March 1991) is 35%, for the financial year 1991 (1 April 1991—31 March 1992) the rate is yet to be fixed.

Assuming the rate for 1991 were 40%, corporation tax for the accounting period would be:

$$\frac{90}{365} \times 1{,}460{,}000 \times 35\% = \quad 126{,}000$$

$$\frac{275}{365} \times 1{,}460{,}000 \times 40\% = \quad \underline{440{,}000}$$

$$\underline{566{,}000}$$

The normal rate of corporation tax for the financial year 1990 is 35%. However, s. 13 ICTA 1988 makes provision for a reduced rate in the case of a company with small profits. For this purpose 'profits' include income profits, capital gains and 'franked investment income' (i.e., dividends from another company except a company in the same group of companies). Loan interest may be deducted in calculating this figure. The reduced rate for the financial year 1990 is 25% and applies where the profits do not exceed £200,000 (the 'lower relevant maximum amount'). Where profits exceed the 'higher relevant maximum amount' (£1,000,000 for the financial year 1990) all profits, not just the excess over that figure are taxed at 35%. Where the amount of the profits falls between the two maximum amounts the effective rate of tax is between the lower and higher rates of tax. In such a case the rate can be calculated for 1990 by treating the first £200,000 as taxable at 25% and the excess at 37.5%. If the profits include franked investment income the calculation is more complicated since only the income profits get the benefit of the lower rate. The Act provides that the tax is first calculated at the full rate and then reduced by an amount expressed by the formula $(M - P) \times (I/P) \times$ (the statutory fraction) where M is the higher relevant maximum amount (£1,000,000), I is the profits other than franked investment income and P the total profits — the statutory fractions for the financial year 1990 is one-fortieth.

3 LOSS RELIEF UNDER THE CORPORATION TAX SYSTEM

Trading losses of companies are relieved in a number of ways; the scheme of the legislation is very similar to the one that applies for income tax (see ch. 14—4). Under s. 393(2) ICTA 1988 a loss made during an accounting period may be set off against any profits of the same accounting period if a claim for relief is made within two years of the end of the accounting period containing the loss. As was stated earlier, 'profits' for corporation tax include both income and capital gains so that, unlike a sole trader or partner, a company may set an income loss (from trade) against the chargeable part of a capital gain. If the loss is not entirely relieved by setting it off against profits of the same accounting period in which the loss was made, the company may also make a claim requiring the unrelieved part of the loss to be set off against profits (including the chargeable part of capital gains) of earlier accounting periods. The period of 'carry-back' allowed may not be longer than the accounting period during which the loss was made — this nearly always means that the carry-back is for one accounting period only. A loss cannot be carried back to a period when the company was not carrying on the business and there are no corporation tax provisions corresponding with s. 381 ICTA 1988 (income tax loss relief for the early years of a new trade).

To the extent that full relief is not obtained under s. 393(2), either because the relief was not claimed or because the profits were not large enough, relief may be claimed under s. 393(1). This is similar to s. 385 and allows the company to carry forward the loss and use it to reduce profits from the same trade in future accounting periods.

For example, a company has accounting periods corresponding with calendar years and its profits and losses are as follows:

	Trade I	*Trade II*	*Capital gains*	*Profits*
	£	£	£	£
1988	100,000	50,000	nil	150,000
1989	(400,000) loss	50,000	30,000	80,000
1990	100,000	50,000	30,000	180,000
1991	200,000	50,000	nil	250,000
1992	200,000	50,000	nil	250,000

If the company makes full use of the relief under s. 393(2) the chargeable profits after loss relief will be:

1988	£150,000 − 150,000	=	nil	(1988 is the preceding accounting period)
1989	£80,000 − 80,000	=	nil	(1989 is the loss-making period)
1990	£180,000 − 100,000	=	£80,000	(relief only against income of same trade)
1991	£250,000 − 70,000	=	£180,000	(full relief has now been given)
1992	£250,000 − nil	=	£250,000	

Alternatively, if the company does not claim relief under s. 393(2) but waits for relief under s. 393(1) the chargeable profits will be:

	£		£
1988	150,000 − nil	=	150,000
1989	80,000 − nil	=	80,000
1990	180,000 − 100,000	=	80,000
1991	250,000 − 200,000	=	50,000
1992	250,000 − 100,000	=	150,000

In deciding which method of relief to use, the company will wish to ensure, so far as possible, that the maximum tax saving is achieved (by setting the loss against those profits which are subject to tax at 35% rather than 25%). However, the cash flow problem of having to meet a tax bill at a time when the cash reserves may be low often means that it is preferable not to carry forward the relief but to claim the relief as soon as possible.

The possibility of carrying forward losses is lost in certain cases where there are substantial changes in both the ownership of the company and in the nature of its trade. This is an anti-avoidance provision designed to prevent the purchase of a company simply to take advantage of its tax losses.

Under s. 394 ICTA 1988 a loss made in the last twelve months of a trade, whether in one accounting period or more, can be carried back and set off against income from the same trade in accounting periods of the last three years, taking later accounting periods before earlier ones. As with income tax, there are provisions to ensure that loss relief is not given unless the trade which produced the loss was being carried on with a view to profit.

If a company makes a capital loss (calculated in the same way as a capital gain) it may be set off against capital gains of the same accounting period, and, if unrelieved, may be carried forward and set off against capital gains of later accounting periods. Although trading losses may be set off against capital gains there are no provisions allowing capital losses to be set off against income profits.

Section 402 ICTA 1988 makes provision for group relief. In outline, where a company is a member of a group it may surrender its loss to another company in the same group. The latter then deducts the loss from its profits as if it were its own loss. Companies are in the same group, broadly speaking, if one is the 75% subsidiary of the other or both are 75% subsidiaries of a third company.

It should be noted that a taxpayer who runs a business liable to income tax and who also owns a company, cannot set off a loss made in the trade against income of the company unless it is paid to him as income (e.g., as director's fees or dividends), in which case relief under s. 380 ICTA 1988 would be available. If the company makes a loss the proprietor cannot set it off against his income at all.

4 CLOSE COMPANIES

A close company is a company controlled by five or fewer participators or participators who are directors (s. 414 ICTA 1988). 'Participators' are shareholders, loan creditors and certain others entitled to participate in the distributed income of the company. 'Control' includes, inter alia, ownership of a majority of the share capital or a majority of the votes or a right to a majority of the dividends. In assessing control, the rights of 'associates' must be added to the rights of a participator — associates include, among others, the participator's spouse, parents, remoter forebears, children, remoter issue, brothers and sisters. The above definition is only a very brief summary but it is sufficient to show that nearly all private companies are close companies (for example, if a company has nine or fewer shareholders, it must be under the control of some five of them even if none of them is related to each other — it will therefore be a close company unless it falls into one of the small number of cases excluded from the definition).

Close companies are subject to certain special tax rules. These are designed to prevent the use of the company as a vehicle for tax avoidance.

If a loan is made to a participator or his associate, then under s. 419 ICTA 1988 the company must pay a levy equal to the rate of advance corporation tax on the loan. This currently means that for every £3 lent an additional £1 must be paid to the Revenue. When the loan is repaid so is the levy, but if the loan is written off or released, the levy becomes irrecoverable. Furthermore, the borrower is liable to income tax on the amount written off or released as if it were a payment of income to him net of basic rate tax. It will be remembered that loans to directors are generally prohibited by the Companies Act 1985, s. 330 (see ch. 3—7.1).

Companies are not normally liable to inheritance tax if they make gifts. However, if a close company makes a gift (or other transfer of value) this is deemed to be a gift made by all the shareholders in the company (except those with very small interests) in proportion to their shareholdings. If the shareholders fail to pay inheritance tax on this deemed gift, the company becomes liable (ss. 94-102 and 202 IHTA 1984).

5 TAXATION ON WITHDRAWAL OF PROFITS

5.1 Introduction

The company law rules dealing with the distribution of profits are set out in Chapter 5 paragraphs 6 and 7 and will not be considered further here. In this section we will be considering the tax consequences of a company distributing its profits by way of payment of dividends, interest on debentures and directors' fees, as well as the effect of a company retaining all or part of its profits.

5.2 Taxation of distributions

5.2.1 Definition of distribution
A shareholder is liable to income tax under Schedule F on any 'distribution' which he receives in respect of shares. The definition of distribution for this purpose is extremely complicated but the following types of receipt are the most important of those included in the definition:

(a) any dividend paid by the company including a capital dividend (s. 209(2)(a) ICTA 1988);

(b) any other distribution out of assets of the company . . . in respect of shares . . . (s. 209(2)(b));

(c) any interest on securities (i.e., debentures) where the interest varies with the profits of the company (s. 209(d)(iii));

(d) in some circumstances, the issue of bonus shares following a reduction of capital or the repayment of share capital after a bonus issue.

The issue of bonus redeemable shares (i.e., shares which do not have to be paid for and which will one day be repaid by the company) is also a distribution, but is described as a 'non-qualifying distribution' and is taxed in a special way. (In general terms, the shareholder receiving the shares pays tax on the value of the shares received but without having to pay basic rate tax (i.e., he is liable to excess liability only) and the company does not have to pay ACT (see below) on the distribution.)

It should be noted that an issue of bonus shares (that is, shares treated as paid up out of the profits of the company), is not a distribution for tax purposes unless share capital has previously been reduced. However, if the shareholders are given a *choice* between receiving a cash dividend (which is, of course, a distribution) or bonus shares, those who choose to take the bonus shares are taxed on the amount of cash dividend forgone in almost the same way as if it were a distribution (s. 249 ICTA 1988).

When a company redeems or purchases its own shares there is usually no income tax liability on the members (this topic will be dealt with in Chapter 17). It is possible to obtain clearance in advance ensuring no income tax liability in respect of such a scheme.

5.2.2   *Tax consequences on the company of distributions*

(a)   *Advance corporation tax*   The payment of a dividend (or other distribution) is neither an expense of a company's business nor a charge on its income. The amount of the dividend cannot, therefore, be deducted in computing the company's liability to corporation tax.

When a company makes a qualifying distribution it must pay advance corporation tax (always referred to as ACT) to the Revenue (s. 14 ICTA 1988). All the types of distribution referred to in paragraph 5.2 are qualifying distributions except the issue of bonus redeemable shares or securities. ACT is payable on a quarterly basis so that a company must usually report the payment of the distribution within, at the most, three months of the payment and must pay the ACT within 14 days of assessment. The ACT serves a dual purpose — it is a prepayment of part of the company's corporation tax liability and also a payment of the shareholders' basic rate income tax (see paragraph 5.2.3). The rate of ACT is calculated by the formula $I/(100 - I)$, where I is the basic rate of tax. Currently the basic rate is 25%, so ACT is $25/(100 - 25) = \frac{1}{3}$. Thus if a distribution of £7,500 is paid the ACT will be £2,500. The amount of ACT is, therefore, equal to basic rate tax, (currently 25%) on the *gross* amount of the distribution, i.e., it is equal to basic rate tax on the amount of the distribution plus the ACT on it.

(b)   *Set-off of ACT*   As we saw in paragraph 2.1, a company is normally liable to pay corporation tax nine months after the end of its accounting period. The amount of ACT paid may be deducted from the corporation tax then due. For example a company makes trading profits of £1,000,000 and pays a dividend of £150,000 during the accounting period. Its corporation tax liability will be £350,000 (35%) but from this the company can deduct the £50,000 (£150,000 × ⅓) paid as ACT. The balance of £300,000 is called mainstream corporation tax (MCT).

From the company's point of view a payment of ACT, therefore, adversely affects its cash flow (since the ACT has to be paid before the normal date for payment of corporation tax), but does not affect the total amount of tax paid. However, the maximum amount of ACT which may be set off against mainstream corporation tax liability for an accounting period is '. . . the amount of advance corporation tax . . . in respect of a distribution . . . of an amount which, together with the advance corporation tax so payable in respect of it, is equal to the company's income charged to corporation tax for that period' (s. 239(2) ICTA 1988). This apparently complicated rule really only means that a company cannot set ACT against MCT if the distribution is paid out of *capital* profits or out of income profits accumulated from an earlier accounting period. The maximum amount of ACT set-off is, therefore, in effect, 25% of *this* year's income profits.

For example, a company has income profits of £1,000,000 in the accounting period ending 31 March 1990 and pays a dividend of £900,000. The ACT will be £300,000 but the maximum ACT set-off is £250,000, i.e., 25% of £1,000,000 (this is because the

ACT on £750,000 is £250,000 — add those together and you have the income profits of £1,000,000), so that the company will pay £300,000 ACT and £100,000 MCT. (The corporation tax liaiblity at 35% on £1,000,000 is £350,000, from which is deducted £250,000.)

In this type of case the company has 'overpaid' corporation tax (in this example, to the extent of £50,000). The amount of overpayment is called surplus advance corporation tax (SACT). SACT may be carried back to the company's six previous accounting periods and may be reclaimed to the extent that *gross* distributions in those years were less than income profits. If the SACT cannot be reclaimed it may be carried forward and used to pay ACT in future accounting periods (subject to the same limit to the amount that may be set off). The effect of these rules is that a company which pays gross distributions in excess of its income profits will suffer a cash flow disadvantage, but the overall amount of corporation tax is not increased in the long run, except in the unlikely event that the distributions for all years taken together exceed the income profit for all years taken together.

5.2.3 Taxation of the recipient

A shareholder who receives a qualifying distribution from a company is liable to income tax under Schedule F on the amount of the 'franked payment'. The franked payment is the amount of the distribution plus the tax credit (i.e., ACT) on it. Thus a shareholder who receives a dividend of £75 is liable to tax on £100 (the ACT or tax credit on £75 being 1/3 or £25). He will be liable to higher rate tax if his *taxable* income exceeds £20,700. However, the recipient is given a tax credit equal to the amount of ACT on the distribution so that he does not have to pay basic rate tax on the franked payment and can reclaim the tax credit to the extent that he is not liable to tax on his income (for example, because he has unused personal reliefs).

It should be noted that profits distributed by certain companies to their shareholders are harshly treated for tax purposes. Where a company is taxed on income profits in excess of the small companies rate, it will have paid tax at more than 25%. However, it can only pass on to a shareholder a tax credit for the ACT paid, which is 25% of the franked payment. A taxpayer whose average rate of tax is less than the company's cannot reclaim from the Inland Revenue any of the tax paid by the company at rates higher than 25%. Furthermore, if the taxpayer is required to pay tax at more than 25% he cannot obtain any allowance for the fact that the company has *already* paid tax at more than 25%. In such a case, the taxpayer does not obtain the full benefit of the gross profit distributed by way of dividend.

5.2.4 Franked investment income

When a company makes a distribution to another company it must pay ACT in the normal way (unless the companies are both members of the same group of companies — i.e., one company owns more than half the shares in the other — when the distribution can be made without payment of ACT). The recipient company does not have to pay corporation tax on the distribution (which, in its hands, is called 'franked investment income'), and when it makes a distribution to its own shareholders out of the franked investment income it does not have to pay ACT. The reason for this is that it would be unfair to tax the same profits over and over again merely because they pass from company to company before reaching an individual shareholder.

5.3   Interest on debentures

5.3.1   Tax consequences on the paying company

Interest is a 'payment by time for the use of money' (per Rowlatt J in *Bennett* v *Ogston* (1930) 15 TC 374). The payment of a distribution to shareholders is not, however, treated as interest even in the case of a fixed dividend paid to preference shareholders. A payment of interest by a company will usually result in a tax saving to the company, either because the interest will be a business expense deductible in computing trading profits or because it is a charge on income deductible from profits before tax is computed on them. This distinction can be important in some cases, since a business expense is deducted when it accrues due, a charge on income when it is paid. There are also small differences in the way that relief is given if a loss results from the payment. Yearly interest is treated as a charge on income and so is short interest paid to a bank in the UK (s. 338(3) ICTA 1988). Short interest paid other than to a bank is deductible as a business expense provided it is 'wholly and exclusively incurred for the purposes of the trade' (s. 74 ICTA 1988; see ch. 14—1.2). 'Short interest' means interest for a period which *cannot* exceed a year and 'yearly interest' means interest for a period which can exceed a year.

5.3.2   Deduction of tax

The company must deduct basic rate income tax (currently 25%) from interest which it pays (s. 349 ICTA 1988). Deduction is not, however, made where the interest is short interest or where it is yearly interest paid to a bank in the UK. When the company deducts tax it must account to the Revenue for the tax deducted. For example, a company borrows £1,000 at 10% interest from an individual. Each year (assuming tax rates remain the same) it will pay £75 to the lender and £25 to the Revenue.

The deduction of tax by the company is required to assist the Revenue with the collection of tax and does not affect the company's liablity to corporation tax. It does not matter to the company whether it pays interest gross to the lender — e.g., £100 is paid to the lender, or net — £75 to the lender and £25 to the Revenue. Deduction is required where the recipient is another company even though companies do not pay income tax (the recipient company will be able to treat the tax deducted as a part payment of its corporation tax).

5.3.3   Taxation of the recipient

The gross amount of interest received by a debenture-holder is taxed under Schedule D Case III. As we have just seen, the company usually deducts basic rate tax from the payment so that the amount received is a net amount. To calculate the amount of tax payable it is, therefore, first necessary to calculate the gross amount of interest. This is done by multiplying the net amount by 100/75 (e.g., £75 × 100/75 = £100). If the basic rate changes so will the fraction — the '75' really represents 100 minus the basic rate of tax.

The gross amount of interest is investment income in the hands of the recipient and is liable to higher rate tax if the recipient's income is large enough. If the recipient has unused personal reliefs the basic rate tax can be reclaimed to the extent that the reliefs are not set against other income. This means that, from the recipient's point of view, the receipt of dividends (or other distributions) and interest are exactly the same. The saving in tax from paying interest rather than distributing profits is made by the company — interest is usually a charge on the company's income whereas a distribution is not.

5.4 Directors' fees

5.4.1 The decision to pay fees
The consequences of the payment of directors' fees were discussed in Chapter 5 paragraph 6.

5.4.2 Deduction of directors' fees in computing corporation tax
Directors' fees are usually deductible as an expense of the business. This is because they are of a revenue rather than capital nature and are wholly and exclusively incurred for the purposes of the company's trade. If fees are paid which are of an excessive amount, only the part of the payment which is reasonable may be deducted (*Copeman* v *William J. Flood and Sons Ltd* [1941] 1 KB 202). However, the Revenue's practice is to permit deduction of any amount of fees in the case of payments to a full-time working director.

5.4.3 Taxation of directors' fees
A directorship is an office and so the emoluments of the office (i.e., the fees) are taxed under Schedule E. (The relevant taxation rules are considered in more detail in Chapter 16 paragraph 3.) The basic (and, if appropriate, higher) rate tax is collected through the 'pay as you earn' (PAYE) system under s. 203 ICTA 1988. The company, therefore, on making payment, deducts tax at source and pays it over to the Revenue.

5.5 Retained profits

5.5.1 Corporation tax
Profits retained by the company are liable to corporation tax at the rates explained in paragraph 2.2. It does not generally matter why the profits are retained, although sums used for certain types of capital expenditure are eligible for relief under the capital allowance system (see ch. 14—3).

5.5.2 Apportionment of income
Until 31 March 1989 close companies and their shareholders were taxed as if income had been distributed in certain cases where income was retained by the company. The Finance Act 1989 (s. 103) abolished these rules.

5.5.3 Future taxation of retained profits
The only tax liability on retained profits *at the time they are made* is corporation tax. However, such profits will usually be subject to tax at some time in the future. Thus, if those profits are distributed in a later year Schedule F tax will be payable by the recipient shareholders. If the profits are retained for many years they will be reflected in the value of the shares in the company so that CGT and IHT liability on disposal of the shares will be increased (capital tax liability on disposal of shares is considered in Chapter 17).

Furthermore, under s. 703 ICTA 1988 the Revenue has wide powers to charge tax so as to counter tax advantages gained on a transaction involving (among other things) the sale of shares at a profit. The profits accumulated in the company and reflected in the value of shares may be taxed in this way when the shares come to be sold. (Section 707 ICTA 1988 provides a procedure for obtaining 'clearance in advance', i.e., the Revenue will state before the transaction is completed whether they will seek to assess tax under s. 703.)

5.6 Conclusion

It is impossible to come to any very general conclusion as to which type of use of profits is most beneficial because the circumstances of each case are so different. However, the tax efficiency of the various possibilities dealt with above can be illustrated by the following example.

An individual decides to set up a company with £1,000,000 on 6 April 1990 and expects the company to make income profits during the first year of £500,000. He wishes to receive £150,000 p.a. from the company before tax. He is single (so his personal relief is £3,005), he has no other source of income and he has no charges on income. When he forms the company he has a choice of investing the money as share capital or of lending it to the company. If the money is lent to the company 15% interest will be paid. If it is invested as share capital the profits may be retained, paid out as directors' fees or used to pay dividends. (For completeness, the effect of retaining *all* the profits will also be considered.)

5.6.1   *Part of profits of £500,000 used to pay director's fees of £150,000*
   (a)   Corporation tax on £350,000 (since the fees can be deducted as a trading expense)

	£
On first £200,000 @ 25%	50,000
On balance of £150,000 @ 37.5%	56,250
Company's total tax	106,250

   (b)   The proprietor's tax under Schedule E on £150,000

	£	
On first £3,005	nil	(personal relief)
On next £20,700	5,175	(basic rate)
On remaining £126,295 @ 40%	50,518	(higher rate)
Proprietor's tax under Schedule E	55,693	(deducted at source under PAYE system)

5.6.2   Part of profits of £500,000 used to pay 15% interest on £1,000,000 (i.e., £150,000)

(a)   Since the interest payment is a charge on income, the corporation tax position is the same as when director's fees are paid.

(b)   The proprietor's/lender's position is basically the same as when director's fees are paid. (The interest is investment income and so, for example, cannot be used as the basis for calculating pension contributions. The basis on which the tax is assessed will be the Schedule D basis not PAYE, so that basic rate tax will be deducted at source and higher rate tax will be paid on the preceding year basis except in the year of the loan.)

5.6.3   Part of profits of £500,000 used to pay dividend of £112,500 net
   (a)   Corporation tax on £500,000

	£
On first £200,000 @ 25%	50,000
On balance of £300,000 @ 37.5%	112,500
Company's total tax	162,500

Note: dividends are neither a business expense nor a charge on income.

The company now has £337,500 from which it can pay a dividend of £112,500. It will have to pay ⅓ of that sum as ACT. Therefore, ACT is £37,500 (payable within three months of the dividend). This sum is deductible from the MCT liability, so that the MCT will be £162,500 − £37,500 = £125,000 (payable nine months after the end of the accounting period).

(b)   The proprietor's/shareholder's income under Schedule F is £112,500 + £37,500 = £150,000. Tax under Schedule F on £150,000 is £55,693 (since the rates of tax are the same as those applying under Schedule E to the director's fees).

5.6.4.   Whole of profits of £500,000 retained in full
   (a)   Corporation tax on £500,000 = £162,500.
   (b)   The proprietor's tax is nil since he has received no income.

5.6.5   Summary
The position can be summarised as follows:

(1)   *Director's fees*

		£
(a) The company is left with £500,000		
− (150,000 + 106,250)		243,750
(b) The proprietor is left with £150,000		
− £55,693		94,307
		338,057

(2)   *Interest*

		£
(a)	The company is left with £500,000	
	− (150,000 + 106,250)	243,750
(b)	The proprietor is left with £150,000	
	− £55,693	94,307
		338,057

(3)   *Dividends*

		£
(a)	The company is left with £500,000	
	− (112,500 + 162,500)	225,000
(b)	The proprietor is left with	94,307
		319,307

(4)   *Retained profits*

		£
(a)	The company is left with £500,000	
	− £162,500	337,500
(b)	The proprietor is left with	nil
		337,500

It can be seen that the most tax-effective ways of distributing profits appear to be the payment of director's fees or interest. We will now examine the reasons for this.

Whether profit is distributed to the proprietor by way of director's fees or interest, the tax effect is the same for the company. Both payments are deductible; the fees are deductible expenses; the interest is a charge on income.

So far as the proprietor is concerned the only tax distinction between fees and interest is that one is earned income and the other is investment income. This distinction is normally of no significance. (Investment income, unlike earned income, can never be taken into account when assessing pensionable income.)

Distributing profit by way of dividend is less tax-effective for the company than either of the other two methods. Dividends are not deductible expenses nor are they charges on income. So far as the proprietor is concerned, distributions by way of dividend may be less tax-effective than the two previous methods. Where profit is distributed by way of dividend by a company which pays tax at a rate of 35%, the company can only pass on to the shareholder a 25% tax credit (see paragraph 5.2.3 above). In such a case the full benefit of the profit distributed by way of dividend is not received by the shareholder.

A company which retains all its profit will have no deductible director's fees nor interest payments to reduce its taxable profits. The proprietor will have received no income from the company and will therefore have no income tax liability relating to it. There may be commercial reasons for retaining some or all of the profit (e.g., to fund expansion of the business), but a proprietor may not be able to do without substantial receipts from the company. If the proprietor cannot do without such receipts, distributions of cash will *have* to be made. If the proprietor can do without such receipts, the company must decide whether it is tax-effective to retain all of its profit or to distribute some.

In cases where the company's average rate of tax is lower than the taxpayer's, it is preferable to retain profits. In cases where the company's average rate of tax is higher than the taxpayer's it is preferable to distribute, *provided* this can be done by way of director's fees or interest. (As explained above, these payments reduce a company's taxable profit.)

Where profit can only be distributed by way of dividend, an overall tax saving cannot be achieved if the company is paying an average rate in excess of 25% and the taxpayer's rate is also in excess of 25%. In such a case, the taxpayer will get only a 25% tax credit and will have to pay higher rate tax from his own resources, getting no benefit from the company's payment of tax in excess of 25%.

From a tax viewpoint, it can be seen that distributions by way of fees and/or interest are likely to be the most effective.

However, tax considerations alone cannot decide the matter. Other relevant factors to be considered are:

(a)   There may be shareholders who are not directors and who therefore cannot receive directors' fees.

(b)   A company may *have* to borrow money on loan for commercial reasons. Thereafter, it will be obliged to pay interest.

16 Taxation of Employments

1 INTRODUCTION

Of all the rights and duties which arise from the employment relationship there can be little doubt that the consideration which is uppermost in the minds of the parties to any employment contract is financial. Thus the employer wants an employee to work for him to increase the employer's profits and the employee wants to receive wages or salary in exchange for his efforts. Since the government will tax the profits of the employer and the wages or salary of the employee, the taxation provisions which are relevant in this context must be considered.

This chapter will be divided into two parts, dealing with the tax rules firstly from the employer's standpoint and secondly from that of the employee. In the first part we will deal principally with the deductibility of the wages or salary as far as the employer is concerned, and in the second part with the taxation principles applicable to wages, salaries, benefits in kind and termination payments.

2 EMPLOYMENT TAXATION FOR THE EMPLOYER

The employer who is carrying on a trade or profession taxable under Schedule D Cases I or II of the Income Corporation Taxes Act 1988 will want to ensure that any payment of salary, pension or compensation for loss of office or any provision of a benefit in kind entitles him to claim a pre-tax deduction, so as to reduce his taxable profits. It will be remembered from Chapter 14 paragraph 1 that, to be deductible, any expense must satisfy two conditions, namely that the payments must be:

(a) of an income nature as opposed to a capital outlay; thus they must be expenses incurred in actually earning profits rather than outlays to put the payer into a position to earn profits;

(b) incurred wholly and exclusively for the purposes of the trade and must not fall within any of the disallowed deductions listed in s. 74 ICTA 1988.

2.1 Limitation on deductibility

The payments that *are* deductible include the payment of salaries, wages, pensions and even lump sum payments in compensation for loss of the employee's office. However, this is subject to certain qualifications.

2.1.1 'Wholly'
In respect of all such payments, the word 'wholly' in s. 74 relates to quantum, so that excessive payments cannot be deducted. In *Copeman* v *William J. Flood and Sons Ltd* [1941] 1 KB 202, it was decided that where such a payment is held to be excessive, such proportion of the payment as is reasonable in the light of the employee's work can be deducted.

With regard to pensions, the pension paid to an ex-employee is deductible even if it is paid voluntarily by the employer. In practice most employers who provide pensions do so by setting up a fund managed by an insurance company. Contributions paid into the fund by the employer are deductible as business expenses provided that the scheme is a retirement benefit scheme as defined by s. 590 ICTA 1988.

2.1.2 Compensation for loss of office

Lump sum payments for loss of office are deductible provided they satisfy the conditions set out above, even though they may be one-off payments. Thus, in *Mitchell* v *B. W. Noble Ltd* [1927] KB 719, compensation payments made to directors who were liable to dismissal because of their misconduct but who resigned to avoid bad publicity, were held to be deductible on the basis that the retirement was in the interests of the business. Conversely, payments made to former employees to persuade them to enter into restrictive covenants have been held not to be deductible, since the payments were intended to buy off potential competitors and so amounted to a capital payment (*Associated Portland Cement* v *Kerr* (1945) 27 TC 108 (CA)). Such a receipt is taxable in the employee's hands under the provision of s. 313 ICTA 1988 (see paragraph 3.6 below). If the employee is redundant and receives a redundancy payment, s. 579 ICTA 1988 provides that such payments are deductible under Schedule D Cases I and II and are treated as having been paid on the last day on which the business was carried on if made after the discontinuance of the trade, profession or vocation. Although s. 579 only deals with statutory redundancy payments, s. 90 ICTA 1988 allows additional payments to redundant employees (subject to a limit of three times the statutory redundancy payment) to be deductible. This includes payments over and above the employees' statutory entitlement made on the cessation of business in accordance with the power to make payments to employees in these circumstances given by s. 719 CA 1985.

2.1.3 The provision of benefits

Many employers provide their employees with benefits over and above their salary, such as company cars, free meals and so on. The cost of providing such benefits will be deductible if the payments are made wholly and exclusively for the purposes of the trade. Thus if cars are provided for salesmen, the outlay will be deductible, but if they are for private use they will only be deductible if they can be regarded as reasonable remuneration.

2.2 Social security contributions

Although it is beyond the scope of this book to consider the social security legislation in detail, it should be noted that the employer is obliged to make social security contributions in respect of each employee (as well as deducting the contributions of the employee before paying over the net wages). The employer's contributions are deductible in computing the tax liability of the employer.

3   TAXATION OF THE EMPLOYEE

3.1   Introduction

Income arising out of an employment is assessable in accordance with the rules of Schedule E of ICTA 1988. Under this heading we will be considering the taxation of the employees' salaries, pensions, receipts of compensation for loss of office, as well as benefits in kind and the deductibility of expenses. In the discussion which follows we assume that the employee is ordinarily resident and domiciled in the UK and that he performs his duties in the UK. In such circumstances the employee's emoluments are liable to tax under Case I of Schedule E as substituted by s. 36 FA 1989.

3.2   The Schedule E charge

Under s. 19 ICTA 1988 as amended, tax under Schedule E is charged in respect of emoluments from an office or employment as well as pensions and income (such as compensation payments) specifically charged to tax under the schedule. Tax is collected on a receipts year basis. That is to say, the employee pays tax on the emoluments received during the tax year whether or not they are for that year or for some other year. The tax is usually collected by deduction at source under the PAYE scheme.

3.2.1   Office
The word 'office' is not defined in the statutes but Rowlatt J in *Great Western Railway Co* v *Bater* [1920] 3 KB 266, said it meant 'a subsisting, permanent, substantive position which had an existence independent of the person who filled it, which went on and was filled in succession by successive holders', although Lord Wilberforce and Lord Lowry, in *Edwards* v *Clinch* [1981] 3 All ER 543, felt the definition should be refined. Lord Wilberforce accepted 'that a rigid requirement of permanence is no longer appropriate . . . and continuity need not be regarded as an absolute qualification. But still, if any meaning is to be given to "office" in this legislation . . . the word must involve a degree of continuance (not necessarily continuity) and of independent existence: it must connote a post to which a person can be appointed, which he can vacate and to which a successor can be appointed'. Over the years office holders have been held to include directors of UK companies, NHS consultants, bishops, judges and personal representatives.

3.2.2   Employment
'Employment' is equally difficult to define, but Pennycuick V-C said in *Fall* v *Hitchen* [1973] 1 All ER 368, that, 'unless some special limitation is to be put upon the word "employment" in any given context, the expression "contract of service" appears to be coterminous with the expression "employment" '. The case involved a ballet dancer who entered into a contract having the attributes of a contract of service, in that he was paid weekly regardless of whether a performance was given or a rehearsal attended, the 'employer' paid national insurance contributions on the dancer's behalf as if he were an employee and the dancer worked only for the employer. This contract was therefore assessable under Schedule E, even though it had been entered into in the normal course of carrying on his profession of dancer. Conversely, if it can

be shown that the taxpayer's method of earning a livelihood does not consist of obtaining a post and remaining in it (as was the case in *Fall* v *Hitchen*), but consists of engagements and moving from one engagement to another, he is assessed under Schedule D and not Schedule E, provided the engagements are entered into as part of his profession (*Davies* v *Braithwaite* [1931] 2 KB 628).

3.2.3 Emolument
Section 131 of ICTA 1988 defines emoluments as including 'all salaries, fees, wages, perquisites and profits whatsoever'. To be assessable the emoluments must arise out of the office or employment and be in money or convertible into money (although there are special stautory rules dealing with benefits in kind which are dealt with below).

3.3 Taxable receipts by employees

3.3.1 What is taxable?
While an employee who receives salary or wages from his employer is obviously assessable under Schedule E, problems arise if the employee receives a gift, a bonus or a tip, especially if the payment is made by a third party. The receipt will only be taxable if the taxpayer holds an office or employment and the receipt derives from the employment. Thus, to be caught by Schedule E, it must be shown that the employment is the source of the payment and that it was paid in respect of services rendered in the course of the employment. This is still the case even if the payment is made voluntarily or is paid without any legal obligation, e.g., tips in restaurants. If, however, the payment is made because of some reason or quality personal to the recipient, such as a special, one-off payment to someone suffering hardship, it is not taxable under Schedule E, since it is not a reward for services. In this case it is immaterial that the payment would not have been made had the employer/employee relationship not existed. Finally, a pension paid to a former employee (or his dependants) is taxable under Schedule E even if it is voluntary or can be discontinued.

3.3.2 Illustrations
The concept of payments being a reward for services rendered can be illustrated by the case of *Calvert* v *Wainwright* [1974] KB 526, in which the tips received by an employed taxidriver were held to be assessable, since they were clearly referable to the service of transportation to the desired destination. One important point made by Atkinson J in his judgment was that while tips were generally assessable, if the tip was unusually large and paid, for example, once a year at Christmas, that might amount to a personal gift thus escaping income tax.

The receipt which was the subject of *Blakiston* v *Cooper* [1909] AC 104, was held to be assessable even though it might appear at first sight to fall within the 'personal gift' category. The case concerned the traditional Easter offerings to a vicar, which were derived from the Easter Sunday collection. Even though this was a 'once a year' payment, it was held to be assessable. In reaching this conclusion Lord Ashbourne said that, 'it was suggested that the offerings were made as personal gifts to the vicar as marks of esteem and respect. Such reasons no doubt played their part in obtaining and increasing the amount of the offerings but I cannot doubt that they were given to the vicar as vicar and that they formed part of the profits arising by reason of his office.'

A receipt will also be assessable if it amounts to an inducement to greater efforts by the employee, even if the payment arises as a result of the employee's personal skills or qualities. In *Moorhouse* v *Dooland* [1955] Ch 284, a professional cricketer was entitled to receive the proceeds of a collection among the spectators if he scored a certain number of runs or took a certain number of wickets. Such proceeds amounted to a reward for his services and so were taxable under Schedule E.

Conversely, in *Seymour* v *Reed* [1927] AC 554, the gate money from a benefit match to which he had no contractual right received by a retiring county cricket player was held not to be assessable, since it reflected the gratitude of his supporters for the enjoyment he had given them over the years rather than a payment to encourage further exertions in the course of his employment. Similarly, in *IRC* v *Morris* (1967) 44 TC 685, an unexpected, once and for all payment of £1,000 to the chief engineer of a construction project, whose efforts ensured the project was completed on schedule, was not assessable since it was decided that the payment was genuinely made as a mark of his employer's appreciation of his special efforts.

3.3.3   Payments made on employee's behalf
Such payments will be assessable if the employer discharges a debt owed by the employee (*Nicholl* v *Austin* (1935) 19 TC 531).

3.4   Benefits in kind

3.4.1   The general rule
The emoluments on which an employee is assessed to tax may include 'perquisites' as well as salary or wages. (The term 'perquisites' in this context includes assets or benefits provided by the employer.) For such receipts to be assessable emoluments, according to normal tax principles, they must be in the form of money or convertible into money (although it is not necessary that the asset or non-cash benefit *is* actually converted into money). Thus, free meals in a staff canteen fail this convertibility test (and so are tax-free) since the employee cannot sell the meal; the mere fact that it saves the employee money is not enough. However, a cash allowance in lieu of such a benefit attracts a tax charge (*Sanderson* v *Durbridge* (1955) 36 TC 239), as does a benefit which is provided in return for a deduction from the salary of the employee (*Machon* v *McLaughlin* (1926) 11 TC 83 (CA)) even if the deduction is voluntary in the sense that the employee is free to restore his income to its original level in exchange for giving up his right to receive the benefit (*Heaton* v *Bell* [1970] AC 728).

If the benefit is convertible into money, the employee is taxed on the monetary value of the benefit to him at the time it was received. This was held, in *Wilkins* v *Rogerson* [1961] Ch 7 (where suits were provided for employees) to mean that the employee should be assessed on the second-hand value of the benefit. If the emolument is a benefit in the form of money (such as a cash allowance), the cash value of the benefit will be the taxable emolument.

These rules make the provision of benefits in kind (this is to say, benefits in the form of assets or services) very attractive since the employees who receive them will either not be taxed at all on them (because their nature is such that they cannot be converted into cash) or be taxed on the second-hand value of the asset (which in the case of clothes, cars and similar items will be considerably less than the 'new value' of the asset). Therefore, to prevent abuse, various statutory provisions have been introduced (these are considered below). While, strictly speaking, the convertibility test applies to all employees, effectively the test is superseded when the special rules apply (see paragraphs 3.4.2 and 3.4.3 below).

3.4.2 Statutory rules applicable to all employees

(a) *Living accommodation* Under s. 145 ICTA 1988, an employee who occupies premises by reason of his employment is taxed on the greater of the rent paid by his employer or the 'annual value' of the accommodation less the rent actually paid by the employee. 'Annual value' means the market rent that could be obtained for the premises on the assumption that the landlord will bear the costs of repair and insurance (s. 837 ICTA 1988). This tax charge can be avoided if the 'representative occupier' exceptions laid down in s. 145 apply. There is, therefore, no charge if the accommodation is supplied:

(i)   where it is necessary for the proper performance of the employee's duties (such as in the case of resident caretakers or lighthouse keepers);

(ii)   for the better performance of the employee's duties and his is one of the kinds of employment in which it is customary for employers to provide their employees with living accommodation (such as in the case of the police or fire officers);

(iii)   where there is a threat to the employee's security and he resides in the accommodation as part of the security arrangements (such as in the case of the Prime Minister).

Under s. 146 ICTA 1988, employees who receive the benefit of taxable living accommodation which costs more than £75,000 to provide will be treated as receiving an emolument equal to 12% of the excess over the £75,000 limit (less any rent paid in excess of the annual value of the accommodation calculated as above). To discover whether the £75,000 limit has been exceeded, the following steps are taken:

(i)   The expenditure incurred in acquiring the estate or interest and the cost of any improvements to the accommodation incurred before the beginning of the tax year for which the charge is made are aggregated.

(ii)   Any reimbursement for such expenditure or cost paid by the employee and any amount which represents consideration for the grant of the tenancy is deducted.

(b) *Vouchers* Where vouchers, stamps or similar documents are provided, which can be converted into money or goods, the employee is taxed on the cost of providing the voucher, etc., incurred by the employer (s. 141 ICTA 1988). However, by virtue of an Inland Revenue concession, luncheon vouchers are exempt up to 15p per day provided they are not transferable.

3.4.3 The statutory rules applicable to directors and higher-paid employees

3.4.3.1 The persons subject to the rules Where the recipient of a benefit is a 'director or higher-paid employee', certain provisions of ICTA 1988 as amended by FA 1989 apply. Under s. 167 the special rules apply if the taxpayer receiving the benefit is an employee earning £8,500 per annum or more or a director. The term 'director' includes any person in accordance with whose directions or instructions the directors of the company are accustomed to act, and a member, if the company's affairs are managed by the members. However, the rules do not apply to:

(a)   a director without a material interest in the company (i.e., his total shareholding together with that of his family, partners, and trustees of a settlement created by him or a relative, does not exceed 5% of the company's ordinary share capital) who works full-time for the company but earns less than £8,500 per annum; or

(b)   a director of a charity or non-profit making body and again earns less than £8,500 per annum.

3.4.3.2   The special rules

(a)   Expense accounts. Under s. 153 ICTA 1988 if an expense account is provided, the director or employee is taxed on its full amount less any expenses incurred wholly, exclusively and necessarily in the course of his employment (see paragraph 3.7 for the deductibility of expenses). Thus, if, for example, the employee has an expense allowance of £1,000 and he uses only £750 'wholly, exclusively and necessarily in the course of his employment' and the rest for his personal benefit, he adds £250 to his taxable emoluments.

(b)   Benefits given to employees and directors. In the case of other benefits in kind which are given outright to the employee, he is treated as receiving emoluments equal to the 'cash equivalent' of the asset, which means the cost to the employer of providing them less any sums paid by the employee. In *Rendell* v *Went* (1964) 41 TC 641 (HL), the employee was assessed on an amount equal to the legal fees paid by his employer arising out of a criminal case. If the employee is given an asset which has depreciated in value, the cash equivalent is its market value at the time of transfer.

(c)   Benefits lent to employees and directors. If the asset is lent to the director or employee, its cash equivalent is the 'annual value' of the use of the asset, plus any expenses incurred by the employer in providing it, less sums paid by the director or employee, or the rent paid by the employer whichever is greater. The annual value depends on the nature of the asset lent.

(i)   Land. The 'annual value' is the market rent on the assumption that the landlord will repair and insure.

(ii)   Cars. The 'cash equivalent' that is to be added to the employee's emoluments where a car is made available for use by the director or higher-paid employee or their families is determined by sch. 6 ICTA 1988 and s. 21 FA 1990, which sets out the cash equivalents by reference to the car's age, its original market value and the cylinder capacity. The cash equivalents are sufficiently low that in practice an advantage is obtained by the person to whom the car is lent. The cash equivalent can be reduced by one-half if mileage covered necessarily in the performance of duties exceeds 18,000 in each tax year, but it is increased by one-half if either the car is used only for private purposes or the business use does not exceed 2,500 miles in each tax year. Cars taken from a pool do not attract the tax charge. The provision of car fuel attracts a charge to tax subject to certain limitations.

(iii)   All other assets. For all other assets lent, the 'annual value' is 20% of its market value at the time it was first put at the disposal of the director or higher-paid employee.

(d)   Beneficial loan arrangements. Generally, beneficial loans would not be benefits in kind, since they are not convertible into money. However, s. 160 ICTA 1988 provides that if an employer makes an interest-free or cheap loan, the recipient director or employee is taxed on its cash equivalent unless this does not exceed £200 or the loan would qualify for interest relief. The 'cash equivalent' is the difference between the official rate of interest fixed by statutory instrument, and currently standing at 15.5%, and the rate paid by the employee. The tax charge arises if the loan is made to the director's or employee's relatives unless he personally derives no benefit from the loan.

If any loan is written off in whole or in part, the amount released is treated as a taxable emolument. Where the release is made on the termination of the employment, there is a tax charge unless the release is caused by the director's or employee's death. If a director or employee (or his family) acquires undervalued shares, the amount of the undervalue is treated as an interest-free loan. Payments made by the director or higher-paid employee reduce the 'notional loan', but it remains outstanding until either: the full value of the shares is paid, or; the debt is released, or; the shares are disposed of, or; the employee or director dies. If the second or third situation arises, the employee or director is taxed as if the amount equal to the outstanding 'loan' had been released or written off.

(e)   School fees. If the employer pays school fees for the children of an employee, the payment is taxable. This will apply even where the fees are paid by the way of scholarships awarded to the children (s. 165 ICTA 1988).

For the purpose of deciding whether an employee or director is earning over £8,500, it is assumed that the special rules apply, (i.e., that the cost of providing the benefit incurred by the employer is added to the employee's salary). Thus if an employee earning £8,400 is given a suit that cost the employer £250 to buy, the cost to the employer is added to his salary to make his emoluments £8,650 and therefore sufficient to make him a 'higher-paid employee' for all purposes. This will be the case even if the second-hand value of the suit was only £50. Furthermore, although the special rules only apply to benefits provided for the director or employee by reason of his employment, s. 168 ICTA 1988 prevents the tax charge being avoided by giving the benefit to the director's or employee's family.

3.5   Terminal payments

3.5.1   General principles
The mere fact that the payment is made on the termination of the contract (or the alteration of its terms) does not preclude its taxation under the rules of Schedule E, if it is 'something in the nature of a reward for services, past, present or future' (per Upjohn J in *Hochstrasser* v *Mayes* [1959] Ch 22). As a result of this, sums paid in accordance with the terms of the employment contract will be taxable since they will represent deferred or advance remuneration (*Dale* v *De Soissons* [1950] 2 All ER 460). Thus if an employee is to be paid £10,000 per year for 10 years but under the contract is to receive a lump sum of £50,000 on either the commencement or termination of the term, the sum is fully taxable under Schedule E (see *Williams* v *Simmonds* [1981] STC 715). Similarly, sums paid to an employee to induce him to withhold his resignation or to work for a lesser salary are assessable, since they represent a reward for future services. However, to fall in this category the payment must represent a reward for services, so that if its purpose is to induce the employee to accept a reduced pension, it is not taxable (*Tilley* v *Wales* [1943] AC 386).

3.5.2   *'Golden handshakes'*

A lump sum payment made to compensate the employee for an early termination of the contract by the employer (sometimes called a 'golden handshake') is not assessable under the general principles. However, it may be taxable under s. 148 ICTA 1988. This taxes a payment on retirement or removal from office or employment that is not otherwise chargeable to tax (under the general principles), 'which is made, whether in pursuance of any legal obligation or not, either directly or indirectly in consideration or in consequence of, or otherwise in connection with, the termination of the holding of the office or employment or any change in its functions or emoluments, including any payment in commutation of annual or periodical payments [such as pensions] (whether chargeable to tax or not) which would otherwise have been made'. The assessment can be made on the personal representatives of a dead taxpayer and payments to a member of the taxpayer's family are also assessable under this section.

Section 148 does not apply if:

(a)   the terminal payment is paid on the death, injury or disability of the holder of the office or employment (s. 188(1)(a));

(b)   the sum falls to be taxed under s. 313 (see paragraph 3.6 below) (s. 188(1)(b));

(c)   the payment does not exceed £30,000 (s. 188(4)). However, any excess over this figure is taxable and the subsection prevents the tax charge being avoided by paying the terminal payments in instalments.

If a terminal payment exceeds the £30,000 limit, the excess is taxable in the year of receipt as earned income.

3.6   Restrictive covenant payments

If an employee receives a payment in consideration of entering into a restrictive covenant, this is regarded as being a capital outlay by the employer (see *Associated Portland Cement* v *Kerr*, paragraph 2.1.2). As such, it should be a capital receipt in the hands of the employee and so not taxable as part of the employee's income. However, s. 313 ICTA 1988 levies tax on such payments. Even though no tax is deducted by the employer, the section requires the employee to gross up the receipt at basic rate and pay tax at the excess rate only. The employee thus pays 15% tax on the grossed up amount if he is a higher rate taxpayer.

3.7   Expenses

(a)   *The test of deductibility (s. 198 ICTA 1988)*   If an employee incurs expenses, they will only be deductible if they are incurred wholly, exclusively and necessarily in the actual performance of his duties. This is narrower than the expenses rule for Schedule D Case I or II taxpayers. Two separate requirements can be extracted. These rules are of limited practical importance since an employee is usually indemnified by his employer for any such expenses which he incurs.

(i)   *Incurred in the performance of duties*   Firstly, the expense must be incurred in the performance of the duties of the office or employment and an expense incurred merely to enable the employee to perform his duties more efficiently will not satisfy this requirement (even where the employee's contract requires him to incur the expense). In *Brown* v *Bullock* (1961) 40 TC 1, Donovan LJ summarised the position by saying: 'The test is not whether the employer imposes the expense but whether the duties do, in the sense that, irrespective of what the employer may prescribe, the duties cannot be performed without incurring the particular outlay.'

(ii) *The expense must be 'necessary'* The second requirement which must be satisfied is that the expense has to be necessary, in so far as the nature of the job itself must be such that it cannot be done without the outlay. If the employee can show the expense is 'necessary' it does not give him a right to claim an unlimited deduction, since not only must the expense be necessary but also the amount of the expense must be no more than is necessary to perform the duties (any excess would not be deductible).

(b) *Travelling expenses* Section 198 provides that the expenses of travelling in the performance of the duties of the office or employment are deductible from the emoluments, provided the employee is necessarily obliged to pay those expenses from his emoluments. The effect of this is that while expenses incurred when travelling on business are deductible (such as travelling from the employer's head office to a sub-office), the expense of travelling from home to the place where the employee is employed is not.

(c) *Subscriptions and business entertainment* While subscriptions to professional societies are not generally deductible, s. 201 ICTA 1988 permits subscriptions to certain professional bodies, including those of architects, dentists, solicitors, and veterinary surgeons, to be deductible even though they are not 'necessary'.

3.8 Social security contributions

The contributions deducted by the employer from the employee's salary (see paragraph 2.2 above) are not deductible when calculating the employee's tax liability. Employees' contributions are greater than those levied on the self-employed but, in compensation, the benefits available to employees are greater than those available to the self-employed. (The details of the benefits are beyond the scope of this book.)

Part IV Restructuring Business and Retirement

17   Disposal of Interest in a Company

1   INTRODUCTION

In this chapter we will consider the various ways in which a shareholder in a company may dispose of his interest in the company either during his lifetime or on death. On disposal of shares tax will often become payable, although there are a number of reliefs available which will be considered later in the chapter. A disposal of shares by a substantial shareholder will alter the control of the company, so that the disposal may affect the rights of the remaining shareholders in the company. The interests of the incoming shareholder and the remaining shareholders have to be balanced against each other, and arrangements for achieving a balance between those interests have to be anticipated and made in advance (usually by drafting suitable articles when the company is formed). It is, therefore, essential that potential problems should be foreseen and suitable arrangements made for the particular circumstances of each company.

2   TRANSFER OF SHARES

2.1   Procedure on transfer

A transfer of shares may be made by means of a sale or a gift *inter vivos*. The death or bankruptcy of a shareholder gives rise to an automatic transmission of shares (which will be followed by a transfer) and the special rules for transmission are dealt with later in the chapter.

A shareholder who wishes to sell his shares may make a contract in any form that he wishes. The contract for sale is sufficient to give the purchaser an equitable interest in the shares. As between vendor and purchaser, the vendor will be liable to account to the purchaser for any dividends received and to vote as directed by the purchaser. However, as we saw in Chapter 4 paragraph 1, membership of the company does not begin until the purchaser is registered as a member in the register of members which the company is required to keep. An entry cannot be made in the register of members until the company has received an instrument of transfer; this is because of s. 183(1) and (2) CA 1985, which says, '. . . it is not lawful for a company to register a transfer of shares in . . . the company unless a proper instrument of transfer has been delivered to it'. The reason for this rule is that stamp duty is payable on a transfer of shares, so the law requires an instrument on which the duty can be charged.

Section 1 of the Stock Transfer Act 1963 provides that a transfer of fully paid shares may be made on a stock transfer form under hand executed by the transferor only and specifying (in addition to the particulars of the consideration, of the description of the number or amount of the securities, and of the person by whom the transfer is made) the full name and address of the transferee. The stock transfer form referred to in the Act is set out in sch. 1 and is a 'proper instrument of transfer' for the purposes of s. 183(1) and (2) CA 1985.

If the shares are not fully paid the Stock Transfer Act does not apply, so that the form of transfer will be whatever is required by the articles (which may require the use of a deed and may require execution by the transferee as well as the transferor).

Once the sale of the shares has been agreed the vendor should execute a stock transfer form (or other proper instrument) and send it together with the share certificate to the purchaser, who pays the stamp duty (1% without any exemption for transfers under £30,000). The purchaser then applies to the company for registration by sending the stamped transfer and share certificate to the company. The transfer must be registered within two months of the application unless the directors have power to refuse registration, and the company must send the purchaser a share certificate within the same period (s. 185 CA 1985). The procedure explained above applies on a gift of shares as well as on a sale (save that no *ad valorem* stamp duty is payable).

A slightly more complicated procedure applies where part of a holding is sold or given away (or where there are two transferees). In such cases the transferor sends his share certificate to the company together with the transfer. The company secretary marks the transfer 'certificate lodged', retains the certificate and returns the transfer. This is then handed to the transferee who pays the stamp duty and then returns the transfer to the company for registration.

2.2   Restrictions on right to transfer

Unless the articles provide to the contrary every shareholder has a *right* to transfer his shares (which in effect means that the transferee has a right to be registered). However, the articles of the company can impose a restriction on the right to transfer shares. In the case of private companies a restriction is extremely common. A restriction is often thought to be desirable since it enables the company (usually through the directors) to refuse to allow unsuitable outsiders to join the company. Article 24 of Table A provides as follows:

> The directors may refuse to register the transfer of a share which is not fully paid to a person of whom they do not approve and they may refuse to register the transfer of a share on which the company has a lien. They may also refuse to register a transfer unless:
>
>   (a)   it is lodged at the registered office or at such other place as the directors may appoint and is accompanied by the certificate for the shares to which it relates and such other evidence as the directors may reasonably require to show the right of the transferor make the transfer;
>   (b)   it is in respect of only one class of shares; and
>   (c)   it is in favour of not more than four transferees.

Thus, the directors can refuse to register the transfer of partly paid shares or fully paid shares over which the company has a lien (however, where Table A applies unamended, there is only a lien for calls on partly paid shares) and fully paid shares (whether or not the company has a lien over the shares) unless the requirements set out in (a), (b) and (c) above are complied with.

The person responsible for drafting the articles of a company should consult his clients to see what restrictions, if any, they require.

Where there are restrictions on the right to transfer shares, the company must decide within two months of application for registration, whether or not to permit the transfer. If within that time the company has not given notice of refusal of registration to the transferee, the company and its officers who are in default are liable to a fine (s. 183(5) and (6) CA 1985) and the transferee becomes *entitled* to be registered.

It is not possible to consider all the possible types of restriction on the right to register but some of the more common restrictions will now be considered.

The directors may, in their absolute discretion and without assigning any reason therefore, decline to register any transfer of any share, whether or not it is a fully paid share.

At one time a company could not be a private company unless there was a restriction, in its articles, on the right to transfer shares. (This requirement was removed by CA 1980, now consolidated in CA 1985.) The inclusion of this particular restriction in Table A before the enactment of the Companies Act 1980 means that it is very common (the number of companies with this provision in their articles is probably very high). As with most restrictions on transfer it is the directors who have power to refuse registration. The power is a negative one, that is, the directors have power to *refuse* registration — their positive approval is not required. This may seem an unimportant distinction but it means that a resolution of the directors is required to refuse registration, and since a resolution requires a majority in favour, an equality of votes will not be sufficient (unless, of course, the chairman has a casting vote and is against registration). This should be borne in mind in the case of 'two-man' companies, since either director will be able to ensure a transfer of his own shares merely by voting against the resolution to refuse registration. The directors' power to refuse registration must be exercised in good faith but it is very difficult to prove bad faith. The directors do not need to give reasons for refusal even if the article does not specifically excuse them from doing so.

It should be noted that this restriction is a restriction on the right to transfer shares, it is not a restriction on the right to sell them. If shares are sold but the purchaser is not registered, the vendor will hold the shares on trust for the purchaser. The purchaser will not be able to sue the vendor for damages (or his money back) unless the vendor guaranteed that registration would take place.

The directors may decline to register a transfer of any share in favour of a person of whom they disapprove or of a share over which the company has a lien.

This restriction gives the directors two grounds for refusing registration. If required to do so, the directors must say on which ground they rely but need not give reasons justifying their decision. However, if they specified refusal on the grounds of a lien and there was no lien over the shares, the transferee would be able to insist on registration. If, however, the directors specified disapproval of the transferee the latter would find it impossible in most cases to establish that they did not disapprove of him. If the directors choose to give reasons justifying their decision the court will enquire into them to see if they are cogent reasons for refusal.

*The directors may decline to register a transfer of any share except a transfer to [a
member of the company or to a member of the family of the transferor].*

This type of restriction may be appropriate to restrict a shareholder in his right to
bring in outsiders against the wishes of other members of the company; it leaves him
free to transfer to insiders or his own family. The words in square brackets could be
adapted to include various other groups of permitted transferees, e.g., named
persons or employees of the company. The term 'family' must, of course, be defined
by the articles.

2.3   Pre-emption rights

The object of restrictions on the right to transfer shares is to keep a private company
private. However, the restrictions referred to above are not entirely sufficient for
that purpose since they are merely restrictions on *transfer* and do not prevent sale or
gift of the equitable title to the shares. If it is decided that the company should be kept
completely private, the articles should, therefore, include pre-emption rights. The
usual provision is that a member who wishes to transfer shares must first offer them
to the existing members of the company. In drafting an article providing for pre-
emption rights the following points should be considered:

(a)   Should the transferring member be free to transfer to any existing member of
the company or should he be obliged to offer his shares to the existing members in
proportion to their present holdings?
(b)   Should the transferring member be obliged to transfer part of his holding to
the existing members if they do not wish to take all the shares which he proposes to
transfer?
(c)   Should any exceptions be made to the pre-emption rights? For example, the
articles may provide that the pre-emption rights do not apply on a transfer to a
member's family as defined by the article.
(d)   How is the price payable to be fixed? It is quite common for the price to be
fixed by agreement or by the auditors if no price can be agreed between vendor and
purchaser.
(e)   How long are the other members to be given to make up their minds? A
period should be specified for the avoidance of doubt.
(f)   How is the transferring member to give notice of his intention to sell? It is
quite common for the article to require notice to be given to the company. The
secretary will then inform the other members of the offer.

A pre-emption right is a right given to the other members of the company. It is also
possible for the articles to provide that a member who wishes to transfer shares shall
have a right to *require* the other members to buy his shares (an example of this type of
right was given in ch. 8—3.2, *Rayfield* v *Hands* [1960] Ch 1).

3   TRANSMISSION BY OPERATION OF LAW

When a member of a company dies his shares vest automatically in his personal
representative, who is entitled to any dividend paid by the company but may not vote

at general meetings. The personal representative does not, however, automatically become a member of the company since membership begins only with an entry in the register of members. A personal representative will have to prove his title to the shares, by production of the grant of representation. Having done so, the personal representative has two courses of action open to him. Firstly, he can apply, by means of a letter of request, for registration by the company as a member (the entry in the register of members will not refer to his representative capacity). If the personal representative is registered as a member, a subsequent transfer to a beneficiary will require a stock transfer form to be completed. Secondly, and alternatively, if the personal representative wishes to sell the shares so as to raise cash for the purposes of the deceased's estate or when he wishes to vest the shares in the deceased's beneficiary, he can do so without himself being registered, by means of a stock transfer form. The articles of the company will usually contain a provision (such as Table A art. 30) permitting the personal representative to be registered as a member.

A restriction on the right to transfer shares does not apply to a transmission on death unless the articles specifically so provide. Although art. 30 of Table A provides that restrictions on the right to registration apply to a personal representative as well as to a transferee, the effect of this article is that the restrictions will be applied only when the directors receive a notice of a transfer (this may be delivered months after the death). If there are pre-emption rights in the articles these should be extended to transmission on death as well as to transfers.

Transmission by operation of law also takes place when a member becomes bankrupt or (if another company) goes into liquidation. The provisions applying to such circumstances are similar to those applying on the death of a member.

4 FINANCIAL INVOLVEMENT BY THE COMPANY

As we have already seen, a company can issue redeemable shares or buy its own shares in certain circumstances (ch. 5— 3.3). If the company buys its own shares it must normally do so out of profits, although purchase out of capital is permitted provided: a special resolution is passed; the directors can certify that the company will be solvent after the purchase and will be able to continue in business for a year; and the creditors do not successfully apply to the court for cancellation (see ch. 5— 3.3).

Sections 151-158 of CA 1985 contain provisions whereby a company can give financial assistance in specified circumstances for the purchase of its own shares without itself buying those shares. The object of this legislation is to facilitate 'management buy-outs', that is, to enable the persons who run the company's business to buy out substantial shareholders (particularly controlling shareholders) who want to dispose of their interests. This is thought to be desirable because in the past, as a result of the fact that financial assistance from the company was not then lawful, companies often had to be put into liquidation when a controlling shareholder wanted to get out of the business and no one concerned with the company had the money to buy him out. The legislation is not limited to cases of management buy-out. The provisions are complex and in some respects obscure.

Section 151(1) of CA 1985 makes financial assistance, direct or indirect, by a company for the acquisition of its own shares prima facie unlawful. Section 151(2) makes it prima facie unlawful for the company to give financial assistance, direct or indirect, for the purpose of reducing or discharging a liability incurred by any person in acquiring the company's shares. Both subsections apply to 'indirect' as well as direct assistance. It is, therefore, prima facie unlawful for a company to guarantee a loan made by a third party (e.g., a bank) to enable someone to buy shares in the company or to guarantee such a loan after the shares have been purchased. A gift is also treated as financial assistance for these purposes and so is any other transaction whereby the assets of the company are reduced (s. 152(1)(a)).

Section 153(1) contains the first exception to the prohibitions referred to above. It applies to all companies, public and private, and says that a company is not prohibited from giving assistance 'for the purpose of an acquisition of shares in it . . .' if:

(a)   the company's principal purpose in giving the assistance is not to give it for the purpose of any such acquisition, or the giving of the assistance for that purpose is but an incidental part of some larger purpose of the company; and

(b)   the assistance is given in good faith in the interests of the company.

This seems somewhat vague and it is not possible to say with any degree of certainty what type of transaction is permitted by it. Section 153(2) contains similar provisions in relation to assistance given after acquisition of shares. Section 153(4) allows financial assistance to be given by the company in connection with acquisition of shares by employees' shares schemes, or by employees (but not directors), and by money-lending companies in the ordinary course of business.

Section 155 CA 1985 contains the second exception to the prohibitions and gives private companies wide powers to give financial assistance for the purchase of their own shares (or for the reduction or discharge of liabilities incurred on purchase). The main requirement of the section is that the assistance must not reduce the net assets of the company or, if it does reduce them, must be provided out of profits available for dividend (s. 155(2)). Financial assistance by way of a loan would not normally reduce net assets since the reduction in assets (cash) caused by the lending would be balanced by the debt owed to the company by the borrower. Financial assistance by way of gift would, of course, reduce net assets.

Before financial assistance can be given under s. 155 a special resolution must be passed approving the assistance (s. 155(4)), and the directors must make a statutory declaration setting out the nature of the assistance and stating the directors' opinion that the company is solvent and will remain so for at least twelve months. The directors' opinion must be confirmed by the auditors in a report annexed to the statutory declaration.

Under s. 157 CA 1985 the special resolution must be passed within a week of the statutory declaration and 10% of the shareholders may apply to the court for cancellation of the resolution within 28 days. The company must send copies of the special resolution, statutory declaration and auditors' report to the Registrar of Companies.

The financial assistance approved by the special resolution must not be given until four weeks after the resolution (or until the court approves it if an application for cancellation is made), and must not be given more than eight weeks after the directors make the statutory declaration.

5 TAX CONSEQUENCES WHERE A COMPANY BUYS ITS OWN SHARES

Where a company redeems, repays or buys its own shares under the provisions referred to in Chapter 5, paragraph 3.3, tax will usually become payable. The amount received from the company is in some cases treated as a dividend (and so is subject to income tax) to the extent that it exceeds the original investment in the company. However, s. 219 ICTA 1988 contains provisions excluding such a payment from the definition of a distribution in certain circumstances. Where the payment is so excluded capital gains tax will be payable on any increase in value of the shares during the period of ownership (the redemption or repayment is treated as a disposal for CGT purposes as if it were a sale).

A redemption, repayment or purchase by the company is excluded from the definition of a distribution if the company is a trading company and the transaction is made 'wholly or mainly for the purposes of benefiting a trade carried on by the company'. Presumably the transaction would be made for such a purpose if the object of it was to enable a shareholder of the company who disagreed with the policy of the directors to retire from the business or if the company had more capital than it required. A transaction designed to enable the proprietors to take an income tax-free profit would not be covered, and this is reinforced by the further requirement that the main purpose or one of the main purposes of the scheme must not be 'to enable the owner of the shares to participate in the profits of the company without receiving a dividend, or the avoidance of tax'. A redemption, repayment or purchase is also excluded from the definition of a distribution if the proceeds are intended to be used (and are used within two years) for the payment of IHT. The IHT must have arisen on a death and the shareholder must show that undue hardship would have arisen if the shares had not been purchased by the company.

In addition to the basic requirements of s. 219, income tax is only avoided if the following conditions are satisfied:

   (a)   that the owner of the shares is resident and ordinarily resident in the UK at the time of purchase;
   (b)   that he has owned the shares for five years;
   (c)   that the sale is of a substantial part of his shareholding taking into account any holding of his associates (which term includes close relatives, partners and trustees of certain settlements);
   (d)   certain special conditions which apply only in the case of groups of companies.

The object of these rules is to ensure that tax avoidance or tax advantages cannot be obtained by a purchase of its own shares by a company, but that 'genuine' transactions should give rise to CGT liability only. It is possible to apply for advance clearance when a scheme to buy back shares is proposed which, if granted, will ensure that putting the proposal into effect will not give rise to an income tax charge.

Payments to buy back members' shares are not deductible in calculating the company's profits for corporation tax purposes.

6 TAX CONSEQUENCES OF SALE OF SHARES

6.1 Capital gains tax

A capital profit on the sale of shares may be liable to income tax under s. 703 ICTA 1988 (see ch. 20—1.6) or where the sale is to the company in which the shares are held (see paragraph 5 above). In other cases the tax liability, if any, will be a liability to capital gains tax. CGT is payable on the 'chargeable gain', that is, broadly speaking, the difference between the sale price of the shares and the purchase price, account being taken of incidental costs of acquisition (including stamp duty) and of disposal. It should be remembered that there is no CGT on the first £5,000 worth of gains during each tax year (6 April-5 April).

In calculating the chargeable gain on a disposal a reduction is available to take account of inflation. The reduction is calculated by reference to the increase in the retail price index from March 1982 or from the end of the month of acquisition, whichever is the later. Inflation before March 1982 is not taken into account. The relevant allowable expenditure (that is, the purchase price and incidental costs of purchase) is increased in proportion to the increase in the retail price index for the period since March 1982 or the month of acquisition.

By way of alternative, the allowance can be calculated by reference to the market value of the asset as at 31 March 1982 where the asset was held on 31 March 1982 by the person making the disposal (rather than by reference to the historic acquisition cost). The claim for this treatment must be made within two years of the end of the tax year in which the disposal was made. The claim for an indexation allowance may have the effect of creating an allowable loss where otherwise a chargeable gain would have arisen or of increasing the size of an allowable loss.

For example: shares are purchased for £10,000 (including incidental costs) on 1 January 1980 and are sold for £15,000 on 1 January 1986 (there are no incidental costs of disposal). Relevant allowable expenditure is therefore £10,000; the indexation allowance is calculated by multiplying this figure by a decimal (calculated to three places) resulting from the formula $(RD - RI) \div RI$ where RD is the retail price index at the time of disposal and R1 is the retail price index for March 1982 (or twelve months after acquisition). Thus, if the retail price index is 340 in January 1986 and 320 in March 1982:

$$(340 - 320) \div 320 = 0.063$$

$$£10,000 \times 0.063 = £630$$

This figure is then deducted from the gain of £5,000 so that the chargeable gain is £4,370. If the shares had been worth £12,000 on 31 March 1982, the allowance could have been calculated (at the disposer's election) by reference to that figure rather than the historic acquisition cost of £10,000.

Calculating the indexation allowance is more complicated where the taxpayer owns shares in a particular company acquired on different occasions and only part of the holding is disposed of.

6.2 Tax relief for the purchase of shares

The purchase of shares in a company is a capital transaction so that income tax relief is not available on the purchase price. However, if money is borrowed so as to buy an interest in a company the interest paid on the loan may be treated as a charge on income under ss. 360ff. ICTA 1988. The relief is only available if, at the time when the interest is paid as well as when the loan is made, the company is a close company (as are almost all private companies), and a trading company. The borrower must also have either a material interest in the company (i.e., he must own at least 5% of the ordinary share capital) or he must own *some* ordinary share capital and work for the greater part of his time in the actual management of the company. If, and to the extent that the company repays capital, the loan is treated as if it has been repaid in the same proportion as the repayment of capital bears to the share capital of the company, the shareholder then loses the right to deduct that proportionate part of the interest.

7 TAX CONSEQUENCES OF A GIFT OF SHARES

7.1 CGT and IHT general principles

A gift of shares may give rise to both CGT and IHT. The CGT is calculated in exactly the same way as on a sale except that market value is substituted for the sale price. IHT is chargeable on the 'loss to the donor's estate'. This normally means the market value of the asset given away but in some cases the loss is considerably more than market value. For example, if a controlling shareholder gives away enough shares to lose control of the company the loss to his estate will be very much more than the value of the shares given away.

A gift of shares by an individual to an individual, to an accumulation and maintenance settlement or to a settlement with an interest in possession (usually a life interest) is a potentially exempt transfer (PET) and does not give rise to any immediate payment of tax. However, where the donor dies within seven years of making the gift, the transfer becomes chargeable. IHT is therefore chargeable on inter vivos gifts only when they do not fall within the definition of a PET or where the donor dies within seven years.

Where tax is payable in respect of a chargeable transfer it may be paid by the donor or the donee. On a lifetime transfer the rate is half the rate on death. Where the tax is paid by the donor 'grossing up' is required. This is because the loss to the donor's estate is not only the loss resulting from the gift of the shares but also the loss resulting from the payment of tax. For example, if shares worth £132,000 are given away (assuming no previous chargeable transfers have been made and that no exemptions are available), the loss to the donor's estate will be £133,000 — the IHT being £1,000 which is the tax on £133,000. (Currently on a lifetime gift the first £128,000 is free of tax and, thereafter, the tax at half the death rate is 20%.)

If the tax is paid by the donee, grossing up is not required, so that tax on a gift of £132,000 would be £800 (20% of the excess over £128,000). However, payment of tax by the donee reduces the effective value of the gift to him and leaves the donor with more property to give away in the future, so that the difference between the two methods of collecting tax is not as great as it may seem (see also the instalment option, below).

If the donor dies within seven years of making a chargeable transfer, then tax at the death rate in force at the date of death will have to be paid (credit being given for any tax already paid). If the donor dies within seven years of making a PET, the PET now becomes chargeable at the death rate. In both cases the primary liability to pay rests on the donee; the donor's estate can be required to pay if the donee does not pay within 12 months after the death. Where the donor dies more than three years after the gift, the tax payable is reduced by tapering relief: 80% of the tax is payable if death is more than three but not more than four years after the death; 60% if more than four but not more than five; 40% if more than five but not more than six; and 20% if more than six but not more than seven). Tapering relief cannot give rise to a repayment of tax already paid at the lifetime rate.

Gifts of interests in businesses, including gifts of shares, are treated favourably for tax purposes compared with other gifts. This is because the government recognises that too high a tax burden on disposal of business interests would lead in many cases to the break-up of businesses as being the only way of raising funds to pay the tax. The various reliefs available specifically for business interests will be referred to in the following paragraphs. It should be remembered, however, that certain reliefs are available in relation to gifts of property of *any* description, including business property. These are:

(a)   the CGT relief of £5,000 per annum and the indexation allowance referred to above;

(b)   the annual IHT exemption of £3,000;

(c)   the IHT exemptions for small gifts (up to £250 per donee);

(d)   the IHT marriage exemption;

(e)   the IHT spouse exemption (which exempts gifts to the donor's spouse completely) and the CGT spouse exemption (by which the donee spouse acquires the property at the donor spouse's base value which effectively postpones the payment of tax until the donee spouse disposes of the property);

(f)   the IHT nil rate band (under which the first £128,000 worth of transfers not otherwise exempt are free of tax although, unlike the exemptions referred to above, such transfers are taken into account in assessing liability on later transfers within seven years of the gift).

7.2   IHT business property relief

Business property relief is available on a gift of shares inter vivos as well as on death. If the donor taxpayer gives away some or all of the shares which gave him control of the company immediately before the transfer, he is entitled to 50% relief and if he gives away other unquoted shares (all shares in private companies are unquoted), he is entitled to 30% relief (ss. 104 ff. IHTA 1984). The shares must have been owned for two years before the transfer otherwise the relief is lost.

The relief takes the form of a reduction of 50% or 30% of the *value* of the shares for tax purposes. The saving of *tax* can, however, be much more than 50% or 30% since the reduction of the value has the effect of saving tax at the highest rates which would otherwise be payable. For example, an inter vivos gift of £200,000 (assuming no previous transfers of value and no other reliefs) is liable to tax of £14,400 (if the tax is paid by the donee and without taking into account CGT). If the 50% relief is available the loss to the donor's estate is treated as £100,000 and the tax is nil.

'Control' for the purposes of this provision means 'control of powers of voting *on all questions* affecting the company as a whole which if exercised would yield a majority of votes capable of being exercised thereon'. A power to exercise control on one particular issue is *not* sufficient. Because of the related property rules, if a husband and wife both own shares in a company and together control it they are each treated as being in control. Similarly, a shareholder may also take into account shares held by trustees of a settlement, the income of which is payable to him, in assessing whether he has control.

7.3 IHT instalment option (ss. 227-229 IHTA 1984)

If the donee pays the tax, *but not if the donor pays it,* the tax may be paid over 10 years by yearly instalments if the taxpayer so elects. This facility applies to a gift of shares giving the transferor control of the company. It also applies to a gift of unquoted shares not giving control provided that:

(a)   the tax could not be paid without undue hardship on the assumption that the donee keeps the shares; or
(b)   the shares are worth more than £20,000 and are at least 10% of all the shares or of the ordinary shares in the company.

'Control' has the same meaning as for the purposes of the business property relief (see paragraph 7.2 above).

When payment by instalments is permitted, the first instalment is generally due six months after the end of the month in which the gift was made. No interest is charged on the tax provided the instalments are paid on time. If the shares are sold during the instalment period all the tax becomes payable immediately.

Although the instalment option does not reduce the amount of tax, the relief is nevertheless very beneficial. The donee will often be able to pay the tax out of income derived from the company if necessary.

7.4 Hold-over relief (CGT) (s. 79 FA 1980)

A *gift* (but not a sale) of shares by one individual to another individual is eligible for hold-over relief. This relief only applies if both donor and donee make a claim for the relief. If a claim is made for relief, the donor's gain is not taxed but the donee is deemed to acquire the asset for its market value, less the amount of the gain. This means that the donee is potentially liable to pay tax on the donor's gain when he comes to dispose of the asset as well as on his own gain. For example, A buys shares for £10,000 and gives them to B when they are worth £15,000. If no hold-over relief is claimed a gain of £5,000 is chargeable (unless A has any exemptions). If hold-over relief is claimed, B is deemed to acquire the asset for £10,000 so if he sells later for £20,000 he must pay tax on £10,000. The donee may, in fact, never have to pay tax on the gain, because he may be eligible for exemption on his later disposal (for example, if he dies owning the shares, no tax will be payable as there is no CGT on death; if he gives the shares away he and his donee may also claim hold-over relief).

If hold-over relief is claimed the whole gain must be held over (so that the donor will 'lose' his annual exemption unless he makes other disposals during the year). However, where the donor is eligible for retirement relief (see paragraph 8 below), only the part of the gain which exceeds the retirement relief has to be held over.

8   CGT RETIREMENT RELIEF

Sections 69 and 70 of and sch. 20 to FA 1985 provide a limited relief from CGT on the disposal, on or after 6 April 1985, of certain business assets. (In the case of disposals made before that date relief is available in a slightly different form.) The relief is available to two categories of individual:

(a)   an individual at age 60; and
(b)   an individual who has not reached 60 if that person has retired on the grounds of ill-health. (In this case, a claim for the relief must be made within two years of the disposal and be supported by medical evidence that the individual is no longer capable of undertaking the kind of work he was doing and that he is unlikely to be able to resume such work.)

There is no requirement that the disposal should be made at the time of the retirement. The relief is not limited to disposals by way of sale or gift. It is also available in respect of the proceeds of an insurance policy or a compensation payment.

Full relief is given on the first £125,000 of gains and 50% relief on gains between £125,000 and £500,000. To qualify for the relief certain conditions (in addition to the requirements that the individual is aged 60 or has retired due to ill-health) must be satisfied. The conditions to be satisfied on a disposal of shares are that:

(a)   The company is a trading company or the holding company of a trading group.
(b)   The company is the transferor's family company (that is, he owns 25% of the voting rights or he owns 5% and he and his family together own more than 50%). ('Family' means the transferor's spouse, brother, sister, ancestor and lineal descendant as well as brother, sister, ancestor and lineal descendant of the transferor's spouse.)
(c)   The transferor is a full-time working director of the company (but see below for the provisions dealing with part-time directors).

To be entitled to the relief at all, the individual must be able to show that these conditions have been satisfied throughout a period of at least one year prior to the disposal. Normally, this period of one year must end with the date of the disposal. However, in certain cases, relief is still available provided the conditions are satisfied by reference to a period ending on an earlier date. Thus, for example, a full-time director who decides to devote less of his time to the company can still claim the relief on a subsequent disposal of his shares if all the conditions set out above (including the requirement that he be aged 60 or be retiring by reasons of ill-health) were satisfied at the time he ceased to work full-time. However, having gone part-time, he can only preserve his right to the relief if he remains a director of the company and devotes at least 10 hours per week to the service of the company in a technical or managerial capacity throughout the period starting with the date he ceases to work full-time and ending with the date of the disposal. There is no limit on the length of time the director can work part-time.

(There are no conditions corresponding to those relating to the transferor being a full- or part-time director of a family trading company or holding company of a trading company (referred to above) where the transferor is disposing of an interest in an unincorporated business, although the other conditions apply equally. Retirement relief on such a disposal is considered in ch. 18 paragraph 3.3.)

The maximum relief is given if all the conditions were satisfied for 10 years preceding the disposal; if satisfied for between 1 and 10 years, the relief is on a sliding scale from 10% to 100%; no relief is available if the conditions were satisfied for less than one year. Thus, if the transferor has satisfied the conditions for seven years and is aged 60 (or more), only 70% of the maximum relief is available; he will therefore be entitled to full relief on 70% of £125,000 and 50% relief on 70% of £375,000 (this being the difference between £125,000 and £500,000).

The amount of the relief is a deduction from the gain realised on the disposal of the shares. However, the relief cannot be used to create a loss and if there is an actual loss, the relief is ignored.

The relief is only given in relation to 'chargeable business assets'. In the case of a disposal of shares it is, therefore, necessary to calculate how much of the gain reflects chargeable business assets of the company (or of the whole trading group where shares in a holding company are being disposed of) and how much reflects other assets (such as stock-in-trade, which is not chargeable at all, and investments, which are not business assets). The relief is then restricted to the part of the gain resulting from chargeable business assets. It should be noted that, although the three conditions referred to above must be satisfied for at least one year (maximum relief after 10 years), there is no requirement that particular assets should have been owned by the company throughout that period.

Where before disposal the business was owned personally by the transferor for part of the 10-year period and by the company in which he owns the shares for part of that period, the period of personal ownership can be counted in calculating the proportion of the maximum relief which is available. Relief is also available where the asset disposed of is something owned personally by the transferor but used by his company (sch. 21 para. 10 FA 1985).

9 TAXATION ON THE DEATH OF A SHAREHOLDER

There is no capital gains tax on death. A person who is given shares under the terms of a will or on intestacy is deemed to acquire them at the market value at death which is, therefore, his 'base value'. The transfer from the personal representative to the beneficiary is ignored. For example, A buys shares for £100,000; he dies when they are worth £150,000, leaving them to B. They are transferred to B when worth £160,000 and B sells them later for £180,000. There is no CGT on A's death or on the transfer from the personal representative to B. When B sells for £180,000 his gain is

£30,000 (the increase in value since A's death) and he will have to pay tax on this sum unless there are any reliefs which he can claim.

IHT is chargeable on death. The rate of tax is double the rate which applies on inter vivos transfers (so that the current rate is 40%). Of the IHT reliefs which were mentioned in paragraph 7.1, only the spouse exemption and the nil rate band are available on death (the latter only to the extent that it was not used up by lifetime transfers, including PET's, in the seven years before death). The business property relief is available on death and so is the instalment option (which may be claimed by the personal representatives).

It should be remembered that in valuing a shareholding for IHT purposes the value of control is taken into account — this applies to the death of a controlling shareholder as well as to an inter vivos transfer. However, in valuing an estate on death, changes in the value of assets resulting from the death are taken into account. If the value of a company's business depends on the expertise of the controlling shareholder, the shares may decline in value dramatically on that person's death, and this may be taken into account in valuing those shares for IHT purposes.

10   TAX STRATEGY

A shareholder, particularly a controlling shareholder, should consider the possible impact of tax on his family from a relatively young age. It should be clear from the rules described above that there is a very considerable fiscal advantage in disposing of shares inter vivos so as to take account of the fact that the IHT lifetime rates are lower than the death rates and tax can be avoided altogether if PETs are made and the donor survives seven years. Since transfers of value are only cumulated for seven years after they are made (i.e., transfers made more than seven years ago are ignored in calculating the amount of tax), there is an advantage to be gained from making gifts of shares over a considerable period of time rather than all at once. However, it should be remembered that at some point one of the gifts will involve loss of control of the company (and consequently a large transfer of value), and that once control is lost the future gifts will be eligible for 30% business property relief, rather than 50% relief.

The burden of IHT can also be reduced in the long run by making use of the spouse exemption to ensure that both husband and wife own enough to take maximum advantage of the nil rate band.

18 Disposals and Acquisitions of Interests in Partnerships

1 INTRODUCTION

An individual may cease to be a partner on the happening of one of the following events:

(a) the dissolution of the partnership;
(b) his retirement; or
(c) expulsion from the partnership.

If the partnership is dissolved, the partnership will come to an end, whereas on retirement or expulsion, the former partners can carry on the business, albeit through the medium of a newly constituted partnership.

In this chapter we will consider the legal and tax consequences of the occurrence of these events, in particular the circumstances in which tax charges can arise. (Exemptions and reliefs will only be considered where they are of special relevance.) We will also consider the position of a new partner joining the firm, whether or not as a replacement for a deceased, retired or expelled partner.

2 DISSOLUTION OF PARTNERSHIP

If an event occurs which causes a partnership to be dissolved, the partnership relationship ceases and the assets of the business must be realised. Under the Partnership Act 1890 certain events result in automatic dissolution unless the partnership agreement provides otherwise. Dissolution is such an extreme step that it is common for partners to provide expressly in their partnership agreement that dissolution is not to occur automatically on the occurrence of the events specified in the Partnership Act.

2.1 The methods of dissolving a partnership

2.1.1 Dissolution by notice
Under ss. 26 and 32(c) PA 1890 one or more partners can, at any time, give notice to their fellow partners to dissolve the partnership. This notice takes effect from the date specified in the notice but if the notice is silent on the point, it takes effect from the date when all partners received the notice. Dissolution under ss. 26 and 32(c) can result in an immediate dissolution of the partnership. This could have disastrous consequences for the business.

However, ss. 26 and 32(c) can be overridden if the partnership agreement contains provisions to the contrary. As a result many partnership agreements require a minimum period of notice to be given before the partnership is dissolved.

2.1.2   Dissolution by agreement
The partnership agreement can specify circumstances which cause the partnership to be dissolved, such as the occurrence of a particular event. The agreement can also specify the manner in which the partnership will be dissolved.

2.1.3   Automatic dissolution
A number of events cause partnerships to dissolve automatically:

(a)   *Bankruptcy, death or charge*   The death or bankruptcy of a partner causes the partnership to be automatically dissolved, unless the partnership agreement contains provisions to the contrary (s. 33(1) PA 1890). Since dissolution is a serious matter for the other partners, many partnership agreements provide that, instead of causing automatic dissolution, the death of a partner shall give rise to the same consequences as a retirement (see below, paragraph 3). A bankruptcy is often treated in the same way as an expulsion (see below, paragraph 5). (If a partner suffers his share of the partnership property to be charged for his personal debts, the other partners have an *option* to dissolve the partnership (s. 33(2) PA 1890).)

(b)   *Illegality*   Partnerships formed to carry out an illegal activity or which are contrary to public policy are automatically dissolved. A change of circumstances can subsequently make illegal a partnership initially formed for a legal purpose. This can arise where, for example, a partnership is formed to carry on a particular activity which is subsequently made illegal by a change in the law. In these circumstances, s. 34 PA 1890 provides that the partnership is dissolved on the happening of the event which makes the business unlawful. (In our illustration, on the date the change in the law takes effect.) It should be noted that, unsurprisingly, a provision to the contrary in the partnership agreement does not override s. 34.

(c)   *By expiration*   Under s. 32(a) and (b) PA 1890, a partnership is dissolved:
(i)   if it was entered into for a fixed term, by the expiration of that term;
(ii)   if it was entered into for a single adventure or undertaking, by the completion of that adventure or undertaking.

A provision to the contrary in the partnership agreement overrides s. 32(a) and (b). (If the agreement is silent and the partnership continues despite the occurrence of the events set out above, s. 27 provides that a partnership at will dissolvable by notice is brought into existence. Such a partnership is subject to the terms of the original agreement to the extent that these do not conflict with the incidents of a partnership at will.)

2.1.4   Dissolution by the court
Finally, a partner may apply to the court for dissolution of the partnership provided one of the statutory grounds for dissolution by the court exists.

Under s. 96 of the Mental Health Act 1983, the court has power, if satisfied after considering medical evidence that a partner is a mental 'patient', to dissolve or give directions for the dissolution of any partnership of which a 'patient' is a member. A 'patient' is a person incapable, by reason of mental disorder, of managing his own property and affairs.

In addition to s. 96 MHA 1983, s. 35 PA 1890 sets out grounds for dissolution by the court. Those grounds which give the partners a remedy in the event of a dispute (that is to say, s. 35(c), (d) and (f)) have been considered in Chapter 11 paragraph 4. The full list of s. 35 grounds is as follows:

Section 35(a)   Repealed by the predecessor to the Mental Health Act 1983.

Section 35(b)   When a partner, other than the partner suing, becomes permanently incapable of performing his part of the partnership contract.

Whether or not a partner has become *permanently* incapable is a question of fact. In *Whitwell* v *Arthur* (1865) 35 Beav 140, a partner had been paralysed for several months but had recovered by the time the action was heard. The court refused to dissolve the partnership since the incapacity was merely temporary. Since there may be difficulties in proving either that the partner is incapable or that his incapacity is permanent, and since there will be difficulties in running a partnership where a partner has a long illness, it is common to include a term in the partnership agreement allowing expulsion or insisting on retirement once a partner has been absent through illness for more than a specified time.

Section 35(c)   When a partner, other than the partner suing, has been guilty of such conduct as, in the opinion of the court, regard being had to the nature of the business, is calculated to prejudicially affect the carrying on of the business.

(See ch. 11—4.2.)

Section 35(d)   When a partner, other than the partner suing, wilfully or persistently commits a breach of the partnership agreement, or otherwise so conducts himself in matters relating to the partnership business that it is not reasonably practicable for the other partner or partners to carry on the business in partnership with him.

(See ch. 11—4.2.)

Section 35(e)   When the business of the partnership can only be carried on at a loss.

This is arguably one of the most important grounds for dissolution. In order for s. 35(e) to be invoked, the circumstances must be such as to make it a practical impossibility for the partnership to make a profit. If the partners who find themselves in this position cannot agree to bring the partnership to an end, an individual partner can apply to have the partnership dissolved. This may be a valuable right if a delay in terminating the partnership will increase the amount of the loss, for which all the partners will be personally liable. It is important to note that a partnership is not necessarily insolvent simply because it is making a loss. It may well have valuable assets which, when sold, will discharge all liabilities and provide a surplus for the partners.

Section 35(f)   Whenever in any case circumstances have arisen which, in the opinion of the court, render it just and equitable that the partnership be dissolved.

(See ch. 11—4.2.)

2.2   The legal consequences of dissolution

2.2.1   Continuing authority of partners for purposes of winding-up (s. 38 PA 1890)
The occurence of one of the events set out in paragraph 2.1 above will cause the partnership to be dissolved but there may be various steps which need to be taken to wind up the affairs of the firm. Section 38 provides that, after the dissolution, the authority of each partner to bind the firm (as well as the other rights and obligations of the partners) continues despite the dissolution but only to the extent necessary to wind up the affairs of the partnership, and to complete transactions begun but unfinished at the time of the dissolution. However, where the dissolution is by order of the court, this authority can be terminated by the appointment of a receiver (who will simply wind up the business) or of a receiver and manager (who will continue running the business but only with a view to the beneficial realisation of the assets by means of, for example, a sale of the business as a going concern). Such appointments are likely to be made where there is a likelihood of dispute if the former partners try to wind up the affairs of the partnership.

2.2.2   Application of the partnership property on dissolution (ss. 39 and 44 PA 1890)
Once the firm has been dissolved, the value of the assets owned by the partnership will be ascertained, as will the extent of the debts and liabilities owed to creditors. In so far as it is necessary, the assets will be sold to raise the funds to discharge the debts. The partners may merely sell the assets used in the business or they may decide to sell the business as a going concern. If the partners decide to adopt the latter course of action, they may be able to sell the business for more than the aggregate market value of the assets used in the business because the sale price may take into account the 'goodwill' attaching to the business.

Goodwill has been defined as 'the whole advantage' whatever it may be, of the reputation and connection of the firm' (*Trego* v *Hunt* [1896] AC 7). This 'advantage' can arise as a result of various factors. If the partners have considerable expertise in their chosen field, their customers may return repeatedly. This 'goodwill' may, however, be largely personal to the partners with the result that it would disappear if they ceased trading. Conversely, if the firm is situated in a prime location (such as the main shopping street in the town), the business may be very successful because of the convenience of access for its customers. In this latter case, the goodwill may attach to the premises rather than the partners, and so may be a very valuable asset of the partnership since it can be passed on to successors.

If the firm has saleable goodwill, a value will be attached to it. The valuation of goodwill is somewhat speculative and any formula for determining its value is inevitably rather artificial. A common formula is to ascertain the net profits of the business for a particular year and then for the parties to agree to multiply the period's profits by an agreed number, often two or three.

Where goodwill is sold, the purchasers will want to protect their investment against the loss of custom arising from the former owners setting up in competition in the same vicinity. Accordingly, the purchaser may wish to include a restrictive covenant in the sale agreement to guard against this possibility. If the purchasers are some of the partners of the dissolved partnership, they too should consider including restrictive covenants to protect their interests.

Once the assets and liabilities have been ascertained, s. 39 entitles each partner to have the property of the partnership applied so that the debts and liabilities of the firm are discharged first. Once these liabilities have been met, any surplus is distributed to the partners (after deducting any sums for which each partner is liable to contribute to the firm, such as contributions to make up losses or deficiencies of capital). In order to ensure that the assets of the partnership are not distributed to the partners personally before the outside creditors are paid off, s. 39 goes on to give partners the right to apply to the court to wind up the business and affairs of the firm in such a way as to ensure that the s. 39 order for application of assets is observed.

Section 44 provides that once the creditors of the firm have been paid, subject to any contrary agreement, the assets of the firm shall be applied in the following order:

(a)   in repaying advances received from partners;

(b)   in repaying the amounts shown as standing to the credit of each partner on his capital account; and

(c)   any balance being divided between the partners in accordance with the profit sharing ratio.

If the partnership has made losses (including losses or deficiencies of capital), these shall be met in the following order:

(a)   from profits;

(b)   from capital;

(c)   from contributions made by the partners in the proportion in which profits are divisible.

Both parts of s. 44 are subject to contrary agreement. In particular the partners may agree to share surplus assets and to contribute to capital losses in a ratio different from the normal profit sharing.

2.2.3   Notification of the dissolution

Section 38 gives partners continued authority to bind the firm after dissolution for the purpose of winding up the business (see paragraph 2.2.1 above). If a partner exceeds this authority, under s. 36(1) PA 1890 outsiders dealing with the firm after a change in the constitution are entitled to treat all apparent members of the firm as still being members until the outsider has notice of the change (see paragraph 3.2.2 below).

In order to protect themselves from liability for unauthorised debts incurred after the dissolution, the partners in the dissolved firm are entitled publicly to notify the fact of the dissolution (s. 37 PA 1890). To obtain protection from liability on unauthorised debts incurred with existing customers, the former partners should give notice personally to the customer. Notice in the *London Gazette* is sufficient to gain protection from liability on debts with new customers (this point is considered in more detail in relation to retirement in paragraph 3.2.2).

2.3 The tax consequences of dissolution

2.3.1 Income tax

The profits of the partnership are normally assessed to tax on the preceding year basis (see ch. 14—2) but if there is a permanent cessation (on a closure of the business) the closing year rules set out in s. 63 ICTA 1988 will be applied (see ch. 14—2.3).

Where there is a change in the persons engaged in carrying on any trade, profession or vocation under Case I or II of Schedule D, s. 113(1) ICTA 1988 provides that the closing year rules will apply to this deemed cessation. However, it is possible for an election to be made under s. 113(2) that the business be treated as continuing for tax purposes provided at least one partner continues.

Where a partnership is dissolved, the business may sometimes be continued for a period pending the final realisation of assets. If, at the time of the dissolution, there is a change in the persons engaged in the partnership (for example, where one partner dies and the surviving partners continue the business pending realisation), the closing year rules will be applied at the time of the dissolution unless the election to have the business treated as continuing is made.

If the partnership has been claiming capital allowances on, for example, the plant and machinery used in the business, balancing charges may be levied if the assets are disposed of for more than their written-down value on cessation. Balancing allowances may be claimed if the market value of the assets is less than their written-down value.

Finally, if the partnership has made losses, loss relief under ss. 380 and 382 ICTA 1988 in respect of the final tax year of the trade may be claimed. Terminal loss relief under ss. 388 and 389 ICTA 1988 will permit the partners to carry back losses made in the final 12 months of the trade against the profits of the same trade during the immediately preceding three tax years. (As to losses generally, see ch. 14—4.)

2.3.2 Capital gains tax

If the partnership property is sold to outsiders following dissolution any gains realised by each partner on the disposal of his fractional share of the assets will be taxable in accordance with general principles. The general principles will also apply when a partner disposes of assets he owns personally but which have been used by the partnership.

The position is more complicated where the assets are disposed of to some of the former partners. In these circumstances para. 3 of the Revenue's Statement of Practice 1/1975 will be relevant. This provides that where a partnership distributes an asset in kind to one or more of the partners, a partner who receives the asset will not be regarded as disposing of his fractional share in it (although the other partners *will* be disposing of their shares in the asset). The Statement of Practice requires that a computation be done of the gains which would be chargeable on the individual partners if the asset had been disposed of at its current market value. Where this results in a gain being attributed to a partner not receiving the asset, the gain will be charged at the time of the distribution of the asset. Where, however, the gain is allocated to a partner receiving the asset concerned there will be no charge on distribution. Instead, his capital gains tax acquisition cost which is to be carried forward will be the market value of the asset at the date of distribution as reduced by the amount of his gain. (The same principles will be applied where the computation results in a loss.)

Example A, B and C decide to dissolve their partnership and agree that, in satisfaction of his right to share in the asset surpluses, A should receive one particular partnership asset which the partnership acquired for £60,000 in 1983 and which is now worth £90,000. (The partners shared profits and asset surpluses equally.) The changes in their respective interests in the asset are as follows:

	Before £	*Current market value* £	*After* £
A	20,000 (⅓)	30,000 (⅓)	90,000
B	20,000 (⅓)	30,000 (⅓)	—
C	20,000 (⅓)	30,000 (⅓)	—

Taking into account para. 3 of the Revenue's Statement, the gain realised on a notional disposal at current market value is calculated. This means that B and C will each be charged to CGT on £10,000 (subject to indexation). A is not charged on a gain of £10,000 (subject to indexation), his acquisition costs for the purposes of calculating his future CGT liability will be the market value of the asset less his share of the notional gain, i.e., £90,000 − £10,000 = £80,000. Thus para. 3 effectively gives rise to an automatic hold-over of A's gain.

2.3.3 Inheritance tax
If the assets of the partnership are disposed of at full market value on dissolution, there will be no reduction in the value of the transferor's estate and, therefore, no transfer of value. If there is no transfer of value there cannot be any IHT liability. However, a charge to tax can arise on dissolution caused by death although (provided the necessary conditions are satisfied) business property relief will be available and this is considered in paragraph 4.4.3 below.

3 RETIREMENT OF A PARTNER

3.1 Circumstances when 'retirement' occurs

The term 'retirement' is most frequently applied to mean a person retiring from full-time work having reached age 60 or 65. However, in the partnership context 'retirement' simply means leaving the partnership voluntarily and so includes the resignation, for any reason, of a relatively young partner.

Partnership agreements can, and should, contain provisions dealing with retirement by partners. This is because the Partnership Act 1890 contains only one provision which specifically deals with retirement. This is s. 26 which deals with 'retirement from a partnership at will' and provides that any partner may 'determine the partnership at any time on giving notice'. If s. 26 notice is given the partnership will be *dissolved*; the section does not permit a partner to retire leaving the partnership otherwise unaffected. To avoid this extreme consequence, suitable provisions must be included in the agreement. One common form of wording provides that the partner wishing to retire should give written notice of a specified length (say, six months or one year). On expiry of the notice period, the partnership is dissolved but only in relation to the retiring partner. The retiring partner may be entitled to some financial settlement from his former partners but otherwise the partnership continues unaffected.

Partnership agreements frequently provide that a deceased person is to be treated as having retired. Additional problems relating specifically to death are considered in paragraph 4 below.

3.2   The legal consequences of retirement

3.2.1   Debts incurred before retirement
The mere fact that a partner retires does not release him from his obligations in respect of debts incurred while he was a partner. Indeed, s. 17(2) PA 1890 provides that 'a partner who retires from a firm does not thereby cease to be liable for partnership debts or obligations incurred before his retirement'.

To avoid the problems of having to meet such debts after retirement, the retiring partner should, if possible, ensure that the debts are paid before he leaves. Since this may be difficult in many cases, the partner will be concerned to gain protection in other ways. In some cases it may be agreed that he shall be indemnified by his former partners or that he will be released from his obligations by the creditor. The indemnity may be more valuable where provision to meet the debts has been set aside at the date of the retirement.

3.2.2   Debts incurred after retirement
While a retired partner must accept liability for debts incurred while he was a partner, he is unlikely to take kindly to liability for debts incurred after ceasing to be a member of the firm.

The general rule is that only partners are liable for debts incurred by the partnership and so ceasing to be a partner prevents the *former* partner becoming liable on future debts. This is because the retirement terminates the agency relationship. However, this general rule is subject to ss. 36 and 14 PA 1890. Under these sections a former partner becomes liable for debts incurred *after* he has left the partnership in certain circumstances.

Section 36(3) provides that the estate of a partner '. . . who, *not having been known to the person dealing with the firm to be a partner*, retires is not liable for partnership debts contracted after the date of the . . . retirement.'

The date at which knowledge is tested for the purposes of this subsection is the date of retirement. If a creditor does not know at that date of the retiring partner's connection with the firm, the former partner will not be liable; the fact that the creditor may subsequently discover the former membership cannot make the former partner liable.

The subsection was considered in *Tower Cabinet Co Ltd* v *Ingram* [1949] 2 KB 397. The facts of the case were that A and B were in partnership. A retired and B continued the business under the old name. After A's retirement, the business ordered goods from a new supplier and failed to pay. The supplier sought to enforce judgment against A. The only knowledge the supplier had of A's connection with the firm was that A's name appeared on headed notepaper which, contrary to A's express instructions, had not been destroyed. The court found that, as the customer had no knowledge prior to A's retirement that A was a partner in the firm, A was completely protected by s. 36(3). (A further question arose of A's possible liability under s. 14(1) — see post.)

In cases where creditors know of the partner's connection with the firm before the former partner retires, s. 36(3) is of no assistance. Section 36(1) provides that 'where a person deals with a firm after a change in its constitution, he is entitled to treat all apparent members of the old firm as still being members of the firm until he has notice of the change'.

It is necessary to consider:

(a)   what constitutes 'notice' for this purpose;
(b) ` what makes a former partner an 'apparent' member of the continuing firm.

3.2.2.1   Notice   Section 36(2) provides that in *respect of persons who had no dealings with the firm before the date of the dissolution or change* a notice in the *London Gazette* (where the firm has its principal place of business in England and Wales) will be sufficient notice.

Thus, to protect himself from liability to new customers who knew of his connection with the firm a retiring partner should ensure that a notice is published in the *London Gazette*.

Notice in the *London Gazette* will not be sufficient to relieve the former partner from liability in respect of customers who *did* have dealings with the firm prior to the dissolution or change. If the retiring partner wishes to be absolutely protected from liability for future debts he should give the customers formal notification. However, it may be that changing the notepaper to remove his name will be sufficient notification although there is no definite authority on this point.

3.2.2.2   Apparent membership   Where persons dealing with the firm know that a person was a partner, that partner will be liable for new debts so long as he is an apparent member of the firm (and until he gives notice). Persons may be 'apparent members' either because a customer has had dealings with them before or because their names appear on the notepaper or on a sign on the door or because the customer has some indirect information about their being partners.

A retiring partner should ensure that his apparent membership of the firm is terminated. He should give actual notice to existing customers and should publish a notice in the *Gazette* to cover the situation where people have not had dealings with the firm but are aware of the partner's connection with the firm.

Liability for subsequent debts may also arise under s. 14 PA 1890.

It will be recalled from Chapter 13 paragraph 3 that s. 14(1) provides that:

Every one who by words spoken or written or by conduct represents himself, or who knowingly suffers himself to be represented, as a partner in a particular firm, is liable as a partner to any one who has on the faith of any such representation given credit to the firm, whether the representation has or has not been made or communicated to the person so giving credit by or with the knowledge of the apparent partner making the representation or suffering it to be made.

Therefore, even if no liability arises under s. 36, the former partner may be liable to any person (whether they had previous dealings with the firm or not) who has given 'credit' to the firm on the faith of a representation that he is still a partner which is made by the former partner or which he has 'knowingly' allowed to be made.

The word 'apparent' in s. 14(1) has the same meaning as in s. 36(1) so that the decision in the *Tower Cabinet* case (see above) is equally relevant in these circumstances. In the case, it was alleged that the former partner had allowed himself to be held out as a partner. However, since the former partner had not authorised the use of the old notepaper, he had not 'knowingly' allowed himself to be held out as an 'apparent' partner and so no liability under s. 14 arose.

A retiring partner should ensure that his name is removed from any signs and that any notepaper is destroyed in order to prevent an accusation that he knowingly allowed himself to be represented as a partner.

3.2.3 Compliance with Business Names Act 1985

After the change in the partnership, the notepaper will normally be changed and care should be taken to ensure that it complies with the requirements of the Business Names Act 1985 (which were considered in ch. 10—6).

3.2.4 Dealing with the finances

Once the partner has retired from the firm, the arrangements for severing, or changing the basis of, the financial connection with the firm will be of considerable importance. These matters are generally covered by the partnership agreement and usually relate to the provision for the partner (and for his dependants) for some form of pension (whether paid by the former partners, under an approved annuity contract, or under a consultancy arrangement — as to all of which see ch. 19—3). In addition, the arrangements will deal with the former partner's entitlement (if any) to payment for his share in the partnership assets (which may include goodwill).

If there is no agreement, the former partner has a right to receive the net value of his share in the partnership property from his former partners.

3.3 The tax consequences of retirement

3.3.1 Income tax

3.3.1.1. Deemed cessation under s. 113 ICTA 1988   On retirement, whenever there is a change in the persons engaged in carrying on any trade, profession or vocation under Case I or Case II of Schedule D, this will result in a deemed discontinuance of the partnership under s. 113(1) ICTA 1988. This deemed discontinuance applies when a new partner joins the partnership (whether or not he replaces a retired partner) and when a partnership is dissolved.

The deemed discontinuance will result in the closing years rules set out in s. 63 ICTA 1988 applying to the partnership as originally constituted and the opening years rules in ss. 60-62 ICTA 1988 applying to the changed partnership. (The opening and closing years rules are considered in ch. 14—2.)

However, the deemed discontinuance imposed by s. 113(1) only applies to the profits of the partnership, not to any losses realised. Therefore, terminal loss relief under ss. 388 and 389 ICTA 1988 will only be available to a retiring partner, not to a continuing partner. Similarly, relief under s. 381 ICTA 1988 (for losses realised by new, unincorporated businesses) will only be available to new partners.

It is possible, under s. 113(2), to elect that the business be treated as continuing. In cases where the opening and closing year rules would be disadvantageous for the business, such an election should be made. Broadly speaking, the deemed discontinuance can be disadvantageous where the profits of the partnership increase regularly from year to year. This is because the preceding year basis (as to which see ch. 14—2.1) ensures that the partners' taxable income, in any tax year, will be less than their actual share of profits received in that year. (The interrelation between the opening and closing years rules is such that a cessation occurring at the end of the fifth year of the life of a firm used to give rise to part of the profit for that five-year period escaping tax. This benefit has been restricted by ss. 61 and 62 ICTA 1988, which is considered below.)

If the profits of the firm remain steady, or actually decline, the deemed discontinuance may be advantageous because the partners will be assessed on the actual profits realised in the relevant tax years, which may be less than the profits on which they would have been assessed under the preceding year basis.

The election must be made within two years of the change. It must be made, in writing, by all partners, both old and new. If a deceased partner is being treated, under the terms of the partnership agreement, as a retiring partner so that the partnership can continue, his personal representatives must join in an election.

Because of the need for all the partners, both old and new, to concur in the s. 113(2) election, the partnership agreement should provide that new partners must agree to the election before joining the firm. Furthermore, there should be a provision to the effect that retiring partners (and the personal representatives of a deceased partner, if appropriate) can be required to concur with the election if the continuing partners so request.

If the election is made, the newly constituted partnership will be assessed on the preceding year basis. In the year of the change, this will mean that the partners in the new firm will be assessed on the profits earned by the partners in the old firm. While this can result in the partners in the newly constituted firm paying tax on profits they never received, this will only be a disadvantage if they pay *more* tax than they would have done had the opening year rules applied.

In order to give protection should any of the partners in the new firm be prejudiced, it is customary for the retiring partners (or the personal representatives of a deceased partner if appropriate) to give an indemnity against any *additional* tax which becomes payable by the partners in the new firm. However, the former partner does not necessarily have to make a payment under the indemnity provision.

It used to be possible to take advantage of the relationship between the opening and closing years rules to gain a tax advantage. Some successful firms made a practice of making a change in the membership of the partnership every five years but not electing for continuance. In order to prevent the opening and closing years rules being abused, ss. 61 and 62 ICTA 1988 were enacted. They provide that (save where the new partnership genuinely carries on a business which is different from that carried on by the old partnership, when ss. 61 and 62 apply) following a change in the persons engaged in the partnership business within s. 113(1), when no s. 113(2) election is made, the opening years of the new partnership will be assessed as follows:

Year of change and the three subsequent years	Actual profits of each tax year
Fifth and subsequent years	Preceding year basis

The partnership will have the option to elect for the actual basis to be applied in assessing the profits of the fifth and sixth tax years.

3.3.1.2 Provision of income for retired partners The methods by which former partners can provide themselves with an income during their retirement are considered in Chapter 19 paragraph 3. The income tax consequences of retirement annuities (whether paid under approved annuity contracts or by the former partners) and consultancy arrangements are not considered further here.

3.3.2 Capital gains tax

It will be recalled from Chapter 14 paragraph 6.2 that disposals by a firm are subject to the normal CGT principles in determining whether a gain has arisen. However, the lack of a comprehensive body of legislation dealing with the taxation of capital gains realised by partners led to difficulties. The Revenue's Statements of Practice SP 1/75 (D/12 (issued on 17 January 1975)) and SP 1/79 set out the Revenue's view of the way in which general capital gains tax principles apply in a partnership context. The underlying principle on which the Statement of Practice of 17 January 1975 is based is that each partner is to be treated as owning a fractional share of each of the chargeable assets of the partnership (including goodwill). This concept forms the basis of the rules which follow.

In this section we will consider the capital gains tax consequences which arise, according to the Statements of Practice, when there is a change in the personnel of the partnership (principally on the retirement of a partner or when a new partner is admitted). In addition, the effect of changing the asset surplus sharing ratio will also be considered.

Where one partner retires from the business he will normally relinquish his interest in the partnership assets in consideration of a capital sum and/or the provision of an income. The retiring partner's present interest in the business is shown on his capital account. He will be treated as making a disposal of that interest to the continuing partners (and to any new partners who are being admitted on his retirement). The continuing (and new) partners will acquire his interest and will thereafter have a greater interest in the business.

Example A, B, C and D share profits (and asset surplus) equally. The assets of the firm were acquired for £60,000. A is retiring and once he has retired, all the profits will be divided equally between B, C and D. The asset-sharing ratio will change as follows:

	Before £	After £
A	15,000 (¼)	(—)
B	15,000 (¼)	20,000 (⅓)
C	15,000 (¼)	20,000 (⅓)
D	15,000 (¼)	20,000 (⅓)

A has disposed of his ¼ interest to the continuing partners and is left with nothing. Each of the continuing partners receives ⅓ of A's ¼ share (i.e., $^1/_{12}$th share in the partnership property).

It can be clearly seen from the above example that the retiring partner has made a disposal to the continuing partners. The question then arises of whether or not the disposal has realised a gain (or a loss). Where the assets have not been revalued in the accounts and the retiring partner receives an amount equivalent to the balance on his capital account, he is simply receiving the return of his original capital contribution. There will be no gain and no loss (SP 1/75 para. 4). For example, in the above illustration, if A was paid £15,000 he would realise neither a gain nor a loss.

However, there will be a gain on disposal where assets have been revalued in the accounts (SP 1/75 para. 5). Where assets have increased in value since the date of acquisition the partners may wish to record this increase in the accounts; the process is referred to as a 'revaluation'. The values of the various assets are increased in the accounts and the balances on the partners' capital accounts are increased by a corresponding amount in order to reflect the increase in the worth of the business. A revaluation of itself gives rise to no charge to CGT since there has been no disposal. However, if after a revaluation there is a change in the asset surplus sharing ratio, for example on retirement, the disponer partner will receive more than his original capital contribution and (subject to indexation and other reliefs) there will be a charge to capital gains tax.

Example The facts are as in the previous example but the partnership decides that prior to A's retirement the assets should be revalued from £60,000 to £90,000. A's ¼ share will be worth £22,500. Therefore A will be treated as disposing of assets for £22,500 which were acquired for £15,000, and will have a capital gain of £7,500.

	Before £	*On revaluation* £	*After* £
A	15,000 (¼)	22,500 (¼)	—
B	15,000 (¼)	22,500 (¼)	30,000 (⅓)
C	15,000 (¼)	22,500 (¼)	30,000 (⅓)
D	15,000 (¼)	22,500 (¼)	30,000 (⅓)
	60,000	90,000	90,000

B, C and D will each be treated as acquiring ⅓ of A's share in the assets and therefore their respective base costs will increase from £22,500 to £30,000. They are, therefore holding assets which have increased in value to them from £15,000 to £30,000. When they realise the assets, there will be a CGT liability (subject to indexation).

An apparent way for a retiring partner to avoid a CGT liability where assets have increased in value would be for the partnership to refrain from revaluing the assets in the accounts and simply to return to the retiring partner the balance on his capital account. After that the continuing partners would make a cash payment to the retiring partner outside the accounts. However, the Revenue's Statement of Practice 1/75 states that when, on a change of partnership sharing ratios, payments are made directly between two or more partners outside the framework of the accounts, the payments represent *an additional consideration* for the retiring partner's share in the assets. Thus, such payments increase the value received by the retiring partner on the disposal.

Example The facts are as in the first example. Instead of revaluing the assets in the accounts, the partners agree that they will pay A the £15,000 due to him on his capital account *and* will pay him an additional £7,500 outside the accounts as a separate matter. As a result of the Statement of Practice, A is to be treated as receiving £15,000 + £7,500 and will, therefore, have a capital gain (subject to indexation) of £7,500.

The members of the partnership, in order to minimise the burden of finding large capital sums, may agree not to revalue assets as and when partners retire. It could be argued that this is a gift by each retiring partner of his share in the increased value of the asset. In the case of a gift (or sale at an under-value), the Revenue can treat the disposal as made for market value unless it was a bargain made at arm's length (s. 29A CGTA 1979). In the case of connected persons, transfers are always treated as otherwise than by way of bargains made at arm's length (s. 62 CGTA 1979). Partners are normally connected but will not be when transferring property to each other provided the disposal *was pursuant to a bona fide commercial arrangement* (s. 63 CGTA 1979). Thus, provided there is some bona fide commercial reason for not revaluing, the Revenue will not seek to substitute market value.

Even where the partners are connected other than by partnership (for example, father and son) the Revenue have stated that they will only seek to substitute market value where the transaction would not have been entered into by persons who were not at arm's length (SP 1/75 para. f).

3.3.2.1 Entitlement to reliefs If a charge to tax arises on the disposal by a partner of his interest in partnership property, the disponer will be entitled to claim the benefit of the CGT exemptions and reliefs in the normal way. One relief which may be of special relevance is the retirement relief given by ss. 69 and 70 of and sch. 20 to FA 1985.

It will be recalled from Chapter 17 paragraph 8 that an individual aged 60 or an individual who has retired under that age on the grounds of ill-health, is entitled to claim a full exemption from charge for gains up to a maximum of £125,000 and an exemption for 50% of gains between £125,000 and £500,000 for gains realised on the disposal of its assets. A former partner who satisfies the age or ill-health condition must have owned the interest in the partnership for at least one year before he qualifies for any relief. Once he has owned the interest for exactly one year he is entitled to a proportion of the full available relief; the limits of £125,000 and £500,000 are scaled down. Thus if a partner has owned an interest for one year he is entitled to a full exemption for gains up to a maximum of one-tenth of £125,000 (i.e., £12,500) and an exemption for 50% of gains from £12,500 to one-tenth of £500,000 (i.e., £50,000).

3.3.2.2 Changes in the asset surplus sharing ratios The principles dealt with above, applicable where one partner is retiring from the firm and giving up his entire interest in the firm, apply equally where a partner gives up part of his interest in a firm. This may be done because new partners are admitted or it may be done in order to give existing partners a greater share in the assets of the partnership.

The partners who are reducing their interest in the assets are treated as making a disposal of part of their interest.

Example   A and B share profits and assets surplus equally. The assets were acquired for £60,000. A and B agree that A will make a disposal to B of one half of A's interest so that, in future, the ratio will be ¾ : ¼.

A is giving up half of his existing entitlement and is, therefore, disposing of assets acquired for £15,000.

	Before £	After £
A	30,000 (½)	15,000 (¼)
B	30,000 (½)	45,000 (¾)

A is making a disposal. As in the case of retirement the question arises of whether there has been a gain (or loss). The same principles apply. Thus, if there has been no revaluation, there is no gain on the disposal. If there has been a revaluation in the accounts there will be a gain on the disposal (subject to indexation). If there is no revaluation but a payment is made outside the accounts the payment is treated as an additional part of any consideration received by the disposing partner.

A partner may decide to dispose of part of his interest in the partnership assets to existing (or new) partners without requiring full consideration. The question will arise of whether or not the Revenue can treat the disponer as disposing of the asset at market value under s. 29A CGTA 1979. As stated above, no such substitution will occur as between partners who are not otherwise connected, provided the disposal is made pursuant to a bona fide commercial arrangement (s. 63 CGTA 1979).

If there is no bona fide commercial arrangement (or if the partners are connected otherwise than by partnership and the transaction is not such as would have been entered into by persons at arm's length), the Revenue can substitute market value. The partners can elect for hold-over relief of the gain attributable to the gift element.

3.3.2.3   Goodwill   Goodwill presents particular problems. In recent years partners (particularly in professional firms) who paid for a share in the goodwill of the firm when they were admitted to partnership have agreed not to charge incoming partners for a share (the burden of finding a large capital sum being regarded as too great). The effect of this is that the old partners write off goodwill. It is clear that when an old partner retires and receives no payment for the goodwill he makes a loss on that asset. Many partnerships have argued that the old partners are entitled to make a claim for CGT loss relief when the value of goodwill is written off. (Section 22(2) CGTA 1979 provides that where an inspector is satisfied that the value of an asset has become negligible he may allow an immediate loss.) The Revenue resist such claims, taking the view that the goodwill still has a value and does not become negligible simply because the partners choose not to charge for it. However, claims for immediate loss relief have been successful in front of the General and the Special Commissioners. The position is unsettled and the practice varies between inspectors, some being prepared to allow such claims and some not.

3.3.2.4   Payment of annuities   A partnership may agree to pay a retiring partner an annuity. The annuity will be subject to income tax in the hands of the recipient partner. If it is more than can be regarded as reasonable recognition of the past contribution of work and effort by the partner to the partnership, the Revenue will treat the capitalised value of the annuity as consideration for the disposal of the retiring partner's share in the assets. An annuity will be regarded as reasonable for this purpose if:

(a)   the former partner had been in the partnership for at least 10 years;
(b)   the annuity is no more than ⅔ of his average share of profits in the best three of the last seven years in which he was required to devote substantially the whole of his time to acting as a partner.

For periods of less than 10 years, fractions other than ⅔ will be used.

3.3.2.5   Disposal of assets owned by partners personally   Where a partner disposes of an asset which he owns personally but which is used by the partnership, the Statements of Practice are not relevant. On such disposals the normal CGT principles are applied to ascertain whether a gain or loss has arisen. Similarly, the disposing partner will be able to claim any relevant exemptions or reliefs, save that retirement relief under ss. 69 and 70 of and sch. 20 to FA 1985 will only be available to relieve the gain realised on the disposal of such an asset if the disposal is associated with the partner's disposal of his share in the partnership on reaching 60 or on retirement under that age on ill-health grounds.

3.3.3   Inheritance tax

Normal principles of IHT apply in the partnership context. Thus, where a partner sells an interest in the partnership for full consideration there is no transfer of value and therefore no charge to IHT arises. If a partner sells an interest for less than full consideration or transfers it for no consideration at all, prima facie a charge to IHT will arise. However, s. 10 IHTA 1984 provides that a disposition is *not* a transfer of value if it was not intended to confer gratuitous benefit and was either made at arm's length between unconnected persons or, if between connected persons, was such as might be expected to be made between unconnected persons. Partners are not connected persons in respect of transfers between partners of partnership assets pursuant to bona fide commercial arrangements. Thus many transfers which might appear to be chargeable may escape IHT on the ground that there was no intention to confer a gratuitous benefit.

It is common for partners to agree that on their retirement (or death) their share of goodwill is to accrue automatically to the other partners without payment. This has the benefit of relieving the partnership of the need to pay for portions of goodwill as and when partners retire. Section 163(1) of IHTA 1984 provides that where a person enters into a contract which excludes or restricts the right to dispose of any property the exclusion or restriction will be ignored in valuing the asset when it is next transferred except to the extent that consideration for the exclusion or restriction was given. The effect of s. 163 is that, unless consideration is given for the accruer clause, the clause will be ignored when the goodwill is valued on the next transfer and the full value of the retiring (or deceased) partner's share in the goodwill will be charged to tax. (There is also a possibility of an immediate charge to tax on the entry into the clause; in that case, however, credit is given on the later transfer for the value brought into charge on entering into the agreement (s. 163 IHTA 1984).) However, it seems likely that the Revenue will follow the approach in *Att.-Gen.* v *Boden* [1912] 1 KB 539, and look at the covenants entered into by all the partners (which may include an agreement to pay an annuity to the former partner) to assess whether what is given up is a fair equivalent of what is received.

In the event that an inter vivos transaction is regarded as the transfer of value it will be potentially exempt. If the transferor dies within seven years the transfer will be treated as if it had always been chargeable. An interest in the partnership is relevant business property qualifying for business property relief at 50% provided:

(a)   the transferor had owned the property for at least two years at the time of the transfer;

(b)   the transferee still owns the property (or replacement property) and it still qualifies as relevant business property.

Where there is a gift of land, buildings, plant or machinery owned by a partner personally but used wholly or mainly for the purpose of the partnership of which he is a member, a reduction of only 30% is available.

The transferor's annual exemption may be available for the tax year of transfer and the preceding tax year, in which case it will reduce the value transferred.

When ascertaining the rate of tax chargeable on the inter vivos transfer it will be necessary to cumulate any chargeable transfers made in the seven years before the transfer in question. Tapering relief will be available if the transferor survives three years from the date of the transfer. The burden of the inheritance tax will fall on the transferee (unless the transferor provides otherwise in his will). In cases where the potential liability is large the transferee may wish to consider insuring the transferor's life. The option to pay inheritance tax by instalments will be available. The first will be due six months after the end of the month of the transferor's death. Interest will not be payable unless an instalment is late.

4   DEATH

4.1   Introduction

As we saw in paragraph 2 above, death causes the automatic dissolution of a partnership. In order to avoid inconvenience to the surviving partners it is common to provide in the partnership agreement that instead of causing an automatic dissolution of the partnership, a deceased partner shall be treated as if he had retired.

There are various specific problems which must be considered in connection with the death of a partner. In this section we will look at the rights and liabilities of the estate of the deceased partner and the tax consequences of death.

4.2   Right of estate to share in profits and obtain amounts due

Section 42(1) of PA 1890 provides that where any member of a firm has died (or otherwise ceased to be a partner) and the surviving (or continuing) partners carry on the business of the firm without any final settlement of accounts as between the firm and the outgoing partner or his estate, the outgoing partner or his estate is entitled at the option of himself or his personal representatives to claim such share of the profits made since the dissolution as the court may find to be attributable to the use of his share of the partnership assets (or to interest at the rate of 5% p.a. on the amount of his share of the partnership assets). Any amount due from the surviving partners to the deceased partner's personal representatives in respect of his share is a debt accruing at the date of the death (s. 43 PA 1890).

Raising a large capital sum to pay to the estate of a deceased partner may strain the resources of a partnership which is continuing after the death of a partner. It is desirable that partners should consider such matters. They may decide to make provision for such sums by taking out insurance cover. They may consider providing in the partnership agreement that on death (and/or retirement) capital sums due should be paid in yearly instalments over a specified period; interest would be payable on the amount outstanding. It is usual to provide in the agreement for a method of calculating the amount due. Frequently such a clause will provide that the deceased (or retiring) partner is to be entitled to a fixed amount in lieu of a share of profits. This avoids the need to apportion profits to the date of death (or retirement).

4.3   Liability for debts

Every partner is jointly liable for debts and obligations of the firm incurred while he is a partner. In addition, s. 9 PA 1890 provides that the estate of a deceased person is severally liable for such debts and obligations so far as they remain unsatisfied *but* subject to the prior payment of the deceased partner's personal debts. A partnership creditor can, therefore, proceed against the estate of a deceased partner in respect of **partnership debts (even after obtaining a judgment against the other partners) provided some part of the debt is unsatisfied.** However, partnership creditors are postponed to the deceased partner's own creditors.

So far as subsequent debts are concerned, s. 36(3) PA 1890 provides that the deceased partner's estate is not liable for partnership debts contracted after the death.

However, if the deceased partner's personal representatives take part in the management of the business they make themselves liable for debts incurred from the time their participation commences.

4.4   The tax consequences of the death of a partner

4.4.1   Income tax
Whether the death is treated in the same manner as a retirement (because of the provisions of the partnership agreement) or as causing a dissolution of the partnership (because the partnership agreement is silent on the point), the death will result in a change in the persons engaged in carrying on the partnership's trade, profession or vocation. There will, therefore, be a deemed cessation of the business under s. 113(1) ICTA 1988 and the closing years rules will apply unless an election under s. 113(2) ICTA 1988 is made to have the partnership's trade assessed on a continuing basis (see paragraph 3.3.1 above). The personal representatives of a deceased partner will have to join in the election if the partnership is not being dissolved and it is, therefore, desirable that the partnership agreement should include a term requiring them to do so.

4.4.2 Capital gains tax

The deceased partner's interest in the partnership assets is *acquired* by his personal representatives at market value on the date of death (s. 49 CGTA 1979). Since a disposal is a prerequisite for liability to CGT, the provisions of s. 49 ensure that no CGT is payable on death and that unrealised gains arising during the deceased's lifetime escape the charge to tax.

The continuing partners may incur a capital gains tax liability if, in order to pay the amount due to the deceased partner's estate (and/or dependants) they have to sell partnership assets which have increased in value since acquisition.

4.4.3 Inheritance tax

The estate of a deceased partner will include his interest in the partnership assets. Under s. 4(1) IHTA 1984, the partner is deemed to make a transfer of value on his death and the value transferred is the value of the assets in his estate immediately before his death. Accordingly, subject to exemptions, reliefs and the deceased partner's cumulative total at the date of death, IHT will be payable in respect of the market value of his share in the partnership.

Changes in the value of assets resulting from death are taken into account for IHT purposes. If all or part of the value of the goodwill of the business was personal to the deceased partner the value of the goodwill, and therefore of the business, will fall as a result of the death. The reduced value of the deceased partner's share in the business will then be included in his estate for IHT purposes.

The value of the deceased's share may be reduced as a result of an option to purchase held by the other partners. Thus, if the partnership agreement provides that on the death of a partner, his fellow partners will have an option to buy the deceased partner's share in the partnership assets for a fixed sum, the value of the assets for the purposes of IHT will be the agreed fixed sum, provided the option was granted for consideration in money or money's worth (s. 163 IHTA 1984) which was considered in more detail in paragraph 3.3.3 above concerning automatic accruer clauses in relation to the goodwill of the business. The points made in connection with such clauses applying on retirement apply equally on death. Therefore, provided full consideration was given for the clause, no IHT liability will arise on the death of one of the partners (*Att.-Gen.* v *Boden* [1912] 1 KB 539).

Where an IHT liability does arise on death it may be reduced by virtue of the relief for business property given by ss. 103-114 IHTA 1984 (and considered above in paragraph 3.3.3).

However, there is no entitlement to claim the relief if the assets are the subject of a binding contract for sale at the time of death. A clause in the partnership agreement to the effect that the surviving partners are *obliged* to buy and the personal representatives of the deceased partner are *obliged* to sell the deceased partner's share may have been included in the agreement for sound commercial reasons but it will result in the loss of business property relief. This is because the Revenue regard such clauses as amounting to binding contracts (see Statement of Practice 12/80 dated 13 October 1980). If there is no *obligation* to buy and sell, the relief is available and so this difficulty can be avoided by the use of an option arrangement or an automatic accruer clause.

IHT attributable to an interest in partnership property can be paid in 10 yearly instalments under ss. 227 and 228 IHTA 1984. The first instalment is due six months after the end of the month of death and no interest is due unless an instalment is late. If the interest in partnership property is sold all outstanding IHT must be paid off. Where the continuing partners purchase the interest of a deceased partner the instalment option will not thereafter be available to the deceased partner's estate.

5 EXPULSION

Section 25 of PA 1890 provides that no majority of the partners can expel any partner unless a power to do so has been conferred by express agreement between the partners. In the absence of an express clause, partners who wished to expel a partner would be unable to do so. The only course open to them would be to dissolve the partnership; they might be unwilling to take such an extreme step.

Where an expulsion clause is included in the agreement it will normally state that breaches of certain terms of the partnership agreement, such as that requiring a partner not to compete with the partnership or to devote the whole of his time to the business, will justify expulsion; it will also usually list specific grounds justifying expulsion, such as intemperance, gambling or scandalous conduct. Bankruptcy is a ground for the automatic dissolution of the whole partnership (s. 33(1) PA 1890) but in order to avoid the consequences of dissolution it is common for the partnership agreement to provide that a bankruptcy will not cause dissolution, rather that it will justify expulsion.

An expulsion clause will generally deal with the manner in which the expulsion is to be effected. It is normal to provide that written notice must be given to the offending partner and that it is to have immediate effect. It is obviously desirable that a partner be expelled as quickly as possible since his activities might be damaging the firm. The partnership agreement will normally distinguish expulsion and retirement in respect of financial arrangements. Thus, if annuities are to be paid the agreement would normally provide that an expelled partner should forfeit his rights.

An expulsion must be carried out in good faith and for the benefit of the firm as a whole, rather than for the personal gain of the continuing partners (*Blisset* v *Daniel* (1853) 10 Hare 493).

The tax consequences of expulsion are the same as for retirement.

6 ADMISSION OF A NEW PARTNER

Although this chapter is primarily concerned with leaving a partnership, the admission of new partners is a topic so closely connected that it seems appropriate to deal with it here.

6.1 Liability

A new partner will be jointly liable with the other partners for all debts incurred after the date of his admission. The position in respect of debts was dealt with in Chapter 13 paragraph 4.

6.2 The tax consequences of a new partner joining the firm

The tax position has been largely dealt with in connection with retirement but for the sake of completeness a brief summary will be given here.

6.2.1 Income tax

When a new partner joins a partnership, there will be a change in the persons engaged in carrying on the partnership's trade, profession or vocation. This will result in a deemed cessation of the business under s. 113(1) ICTA 1988 and the application of the closing years rules (see paragraph 3.3.1 above) unless an election under s. 113(2) is made by all the partners both old (or their personal representatives, if appropriate) and new. Since the s. 113(2) election will result in the partnership's profits being assessed on the preceding year basis, the new partner will be assessed on profits he never received. To avoid him being prejudiced by this, the partnership agreement should contain a clause under which the partners in the old firm will indemnify him against this additional tax liability.

6.2.2 Capital gains tax

A newly admitted partner will acquire an interest in the partnership assets either by purchase or by gift. Thus, if the old partners give the incoming partner a one-third share in profits and asset surpluses, he will acquire one third of the value of the partnership assets at that date. That value will be his acquisition value.

Example A and B, who share profits and assets equally, decide to admit C and to share profits and assets equally thereafter. The partnership assets are shown in the accounts as worth £120,000 a the date of C's admission.

	Before £	After £
A	60,000 (½)	40,000 (⅓)
B	60,000 (½)	40,000 (⅓)
C	—	40,000 (⅓)

C's acquisition value is, therefore, £40,000. A and B have disposed of a part of their share in the assets surplus. As discussed above there will be no charge to CGT on such a disposal provided there has been no upward revaluation of the assets in the accounts and provided no payment is made. The old partners are treated as making a disposal for a consideration equal to their capital gains tax cost so that there will be neither a chargeable gain nor an allowable loss at that point. They will carry forward a smaller proportion of cost to set against a subsequent disposal of their assets. The Inland Revenue will not seek to substitute market value in such a case since the transaction is likely to be a bona fide commercial transaction where the continuing partners dispose of a share in the asset surpluses but in consideration of the incoming partner covenanting to devote himself to the partnership. If there has been an upward revaluation in the accounts there will be a potential charge to CGT.

If the incoming partner makes a payment of cash the effect of such a payment depends upon whether it is a contribution of capital which is to be credited to his capital account or whether it is a payment to the old partners. In the former case no cash has been paid to the old partners and so there is no assessment to CGT; in the latter case there can be an assessment to CGT irrespective of whether the payment is made through the accounts (in which case the amount paid will be credited to the capital accounts of the old partners) or whether it is made outside the accounts to each partner individually.

6.2.3   *Inheritance tax*

Inheritance tax is unlikely to be an immediate problem for a newly admitted partner. However, he might be the recipient of a potentially exempt transfer of value. If so, it is possible that the transfer will become chargeable if one or more of the transferor partners dies within seven years. The donee of an inter vivos transfer of partnership property may exercise the right to pay by way of 10 equal yearly instalments, the first due six months after the end of the month of transfer. Interest is not charged unless an instalment is late.

19 Retirement Provision

1 INTRODUCTION

Ensuring financial security during retirement is a matter which becomes of increasing concern to many individuals as they progress through their working lives. This chapter is concerned with the principal methods of providing for retirement which are available to directors, and employees, of companies and to partners. Different individuals will have different priorities and requirements so far as retirement provision is concerned. For some building up a capital fund during their working lives which can be invested to produce income and further capital growth will be of paramount importance; for others, the main aim will be to ensure they have a steady source of income.

For individuals who wish to enjoy the benefits of a capital fund on retirement, the sale of shares in their trading company or the sale of their interest in a sole proprietorship or partnership may be a convenient way of achieving their aim. The consequences of following this course of action were considered in Chapter 17 (where the individual wishes to leave a company) and Chapter 18 (where the individual wishes to leave a partnership). However, this option may not be available, or may be unattractive to the individual involved who may, therefore, need to ensure he receives a pension during his retirement.

This chapter is primarily concerned with the provision of income during retirement, whether from some form of pension fund or by means of payments from the former employer or former partners of the individual.

2 RETIREMENT PROVISION FOR DIRECTORS AND EMPLOYEES

2.1 Private occupational pension schemes (ss. 590-612 ICTA 1988)

Many (though not all) employers provide private occupational pension schemes for their employees. The funds which provide the pensions are built up by contributions from the employer and the employee. These funds are usually managed by trustees who not only invest the contributions received but also administer the payment of pensions. Alternatively, under some schemes the contributions are paid, by way of premiums, to an insurance company which provides the pensions.

In theory a very wide range of schemes could be made available. However, one type of scheme (an 'exempt approved retirement benefits scheme') is eligible for very favourable tax treatment and so is very widely used. Such a scheme is one which is approved by the Occupational Pensions Board and accepted as exempt by the Inland Revenue Superannuation Funds Office. (The Revenue will grant exemption where the scheme is established under irrevocable trusts or where there are special circumstances justifying exemption.)

To be an approved scheme the following requirements must be complied with:

(a)   The scheme is bona fide established for the sole purpose of providing benefits in respect of the service of the recipient as an employee.

(b)   The scheme is established in connection with a trade or undertaking carried on in the UK by a UK resident.

(c)   The administrator of the scheme is a UK resident.

(d)   The scheme is recognised by both the employer and employees, and every employee has been given written details of its principal provisions.

(e)   The employer is a contributor to the scheme.

(f)   Contributions made by the employees under the scheme cannot be repaid.

(g)   The benefits are payable to the employee or his surviving spouse, children, dependants or personal representatives.

(h)   Any benefit for an employee is a pension on retirement which is first paid at an age not before 60 (for men) or 55 (for women) and not after 70, which does not exceed $\frac{1}{60}$th of the employee's average annual remuneration for the last three years of service for each year of service up to a maximum of 40 years.

(i)   Any benefit for the employee's spouse is a pension on the death or retirement of the employee which does not exceed $\frac{2}{3}$rds of the pension which would have been payable to the employee.

(j)   It must not be possible to surrender, commute or assign the pension in whole or in part, save that commutation in exchange for a lump sum is allowed provided the lump sum does not exceed $\frac{3}{80}$ths of the employee's final annual remuneration multiplied by the number of years of service up to a maximum of 40 (subject to an overall maximum of 1½ times the final remuneration).

(k)   No other benefits are payable under the scheme.

An earnings limit of £60,000 applies for the purpose of calculating certain benefits paid and contribution levels for approved schemes established on or after 14 March 1989 (this limit also applies to new entrants to existing schemes who join on or after 1 June 1989).

The Inland Revenue have a discretion to grant approval to schemes which do not satisfy certain of the requirements relating to the amount or type of benefit which can be received under the terms of the scheme. This discretion can be exercised to grant approval for schemes, providing, *inter alia*, higher pensions, death in service pensions for spouses, lump sum death in service benefits of up to four times the final remuneration or refunds of contributions.

If the scheme is a qualifying exempt approved scheme, the tax consequences are as follows:

(a)   Income derived from investments and deposits held for the purposes of the scheme are exempt from income tax.

(b)   The contributions to the scheme made by the employer can be deducted from profits when computing liability to tax under Schedule D Cases I and II.

(c)   The employee is allowed to deduct any ordinary annual contribution paid under the scheme when calculating his liability to Schedule E tax.

(d)   All pensions and annuities paid under the scheme are chargeable to tax as earned income under Schedule E. (The PAYE system applies for the purposes of collection of tax.)

2.2 Retirement annuity schemes

An employee whose employer has not set up an occupational pension scheme is in the same position as a self-employed person. Accordingly, employees who are in non-pensionable employment often provide for their own retirement by means of a personal pension scheme (see paragraph 3.1).

2.3 Fees paid to non-executive directors

In cases where the employee wishing to ensure security of income during his retirement is a director of a company, it may be possible to secure an appointment as a non-executive director. Such an appointment is akin to an appointment as a consultant to a partnership. Provided the fees can properly be regarded as deductible expenses, the employer will be able to deduct the fees in calculating its taxable profits. The recipient will be receiving emoluments deriving from an office and will be assessed to tax under Schedule E. However, the company could remove the non-executive director from office and so this may not be a very secure method of providing for retirement.

2.4 The state pension

In addition to the possible sources of pension benefits referred to above, a statutory state pension is available to every individual who has made National Insurance contributions.

The state pension scheme is funded by contributions made by both the employer and the employee. The terms of the state scheme provide for two types of pension, namely the flat-rate pension and the earnings-related pension (although the government is considering abolishing the earnings-related pension).

The flat-rate pension is payable at 65 (for men) and 60 (for women) to every individual who has contributed to the scheme for $^9/_{10}$ths of his or her working life.

In contrast the earnings-related scheme (under which an additional pension is provided, the amount of which is linked to the employee's earnings) is only available to employees whose employers have not 'contracted out' and there is a limit on the amount of earnings which are pensionable. (An employer can contract out if a private pension scheme is provided.)

The employee is not entitled to deduct any National Insurance contributions when calculating his tax liability.

3 RETIREMENT PROVISION FOR SOLE PROPRIETORS AND PARTNERS

3.1 Retirement annuity contracts

On 1 July 1988 it ceased to be possible to take out new retirement annuity contracts since they were replaced by personal pensions (see para. 3.2 below). Since it is possible to continue to contribute to existing contracts, such contracts will continue to be of relevance for some years to come. Their key elements are explained below.

These schemes are available to the self-employed, employees whose employers do not run an occupational scheme and employees who opt out of their employer's scheme. The future pensioner gets income tax relief on contributions to a personal pension scheme up to a maximum of 17½% of net relevant earnings. Higher percentages apply where the premium is paid by a taxpayer aged 51 or older. On retirement, an annuity is purchased with the money in the accumulated fund. At that stage no capital gains tax is payable although the annuity when received is, of course, liable to income tax. A lump sum may be taken in cash on retirement provided that it does not exceed £150,000 nor 25% of the fund.

3.2 Personal pensions

Such pensions (which replace retirement annuity contracts) can be taken out by the self-employed. They can also be taken out by employees in non-pensionable employment or those in pensionable employment who wish to 'top up' their occupational pensions or who have 'contracted out' of their occupational schemes.

As with the retirement annuity contracts, the future pensioner will get income tax relief on his contributions up to a maximum of 17½% of net relevant earnings. However, if the taxpayer is aged 36 or over, the percentage for which relief is available increases on a sliding scale dependent on the payer's age.

As with occupational pensions, the tax relief is limited to contributions on earnings of up to £60,000 per annum. For personal pension plans entered into on or after 27 July 1989 the £150,000 ceiling applicable to the maximum tax free lump sum has been removed. Instead the maximum lump sum which can be taken at retirement is 25% of the total fund; the rules for determining the 'total fund' are beyond the scope of this book.

3.3 Partnership annuities

While personal pensions may be the only method of providing a pension which is available to sole proprietors and employees in non-pensionable employment, it may be possible for a retiring partner (or his spouse and dependants) to receive an annuity from the continuing partners.

The terms of the payment of such an annuity are a matter to be agreed between the partners and that agreement should be reached well in advance of the retirement date.

This method of providing a pension has the attraction, so far as the retiring partner is concerned, of not requiring him to make payments prior to retirement (as is the case with a personal pension). However, the continuing partners may object since they will be supporting a person who is no longer contributing to the profits of the business.

The amount of the annuity will be a matter of negotiation. It can be linked to the profits of the partnership and so it may be possible to ensure that the income of the retired partner keeps pace with inflation.

Where an individual has ceased to be a member of a partnership on retirement, by reason of age or ill-health, or on death and an annuity is paid for his benefit or the benefit of his widow or dependants the annuity is treated as earned income, subject to a limit. The annuity must be paid under the partnership agreement, or an agreement replacing or supplementing the partnership agreement, or an agreement with an individual who has acquired all or part of the partnership business; it will be paid net of basic rate tax (see below).

So far as the continuing partners are concerned, they will each bear the cost of the annuity in the same proportions as they share profits. The gross amount of the annuity payment is treated as a charge on their incomes and so will reduce their taxable share of profits. They will pay the annuity to the former partner net of basic rate income tax.

3.4 Appointment as a consultant

The retiring partner may wish to retain some contact with the activities of the business by continuing to be involved as a consultant. Such an arrangement may give rise to the practical advantage that the partnership retains the benefit of the personal goodwill the retiring partner has built up over the years.

From a tax viewpoint, as the consultant is no longer a partner, the consultancy fees can be deducted in computing the partnership's profits provided they are wholly and exclusively incurred for business purposes.

The consultant will receive earned income taxable under Schedule E, although the nature of the consultancy arrangement may be such that he can show he is exercising a profession or vocation in which case he will be assessed under Schedule D Case II. This is more likely to be the case if the retiring partner has a number of consultancy arrangements.

3.5 The state pension

Self-employed individuals, such as partners, pay Class 2 and Class 4 National Insurance contributions. Class 2 contributions are paid at a flat rate and, subject to satisfying certain requirements as to contribution history, entitle the individual to receive the flat-rate state retirement pension at 65 for men and 60 for women (but not the earnings related pension). Class 4 contributions are based on a percentage of taxable profits within certain limits. The payment of Class 4 contributions does not give rise to entitlement to any benefits; in effect, they operate as a form of additional income tax. Section 617 ICTA 1988 introduces provisions which allow tax relief to be given on 50% of the Class 4 contributions paid by a self-employed individual.

20 Choice of Business Medium and Transfer of a Business to a Company

1 CHOICE OF BUSINESS MEDIUM

1.1 Introduction

The purpose of this section is to make a comparison between companies, on the one hand, and partnerships or sole traders on the other, with a view to explaining the various factors which ought to be taken into account when a choice is made between the two business media.

This choice will first be made when a new business is set up, but should be kept under review as circumstances (and the law) change. For the sake of clarity, the differences between companies and partnerships are considered under various headings. It is important to realise that in making a choice each factor should be taken into account. In particular cases one factor may outweigh all the others, but generally each medium has some advantages and some disadvantages so that often the choice will be a difficult one.

1.2 Risk of capital

All business involves a risk of capital. The degree of risk obviously varies considerably depending on the nature of the business, the economic climate and the skill of the people running the business. The amount of capital which is at risk also varies considerably — some types of business require a great deal of capital, others very little.

One advantage of a company over a partnership is that a company can be formed with limited liability. This means that the shareholders must contribute the amount unpaid on their shares, but no more, if the company goes into liquidation when it is insolvent. In the vast majority of cases the shares will be fully paid, so that no contribution towards the company's debts has to be made. However, the shareholders will lose their shares when the company fails so that, realistically, the limit to their liability is what they have invested in the company. A shareholder who is also a director will also lose his livelihood. A director (including a shadow director) may also become personally liable if he is judged to be guilty of wrongful trading (see chapter 21 paragraph 7.3).

If a partnership becomes insolvent, each of the partners is jointly and severally liable for all the debts of the partnership. This means that he stands to lose not only what he has invested in the business but also any other property which he owns. The liability of partners is, therefore, unlimited in amount. The partnership agreement may make provision as to how losses are to be shared between the partners but this does not prevent creditors claiming in full from a rich partner whose poor partners are unable to pay their share of the loss.

At first sight limited liability would seem to be an enormous advantage to the proprietors of a business in every case. However, there are at least two circumstances where limited liability is not very significant:

(a) *Where there is little risk of substantial loss of capital* — The clearest example of this is a business involving the giving of advice, such as a consultancy. The proprietor expects to make profits by providing expertise in return for payment; comparatively little is required in the way of capital expenditure on equipment and the running costs of the business will be small. In many cases the biggest potential loss will be claims for damages if bad advice is given to clients and this can be covered by insurance.

(b) *Where the proprietor risks everything he owns in the business* — If the proprietor's only assets are what he has invested in the business, he will effectively lose everything when the business fails whether it is a company or partnership. (This is, of course, only true while all the capital remains in the business, so that limited liability will become relevant once the proprietor starts to take profits out of the business on a large scale.)

Sometimes limited liability would be very desirable but cannot realistically be achieved because credit is needed but cannot be obtained without a personal guarantee. Many businesses rely on borrowed money. A bank lending to a small company will often require a personal guarantee from the directors or shareholders, so that if the company cannot repay the loan the bank has further security. This may wipe out the advantage of limited liability to a large extent.

Limited liability is most significant (and can realistically be achieved) where there is a substantial risk of loss of capital invested and the proprietor (or one of the proprietors) has private wealth not invested in the business. In such cases limited liability may be so desirable that it far outweighs any other consideration, and therefore the business must be run as a company.

1.3 Expense

Certain expenses must inevitably be incurred when a company is formed. These include the Registrar's fee of £50 and the cost of preparing the memorandum and articles. If a partnership is formed these expenses need not be incurred since there are no registration requirements. However, in most cases the partners will want a properly drawn up partnership agreement and will wish to instruct a solicitor to draw it up for them.

It is difficult to make any general comparison between costs of formation, since they will depend largely on the complexity of the proposed memorandum and articles or partnership agreement. The legal fees payable for formation are about the same in both cases where the documents have to be drafted by a solicitor. Where a company is bought 'off-the-peg' from a law stationer the costs are likely to be in the region of £150 (including the Registrar's fee), which is likely to be less than the cost of drawing up a partnership agreement of similar complexity.

In addition to legal advice, the proprietors of a new business will often wish to seek advice from accountants. Again, the amount payable for the advice will depend on the complexity of the advice given rather than the business medium used. Similarly, certain printing costs will be incurred for business letter paper. These expenses are only *necessary* in the case of a company (which must comply with the provisions of the Companies Act relating to the name, number and address of the company), but in the case of a partnership printed letter paper will normally be used even though it is not required by law.

With both media formation expenses are likely to be fairly substantial (for a small business, hundreds rather than thousands of pounds) but are unlikely to influence the *choice* of business medium.

After formation the major administrative costs of a business will again depend on the complexity of the business. However, in respect of accounts a company is at a disadvantage when compared with a partnership. All types of business will wish to keep accounts and prepare final accounts annually. Nearly all businesses will wish to pay a qualified accountant to draw up these accounts (if only so as to make sure that advantage is taken of tax reliefs and exemptions). A company, however, must draw up the accounts in a particular way so that they comply with the Companies Act 1985. This means that the accounts must in some respects show more information than the accounts of a partnership and for a small business this may involve considerable extra cost. (It should be remembered that the partial exemption of 'small' companies from accounting requirements applies only to the published accounts — full accounts must be prepared for the members.) Furthermore, once the accounts have been produced they must be audited by an independent qualified accountant. This means that a company must incur two lots of accountants' fees annually, whereas a partnership need only incur one.

A company is also required to prepare an annual return and to pay a fee of £20 on filing it with the Registrar. The Companies Act also requires many other returns to be filed from time to time (e.g., particulars of directors, charges and address of registered office); although fees are not payable on the filing of these returns, their preparation will add to the running costs of the business if it is a company. Many company directors will not feel able to deal with these matters themselves and so will have to hire a qualified company secretary or take legal advice.

The running costs of a company will be more than those of a partnership although the difference is not likely to be great enough to be significant except in the case of small businesses.

1.4 Management

The Companies Act lays down certain rules as to the management structure of companies. A company is, for example, required to have at least one director and a secretary. Certain obligations are imposed on these officials in relation to filing returns. However, a company is entitled to lay down in its articles rules as to management of whatever type it chooses. A partnership may also establish its own rules for management of the business. The Partnership Act 1890 lays down certain presumptions (e.g., that, in the absence of contrary agreement, decisions are taken by a majority vote of the partners except in a limited number of cases where unanimity is required). The partners are free to vary these presumptions by agreement or by a course of dealings. Both types of business medium are, therefore, entitled to choose a management structure which is suitable for the particular case.

1.4.1 Internal flexibility

After a suitable management structure has been chosen it may need to be changed because of changed circumstances. In the case of a company, changes to the articles require a special resolution (i.e., a 75% majority of the shareholders). However, many changes of management structure can be made without a change in the articles. Thus if the articles are in the usual form, the maximum number of directors can be increased and new appointments can be made to the board by an ordinary resolution (simple majority of shareholders) and a managing director can be appointed by the board. The board may also decide on its own procedures for taking decisions and may delegate decision making powers as and when necessary. If it is considered that the structure is too flexible, the articles may provide for special resolutions in circumstances where an ordinary resolution would otherwise be sufficient (except in the case of removal of directors from office, where an ordinary resolution is always sufficient (s. 303 CA 1985)). The articles may also restrict the powers of the board and require the approval of the members in general meeting for major decisions. An extreme degree of inflexibility can be achieved, if desired, by including in the memorandum provisions which could have been included in the articles and by making these provisions unalterable.

In the case of a partnership, the agreement between the partners can be altered. This normally requires the approval of all the partners so that the 'constitution' of a partnership is more rigid than that of a company. However, if, when the partnership agreement is drawn up, it is decided that a greater degree of flexibility is required, the agreement can provide for alteration by a majority (without unanimous agreement), either in general or in particular cases.

It is, therefore, possible for either business medium to have a very flexible or a very rigid management structure, as the proprietors wish.

1.4.2 Security of tenure

Just as the profits of a partnership are divided between the partners so, in the case of most small companies, the profits will be divided between the directors. Security of tenure as a partner or director is, therefore, of vital concern to the proprietors of a business.

A director is always subject to removal by an ordinary resolution of the members. However, a director who has the majority of votes (or a majority of votes on a resolution for his removal — see *Bushell* v *Faith* [1970] AC 1099, ch. 8—2) is effectively irremovable. A director who does not have a majority of votes but who has a service agreement may be entitled to substantial compensation if removed from office, and so to that extent may be protected. If the company is a 'quasi-partnership' (see ch. 8—2), removal of a director from office may also lead to liquidation of the company.

In the case of a partnership, removal of a partner will, subject to contrary agreement, involve the dissolution of the partnership. At first sight this would seem to put a partner in a stronger position than a director. However, in practice, this is not necessarily so. In some cases it will be possible for some of the partners to get rid of one of their colleagues and then set up a 'new' business after the dissolution, which will in effect be a continuation of the old business. This will be possible particularly if those who remain own the premises where the business is carried on. The position of a junior partner is not, therefore, necessarily stronger than that of a director who is not in control of the company.

The practical reality of the situation is that if a director or partner is vital to the business he cannot be removed without bringing the business to an end. However, where a director or partner is really no more than a senior employee, he can be removed on payment of any compensation provided for in his service contract or in the partnership agreement. A director, but not a partner, may also be entitled to compensation for unfair dismissal or redundancy.

1.4.3 Succession to the business

The articles of a company may restrict the right to transfer shares, thus preventing a shareholder from selling out or giving away shares to anyone he pleases. Such restrictions may be coupled with pre-emption rights given to the other shareholders. Alternatively, shares may be freely transferable. It is, therefore, possible to make provision for succession in advance, provided that sufficient thought is given to the problem at the time when the articles are drafted. Similarly, a partnership agreement may make provision for bringing in new partners and for payment to the existing partners on leaving. If no other provision is made, unanimity is required for the admission of a new partner. Since the partners have to be able to work together in running the business, it is unlikely that they would be willing to allow admission of new partners without such agreement.

It is, therefore, possible to lay down rules for succession with either type of business medium. In practical terms the problem of succession is one which can only be solved if suitable purchasers can be found or if suitable donees willing to carry on the business are available. The management buy-out provisions of the Companies Act 1985 (see ch. 17—4) may assist considerably in the case of small private companies. It is also generally easier to achieve succession in the case of a company, since the sale of a majority shareholding passes control to the purchaser. The majority shareholder will usually be free to sell out since he is in control of the board who will, therefore, approve any transfer of his shares unless there are any pre-emption rights.

1.4.4 Legal status of business media

There are a number of ways in which the legal status of a company differs from that of a partnership, for example:

(a) A company is a separate legal person whereas a partnership is not.

(b) Only companies can create floating charges.

(c) A company is bound by the ultra vires doctrine (although following the enactment of the Companies Act 1989 this doctrine has been greatly modified in its effect) whereas a partnership is not, so that a partnership is free to change the nature of its business (unanimous agreement of the partners is required but outsiders will not be affected by the absence of such agreement).

(d) An unlimited number of persons may be members of a company at any time whereas partnerships (other than in certain professions) are limited to 20 members.

None of these differences is likely to affect the choice of business medium in most cases.

1.5   Publicity

As we saw in Chapter 9, a company is required to make a considerable amount of information, including annual accounts, available to the public. A partnership is not required to make such information available. A desire to keep the affairs of the business secret may influence some businessmen to prefer a partnership to a company, but it is not likely to be a major factor in most cases, especially since the partners will, in practice, be required to show their accounts to any prospective lender.

1.6   Taxation — trading profits

The reader is advised to re-read Chapters 5, 14 and 15 before reading the rest of this section. As was explained in Chapter 5, a company has a choice as to how to use its profits — they may be used to pay dividends, interest, or directors' fees, or they may be retained in the business. Each of these four possibilities has different tax consequences. Generally speaking, the payment of directors' fees is the most tax-efficient use of profits, and for a small private company most of the profits will normally be used for this purpose for non-tax reasons anyway. This is because the directors must be compensated for the work that they do for the business and often little profit will be left over for other purposes.

Where profits are sufficiently large, however, a company can be used as a means of tax planning by deciding to retain profits or pay dividends. Retained profits are liable to corporation tax at 25% or 35% (depending on the size of the profit). The rate can be kept down to 25% if sufficient is paid in directors' fees to keep the profits below the threshold for the higher rate of corporation tax. This rate of tax may be somewhat less than the shareholder's rate of income tax (which may be 40%). However, the future consequences of capital taxes must also be taken into account. The accumulated profits will be reflected in the value of the shares in the company so that on a disposal of shares CGT (in rare cases income tax where the company buys back its own shares or under s. 703 ICTA 1988) and/or IHT may be payable, thus reducing the effectiveness of the income tax saving resulting from retention of the profits.

A decision to pay dividends may be taken for non-tax reasons, since it is the only way to provide a shareholder who is not also a director with a return on his investment. However, as we saw earlier, a dividend may be tax-inefficient in the case of a company where profits are high.

A partnership offers less scope for tax planning in relation to income profits than a company. All the income profits are taxed as income of the partners whether they are actually paid to them or are retained in the business (unless a capital allowance is available). To the extent that profits are withdrawn from the business a partner is in the same position as a director receiving directors' fees — both pay income tax on the sums that are received.

It should be noted, however, that partners pay tax on the preceding year basis, that is, in each tax year they pay tax on the profits of the accounting period ending in the preceding year of assessment. A director pays tax on his fees under the PAYE scheme immediately, so that there is a cash flow advantage in paying tax on partnership income rather than on directors fees.

To the extent that profits are retained in the business, a partner pays the same tax as if the profits had been withdrawn. This will be an advantage when compared with a company where the partner's rate of tax is less than the rate of corporation tax, and a disadvantage when it is more.

It is, unfortunately, not possible to come to any general conclusions about which business medium is most suitable from the point of view of income taxation. Probably in most circumstances there is now little to choose between the two. This is partly the result of the fact that relatively small differences now exist between the rates of tax applying to individuals and companies. In any case, in most businesses, substantially all the profits will be used to pay directors' fees or will be withdrawn by the partners. Where profits are sufficiently large that there is a real possibility of tax planning, the greater flexibility provided by the system of company taxation may be advantageous.

1.7   Interest relief

A payment of interest must generally be paid out of taxed income. However, in some cases interest paid may be deducted from income before it is assessed to tax as a 'charge on income' (so that tax relief is available on the interest payment). This relief is available where money is borrowed to buy an interest in a partnership. Relief is also available where money is borrowed to buy shares in a close company provided that either:

(a)   the shares give the borrower a 'material interest' (i.e., more than 5% of ordinary share capital or a right to more than 5% of the income);

(b)   the borrower owns some shares and, from the time when he used the loan until the time when the interest was paid, he was working for more than half his time in actual management of the business; or

(c)   the borrower is a full-time employee of the company (whether a close company or not), the loan is used to buy shares in the company, and the company is an employee-controlled company (i.e., 51% of share capital and voting power is beneficially owned by employees and their spouses).

1.8   Losses

A trading loss made by a company may be set against the profits (including capital gains) of the loss-making period and the *previous* period of equal length (provided the loss-making trade was then being carried on). To the extent that relief is not claimed for those periods, or is claimed but full relief is not available because the profits are smaller than the loss, the relief may be carried forward and set against future income from the same trade. Broadly similar rules apply to a partnership. The partners may set a loss off against income (of any type) in the year of assessment when the loss is made (which may include profits from the same trade earned in the previous accounting period and now taxable on the preceding year basis), and, provided the trade is still being carried on, in the *next* year of assessment. To the extent that this does not give full relief, the loss may be carried forward and set against future profits of the same trade.

These rules give a company one advantage over a partnership, in that it may set a trading loss off against capital gains, whereas a partnership cannot. However, losses made by a company can only be set off against profits of the company, not against other income of its shareholders, whereas a partner with another source of income (for example, dividends on shares which he owns) may set the loss off against that other income. Furthermore, a loss made in the first three years of a new unincorporated trade may be carried back and set off against income of the partners in the three years before the trade was set up. A person who sets up a company gets no such relief for losses made in the early years of the company's trade.

1.9   Capital gains

A company pays corporation tax at the rate of 25% or 35% of any capital gain which it makes. The disposal of assets by a partnership gives rise to tax at the appropriate rate or rates of the partners (which may be 25% or 40%). However, a company and its proprietors suffer two disadvantages in respect of capital gains. Firstly, the profit made on the disposal of a capital asset (after payment of tax) will be reflected in the value of the shares in the company and further capital gains tax will be payable on disposal of those shares. (For example, an asset is purchased for £10,000 and sold for £20,000. Tax of (say) £2,500 will be paid, leaving a net profit of £7,500. This profit will be reflected in the value of the shares so that if they are disposed of, a further gain of £7,500 will be taxed. This extra charge to tax can be avoided if the disposal of the shares is tax-free (e.g., because they are given away on the death of the shareholder).) Secondly, a company is not entitled to an annual exemption, whereas in the case of a partnership each partner is entitled to an annual exemption for the first £5,000 worth of gains during each tax year.

There are also differences between companies and partnerships in respect of various capital gains tax exemptions; thus:

(a)   Retirement relief is usually available to a partner who disposes of an interest in a partnership when he is over 60. As we have already seen (ch. 17), similar relief is available in the case of a disposal of shares, but only if the company is a trading company and a family company and the disposal is by a full-time working director.

(b)   Roll-over relief is available on the disposal and replacement of certain types of business asset (including land, goodwill and fixed plant and machinery). When such assets are disposed of the gain is not taxed (if the disposer so elects) but instead the gain is deducted from the allowable expenditure on the replacement assets (so that when they are disposed of both gains are taxed). The relief is available to a partner and to a company. It is also available to a shareholder who owns an asset which is used by his company provided the company is his family company (i.e., he owns 25% of the voting rights or he owns 5% and he and his family together own more than 50%).

1.10   Inheritance tax

A company cannot normally be used as a means of avoiding IHT, since gifts by a close company are attributed to the shareholders in the company (s. 94 IHTA 1984). Nearly all small companies come within the definition of a close company. Similarly, gifts of partnership assets will be liable to tax as gifts of the individual partners. Inheritance tax is, therefore, generally a neutral factor in the choice of business medium.

There are, however, a number of differences between the ways in which IHT business property relief operates in respect of a company and a partnership. It will be remembered that the relief operates as a reduction in the value transferred of 50% in the case of a gift of shares giving control of the company (see ch. 17—7.2). Fifty per cent relief is also available on a gift of an 'interest in a business', which includes a partner's share of partnership assets. However, relief is available at a rate of only 30% in the case of a minority shareholding. A minority shareholder is, therefore, less favourably treated than a partner (who is entitled to the 50% relief however small his interest in the partnership). There is also a difference in the relief given where an asset is owned by an individual partner or shareholder but used by the partnership or company. A partner whose private property is used by his partnership is entitled to relief of 30% when he gives the property away. Similar relief is available to a shareholder but only if he owns shares which give control of the company.

Business property relief is, therefore, neutral as between a partner and a *majority* shareholder, but treats a partner more favourably than a *minority* shareholder.

1.11   Pensions and social security

There are a number of ways in which businessmen may provide for their retirement (see ch. 19). The most favourable method from the tax point of view is an 'exempt approved pension scheme'. Such a scheme affords generous tax relief on contributions by both employers and employees and further relief from capital taxes to the managers of the scheme. Its purpose is to provide a pension and, in some cases, a lump sum on retirement. Such schemes are not available to the self-employed (such as partners). Partners are able to get the relief by means of a personal pension. Contributions are deductible from taxable income up to a certain percentage of relevant earnings depending on the age of the contributor. However, the relief is limited to the appropriate percentage of £60,000 in the case of partners whose income exceeds this figure.

Social security also operates differently in respect of employees and the self-employed. Contributions must be made by both employer and employee in respect of an employed person; a self-employed person must contribute at a rate higher than the employee's contribution but lower than the employer's and employee's contributions combined. The benefits to which an employed person is entitled are correspondingly higher than those to which a self-employed person is entitled. The overall effect of the differences between the two schemes is controversial but many consider that the self-employed are at a disadvantage.

1.12   Conclusion

It is not possible to lay down any hard and fast rule as to which business medium is most beneficial since there are too many variables. In a significant number of cases the desirability of limited liability will indicate company formation as the only real possibility. Where limited liability is not of great importance, the tax factors will be more significant. Generally speaking, a company will be more likely to be required where profits are large and a partnership where they are small, but really the only sound advice is that each case must be determined according to the particular circumstances.

2 INTRODUCTION TO TRANSFER OF A BUSINESS

A sole trader or partnership may decide, for a variety of reasons, to incorporate the business. If this step is taken, although the business will remain unchanged, the incorporation will give rise to a number of tax and other problems. In this section we will consider these problems and how they can be avoided, or at least mitigated. As we shall see, the tax rules are the most important in this area, since if they are not appreciated the payment of an unexpected tax bill can cause very serious cash flow problems. As an aid to understanding these problems, it is helpful to bear in mind that when the trader (which for these purposes includes partnerships) incorporates the business, it is transferred to a separate legal entity, the company. This means that the trader ceases to trade as an unincorporated business and disposes of the business and its assets to the company. The fact that the former proprietor or proprietors own the company and operate the business in exactly the same way as before is immaterial since the members of the company are distinct legal entities (*Salomon* v *A. Salomon & Co Ltd* [1897] AC 22).

It may therefore come as a surprise to many traders who incorporate their businesses to discover that incorporation can lead to the payment of income tax, capital gains tax and stamp duty. In this section these tax liabilities will be considered in turn.

3 INCOME TAX

3.1 The closing years rules

Of the possible tax liabilities which can arise, the one which may cause the most difficulties, if it is not provided for, is the liability to income tax. Transferring the business to the company means that the unincorporated trader has permanently stopped trading, with the result that the closing years rules of assessment set out in s. 63 ICTA 1988 will apply. To recapitulate, the effect of s. 63 is as follows:

(a) In the tax year in which the business is sold to the company, the trader pays tax on the profits made from 6 April to the date of discontinuance, that is, the date the business is transferred to the company. If the trader has no accounts which cover this period, the profits made in the final accounting period will be apportioned on a time basis.

(b) In the penultimate and pre-penultimate tax years, the preceding year basis will apply, so that the trader will be assessed on the profits made in the accounting period which ended in the tax year immediately preceding the relevant year. The Inland Revenue have a right to tax both the penultimate and the pre-penultimate tax years on an actual or current year basis (that is, the profits from 6 April to the following 5 April) if the profits for those periods are higher.

The problems that can result from these rules are best illustrated by applying the rules to a set of facts. If a trader makes up his accounts to the 5 July each year and transfers his business to a company on 6 July 1990, the profits on which he will be assessed, if the Revenue do not make their election, are as follows:

(a)   Final tax year (1990/91) — profits made from 6 April 1990 to 5 July 1990. As he has no accounts covering this three-month period he will pay tax on ¼ of the profits made in the final accounting period which ends on 5 July 1990.

(b)   Penultimate tax year (1989/90) — profits made to 5 July 1988, since the preceding year basis is applicable.

(c)   Pre-penultimate tax year (1988/89) — profits made to 5 July 1987 (since, again, the preceding year basis applies).

This shows that there is a 'tax-free' gap from 6 July 1988 to 5 April 1990. Clearly, were it is not for the Revenue's right to elect to tax the trader on the actual basis for the penultimate and pre-penultimate tax years, the sensible trader would ensure that he completed as much work as possible (assuming he is assessed on the earnings basis, see ch. 14—1.4) during the accounting period ending on 5 July 1989, since the profits arising would fall into this 'tax-free gap'. If the trader's profits are higher during these two tax years the Revenue will make their election, which means the profits on which he will be assessed are as follows:

(a)   Final tax year — as above.

(b)   Penultimate tax year — profits made between 6 April 1989 and 5 April 1990, apportioning accounts for the appropriate accounting periods on a time bais.

(c)   Pre-penultimate tax year — profits made between 6 April 1988 and 5 April 1989, again apportioning the accounts.

The election has the effect of wiping out the 'tax-free gap' from July 1988 to April 1990, but since the tax year before the pre-penultimate one (1987/1988) is assessed on the preceding year basis, so attracting tax on the profits made to July 1986, the 'tax-free gap' merely appears earlier in the accounts. Now, no tax will be paid based on the profits made between 6 July 1986 to 5 April 1988.

The end result is that whether or not the Revenue make their election, a tax-free gap of between 12 and nearly 24 months (depending on the date the accounts are made up to) will appear somewhere in the accounts of the last four years of the business.

3.2   The additional tax liability

While the 'tax-free' gap may be a considerable advantage, the closing years rules as a whole can lead to a serious cash flow problem when the Revenue do elect to tax the trader on the actual basis (which they will do if his profits have been increasing). The problem stems from the dates for payment of tax, which for Schedule D Cases I and II taxpayers are 1 January in the relevant tax year and the immediately following 1 July.

Since the Revenue's right to elect relates, in the illustration, to the tax years 1988/89 and 1989/90, by the date of transfer (6 July 1990) the dates for payment of tax in respect of both these years will already have passed. The result of this is that any extra tax is immediately payable, subject only to the time it takes for the Revenue to consider the accounts for these periods and to produce a revised assessment for the two tax years. (It should be remembered that the Revenue will already have calculated, and probably have received, the tax payable for these two years on the preceding year basis, so that only the difference between the tax already assessed and the tax liability that has arisen on the actual basis will now be payable.) If the profits have been rising sharply, or if the rates of tax have increased, the extra amount that is now payable could be a considerable burden, especially if provision has not been made to meet it.

3.3 Funds used to pay additional tax liability

If steps have not been taken to guard against this eventuality and the trader has transferred all the assets of the business to the company, he faces serious problems trying to raise the money to pay this tax. If he tries to borrow money from a bank, he will have to pay interest charges and he will not be able to borrow money from the new company since he will, presumably, be a director and loans to directors are generally forbidden. If he is merely a shareholder in the company it could lend him the money, but since it will almost certainly be a close company, it will have to pay a sum equivalent to ACT until the loan is repaid and should it be written off, the trader will have to pay income tax on the amount of the loan grossed up at basic rate.

Since the company cannot simply pay the tax liability on the trader's behalf, the only other method of receiving money from the company is in the form of either directors' fees or dividends. Since these are themselves taxable as income receipts, he would have to bear income tax on them so he would need to receive sufficiently large fees or dividends to leave him, after tax, with enough to live on and to meet the additional tax liability. Such a payment could place an intolerable burden on the new company.

If these methods were unavailable to the trader, his only alternative would be to sell his personal assets, which would include the shares in the new company. Thus a lack of foresight could lead to the trader having to sell all his shares, or at least introduce an unwanted 'partner' and, to add insult to injury, possibly having to pay capital gains tax on the sale of these personal assets.

The problems outlined above can be avoided by, for example, the trader retaining any cash that he set aside out of the business profits as a tax provision or the book debts of the business. However, when considering this, care must be taken to ensure that retaining such sums or assets does not deny the trader relief from other taxes. As will be seen later (paragraph 4.2), retaining cash has no effect on the trader's entitlement to capital gains tax roll-over relief, but retaining an asset such as the book debts can cause the trader to lose this relief altogether (although it will save stamp duty; see paragraph 6).

3.4 Loss relief

If a loss was made in the final 12 months' trading, it could be carried across against other income under s. 380 ICTA 1988, and any unabsorbed loss carried back and set against the profits of the three tax years immediately preceding the year of incorporation, taking later years before earlier ones (s. 388 ICTA 1988). This would have the effect of reducing, if not wiping out, the profits, made during the last months of the unincorporated business's life and would almost certainly prevent the Revenue making their election. If, having made use of both provisions, there is still an unabsorbed loss, it cannot be used by the company. However, s. 386 permits the former proprietors, provided they sold the business in exchange wholly or mainly for shares in the new company, to set the remaining loss against income received from the company while they continue to own the shares. They must reduce earned income (such as directors' fees) before investment income (such as dividends).

Although it may appear strange that a loss-making business should be incorporated there may be sound reasons for doing so. For example, the business may be entering a temporary period of recession and the trader may want to protect himself from personal liability for future debts, or the loss may have been deliberately created by claiming capital allowances in respect of items of plant and machinery bought shortly before incorporation.

3.5 Capital allowances

Whether or not the purchase of an item attracting capital allowances has created the final year loss, the trader's capital allowance position is the remaining income tax point which needs to be considered. The rules relating to capital allowances have already been considered (see ch. 14). The important point to be considered in the context of incorporating a trader's business, is that the transfer to the company, even if the purchase price is to be paid in shares, will be a disposal. If the capital allowances claimed exceed the amount by which the assets have depreciated in value, the Revenue have a right to levy a balancing charge under Schedule D Case VI. This means the Revenue recovers the tax lost as a result of the over-deduction of allowances. Thus there can be another additional income tax bill arising on the incorporation. This bill can be avoided provided the provisions of sch. 8, para. 13, FA 1971 are satisfied. To summarise them, if the company buys the assets for more than their written-down value, the transfer is not to be regarded as a discontinuance of the trade for the purposes of capital allowances provided:

(a)   the trader and persons connected with him (which includes partners) are the majority shareholders in the new company; and

(b)   an election is made to the effect that if there is no discontinuance, there is no disposal and the balancing charge does not arise. The result is that the new company takes over the trader's capital allowance position and makes the appropriate claims for writing-down allowances in respect of the, as yet, unallowed expenditure.

4   CAPITAL GAINS TAX

4.1   The disposal

The incorporation of the old business not only means there is a discontinuance for income tax purposes, but that there is also a disposal for CGT purposes. This disposal arises because the business, its assets and connections (i.e., goodwill) are being *sold* to the company in exchange for shares. This is a chargeable disposal within the Capital Gains Tax Act 1979 and the trader will be liable for any gain that is realised.

The gain is calculated in the normal way by deducting the allowable expenditure from the market value of the assets transferred. Allowable expenditure includes the expenses incurred in acquiring, improving and disposing of the assets. Any indexation allowance which is available is also deducted. This liability cannot be avoided by the company issuing shares of a purely nominal value in exchange for the assets, as the Revenue have a right to substitute the market value of the assets in such circumstances. This gain could be considerable, especially if the business is successful and was set up several years previously. However, relief is available to the trader if the requirements of s. 123 CGTA 1979 are satisfied.

4.2   Relief under s. 123 CGTA 1979

4.2.1   The basic rule

Section 123 of CGTA 1979 applies where a person (not being a company) 'transfers to a company a business as a going concern, together with the whole assets of the business, or together with the whole of those assets other than cash, and the business is transferred wholly or partly in exchange for shares issued by the company to the person transferring the business'. The section permits a deduction to be made from the gain arising when the business and its assets are disposed of. Section 123(4) provides that this deduction is the gain reduced by the fraction A/B, where A is the 'cost of the new assets' (that is, the value of the shares issued to the former owner), and B is the whole of the consideration received by the former owner in exchange for the business. Thus, if the former owner transfers a business with assets worth £100,000 to the new company and receives £90,000 worth of shares and £10,000 worth of debentures in exchange, his gain will be reduced by the fraction £90,000/ (£90,000 + £10,000), i.e. $^9/_{10}$ths. This means that the former owner only pays tax on $^1/_{10}$th of the gain realised on the disposal of the business; the remaining $^9/_{10}$ths are, however, taxable when he disposes of the shares at some time in the future. If he only receives shares, the whole of the tax liability on the gain would be postponed in this way, or 'rolled-over' as the Act describes it.

It should be noted that the relief only applies to the former owner and his tax liability. The company's acquisition price of the assets will be their full market value at the date of the disposal.

4.2.2   The assets transferred to the company

Although these rules may appear complex at first sight, two simple requirements can be extracted from them. Firstly, to claim the relief at all, the whole of the assets of the business (other than cash) at the date of incorporation must be transferred to the company, and secondly, the relief may only be claimed in full if the consideration received was entirely in the form of shares. Provided these conditions are satisfied, the effect of s. 123 is that the former owner acquires the shares at a value equal to his original acquisition price of the assets that have just been transferred to the company, so tax is only paid when they are later sold or given away (by which time he may qualify for retirement relief under s. 124 CGTA 1979). Since s. 123 relief can be obtained so easily by following these rules, it may seem strange that a number of traders choose not to follow them. There are, however, two good reasons for this:

(a) To provide a fund from which the extra income tax liability, arising as a result of the Revenue's election under the closing years rules, can be paid. The section itself envisages the retention of a cash fund but other assets, such as book debts owed to the business at the date of transfer, might be kept by the former owner and would perform the same function as such a fund. Furthermore, the retention of non-cash assets can lead to a stamp duty saving (see paragraph 6 below).

(b) To avoid the 'double capital gains tax charge', which is a problem where companies own appreciating assets, such as land or buildings. If a company owns such an asset and disposes of it realising a gain, the company will pay corporation tax on that gain. The post-tax gain will then increase the value of the company's asets, which in turn has the effect of increasing the value of the shares. This will result in the shareholder making an increased gain, and so paying more capital gains tax, on a later disposal of the shares. Retaining the asset in the former owner's hands ensures that there is only one capital gains tax charge if the asset is disposed of. It may also produce a stamp duty saving (see paragraph 6). However, this is at the cost of the potential loss, or at least reduction, of certain capital tax reliefs (retirement relief and business property relief; see paragraph 5).

For either of these reasons, therefore, the former owner may retain assets even though, prima facie, this means the loss of the s. 123 relief. However, if the trader is sufficiently careful, it may be possible to retain assets without forfeiting the relief.

Section 123 relief is lost if all of the assets in the business *at the date of transfer* are not transferred, but there is nothing to prevent the trader transferring assets out of the business prior to incorporation and the company receiving all that is left. Provided the assets retained did not prevent the business being transferred as a 'going concern', the only stumbling block is convincing the Revenue that the assets no longer form part of the business. One method would be to make appropriate entries in the business' books, by debiting the trader's capital account with the value of the assets involved, but this would not amount to conclusive evidence that the asset had become 'private' property. Such conclusive evidence would be provided by transferring the assets to someone else, but unless an exemption was available, a tax charge would arise as a result of that transfer. An exemption is, of course, available if the assets are transferred to the former owner's spouse. However, the decision in *W. T. Ramsey v IRC* [1981] 2 WLR 449, which created a form of 'associated operations' for capital gains tax, might lead the court to decide that the transaction was made simply with a view to avoiding tax, thereby denying the former owner the right to take advantage of s. 123.

4.2.3 Method of payment for assets

Even if the Revenue are convinced that all the assets comprised in the business have been transferred, the relief can only be claimed in full if the company 'pays' for the assets in shares. As has already been explained, if the consideration is wholly or partly in debentures and/or cash the roll-over relief is wholly or partly denied to the former owner. Despite this, a trader might want to be paid either in cash or debentures for the following reasons. The advantage of receiving cash is that it provides a fund from which the former owner can pay the extra income tax liability arising on discontinuance. Since s. 123 permits cash to be retained without loss of the relief, this form of payment will only be necessary if the business had insufficient cash at the date of transfer to meet the tax liability, but was able to raise cash (for example, by collecting debts) shortly after incorporation.

It is much more common for the former owner to be paid in shares and debentures. Debentures have advantages for both the holder (in the form of security of both capital and income) and the company (in the form of a pre-tax deduction in respect of the interest payments), and these advantages may compensate the former owner for partial loss of capital gains tax relief. It should be remembered that receiving part of the consideration in debentures means only a proportionate part of the gain is taxable, and the taxable gain could be reduced or wiped out by the annual £5,000 exemption. This has the attraction of reducing any future taxable gain and also of ensuring that he does not lose the benefit of the annual exemption for the year of incorporation.

4.3 VAT relief

If the trader is registered for VAT, VAT may be chargeable on the transfer of the assets unless the business is transferred as a going concern (s. 33 Value Added Tax Act 1983).

4.4 Relief for gifts of business assets (s. 126 CGTA 1979)

Section 126 gives 'hold-over' relief where an asset used by the trader in his trade, profession or vocation is transferred to a company, provided the transaction is not a bargain at arm's length. This means that if the asset is 'sold' at an under-value, or even given to the company, the trader and the company can elect that the company acquires the asset for a consideration equal to the trader's acquisition cost (if there is an outright gift) or the sale price (if there is a sale at an under-value). The effect of the relief is to postpone the payment of tax until the asset is disposed of, when the *company* will be liable to pay the tax, not the trader.

5 CAPITAL TAX RELIEF AND RETAINED ASSETS

Retaining business assets can have the immediate disadvantage of denying the former owner the relief given by s. 123 and it can also have the long-term disadvantage of affecting his entitlement to both capital gains tax and inheritance tax reliefs. There are three such reliefs that the retention puts at risk.

5.1 Roll-over relief (ss. 115-121 CGTA 1979)

Firstly, it will be remembered that ss. 115-121 CGTA 1979 give traders, be they companies or individuals, the right to roll over any gain made on the disposal of specified business assets into replacement assets. Obviously, if the company receives the asset and deals with it in this way, relief can be obtained and the payment of tax postponed. However, the former owner may retain an asset (perhaps to avoid the double capital gains tax charge) intending to let the company make use of it. A problem may arise if he wishes to replace it with another. To obtain the roll-over relief an additional requirement must be satisfied.

Section 120 of CGTA 1979 permits the tax to be postponed only if the asset is disposed of by him and it was used in a business carried on by his 'family company'. A 'family company' is defined in s. 124(8) CGTA 1979 as meaning one in which the voting rights are:

(a)   as to not less than 25% exercisable by the individual; or
(b)   as to not less than 51% exercisable by the individual together with members of his family, and, as to not less than 5% exercisable by the individual himself. (For these purposes 'family' covers spouse, and brothers, sisters, ancestors and lineal descendants of either the former owner or his spouse.)

This will obviously not cause any problems if the former owner was the sole proprietor of this business, but clearly difficulties may arise if a partnership business has been incorporated, since some of the former partners may well own less than 25% of the shares.

5.2   Retirement relief (ss. 69 and 70 FA 1985)

A more serious problem arises in relation to retirement relief. Sections 69 and 70 FA 1985 give relief to an individual who disposes by sale or gift of the whole or part of a business or shares or securities of a company, having reached the age of at least 60, or who retires through ill-health below that age (see ch. 17—8).

5.3   Business property relief (ss. 103-114 IHTA 1984)

The third, and final, capital tax relief that is affected, is the relief for business property from capital transfer tax. This enables the transferor to claim a 50% reduction in the value transferred if shares forming part of a controlling holding are given away. While the value transferred will reflect not only the value of the underlying assets, but also the value of the controlling interest, the reduction will, in effect, be a 50% reduction in the asset's value. However, if the asset given away has been kept out of the company, a 30% reduction in the value transferred is all that can be claimed and only then if the transferor controls the company that used the asset. The retention therefore means that, in effect, the trader will face a liability to IHT on an additional 20% of the value of the asset. This could lead to a considerable tax liability.

Therefore, when deciding whether or not to retain assets, the trader must weigh up the advantage of avoiding the double capital gains tax charge against the loss of s. 123 relief and the payment of additional capital transfer tax when the asset is given away at some time in the future.

6   STAMP DUTY

6.1   Introduction

So far we have considered the tax liabilities of the trader personally; now we will consider the liabilities of the company to stamp duty. When a business is incorporated sufficient provision must be made to enable the company to meet this liability. In this section we do not intend to consider the duty in great detail, but will look at the particular points relevant on the incorporation of an existing business.

6.2 The charge to tax and s. 59 of the Stamp Act 1891

When dealing with stamp duty it is necessary to decide whether the assets transferred attract the duty at all, whether duty is paid on the contract or the conveyance, and finally, what the rate of duty should be.

Stamp duty is only payable if a transaction is evidenced by written instrument. Thus, oral contracts do not attract the duty, neither do transactions where ownership of the asset passes by delivery. Where a written instrument is used, stamp duty is payable, by s. 54 of the Stamp Act 1891, on the conveyance on sale but not on a mere contract to convey. Since a binding contract transfers the equitable title, if a purchaser is satisfied with the equitable title, it is prima facie possible to avoid stamp duty by never executing the conveyance. Normally a purchaser will not be satisfied with such title, but where a business is being incorporated, the new company will frequently be prepared to accept this. To prevent the loss of revenue that would result from this situation, s. 59(1) of the Stamp Act 1891 provides that the purchaser shall pay duty on the contract for the sale of any equitable interest or interest in any property or for the sale of any estate or interest in any property, except (*inter alia*) land, goods, wares or merchandise, or marketable securities or any ship or vessel, as if it were an actual conveyance on sale of the estate, interest, or property contracted or agreed to be sold.

The effect of the section is to levy duty on any contract to sell many of the assets that are likely to be transferred when incorporating an existing business (for example, goodwill, book debts, patents, 'know-how', the benefit of pending contracts, tenants' fixtures on *leasehold* property, *equitable* interests in freehold property and cash on deposit). If there is a subsequent conveyance no further duty is payable on that conveyance but if the duty was not paid on the contract no penalty becomes payable (other than one for late stamping), provided a conveyance or transfer is presented for stamping within six months of its execution (or within such longer period as the Commissioners of Inland Revenue may think reasonable in the circumstances of the case).

6.3 Treatment of items outside the s. 59 charge

Of the items excepted by s. 59, those falling into the category 'goods, wares or merchandise' are totally exempt from the charge provided title in them passes by delivery. This will be so in relation to stock-in-trade, plant and machinery, cash in hand and cash in a current bank account, but only if they are not specifically dealt with in the later conveyance (s. 34(4) Finance Act 1958). With regard to the cash, the exemption only applies to cash in hand or in a current account, since the Revenue regards such money as not being 'property' within the meaning of s. 59(1). However, cash on deposit is a debt to the customer by the bank (*Foley* v *Hill* (1848) 2 HL 28) and so is caught by the section

Where a legal estate in land (which includes fixtures on freehold property), marketable securities or ships is transferred, duty is paid, but on the conveyance or transfer, if there is one, and not the contract, so that it is theoretically possible to avoid stamp duty in respect of these items, although in practice a conveyance will normally be required.

Once the items that are subject to the duty have been valued, all the values are aggregated to calculate the rate of duty that is payable. If the business has liabilities that the new company is taking over, s. 57 of the Stamp Act 1891 requires duty to be paid on the total value of the dutiable assets being transferred without the deduction of the liabilities. This is because the agreement to pay the debts is part of the consideration given in exchange for receiving the assets (one practical point, unrelated to stamp duty, is that in such a case the agreement of the creditor will have to be obtained).

6.4   The stamp duty rates

The full rate of tax is £1 per £100 or part thereof of the value of dutiable items being transferred. However, if the instrument contains a certificate of value certifying that the value of the dutiable items does not exceed £30,000 no duty is payable. The usual wording for the certificate is:

> It is hereby certified that the transaction hereby effected does not form part of a larger transaction or of a series of transactions in respect of which the amount or value or the aggregate amount or value of the consideration exceeds £30,000.

It is important to note that the certificate of value relates to the total value passing under the transaction as a whole, so that where some assets pass under the contract and others under a conveyance, the values of property passing under both the contract and the conveyance must be aggregated. The calculation of the duty paid on the contract is made by apportioning the total consideration on the form 'Stamps 22'.

6.5   Saving stamp duty

Stamp duty can be saved in two ways: either by not transferring dutiable items to the company, or by converting ones that attract the duty into ones that do not. Thus the trader can retain book debts to provide a source of money to meet his additional income tax liability or to pay his existing trade creditors. Another possible way of saving stamp duty is to transfer cash on deposit into a current account. This need only be done for the day of the transfer.

7   SUBSIDIARY MATTERS

The tax matters already dealt with will, of course, be important to the former owner but there are a number of other points that must not be overlooked.

7.1   The transfer and employment law

Firstly, the effect of the transfer on the business' employees. The general rule used to be that the transfer of the business terminated the contracts of employment of all the employees and, if common law and statutory claims were to be avoided, the employees had to be notified of the transfer and offered employment with the new company on the same, or suitable, terms before the transfer took place. However, as a result of the Transfer of Undertakings (Protection of Employment) Regulations 1981 (SI 1981 No. 1794), this is no longer the case, since regulation 5(1) provides that a 'relevant transfer' shall not terminate a person's contract of employment and the contract shall have the effect after the transfer as if it had originally been made between the employee and the transferee. (A 'relevant transfer' is defined in regulation 3(1) as being 'a transfer from one person to another of an undertaking situated immediately before the transfer in the United Kingdom or of a part of one which is so situated'.) Thus, if a business is transferred to a company, the employees are treated as if their contracts had originally been made with the new company, which takes over all the trader's rights, powers, duties and liabilities under the employment contracts. Therefore the employee's period of continuous employment is preserved as are any pre-existing rights against the old employer for breach of contract, or duty. As a result, the new employer could be faced with liability for a constructive dismissal arising from the old employer' breach, for example, and should obtain suitable indemnities.

While these regulations do not prevent an employee bringing a claim against the trader if there is a substantial change made in his working conditions, no action can be brought simply because the identity of the employer has changed, unless the employee shows the change to be significant and to his detriment.

Regulation 5 does not enable the fact of the transfer to be kept from the employees. Regulation 10 imposes an obligation on the transferor to inform and consult with trade union representatives.

7.2 The transfer and company law

In addition to the matters that always arise on the formation of a new company, one special problem particularly relevant to this kind of transfer must be considered. On the assumption that the transferor of the business is to be made a director of the new company, the consent of the members in general meeting will almost certainly be needed to the purchase by the company of the assets. Section 320 CA 1985 requires such consent to be obtained if a director sells to (or buys from) the company a non-cash asset or assets of the 'requisite value', which means assets worth £50,000 or representing at least 10% of the company's assets (subject to a minimum value of £1,000). If the consent is not obtained, the transaction is voidable at the instance of the company and the director will have to account to the company for any profit made and indemnify it for any loss or damages arising. In order to obtain the necessary consent, a general meeting of the company will have to be held immediately after incorporation and before the transfer takes place.

Furthermore, the transferor must make sure that the new company's name appears on all letters, cheques and order forms as required by s. 348 CA 1985, and that the letters have printed on them the information required by ss. 305 and 351 CA 1985.

7.3 The transfer and other miscellaneous matters

Further practical points to be dealt with include:

(a)   The local inspector of taxes must be notified that there is a new employer for PAYE purposes as well as there being a new company liable to corporation tax.

(b)   If the business' turnover exceeds £25,400 (and so is registered for VAT), its VAT registration must be cancelled and the company must apply to have itself registered. In order to ensure there is no gap in the VAT registration it is advisable to cancel the old one after the company's registration has been confirmed.

(c)   The consent of a landlord to the assignment of a lease must be obtained. If the new company is taking over responsibility for hire-purchase contracts, the consent of the finance house must be obtained.

(d)   The former owner can bring his personal liability to existing creditors to an end by entering into a contract of 'novation'. However, the consent of the creditors is required.

(e)   The company must take out appropriate insurance cover and have any vehicles transferred into its own name.

Part V   Insolvency

21 The Insolvent Company

1 INTRODUCTION

All statute references in this chapter are to the Insolvency Act 1986 except where otherwise stated.

In this chapter we deal with the procedures which are available when a company is insolvent and with the procedures which are designed to prevent insolvency where a company is having financial problems.

The law relating to these matters is now largely contained in the Insolvency Act 1986. There are four principal procedures available where a company is insolvent or has financial problems:

(a) Administration order. This is a procedure which may be ordered by the court with a view to saving the business of the company (or part of it), or with a view to a more beneficial realisation of assets than could be achieved by winding up, or with a view to obtaining approval for a voluntary arrangement.

(b) Voluntary arrangement under the Insolvency Act 1986. This procedure enables a variety of schemes to be implemented (with the agreement of the company and its creditors) either so as to avoid or to supplement other types of insolvency procedure.

(c) Administrative receivership. An administrative receiver is appointed by a lender who holds a floating charge. The main responsibility of the receiver is to take control of the company so as to pay off the appointing creditor. However, the law recognises that this may have a considerable and permanent effect on the company and its other creditors and so various statutory powers are granted to the receiver and a number of obligations are imposed on him.

(d) Liquidation (or winding up). There are three types of liquidation: liquidation by the court (or compulsory winding up), members' voluntary liquidation and creditors' voluntary liquidation. There are many procedural and other differences between these types of liquidation but each is designed to achieve the same thing, that is, the collection and distribution of all the company's assets. The effect of liquidation is that the company ceases to exist as a *commercial* entity. When the liquidation is over the company is 'dissolved', that is, it ceases to exist as a *legal* entity.

The administration procedure and liquidation by the court are initiated by petition, applications to the court are required at various stages of the procedures for these remedies and also in relation to voluntary schemes, administrative receivership and voluntary winding-up. The High Court has jurisdiction to deal with any such petition or application where the company is registered in England and Wales. This type of business is assigned to the Chancery Division. In addition the county court of the district in which the company's registered office is situated has concurrent jurisdiction where the company's paid-up share capital does not exceed £120,000.

2 ADMINISTRATION ORDERS

The concept of administration was introduced for the first time by the Insolvency Act 1985, now consolidated in the Insolvency Act 1986. Administration is intended as an alternative to winding up. It is to be used principally in circumstances where a company is in difficulties but where something can be saved.

2.1 Application and grounds

A petition for the making of an administration order may be presented by the company, or its directors, or by a creditor or creditors (including any contingent or prospective creditor or creditors) or by any or all of those people together.

The petitioner must show that the company is unable to pay its debts or is likely to become unable to pay its debts. The petitioner must swear an affidavit setting out the grounds for the petition. This may be supported by a report from an independent insolvency practitioner which sets out the practitioner's reasons for believing that at least one of the objectives can be achieved. If no such report is annexed to the petition the petitioner must explain why none has been produced. In practice a petition not supported by a report is unlikely to succeed except perhaps in cases of great urgency.

The circumstances in which a company is treated as being unable to pay its debts are the same as for compulsory winding up (see paragraph 5.2.1). In addition to proving inability to pay debts the petitioner must also satisfy the court that the making of the administration order would be likely to achieve one or more of the following objectives:

(a)   the survival of the company, and the whole or any part of its undertaking as a going concern;

(b)   the approval of a voluntary arrangement or a composition in satisfaction of the company's debts, or a compromise or arrangement between the company and some or all of its members under s. 425 CA 1985; or

(c)   a more advantageous realisation of the company's assets than would be effected on a winding up.

As we will see shortly, the making of an administration order imposes a moratorium on the collection of debts by the company's creditors. A 'breathing space' is, therefore, created during which the administrator appointed by the court can seek to do one of these three things for the benefit of the creditors of the company generally.

The court has a discretion as to whether or not it will make an administration order. Very many companies are insolvent (unable to pay their debts) because of the 'balance sheet test' (that is, the value of the assets is less than the amount of the liabilities taking into account contingent and prospective liabilities). However, the court will exercise its discretion and refuse to make an administration order in cases where the company is viable even though technically insolvent.

2.2 Consequences of petition

The presentation of the petition for an administration order has an immediate and dramatic effect on the company. From the time when the petition is presented until the time when the court decides to make the order or to dismiss the petition a 'moratorium' is imposed on the company's debts. This means that creditors may not:

(a)   take any steps to enforce any security over the company's property (this does not, however, prevent appointment of an *administrative* receiver — see paragraph 2.5);

(b)   repossess goods in the company's possession under a hire-purchase agreement, a conditional sale agreement, a chattel leasing agreement or an agreement under which the vendor has retained title;

(c)   commence or continue proceedings, execution or other legal process against the company or its property;

(d)   levy distress against the company's property.

However, any of these things can be done with leave of the court. The object of these rules is to preserve the assets of the company so that if an order is made the administrator will have a better chance of saving the business. If each creditor was entitled to enforce his own security during this crucial period then the administrator's chances of saving the business would be greatly reduced.

During the period between the petition and the making of the order or the dismissal of the petition the company cannot be wound up. (A petition for winding up may, however, be presented — it will be considered only if the court dismisses the petition for administration.)

2.3 Consequences of administration order

The administration order directs that the affairs, business and property of the company are to be managed by an administrator appointed by the court. The administrator must be a qualified insolvency practitioner. Once the order is made any petition for the winding up of the company is dismissed, any administrative receiver vacates office (see paragraph 4.2 for the definition of an administrative receiver and note that an administration order cannot normally be made where an administrative receiver is in office — see paragraph 2.5). The administrator can also require any other receiver to vacate office.

While the administration order is in force the moratorium preventing creditors from enforcing their rights continues. The restrictions are the same as those following the petition (see paragraph 2.2 above) save that the restrictions can be waived by the administrator as well as by the court. In addition, no appointment of an administrative receiver is possible while the order is in force.

The fact that the company is subject to an administration order and the name of the administrator must be stated on every invoice, order for goods and business letter on which the company's name appears.

2.4 The administration process

2.4.1 Powers and duties of the administrator

As we have already seen the administrator is appointed to run the company and its business with a view to saving the viable parts of the business or with a view to obtaining approval for a voluntary scheme or with a view to advantageous realisation of assets. The administrator is given very wide powers to achieve these things. He is given power to do 'all such things as may be necessary for the management of the affairs, business and property of the company' (s. 14(1)(a)) and also certain particular powers listed in sch. 1. These include power to bring and defend proceedings, sell assets, borrow money, insure and appoint agents. In cases of difficulty the administrator may apply to the court for directions.

Section 15 gives the administrator power to deal with certain property of (or in the possession of) the company free from the claims of other persons. Section 15(1) allows the administrator to dispose of property which is subject to a floating charge as if the property were not subject to the floating charge. This provision applies also where the property is subject to a charge which was a floating charge when created even though it has since crystallised and thus turned into a fixed charge. Where property is disposed of by the administrator under s. 15(1), the holder of the floating charge (or former floating charge) is entitled to the same priority in respect of the property directly or indirectly representing the property disposed of as he would have had in respect of the property which was subject to the charge and which was disposed of by the administrator. Thus the position of the floating chargee is, in theory, as secure as it was before the administration order was made. However, the holder will have to wait for payment, possibly for a considerable time, and formidable problems may arise in trying to identify what property is to be regarded as 'directly or indirectly representing the property disposed of'.

Section 15(2) allows the administrator to dispose of property which is subject to a fixed charge and of property in the possession of the company under a hire-purchase agreement, a conditional sale agreement, a chattel leasing agreement or a retention of title agreement. However, in this case the administrator can only dispose of the property with the agreement of the court which must be satisfied that the disposal is likely to promote the purpose for which the administration order was made. The court order must direct that the proceeds of sale (and any sum required to make good any difference between the proceeds and market value of the assets) shall be used to discharge the company's liability to the secured creditor or owner of the goods which have been disposed of as the case may be. The need to apply to the court can be avoided if an agreement can be reached by the administrator and the creditor or owner of the goods.

2.4.2 Publicity and statement of affairs

Section 21 requires the administrator to send notice of the order under which he was appointed to the company forthwith, an office copy to the registrar of companies within 14 days and, unless the court otherwise directs, notice to all creditors (so far as he is aware of their addresses) within 28 days.

The administrator must also require a statement of affairs to be prepared (s. 22). This will usually be required from the directors but the secretary, former directors, certain employees and former employees and the directors and certain employees of certain associated companies may also be required to make the statement. The statement must usually be prepared within 21 days but the administrator or court can extend this period. The statement must set out details of the company's assets, debts and liabilities, creditors and securities.

2.4.3 Proposals

Because of the moratorium created by an administration order the creditors of the company are forced to bear some of the risk inherent in the whole process of administration (that is the risk that, if the administration fails to save the business, the company will be in a weaker position when the administration ends than when it began). The creditors are, however, given a measure of control over the administration process. Section 23 requires the administrator to prepare proposals as to how he is going to achieve the purpose for which he was appointed. These proposals must be sent to the registrar of companies and to all creditors (so far as the administrator is aware of their addresses) within three months of the making of the order unless the court extends the period. Copies of the proposals must also either be sent to all the members or the members must be given an opportunity to ask for free copies.

The administrator must hold a meeting of the creditors within three months of the order (unless the court extends the period) at which the proposals are considered. If the proposals are accepted by the creditors' meeting then the administrator must manage the company in accordance with the proposals. The creditors' meeting may propose modifications to the proposals but, as he is the person who will have to implement them, the administrator can reject such modifications.

If the creditors' meeting rejects the proposals the administrator must go back to the court. In such a case the court will usually discharge the administration order but it may also make any other order as it sees fit including a further administration order.

During the course of the administration the administrator may need to revise the proposals which have been accepted by the creditors. If he does so, and the revision appears to him to be substantial, then he must seek approval of the revision from a creditors' meeting (s. 25).

2.4.4 Discharge of administration order

The administrator may apply to the court for discharge of the order at any time. He *must* make such an application when it appears to him that the purpose for which the order was made has been achieved or has become incapable of achievement or when required to do so by a creditors' meeting. The court has a wide discretion to discharge the order in such cases or to make such other order as it sees fit. In most cases it will discharge the order. Ten per cent by value of the creditors are given a right to require the administrator to summon a meeting at any time (s. 17(3)).

2.4.5 Unfair prejudice (section 27)

At any time when an administration order is in force any creditor or member may petition the court on the grounds that the company's affairs, business and property are being or have been managed by the administrator in a manner which is unfairly prejudicial to some or all of the members or creditors (including the petitioner) or that any actual or proposed act or omission would be so prejudicial. Where unfair

prejudice is proved the court has a wide discretion to make such order as it sees fit to
end the prejudice (including power to discharge the administration order).

2.5   Administration and other remedies

Administration is an alternative to winding-up. An administration order cannot,
therefore, be made once the company has gone into liquidation. This means that the
passing of a winding-up resolution by the company (see paragraph 5.3.1) or the
making of a winding-up order (see paragraph 5.2.2) preclude the making of an
administration order. Similarly the making of an administration order prevents
winding-up. Once the administration order is made any winding-up petition is
dismissed, no new petition may be presented and the company loses the right to pass
a winding-up resolution while the administration order is in force.

   Administration and administrative receivership are also mutually exclusive. Thus
when a petition for an administration order is presented notice must be given to any
person who has appointed or is entitled to appoint an administrative receiver (see
paragraph 4.2 — broadly speaking a floating charge holder can make such an
appointment). An administration order cannot be made if, by the time of the
hearing, an administrative receiver has been appointed unless either the creditor
who made the appointment consents or it is shown that his charge would be liable to
be set aside under ss. 238, 239 or 245 (see paragraphs 7.4 and 7.6). Once an
administration order has been made no appointment of an administrative receiver is
possible. These rules give a creditor who can appoint an administrative receiver a
right to veto administration but if he wishes to do so he must act quickly as the right to
veto is lost if no appointment has been made by the time the petition for
administration is heard.

3   VOLUNTARY ARRANGEMENTS (SECTIONS 1 TO 7)

3.1   Proposals and nominee's report

The Insolvency Act 1986 seeks to promote agreement between a company in
difficulties and its creditors. The directors or (where the company is being wound up)
the liquidator or (where an administration order is in force) the administrator may
make proposals to the company and its creditors. These proposals must, if they are to
be put into effect under the Act, nominate a qualified insolvency practitioner to act in
relation to the composition or scheme which is proposed. Where the nominee is not
the liquidator or administrator, the person making the proposal (that is, the
liquidator, administrator or directors) must submit details of the proposals and of the
company's creditors, debts, liabilities and assets to the nominee. The nominee must
then submit a report to the court stating whether or not he thinks that meetings of
members and creditors should be called to consider the proposals.

3.2   The meetings

Where the nominee recommends that meetings should be held he may call the
meetings unless the court orders otherwise. Where the nominee is also the liquidator
or administrator of the company he may call such meetings without reporting to the

court. Notice must be given to every creditor of whose claim and address the person calling the meeting is aware.

The meetings of members and creditors then consider the scheme, which they may reject, approve or approve with modifications. A simple majority is required at the members' meeting (members having the voting rights attached to their shares by the articles). The position is more complicated at the creditors' meeting but basically the resolution is only validly passed if approved by at least three-quarters (by value) of the unsecured creditors *and* by a simple majority (by value) of the unsecured creditors together with such of the secured creditors as are not connected with the company.

The result of the meetings must be reported to the court. Any person who considers that he is unfairly prejudiced by the scheme or that there was a material irregularity in the conduct of either of the meetings can apply to the court under s.6. The application must be made within 28 days of the result of the meetings being reported to the court. If the court is satisfied that there has been unfair prejudice or a material irregularity it can revoke or suspend the approval of the scheme or order further meetings. Application for such an order may also be made by any liquidator or administrator of the company or by the nominee.

3.3 Implementation of scheme

Where both meetings approve a scheme and the scheme is not successfully challenged in court the scheme becomes binding on all persons who had notice of the shareholders' or creditors' meeting and were entitled to vote at that meeting. However, unless he agrees, the scheme cannot affect a secured creditor's right to enforce his security nor a preferred creditor's preference (see paragraph 8 for definition of preferred creditor).

Once approved, the scheme is implemented by the supervisor (who is the same person as the nominee unless the court or meetings decide otherwise). Any person who is dissatisfied with the way in which the scheme is being implemented may apply to the court which may give directions to the supervisor.

3.4 Relationship between voluntary schemes and administration

The proposal that a voluntary scheme should be implemented does not create a moratorium so that, unless and until the scheme is approved, any creditor can seek payment of his own debt (by court action, petition for winding up, repossession or any other lawful means available to him). Even when the scheme is approved it does not prevent secured creditors enforcing their security. A voluntary arrangement is, therefore, more likely to succeed if an application for administration is made first thus giving rise to the moratorium. The administrator may then be able to put together a satisfactory voluntary scheme which he can supervise.

4   RECEIVERSHIP

4.1   Nature of receivership

A receiver is a person who is appointed by or on behalf of a creditor to realise a security. His principal duty is to the appointing debenture holder. Receivers may be appointed by the debenture holder (provided that the debenture so provides) or by the court. In practice nearly all appointments are made by the debenture holder. The powers of the receiver are derived from the debenture although administrative receivers as defined by the Insolvency Act 1986 have certain statutory powers. Certain restrictions and duties are imposed on all receivers of company property including:

(a)   A power of the court to fix the amount of the receiver's remuneration if the company goes into liquidation.

(b)   A requirement that invoices, orders for goods and business letters should state that a receiver has been appointed.

(c)   Certain duties requiring the receiver to file returns with the registrar.

4.2   Administrative receivers — definition

Most receivers come within the definition of an 'administrative receiver' (s.29(2)). The Insolvency Act 1986 imposes certain duties on and grants certain powers to administrative receivers which do not apply in the case of other receivers. Only a qualified insolvency practitioner can be appointed as an administrative receiver. An administrative receiver is:

(a)   a receiver or manager of the whole (or substantially the whole) of a company's property appointed by or on behalf of the holders of any debentures of the company secured by a charge which, as created, was a floating charge, or by such a charge and one or more other securities; or

(b)   a person who would be such a receiver or manager but for the appointment of some other person as the receiver of part of the company's property.

In practice the person with a floating charge over the whole or substantially the whole of the company's property will usually be a bank. The bank is also likely to have fixed charges over land owned by the company and certain other assets (e.g., book debts) but these do not prevent it from appointing an administrative receiver.

4.3   Administrative receivers — powers and duties

The administrative receiver, when appointed, effectively replaces the directors in the management of the company. His appointment is, therefore, a matter of great importance to the members, creditors and employees of the company. The law recognises this and so grants powers to and imposes obligations on an administrative receiver which make his position very similar to the position of an administrator. The administrative receiver is chosen by the debenture holder, not by the court, but can only be removed by the court.

4.3.1 General powers

An administrative receiver has all the powers conferred on him by the debenture under which he is appointed and also certain powers listed in the Insolvency Act 1986. The statutory powers include power to deal with the assets of the company, take or defend proceedings in its name and power to carry on the business of the company. These powers are the same as those granted to an administrator.

Section 43 gives an administrative receiver power to go to court to obtain an order for the sale of assets free from any security with priority over the debenture under which he was appointed. The court may only authorise the administrative receiver to dispose of such property if it is likely to promote a more advantageous realisation of the company's assets. The court might, for example, authorise such a disposal so as to enable the receiver to sell the business of the company as a going concern. The proceeds of disposal (plus any difference between those proceeds and market value) must be paid to the person who was entitled to the security.

4.3.2 Legal position

The administrative receiver is deemed to be the agent of the company (s.44). Any contract which he makes is, therefore, binding on the company. The agency, however, ends when the company goes into liquidation. Section 44 also makes the administrative receiver personally liable on any contract which he himself makes and on any contract of employment which he 'adopts'. What amounts to an adoption of a contract is unclear. The administrative receiver is entitled to an indemnity against personal liability out of the assets of the company and, if the debenture so provides, will have an indemnity from his appointor.

4.3.3 Duty to pay preferential creditors

The primary duty of any receiver is to realise the security of the debenture holder who appointed him. A receiver appointed on behalf of a floating charge holder (whether or not he is an administrative receiver as defined) is, however, under a duty to pay preferential creditors (see paragraph 8) in priority to the debt secured by the floating charge.

4.3.4 Investigation etc. (sections 46 to 49)

An administrative receiver is entitled to a statement of affairs from the directors (or in certain cases other officials) of the company. Within three months of his appointment (or longer if the court so directs) he must make a report which he must send to the court and to creditors.

The report must give details of the events leading to the appointment of the receiver, his dealings with the property of the company, his payments to the creditor who appointed him and to preferential creditors and an assessment of what will be available (if anything) to ordinary creditors.

4.4 Choice of remedy

A bank or other creditor with a floating charge will often be faced with a choice if its customer gets into difficulty. It may go to court to seek an administration order, or it may appoint its own administrative receiver, or it may seek winding-up. As we have already seen (paragraph 2.5) the debenture holder loses the right to appoint an administrative receiver once an administrator has been appointed but, until that time, can effectively veto administration by appointing an administrative receiver.

Administration and administrative receivership are in many ways very similar but are different from each other in the following principal respects:

(a)   The administrative receiver is chosen by the debenture holder, the administrator is appointed by the court.

(b)   The administration procedure leads to a moratorium, administrative receivership does not.

(c)   Administration blocks winding-up petitions by other creditors.

(d)   In administration certain transactions may be set aside (see paragraph 8).

(e)   In administration owners of goods in the company's possession under hire-purchase and retention of title agreements cannot repossess without leave of the administrator or court.

5   LIQUIDATION OR WINDING-UP

5.1   Types of winding-up

There are two types of winding-up: compulsory liquidation and voluntary liquidation. Compulsory liquidation is initiated by petition to the court. Voluntary liquidation is initiated by a decision of the members of the company. Both types of winding-up are designed to bring the existence of the company to an end and to distribute its assets to those entitled to them.

5.2   Compulsory winding-up

5.2.1   Grounds

Compulsory liquidation begins with a petition to the court (Chancery Division or, in some cases, county court — see paragraph 1 above). A petition can be presented on a number of grounds. By far the most common ground is that the company is unable to pay its debts. A company is treated as being unable to pay its debts if:

(a)   a demand for payment, in the prescribed form, for more than £750 (this figure may be changed from time to time by regulations) has been left at the company's registered office and the company has neglected to pay the debt, or to secure or compound for it (that is, agree to a reasonable compromise) to the reasonable satisfaction of the creditor for three weeks; or

(b)   execution or other process issued on a judgment, decree or court order is returned unsatisfied; or

(c)   it is proved that the company is actually unable to pay taking into account contingent and prospective liabilities; or

(d)   it is proved that the value of the company's assets is less than the amount of its liabilities taking into account contingent and prospective liabilities.

Apart from inability to pay debts there are other grounds on which a company may be wound up. These are, however, seldom resorted to and are not considered in this book save that the 'just and equitable' ground is considered in Chapter 8 paragraph 7.

5.2.2 Locus standi

A petition for compulsory winding-up may be presented by the company itself, any creditor or creditors (including contingent or prospective creditors), any contributory or contributories (the term 'contributory' includes the members of the company and certain former members) and, in very limited circumstances, by the Department of Trade and Industry. In practice the overwhelming majority of petitions are presented by creditors.

Even where a creditor has proved grounds for winding up, the court has a discretion to refuse to make an order winding up the company. An order will normally be refused where:

(a)   The petitioning creditor (together with any supporting creditors) is owed £750 or less. This is by analogy with the rule whereby a statutory demand for more than £750 can be used as proof of inability to pay debts.

(b)   The majority by value of the creditors oppose the winding-up of the company.

5.3   Voluntary winding-up

5.3.1   Commencement

By s.84 a company can be wound up voluntarily if:

(a)   a special resolution to wind up is passed; or

(b)   an extraordinary resolution is passed to the effect that the company should be wound up as it cannot continue in business because of its debts (that is, the company is, in effect, insolvent).

The winding-up commences from the date of passing the appropriate resolution. A notice of the resolution must appear in the *London Gazette* within 14 days of its being passed.

5.3.2   Types of voluntary winding-up

There are two types of voluntary liquidation; a members' voluntary winding-up and a creditors' voluntary winding-up.

The liquidation will be a members' voluntary winding-up if, within the five weeks immediately preceding the date of the resolution (or on that date but before the resolution is actually passed) the directors (or the majority of them if more than two) make a statutory declaration, setting out the company's assets and liabilities, and stating that they have made a full enquiry into the company's affairs and are of the opinion that the company will be able to pay its debts in full within 12 months of the commencement of the winding-up. The declaration must be delivered to the registrar within 15 days after the day the resolution was passed.

If no such 'declaration of solvency' is filed the winding-up is a creditors' winding-up. A meeting of the creditors must be called for a day not later than the 14th day after the day on which the meeting at which the members pass the winding-up resolution is held. Notice of the meeting must be posted to the creditors at least seven days before the creditors' meeting and the meeting must also be advertised in the *Gazette* and at least two newspapers.

During the course of a members' voluntary winding-up, it may become clear that the company will be unable to pay its debts within 12 months of commencement of the winding-up. If this happens the liquidator must report the fact to the creditors, call a creditors' meeting and convert the liquidation into a creditors' voluntary winding-up.

6 LIQUIDATORS

6.1 Compulsory liquidation

When a winding-up order is made the official receiver of the court becomes the liquidator of the company and continues in office until someone else is appointed (s. 136(2)). The official receiver may summon meetings of creditors and contributories with a view to the appointment of a liquidator. He must either do so or give notice that he intends not to do so within 12 weeks of the winding-up order and may be required to call such meetings by one-quarter (by value) of the creditors.

Where meetings of creditors and contributories are held each meeting may nominate a liquidator. If the same person is nominated by each meeting, he becomes the liquidator. If different people are nominated the creditors' nominee takes office unless a creditor or contributory successfully applies to the court for the appointment of the contributories' nominee (either alone or jointly with the creditors' nominee) or of some other person.

Any liquidator must be a qualified insolvency practitioner.

6.2 Creditors' voluntary winding-up

As we have already seen, in a creditors' winding-up a meeting of creditors must be held within 14 days of the meeting (of the members) at which the winding-up resolution was passed. The creditors may nominate a liquidator at their meeting. He will then become liquidator of the company but any director, member or creditor may apply to the court for the appointment of the members' nominee (either alone or jointly with the creditors' nominee) or of some other person.

The members will often have appointed a liquidator at the meeting at which the resolution for creditors' winding-up was passed. Such a liquidator is entitled to act until the creditors' meeting is held but during that period his powers are restricted to collecting the company's property, disposing of perishable goods or other goods which may decline in value and taking other steps to protect the company's assets.

The liquidator must be a qualified insolvency practitioner.

6.3 Members' voluntary winding-up

The liquidator (who must be a qualified insolvency practitioner) is appointed by the members in general meeting.

6.4 Functions of liquidators

The function of the liquidator of a company is to collect in the assets of the company and to pay their value to those creditors who are entitled according to the statutory order for payment (see paragraph 8). If there is anything left after all creditors have been paid their debts and interest, the surplus goes to the members. If there are two or more classes of shares some members may have priority over others in claiming the surplus.

Sections 165 and 167 give liquidators extensive powers to assist them in performing their functions. These powers include:

(a)   Power to pay any class of creditors in full.

(b)   Power to enter into a compromise or arrangement with creditors (this can be made binding without the agreement of all the creditors in certain cases provided that the voluntary arrangements procedure (paragraph 3 above) is used).

(c)   Power to compromise claims to which the company is entitled.

(The liquidator can only exercise the above powers with the sanction of an extraordinary resolution in the case of members' winding-up, of the court, a committee of creditors or creditors' meeting in the case of creditors' winding-up and of the court or committee in the case of compulsory winding-up.)

(d)   Power to bring or defend legal proceedings.

(e)   Power to carry on the company's business for the purpose of beneficial winding-up.

(Sanction is required in the case of compulsory winding-up only.)

(f)   Power to sell the company's property.

(g)   Power to execute documents (including deeds).

(h)   Power to borrow on the security of the company's assets.

(i)   Power to act through agents.

(j)   Power to do 'all such other things as may be necessary for winding up the company's affairs and distributing its assets'.

(No sanction is required for items (f) to (j) in any type of winding-up.)

6.5   Proceedings against the company

It would obviously be unfair if one creditor could start an action after the liquidation had begun and so obtain priority over the other creditors. Therefore, once an order for compulsory winding-up has been made, no action can be started or proceeded with unless the leave of the court is obtained (s.130), and at any time between presentation of the petition and the making of the order, the company, or any creditor or contributory, can apply to have any action pending against the company stayed (s.126). Furthermore, any execution, attachment, sequestration or distress started after the commencement of a compulsory liquidation is void. However, if the attachment or execution was begun before presentation of the petition it can only be avoided by the liquidator if it was completed after commencement of the liquidation. This last provision also applies to voluntary liquidations, the operative date being the date the resolution to wind up the company was passed.

With regard to voluntary liquidations, the liquidator, any creditor or member, may apply to the court to have actions stayed. Such a stay is not granted automatically although, if the action is begun after the date of passing the resolution to wind up an insolvent company, it will normally be granted.

7 COLLECTION AND DISTRIBUTION OF ASSETS IN LIQUIDATION

7.1 Property of the company

The company's assets do not vest automatically in the liquidator but the court may, on the application of the liquidator, direct that all or any of the property of the company vest in the liquidator and that he may bring or defend actions in his own name. This power is rarely used because the liquidator's statutory powers are sufficient in most circumstances. Whether or not the asset is vested in his name the liquidator has power to sell or mortgage the property and to satisfy the claims of the various people entitled in the company's liquidation (see paragraph 6.4 above).

An important power of the liquidator in relation to the company's property is the right of disclaimer given by s.178. The section gives the liquidator power to disclaim any of the company's property which consists of unprofitable contracts, or other property that is unsaleable or not readily saleable. This means that the liquidator can rid himself of property that will reduce the value of the company's assets. Once he has disclaimed the property, s.178(4) provides that the title, rights, interests and liabilities of the company are terminated but other persons' rights and liabilities are unaffected except so far as is necessary to release the company and its assets from liability.

The liquidator loses the right to disclaim if he has served on him, by an interested person, a written demand requiring him to decide whether or not to disclaim the property to which he does not reply within 28 days.

7.2 Fraudulent trading (section 213)

If it appears that a company has carried on business with a view to defrauding creditors or for any fraudulent purpose, the court, on the application of any liquidator, creditor or contributory, may order that any person knowingly engaged in such trading shall be personally liable to make such contributions to the company's assets as the court thinks proper. Normally, such a person's maximum liability is limited to the debts incurred while the fraudulent trading was carried on, although it is possible that the court may order that a greater contribution be made.

In general terms, an allegation of fraudulent trading can be made if the company trades, and incurs debts, when the directors know that the company has no reasonable chance of meeting its liabilities. Furthermore, the powers of s.213 can be invoked even if only one transaction is involved and only one creditor is defrauded. The order would normally be made against the company's directors, but since the section is widely drafted it can catch creditors if they know the trade is being carried on fraudulently with a view to making a payment to them.

7.3 Wrongful trading (section 214)

The directors of a company which is being wound up may be made liable, by the court, to contribute to the assets of the company if they are found to be guilty of wrongful trading. A person is guilty of wrongful trading where:

(a)   the company goes into insolvent liquidation;
(b)   that person knew or ought to have concluded (at some time before the commencement of winding-up) that there was no reasonable prospect that the company would avoid going into insolvent liquidation; and
(c)   that person was a director of the company at that time.

A defence is available to a director who shows that he took every step with a view to minimising the potential loss to the company's creditors as he ought to have taken. However, in judging whether this defence is available the court must assume that the director knew what a reasonably diligent person having the general knowledge, skill and experience that it is reasonable to expect of a person carrying out his functions in relation to the company would have as well as taking into account the general knowledge, skill and experience which he actually had.

The steps which a director must take to avoid liability for wrongful trading will vary depending on the circumstances of the case. They might include, for example, proposing that the board should apply to the court for an administration order.

7.4 Transactions at an undervalue and preferences

Certain transactions which a company has entered into may be set aside on the ground that they are transactions at an undervalue or preferences. An application to the court by the liquidator is required for such transactions to be set aside. (The same rules apply where an administration order has been made save that the application is then made by the administrator.)

An undervalue is defined (by s.238) as a transaction where the company makes a gift to any person and where the company receives no consideration or where the consideration is worth significantly less than the consideration provided by the company. However, an undervalue cannot be set aside if it was entered into in good faith for the purpose of carrying on the company's business and at a time when there were reasonable grounds for believing that the transaction would benefit the company. For this reason a transaction cannot be set aside when the company sells stock or other assets at a reduced price so as to overcome cash flow problems.

A preference (s.239) is given if the company does anything or suffers anything to be done which puts a creditor, or a surety or guarantor of a debt of the company, into a better position on liquidation than he would have been in if that thing had not been done. Examples of preferences include payment of a debt to a particular creditor who would only have received partial payment on winding up or the giving of security to a creditor. However, a transaction cannot be set aside as a preference unless the company was influenced in deciding to give the preference to a person by a desire to put that person into a better position on liquidation than he would have been in if it had not been done. Such a desire is presumed where the preference was given to a connected person, which includes any director of the company. Where payment was made or security was given to a creditor because he was threatening proceedings or otherwise insisting on payment he will usually be able to show that this defence is available.

Where it is shown that a transaction can be set aside as a transaction at an undervalue or preference the court can make such order as it sees fit for restoring the position to what it would have been if the transaction had not been entered into. This could include, for example, ordering the person who entered into the transaction or who received the preference to return property or its value to the company. The position of a bona fide purchaser for value is, however, protected.

Undervalue transactions and preferences can only be set aside if they were entered into at a 'relevant time', that is, a time when both of the following requirements are satisfied:

(a)   in the case of a transaction at an undervalue, the time is within two years before commencement of winding-up or presentation of the petition for administration or, in the case of a preference, within six months before that date; and

(b)   in the case of either an undervalue or preference, the time is a time when the company is insolvent or a time when the company becomes insolvent as a result of the transaction.

Where a preference has been given to a connected person the six-month limit is extended to two years. Where an undervalue transaction has been entered into with a connected person insolvency is presumed unless it can be disproved.

7.5   Transactions defrauding creditors

Sections 423-425 contain another provision by which transactions at an undervalue can be set aside. This provision is not restricted to cases of winding-up or administration orders and the undervalue transaction can be set aside whenever it was made. However, the person who applies to the court to have the transaction set aside under this provision must show that the company in entering into the transaction did so with the purpose of putting assets beyond the reach of that person.

7.6   Floating charges (section 245)

A floating charge is prima facie invalid if:

(a)   it was made within 12 months before the presentation of a successful petition for winding-up or for an administration order or before the passing of a winding-up resolution; and

(b)   it was made at a time when the company was unable to pay its debts or became unable to do so as a result of the charge.

Where the company has created a floating charge in favour of a connected person the charge is prima facie invalid if it was made within *two* years before the petition or resolution. The charge is prima facie invalid in such a case even if the company was (and remained) solvent when the charge was created.

A floating charge created within the time-limits (and so prima facie invalid) is valid to the extent of:

(a) consideration for the charge consisting of money paid or goods and services supplied to the company at or after the creation of the charge; and

(b) consideration consisting of discharge or reduction of any debt of the company at or after the creation of the charge; and

(c) interest on (a) and (b) above.

Section 245 is designed to prevent a company benefiting a creditor by giving a charge for existing debt. The exceptions are designed to ensure that a company may still give security in order to obtain money or supplies even though in some difficulty. This should not in principle cause any harm to existing creditors.

7.7 Assets in the hands of the company

The creditors of an insolvent company are entitled to payment from its assets. They are not entitled to any assets of which the company is the legal owner but which it holds on trust for a third party. This has been held to apply in certain cases where a company holds cash for its customers. In *Re Kayford Ltd* [1975] 1 All ER 604, the company put money received from mail order customers into a special trust account from which it only made withdrawals when goods were delivered to the customers. When the company went into liquidation it was held that the money in the account belonged to the customers whose orders had not been fulfilled and so was not available to the liquidator.

Many suppliers of goods supply goods under contracts which contain retention of title clauses. These are clauses which state that the vendor retains title to the goods supplied until the purchaser pays for them. Such clauses have been considered in a number of reported cases (the leading case is *Aluminium Industrie Vaasen BV* v *Romalpa Aluminium* [1976] 2 All ER 552). Their effect varies depending on the exact wording which is used and on the circumstances of the case. A straightforward reservation of title clause is effective in ensuring that the vendor, not the liquidator, is entitled to the goods (or the proceeds of their further sale) if the company becomes insolvent. However, clauses which have tried to extend the unpaid vendor's rights (for example, by purportedly transferring them to newly manufactured goods only partly consisting of the goods which he originally supplied) have generally failed. (For the powers of an administrator to dispose of goods despite a retention of title clause see paragraph 2.4.1 above.)

8 ORDER OF ENTITLEMENT TO ASSETS

The principal duty of the liquidator of a company is to distribute the assets to those entitled. In a large majority of cases there will be insufficient funds available to pay all the creditors in full. There is, therefore, an order in which the assets must be paid to the creditors.

(a) Creditors with fixed charges are entitled to payment out of the assets which are charged to them before those assets are used for any other purpose. As between creditors with fixed charges over the same assets priority is governed by registration under s. 395 CA 1985 (but remember that a fixed charge gives priority over a floating charge, even though the latter is created and registered first, unless the floating charge prohibited the creation of later fixed charges ranking in priority to it and the fixed chargee had notice of this prohibition when he took the charge).

If the security of a fixed charge is inadequate (that is, the value of the charged assets is less than the amount of the debt), the chargee may claim the balance of the debt as an ordinary creditor. If the debt is oversecured (that is, the value of the charged assets is more than the amount of the debt), the chargee will be paid in full and the balance will be available for other creditors.

(b)   Costs of winding up, including liquidators' fees and expenses, are paid in full before any other creditors (except those with fixed charges who are paid first to the extent of their security).

(c)   After payment of costs and expenses the next category of creditor is the preferred creditor. Preferred debts are:

(i)   Sums owed to the Inland Revenue for PAYE deducted from employees' wages in the 12 months before the relevant date.

(ii)   VAT (and certain other sums due to Customs and Excise) referable to the six-month period before the relevant date.

(iii)   Certain social security contributions and contributions to occupational pension schemes.

(iv)   Wages owed to an employee in respect of the four months before the relevant date up to a maximum of £800 per employee (this figure may be varied from time to time by statutory instrument). Certain categories of holiday pay are also preferential.

(v)   Money lent to an employer so as to enable it to pay debts in category (iv) above and which was in fact used for that purpose. (Thus a bank is a preferential creditor if it allows an employer to overdraw a 'wages account' so as to keep on the workforce in the four months before the relevant date.)

The 'relevant date' is usually the date of the winding-up resolution, appointment of liquidator or date of appointment of a receiver.

Preferred creditors (to the extent of their preference) are entitled to payment in full before ordinary creditors or holders of floating charges receive any payment. If the assets are insufficient to pay the preferred creditors in full they rank equally *inter se* and so each is paid the same proportion of the preferred debt.

(d)   Floating chargees rank after preferred creditors but, to the extent of their security, before ordinary creditors. Priority is determined by date of registration where there are two or more floating charges over the same property.

(e)   Ordinary creditors rank after all preferred creditors and secured creditors. They rank equally *inter se*.

(f)   Once all creditors have been paid in full any surplus is first used to pay interest on debts from the date of liquidation. This interest is paid to all creditors equally regardless of whether their debts ranked equally for payment.

(g)   Any surplus after payment of debts and interest goes to the members according to the rights attached to their shares.

9 DISSOLUTION

Once winding-up is complete the company may be dissolved. This is achieved in the following ways:

(a)   In compulsory liquidation the liquidator gives notice to the registrar of companies that he has completed the winding-up. This company is then automatically dissolved three months later.

(b)   In voluntary winding-up the liquidator holds a final meeting and files certain returns with the registrar of companies. The company is then automatically dissolved after three months.

(c)   The registrar may dissolve a company by striking it off the register in certain circumstances where the company has ceased to trade.

22 Bankruptcy

1 INTRODUCTION

The risk of personal bankruptcy is a spectre which haunts many partners and sole traders. If a partner or sole trader finds that he is unable to pay his debts as they fall due, he may be made personally bankrupt. Thus, the partner or sole trader may be made bankrupt if his liabilities exceed his assets; he faces the same risk if he has insufficient liquid assets to pay his current liabilities even if the value of his total assets exceeds the value of his total liabilities.

It is to avoid this risk that many entrepreneurs choose to trade through a limited company. However, it should not be forgotten that the directors and members of a company may face personal bankruptcy where, for example, a director or shareholder has personally guaranteed a loan to the company or where a director is liable for 'wrongful' trading.

The members or partners may, of course, also find themselves facing bankruptcy as a result of a financial collapse entirely unconnected with the business of their own company or partnership.

The law of bankruptcy was reviewed and revised in the Insolvency Act 1985 which repealed the Bankruptcy Act 1914. The 1985 Act has itself been consolidated with the provisions relating to corporate insolvency contained in the Companies Act 1985 and the consolidated legislation is now contained in the Insolvency Act 1986 together with delegated legislation made under its provisions.

In this chapter we will summarise the law under the following headings:

(a)   The procedure for making a person bankrupt, including the persons who can present a petition for bankruptcy, the grounds on which the petition is based, the consequences of presenting the petition and the procedure following the making of the order.

(b)   The appointment, function and removal of the trustee in bankruptcy.

(c)   The effect of the bankruptcy order on the bankrupt personally.

(d)   The provisions relating to the assets in the bankrupt's estate.

(e)   The distribution of the bankrupt's assets.

(f)   The duration of the bankruptcy and the discharge of the bankrupt.

(g)   The rules governing the new voluntary arrangements contained in the Insolvency Act 1986.

A debtor who finds himself unable to meet all his debts in full may:

(a)   be adjudicated bankrupt (whether on his own application or on application by certain others) if the full bankruptcy procedure is followed (where the debtor's liabilities are below the small bankruptcy level, currently £20,000, the court has power to order a summary administration); or

(b)   have his estate administered by a qualified insolvency practitioner under a voluntary arrangement (see paragraph 6 below).

2 THE BANKRUPTCY PROCEDURE

2.1 Introduction

In this section of the chapter we consider the 'full' bankruptcy procedure. Bankruptcy proceedings are commenced by the presentation of a petition for a bankruptcy order. The petitioners (who, broadly speaking, simply have to prove that the debtor is unable to pay his debts) are:

(a)   a creditor (or creditors jointly) whether secured or unsecured; or
(b)   the debtor personally; or
(c)   a supervisor of, or a person bound by, a voluntary scheme; or
(d)   the Director of Public Prosecutions.

2.2 Procedure on a creditor's petition

2.2.1 *Prerequisites for presentation of a creditor's petition*
The court will only entertain a petition presented by a creditor or creditors if certain conditions are satisfied:

(a)   The debtor must be domiciled or personally present in England and Wales when the petition is presented (although in certain circumstances petitions can be presented against persons who do not satisfy these requirements, provided, during the three years prior to presentation of the petition, the debtor was ordinarily resident, or had a place of residence, in England and Wales or carried on business there, whether personally or by means of an agent or manager, or was a member of a partnership which carried on business in England and Wales).

(b)   The debt (or debts) which are the basis of the petition must be for a liquidated sum (whether payable immediately or at some time in the future).

(c)   The debt (or debts) must amount to at least £750. (This sum can be changed from time to time by statutory instrument.)

(d)   The debt must be unsecured. At first sight this requirement may seem harsh on secured creditors but it should not be overlooked that a creditor who has security for his debt may take that security if the debtor fails to discharge his liability. However, there may be circumstances when the security taken by the secured creditor is not adequate (for example, if the value of the security is less than the debt outstanding). In such circumstances the secured creditor can present a petition but only if he states in the petition that he is willing to relinquish his security or petition only for the unsecured balance (if any) of the debt.

2.2.2 *Grounds for presenting a creditor's petition*
Having satisfied the prerequisites for presenting a creditor's petition, the petitioning creditor (or creditors jointly) must allege that the debtor appears either:

(a)   to be unable to pay, or
(b)   to have no reasonable prospect of paying

the debt or debts specified in the petition and that there are no outstanding applications to have a 'statutory demand' set aside. (A 'statutory demand' is a demand in a form which complies with the Insolvency Rules 1986, r. 6.1). The functions of the demand are described below.

Before the court will make the order, the debtor's inability to pay his debt or debts may be proved in one of two ways:

(a)   By showing that a 'statutory demand' served on the debtor requiring him to pay, secure or compound for the debt to the satisfaction of the petitioning creditor has not been complied with within three weeks. (A petition may be based on a period of non-compliance with the 'statutory demand' of less than three weeks if there is a 'serious possibility' that the debtor's property, or its value, would be diminished to a significant extent if the full period elapsed.)

(b)   By showing that execution or other process issued in respect of the debt as a judgment or order of any court has been returned unsatisfied in whole or in part.

Once a petition has been presented by a creditor the court may dismiss the petition if it is shown that the debtor can pay all his debts, including contingent and prospective debts; if the creditor has unreasonably refused any offer made by the debtor in response to a 'statutory demand'; or if it is appropriate to dismiss the petition for any reason, including a breach of the rules.

The court *must* dismiss a petition if a 'statutory demand' (whether to pay, secure or compound the debt or to show 'reasonable prospects' of payment) has been complied with.

2.3   Procedure on a debtor's own petition

The debtor himself may present a petition provided he has a connection with England and Wales. Accordingly the debtor must be able to show that he satisfies the requirements set out in paragraph 2.2.1 (a) above.

Provided the debtor has a sufficient connection with England and Wales to enable a petition to be presented, the only ground on which the petition can be based is that the debtor is unable to pay his debts. When presenting the petition, the debtor must lodge a 'statement of affairs' giving full details of his assets, liabilities and creditors. Once presented, the petition can only be withdrawn with leave of the court.

While the court will normally make the bankruptcy order which the debtor is seeking, the court *must* not make the order if:

(a)   the unsecured debts are less than the 'small bankruptcies level' (currently £20,000);

(b)   the value of the assets is at least the 'minimum amount' (currently £2,000);

(c)   during the five years preceding the presentation of the petition the debtor has not been adjudged bankrupt or made a scheme or composition with his creditors; and

(d)   it would be appropriate to obtain a report from a qualified insolvency practitioner.

In the circumstances set out above, the insolvency practitioner will inquire into the debtor's affairs and report on whether the debtor is willing to make a proposal for a composition with his creditors and/or whether the creditors should be summoned to a meeting at which they will consider such a proposal. Having considered the report of the insolvency practitioner the court can, if it considers it appropriate, make a bankruptcy order. Otherwise the voluntary composition will be pursued or the court can issue a certificate of summary administration.

2.4   Presentation of a petition by a supervisor of, or a person bound by, a voluntary scheme

The supervisor of, or a person bound by, a voluntary scheme (the details of which are considered below in paragraph 8) may base a petition on the following grounds:

(a)   that the debtor has failed to comply with his obligations under the scheme (or failure to comply with the supervisor's reasonable requests in connection with the scheme);

(b)   that the debtor has provided false or misleading information in connection with entry into the scheme.

2.5   Presentation of a petition by the Director of Public Prosecutions

The DPP has power (under the Powers of Criminal Courts Act 1973) to apply to have a person made criminally bankrupt if the person has been convicted of an offence where loss in excess of a specified value has occurred. Having obtained a criminal bankruptcy order, the DPP can apply to have the criminal made bankrupt under the Insolvency Act 1986. The application must be granted unless an appeal against the criminal bankruptcy order is successful.

2.6   Consequences of presenting a petition

2.6.1   Restrictions on dispositions

A debtor who is the subject of a bankruptcy petition may be tempted to dispose of property before he is adjudicated bankrupt. The Insolvency Act 1986 makes void any disposition of property or payment of money made after the presentation of a petition if the debtor is subsequently adjudicated bankrupt unless the court approves the transaction either before or after it takes place. (If the court does not give its approval, the transferee holds the property as part of the debtor's estate.)

An innocent third party dealing with the debtor could be prejudiced by this provision and so the Act gives persons dealing with the debtor in the period between presentation of the petition and the making of the bankruptcy order limited protection. The protection takes the form of denying any remedy against a person who has, during the period referred to above, dealt with the debtor provided that person acted in good faith, for value and without notice of the presentation of the petition.

2.6.2   Restrictions on proceedings

The court has power to stay any action, execution or legal process against the debtor or his assets while bankruptcy proceedings are pending. The court can act simply on the basis of proof that the petition has been presented.

2.6.3   Appointment of interim receivers

If it is necessary for the protection of the debtor's estate, the court may appoint an interim receiver following the presentation of the petition.

If an appointment is considered necessary, the official receiver will be appointed as 'interim receiver' unless the petition was presented by the debtor and an insolvency practitioner has been appointed to prepare a report on the debtor's affairs. In that case, the insolvency practitioner may be appointed as the interim receiver.

The court can determine the powers of the interim receiver. These may include power to sell perishable goods or goods which are likely to diminish in value, power to take steps to protect the estate and all the powers which a receiver and manager appointed by the High Court enjoys.

2.7   Making the bankruptcy order

Once the petition has been presented, the court may exercise its discretion to make a bankruptcy order (or, in the case of a petition presented by the debtor personally, to make an interim order so that a voluntary composition with the creditors can be arranged).

2.8   Procedure following the making of the bankruptcy order

2.8.1   The official receiver becomes receiver and manager of the estate

Unless a trustee in bankruptcy is appointed at the time the bankruptcy order is made, the official receiver will become the receiver and manager of the bankrupt's estate on the making of the order, pending the appointment of a trustee in bankruptcy.

If the official receiver does become the receiver and manager of the estate, he has all the powers of a receiver and manager appointed by the High Court and can sell goods which will perish or diminish in value as well as taking any steps necessary to protect the bankrupt's assets. However, in performing his functions, he must not incur expenditure without the permission of the Secretary of State.

One danger faced by the official receiver in performing his functions is that he may take or dispose of an asset which does not belong to the debtor (such as property which is being purchased on hire-purchase). In these circumstances, no liability will arise provided the official receiver can show he had reasonable grounds for believing that the assets belonged to the debtor and that he was not negligent in acting as he did.

While the official receiver must investigate the conduct and affairs of the bankrupt (including investigating events which occurred prior to the making of the bankruptcy order), he need only report on his investigations if he thinks fit.

In certain circumstances, a trustee in bankruptcy is appointed at the time the bankruptcy order is made so that the official receiver does not become receiver and manager of the estate of the bankrupt. (The powers and duties of the trustee in bankruptcy are considered in paragraph 3 below.)

A trustee in bankruptcy will be appointed with effect from the date of the bankruptcy order in the following circumstances:

(a)   In the case of criminal bankruptcy proceedings or where the bankruptcy is a small bankruptcy (that is to say, where the circumstances justify a summary administration), the official receiver is appointed as trustee in bankruptcy on the making of the order.

(b)   If the petition was presented by the debtor personally and, having considered the report on the debtor's affairs prepared by a qualified insolvency practitioner, the court decides to make a bankruptcy order, the practitioner may be appointed to take office as trustee in bankruptcy with immediate effect.

(c)   If the petition was presented as a result of non-compliance with the terms of a voluntary scheme, the supervisor of the scheme may be appointed as trustee in bankruptcy on the making of the bankruptcy order.

2.8.2   Statement of affairs by the bankrupt

Having been adjudicated bankrupt, the bankrupt must, unless the official receiver dispenses with the requirement, prepare a statement of his affairs within 21 days (although this time-limit may be extended by the official receiver). Failure to do so will be contempt of court.

When the debtor presents his own petition he must prepare a statement of affairs which is lodged with the petition.

A statement of affairs must give details of the creditors and the debts they are owed as well as particulars of the bankrupt's assets and any other matter specified in delegated legislation.

2.8.3   Public examination of the bankrupt

At any time after the order is made and before the bankrupt is discharged, the official receiver can apply for an order that the bankrupt be required to attend a public examination of his affairs. (The official receiver must make such an application if he is required to do so by at least one-half (by value) of the creditors.)

If the order is made, the bankrupt must attend to give details of his assets and affairs as well as explaining the reason for his bankruptcy. Failure to attend without good cause amounts to contempt of court.

The examination can be attended by the official receiver, the trustee in bankruptcy, the special manager (if there is one — see paragraph 2.8.4 below), the DPP (in cases of criminal bankruptcy) and any creditor who has proved his debt.

2.8.4   Appointment of a special manager

Once the debtor has been adjudicated bankrupt, the official receiver or trustee in bankruptcy can apply to the court for the appointment of a special manager to manage the bankrupt's estate, property or business if the nature of the estate, property or business justifies it. He will be given such powers as the court may prescribe.

2.8.5   Appointment of a committee of creditors

Following the making of the bankruptcy order, a committee of creditors can be appointed by the creditors (unless the official receiver has been appointed as trustee in bankruptcy in which case the Secretary of State performs the function of the committee).

3   THE TRUSTEE IN BANKRUPTCY

3.1   Introduction

The Insolvency Act 1986 provides that the administration of a bankrupt estate should be carried out by a trustee in bankruptcy and in this paragraph we will consider his appointment, functions, duties, powers, liabilities and removal.

3.2   Appointment

The procedure for appointing a trustee in bankruptcy and the date on which his appointment takes effect differ depending on who makes the appointment.

(a)   *Creditors*. If the official receiver is acting as receiver and manager of the bankrupt's estate, he has 12 weeks from the making of the order to decide whether to call a meeting of the creditors for the purpose of appointing a trustee. If he decides to call such a meeting he must notify the creditors within the 12-week period. He *must* call such a meeting if one-quarter (by value) of the creditors demand it and if he decides not to call a meeting, one-quarter (by value) of the creditors can override his decision. If no meeting is to be called the official receiver must notify the court and all the creditors of whom he is aware or who are identified in the statement of affairs prepared by the bankrupt, of his decision. Provided the creditors do not object to no meeting being called, on notifying the court that no meeting will be held, the official receiver automatically becomes the trustee. If a meeting is held and someone other than the official receiver accepts the appointment, the appointment takes effect from the date indicated in the certificate of appointment (which is the statement confirming the appointment).

(b)   *The court*. Where the bankruptcy is dealt with by the summary administration procedure, the court can appoint someone other than the official receiver to act as trustee. If the order is based on the debtor's own petition, the insolvency practitioner who is appointed to report on the debtor's affairs can be appointed as the trustee. Where the order follows the debtor's failure to comply with a voluntary scheme, the supervisor of the scheme may be appointed on the making of the order. Any appointment made by the court takes effect from the date specified by the court when the order is made.

(c)   *The Secretary of State* has power to appoint the trustee if the creditors fail to make an appointment at their meeting. The official receiver can apply at any time to the Secretary of State to be replaced by an insolvency practitioner. Any appointment by the Secretary of State takes effect at the time specified in the certificate of appointment.

3.3   Functions of the trustee

The function of the trustee is to get in, realise and distribute the bankrupt's estate in accordance with the provisions of the Act. In carrying out that function and in the management of the bankrupt's estate the trustee is entitled to use his own discretion.

3.4 Duties of the trustee

There are a variety of duties imposed by the Act on the trustee, these include:

(a) taking possession of books, papers and other records relating to the affairs of the bankrupt;

(b) notifying the committee of creditors of disposals of assets;

(c) convening meetings of creditors if required to do so by one-tenth by value of the creditors;

(d) keeping, producing and auditing his books, records and accounts;

(e) calling a final meeting once the administration is complete at which a report of the administration is given.

3.5 Powers of the trustee

The Act gives the trustee wide powers which he may exercise in the course of administering the bankrupt's affairs. He may:

(a) Sell any part of the property for the time being comprised in the bankrupt's estate, including the goodwill and book debts of any business.

(b) Give receipts for any money received by him.

(c) Prove, rank, claim and draw a dividend in respect of such debts *due* to the bankrupt as are comprised in the bankrupt's estate.

(d) Exercise in relation to any property comprised in the bankrupt's estate any powers which the Act vests in him as trustee.

(e) Exercise all the powers of a receiver appointed by the High Court to enable him to collect or retain the bankrupt's estate.

(f) Exercise all the powers the bankrupt could exercise to transfer shares, stock or other property.

(g) Exercise extensive powers to require delivery, production or inspection of books, documents and records.

(h) Apply to the court for orders directing the bankrupt to do any act in connection with the administration of the estate.

(i) Hold property, make contracts, sue and be sued, employ agents, execute documents and do any act which may be necessary or expedient for the exercise of his powers.

There are, however, certain further powers which are only exercisable with the consent of the committee of creditors (see paragraph 2.8.5 above) or of the court. These include:

(a) Power to carry on the bankrupt's business with a view to a beneficial winding up.

(b) Power to mortgage or pledge assets with a view to raising money for the estate.

(c) Power to make any compromise or arrangement as may be expedient with the creditors of the estate.

(d) Power to require the bankrupt to do any acts in the management of carrying on or the bankrupt's business.

3.6 Power to disclaim onerous property

In addition to the powers listed in paragraph 3.5, the trustee may also disclaim onerous property such as unprofitable contracts, unsaleable property or property which may give rise to a liability to pay money or perform onerous acts. Having disclaimed such property, all rights, liabilities and interests of the bankrupt in the property are determined and the trustee is discharged from any personal liability (but the rights and liabilities in the property of any other persons are not affected by the disclaimer except so far as is necessary for the purpose of releasing the bankrupt, the bankrupt's estate and the trustee from any liability).

3.7 Supervision of the trustee

(a) *By the committee of creditors.* We have already seen that certain powers of the trustee can only be exercised with the consent of the committee of creditors.

(b) *By the court.* All bankruptcies are under the general control of the court. Thus, the bankrupt, any of the creditors or any person who is dissatisfied with the acts or proposed acts of the trustee has the right to apply to the court which will make whatever order it thinks fit.

3.8 Liabilities of the trustee

If the trustee has misapplied, retained or become accountable for any money or property of the estate or has caused the bankrupt's estate to suffer loss as a result of misfeasance or breach of duty, the remedy may be sought by application to the court by the official receiver, any creditor, the Secretary of State or the bankrupt himself. However, if the trustee seizes or disposes of property that does not in fact belong to the bankrupt the trustee will not be liable provided he acted without negligence and with reasonable grounds for believing he was entitled to seize or dispose of that property.

3.9 Retirement, removal and release

3.9.1 Resignation
A trustee in bankruptcy may resign only if the resignation is accepted either by a creditors' meeting or by the court. Resignation must arise out of ill-health, retirement from practice, conflict of interest or other sufficient causes.

3.9.2 Removal
The appointees of creditors can be removed either by the court or by the creditors themselves at a general meeting summoned specially for the purpose. The Secretary of State or the court may remove their appointees from office at any time. Appointees of the Secretary of State or the court can only be removed by the creditors at a meeting called by the trustee (he *must* call such a meeting if required to do so by one-quarter, by value, of the creditors). However, the official receiver cannot be removed from office by the creditors in criminal bankruptcy or summary administration cases.

After the final meeting of creditors has been held the trustee must notify the court of the decisions of that meeting and having given notification he vacates his office.

3.9.3 Release

If a trustee in bankruptcy ceases to hold office, he will wish to be released from his duties and obligations. If the trustee is the official receiver who has been replaced by the appointee of creditors or of the Secretary of State his release takes effect from the time of giving notice of the replacement to the court. If the court orders the replacement, the court will specify the date from which the release takes effect. If the cessation of office is as a result of completing the administration, on notifying the Secretary of State of this fact, the Secretary of State will specify the release date. Where the trustee is a qualified insolvency practitioner who has been removed by a creditors' meeting, his release takes effect from his notifying the court of the removal. If the insolvency practitioner has completed the administration, the release is operative from the date he vacates office. In both these last two cases, the meeting may decide that the insolvency practitioner should not be released, in which case the release date is determined by the Secretary of State.

4 EFFECT OF THE BANKRUPTCY ORDER ON THE BANKRUPT PERSONALLY

If the court exercises its discretion to make a bankruptcy order against the debtor, he will become an undischarged bankrupt and will be deprived of the ownership of his property. The bankrupt must give up all his assets and papers to the official receiver or trustee in bankruptcy and he must assist in the protection and recovery of his property. A full inventory of his estate must be provided by the bankrupt who can be required to attend on the official receiver or at court for questioning on his affairs (see above, paragraph 2.8.3).

An undischarged bankrupt suffers certain disabilities, for example he cannot practise as a solicitor or barrister nor act as a director, nor be involved in the management, of a company. Furthermore, an undischarged bankrupt faces criminal liability if he commits one of the offences specified in the 1986 Act. We set out below some of the more important offences.

4.1 Offences relating to property dealings

(a) An offence is committed if a bankrupt makes, or causes to be made, or, within five years before the bankruptcy order, has made or caused to be made any gift or transfer of or charge on his property or has caused, or connived at the levying of execution upon his property.

(b) Concealing or removing property within two months before or at any time after a money judgment was unsatisfied is an offence.

(c) An offence is committed if an undischarged bankrupt fails to disclose his status when obtaining credit or entering into a hire-purchase or conditional sale agreement.

4.2 Failing to deliver up property

Unless the bankrupt can show he did not intend to defraud his creditors, he will be guilty of an offence if he fails to deliver up property which is in his possession or control to the official receiver or trustee in bankruptcy.

4.3 Other offences

There are a variety of offences arising out of the bankrupt's failure to make a full disclosure of his conduct, dealings, affairs or property. Furthermore, misleading creditors with a view to inducing them to enter into any agreement relating to his affairs or bankruptcy amounts to an offence.

5 ASSETS IN THE BANKRUPT'S ESTATE

5.1 Introduction

The trustee in bankruptcy is under an obligation to collect the bankrupt's assets and distribute them among the bankrupt's creditors. In this section, we consider which assets can be claimed by the trustee towards payment of the bankrupt's debts.

5.2 Avoidance of dispositions made after the presentation of the petition

Any disposition made by the bankrupt in the period between presentation of the petition and the date the estate of the bankrupt vests in the trustee in bankruptcy is void, unless the court gave prior consent (or subsequently ratifies) the disposition. (The date the estate of the bankrupt vests in the trustee is considered in paragraph 5.3 below.) As was explained in paragraph 2.2.1 above, transferees who acted in good faith, for value and without notice of the presentation of the petition are protected from having their disposition avoided but only if the transaction took place before the bankruptcy order was made. If the transaction took place after the date of the order, protection is only available if the court sanctions the transaction (even if the transferee acted in good faith, for value and without notice of the petition or order).

5.3 Vesting the assets in the trustee

Once the bankruptcy order is made, the undischarged bankrupt is deprived of the ownership of his property. However, while the trustee in bankruptcy is entitled to the bankrupt's assets from that date, the property does not actually vest in the trustee until his appointment takes effect (which will be the date specified in his certificate of appointment). In cases where the official receiver becomes trustee the property vests on the date he becomes trustee.

Once the property has vested in the trustee, he may take steps to avoid dispositions of property made by the bankrupt since presentation of the petition (unless the dispositions are protected — see paragraph 3.2 above). Furthermore, the trustee can claim property to which the bankrupt becomes entitled after the date of the order by serving notice in writing on the bankrupt within 42 days after acquisition or devolution comes to the trustee's notice. Once the time-limit has expired, the trustee will need to obtain a court order before being able to serve the notice. Having claimed the property the trustee's title relates back to the date the bankrupt became entitled to the asset. If the asset has been transferred to a third party, the trustee can still take the asset unless the transferee is a bona fide purchaser for value without notice of the bankruptcy order.

The property to which the trustee is entitled vests in him automatically without the need for any conveyance, assignment or transfer and the trustee takes the same title and subject to the same rights as the bankrupt. Thus, if the bankrupt entered into a contract which could have been rescinded against the bankrupt, the third party can rescind the contract against the trustee. 'Property' for these purposes is defined to include 'money, goods, things in action, land and every description of property wherever situated and also obligations and every description of interest, whether present or future or vested or contingent, arising out of, or incidental to, property'.

5.4 Property not available to the trustee

If the bankrupt enjoyed a purely personal right, such as the benefit of the Rent Act statutory tenancy, this is not available to the trustee. Neither are the following items available for distribution:

(a)   Property held by the bankrupt in trust for any other person.

(b)   The tools of his trade, as well as such wearing apparel and bedding as is necessary to satisfy the basic needs of the bankrupt and his family.

(c)   The personal earnings of the bankrupt to the extent that those earnings are not in excess of what is required to satisfy the reasonable domestic needs of the bankrupt and his family.

(d)   The benefit of the right to bring a personal action (such as damages for injury to credit) are not available (although the benefit of actions for damages for injury to the bankrupt's property are).

(e)   Property subject to a retention of title clause. (See Chapter 21 paragraph 7.7.)

5.5 Extension of trustee's title to bankrupt's property

The Act gives the trustee power to claim assets which are no longer in the possession or ownership of the bankrupt in the circumstances set out below.

5.5.1 Transactions defrauding creditors (sections 423 to 425)

Section 423 of the Insolvency Act 1986 can be used to give relief in respect of transactions defrauding creditors. To be within the scope of s. 423 a transaction must be a transaction at an undervalue entered into between one person and another, and be accompanied by the requisite intent, namely that it is done for the purpose of putting assets beyond the reach of a person who is making, or may at some time make, a claim against the relevant person, or of otherwise prejudicing the interests of such a person in relation to the claim which he is making or may make.

The transaction which is the subject of an action under s. 423 can have taken place at any time; there is no time-limit.

The application can be made by any person who is or is capable of being prejudiced. However, where a bankruptcy order has been made the official receiver or the trustee in bankruptcy should apply (the persons prejudiced can, in this case, only apply with leave of the court). The section goes on to provide specifically that all applications under its provisions are to be treated as made on behalf of every person who is (or is capable of being) prejudiced by the transaction.

To be actionable, the transaction must have been 'at an undervalue', which term is defined as consisting of:

(a)   A gift or other transaction whereby no consideration will be received by the relevant person.

(b)   A transaction entered into by the relevant person in consideration of marriage.

(c)   A transaction with another person for a consideration the value of which in money or money's worth, is significantly less than the value, in money or money's worth, of the consideration provided by the relevant person.

If the other party to the transaction provides consideration of some description, the court will decide whether that consideration is 'significantly' less than the consideration provided by the relevant person.

If the court is satisfied that an objection to the transaction has been entered into, it may make such orders as it thinks fit:

(a)   To restore the position to what it would have been if the transaction had not been entered into.

(b)   For protecting the interests of the persons on whose behalf the application is treated as having been made.

The powers which the court can exercise include restoring property, following the proceeds of a sale and ordering payment by those who have benefited. However, persons who have acquired an interest in property or received a benefit will not be prejudiced by the order of the court provided they acted in good faith, for value and without notice of the relevant circumstances.

5.5.2   Undervalue transactions

If a person who is subsequently made bankrupt has transferred property to, for example, a member of his family or to trustees to hold for the benefit of his family with a view to putting assets beyond the reach of his creditors the transaction may be voidable under s. 339 of the Insolvency Act 1986.

If the transaction is at an undervalue (which has the same meaning as under s. 423 referred to in paragraph 5.5.1 above) and is with a person who is not an associate of the transferor, it is voidable at the instance of the trustee in bankruptcy (or administrator where a voluntary arrangement has been made) if the transaction took place within the five years ending with the day the bankruptcy petition which ultimately led to the individual being adjudged bankrupt was presented (unless the debtor was solvent at the time of, and despite entering into, the transaction). However, if the individual entered into the transaction at an undervalue within two years of the presentation of the relevant bankruptcy petition, the transaction is voidable irrespective of whether the debtor was insolvent at the time of, or as a result of, the transaction.

In circumstances where the transferee is an 'associate' of the transferor, transactions entered into during the period of five years preceding the presentation of the petition are presumed, unless it can be *proved* to the contrary, to have taken place at a time when the transferor was insolvent. There is therefore a rebuttable presumption of insolvency in these circumstances. 'Associate' is defined as the bankrupt's spouse or former or reputed spouse, and, in relation to any of them or the bankrupt, a brother, sister, uncle, aunt, nephew, niece, lineal ancestor or lineal descendant (including relatives of the half-blood and stepchildren and adopted children; illegitimate children count as legitimate children). Equally a company controlled by the bankrupt or any associate(s), as defined, is an associate; control includes cases where the board of a company, or of any company which controls it, acts customarily in accordance with a person's instructions and includes cases where a person can exercise one-third of the voting power of the company or of any other company which controls it.

5.5.3 Voidable preferences

A debtor who is in financial difficulties may not only make an undervalue transaction (as described in paragraph 5.5.2 above) but he may also be tempted to give a 'voidable preference' (Insolvency Act 1986, s.340).

A 'voidable preference' consists of the debtor doing or suffering anything to be done at a time when he is insolvent which 'has the effect of putting [the person who benefits from the preference] into a position which, in the event of the [debtor's] bankruptcy, will be better than the position he would have been in if that thing had not been done'. Thus, a debtor discharging one of his unsecured, ordinary creditor's debts in full at a time when his assets are insufficient to discharge *all* his debts in full may have given a voidable preference.

If the trustee in bankruptcy considers that a voidable preference has been made, he may apply to the court to remedy the preference. However, an order can only be made where it can be proved that the debtor was 'influenced in deciding to give it by a desire' to improve the position of the creditor. Under these provisions the intention to prefer the particular creditor need not be the *dominant* intention; it can merely be an influential one. The term 'desire' is not explained in the Act but discharging a debt owed to a creditor who is applying pressure (for example, threatening to sue the debtor if the liability is not discharged) will probably not amount to a voidable preference since the debtor can hardly be said to desire (in the sense of 'wish') to produce the eventual result of improving the creditor's position.

In cases where the preference is given by an individual to his 'associate' (see paragraph 5.5.2 above), there is a *presumption* that the debtor was influenced by the desire which would make the preference voidable, unless the contrary is proved.

A preference is voidable if it takes place within the two years ending with the presentation of the bankruptcy petition, if the person preferred is an associate, but in other cases the preference is only actionable if it took place in the six months preceding the presentation of the petition.

If the court considers that the debtor has preferred one or more of his creditors, it has a wide range of powers to remedy the preference. These include power:

(a)   To require any property to be transferred to the trustee.

(b)   To require any person who has benefited from the preference to pay such sums as the court directs.

(c)   To trace the transferred property into sale proceeds.

(d)   To reimpose obligations discharged by the preference.

While these remedies may affect the other party to the preference they may also affect third parties. In that case, the third party will be protected if either he acquired property or received a benefit from a party to the preference in good faith for value without notice of the circumstances.

5.5.4   Execution and distress

Judgment creditors are not obliged to return property provided the execution was completed before the making of the bankruptcy order.

If the sheriff or bailiff has levied execution on goods, on being informed of the bankruptcy order, he must hold the goods (or their sale proceeds, if appropriate) for the trustee in bankruptcy.

Where execution is for an amount in excess of £500 (this limit may be increased from time to time), those proceeds must be held by the sheriff or bailiff for 14 days. If during that period he is notified of a petition he must not hand the proceeds to the judgment creditor.

So far as the debtor's liability for unpaid rent is concerned, the landlord may levy distress for rent due for up to six months before the making of the bankruptcy order. This right can still be exercised even after the estate has vested in the trustee in bankruptcy. However, this right is subject to certain limitations. Thus, the right cannot be exercised if, as a result, the landlord is paid in priority to the preferential creditors (see paragraph 6.3 below).

5.5.5   Family homes

The Insolvency Act contains provisions designed to protect the family home of the bankrupt for the benefit of his family.

If the family home is owned in the sole name of the bankrupt the 1986 Act charges the right of occupation of the spouse of the bankrupt on the interest of the trustee in bankruptcy in the matrimonial home. If an application is made to realise the bankrupt's interest in the house the court will consider certain factors when deciding whether to grant an application for sale of the house. These factors include the creditors' interests, the needs and resources of the spouse, the needs of the children, whether the spouse's conduct contributed to the bankruptcy and all other relevant circumstances. (If the matrimonial home is owned in joint names by the bankrupt and his spouse, the discretionary factors listed above will be taken into account when the trustee applies under s.30 of the Law of Property Act 1925 to realise the bankrupt's interest.) If the application is made after one year has elapsed since the bankrupt's property vested in the trustee in bankruptcy, the interests of the creditors will be paramount.

If the bankrupt's minor children lived in the home at the time of presenting the petition and when the bankruptcy order was made, the bankrupt cannot be evicted without a court order. The court will consider the creditors' interests, the bankrupt's financial resources, the needs of the children and all the circumstances when deciding whether to make the eviction order. If the application is made after one year has elapsed since the bankrupt's estate vested in his trustee the interests of the creditors will outweigh all other considerations, unless the circumstances are exceptional.

6 DISTRIBUTION OF THE BANKRUPT'S ASSETS

6.1 Proof of claims

Once the assets of the bankrupt have been collected, the trustee will distribute them among those entitled in accordance with the rules on priority of payment. A creditor can only participate in the distribution if the debt owed is a provable debt. Section 322 provides that delegated legislation is to specify the manner in which debts are to be proved; such legislation will lay down the trustee's powers to accept or reject proofs. Where the value of any debt is uncertain, the trustee has the responsibility for valuing it (subject to appeal to the court) and the proof will then be admitted at his (or the court's) valuation.

6.2 Distribution procedure

Having realised as much of the bankrupt's assets as possible without needlessly protracting the administration of the estate, the trustee must notify the creditors that he intends to declare a final dividend (or that no dividend will be declared). The notice must also state a final date for the proving of claims (although the court has power, on application by any person, to postpone this date). Subject to any postponement, any creditor who fails to prove by the final date may be ignored in the final dividend.

Before calculating the dividend, the trustee must have taken into account all the expenses of the administration, such as the cost of calling and holding the final meeting of creditors (at which the trustee delivers his report of the administration and the creditors decide whether to grant the trustee his release; this meeting is, however, only held when the trustee is not the official receiver).

Once the expenses have been taken into ,account, the dividend is paid in accordance with the order of priority for payment of debts.

6.3 Order of priority for payment of debts

The distribution of the bankrupt's assets must be made strictly in accordance with the statutory order for payment of debts which is as follows:

(a) Secured creditors, who take the mortgaged or charged property in priority to all other claims. However, if the security is insufficient to meet the debt, as far as the excess is concerned, the secured creditor claims as an ordinary creditor.

(b) The administration costs of the bankruptcy paid to the official receiver, the trustee in bankruptcy and others, including professional advisers who have given assistance.

(c) Certain sums paid to masters by their apprentices.

(d) The preferential debts which are the same as those relevant on a company liquidation. These debts are calculated by reference to the 'relevant date', which, generally, is the date the bankruptcy order is made (unless an interim receiver is appointed following the presentation of the petition in which case the date is that on which the receiver is first appointed), and include:

(i)   Sums due from the debtor in respect of deductions of PAYE from his employees' wages in the 12 months prior to the relevant date.

(ii)   VAT claims up to six months before the relevant date.

(iii) National insurance contributions for 12 months prior to the relevant date (for Class 1 or 2 social security contributions) or one year's assessment of Class 4 contributions before 5 April prior to the relevant date.

(iv)   Employees' arrears of wages or salary (including time or piece work and commission) for four months prior to the relevant date subject to an overall financial limit prescribed by delegated legislation (currently £800). These sums include sick pay, protective awards, and payments for time off work, such as on trade union work.

(v)   Accrued holiday remuneration.

(e)   The ordinary and unsecured creditors.

(f)   Statutory interest which will be paid if a surplus remains after all previous claims have been paid. This interest is paid from the date of the order to the date of payment and the rate is the greater of the rate provided for in s.17 of the Judgments Act 1938 and the rate the bankrupt would have had to pay on the debt if he had not been made bankrupt.

(g)   The postponed creditors such as the spouse of the bankrupt who has a provable debt as a result of a loan to the bankrupt spouse.

(h)   The bankrupt receives any surplus.

As with companies in liquidation, each class of creditor must be paid in full before the next class receives anything. If the assets are insufficient to meet the debts owed to the creditors of the class, they are paid rateably according to value. If there are mutual debts between the bankrupt and one of his creditors, there is a statutory set-off so that only the balance owed to the creditor will be proved and (subject to the availability of assets) paid to the creditor.

7 DURATION OF THE BANKRUPTCY AND DISCHARGE OF THE BANKRUPT

7.1 Duration of the Bankruptcy

In view of the disqualifications and disadvantages suffered by an undischarged bankrupt (such as the criminal liability which can arise if an undischarged bankrupt fails to reveal his status when seeking credit), the duration of a bankruptcy will be of some importance to the individual involved. The bankruptcy commences with the day on which the order adjudicating him to be bankrupt is made and the bankruptcy ends once the bankrupt obtains his discharge.

7.2 Discharge of the bankrupt

The Insolvency Act 1986, in relation to the majority of bankruptcies, provides for a bankrupt to be automatically discharged once the period of time specified by the Act has elapsed. However, as will be seen, the Act contains provisions which will prevent the 'automatic' discharge being available if the circumstances justify it.

An individual's bankruptcy will be discharged:

(a) In the case of summary administrations, two years after the bankruptcy order is made.

(b) In the case of criminal bankruptcies, the court's consent is required and an application for such an order of the court cannot be made until five years have elapsed since the adjudication of bankruptcy. When considering the application, the court has power to allow, refuse, suspend and/or place conditions on the discharge.

(c) In the case of individuals who have suffered repeated bankruptcies, the order of the court is required. If the individual was an undischarged bankrupt within the 15 years prior to the date the bankruptcy order currently in force was made, the bankrupt has to wait five years after the commencement of the current bankruptcy before applying for a discharge. When considering the application, the court has the same discretion as in the case of criminal bankruptcies. If the individual was an undischarged bankrupt more than 15 years before the date the current bankruptcy order was made, the procedure is set out in (d) below.

(d) In all other cases, the bankruptcy is automatically discharged once three years have elapsed from the making of the bankruptcy order. However, the discharge will not be automatic if the official receiver is able to convince the court that there is or has been a failure by the bankrupt to 'comply with any of his obligations under' Part IX of the 1986 Act (which contains all the bankruptcy provisions). If the court is satisfied that it should exercise its discretion, it can order that time shall stop running in respect of this three-year period for the period specified in the order or until any condition it imposes is fulfilled.

7.3 Effect of discharge

Once the bankrupt has been discharged, he is normally freed from the disqualifications suffered by undischarged bankrupts and from liability to meet his bankruptcy debts. However, the 1986 Act provides that certain liabilities and obligations can survive the discharge. These include the following.

(a) Creditors may still prove their debts and the bankrupt will still be under an obligation to meet non-provable debts.

(b) Creditors who have retained security for their debts can still realise that security.

(c) The bankrupt will remain liable for provable debts where the liability is based on fraud or fraudulent breach of trust or where the liability is for personal injuries caused by negligence, nuisance, breach of contract or breach of statutory or any other duty.

8   VOLUNTARY ARRANGEMENTS

8.1   Introduction

While formal bankruptcy may be the appropriate method of dealing with many debtors who find themselves in financial difficulties, there will be certain cases where the debtor involved may be able to come to terms with his creditors without involving the full rigour of the bankruptcy procedure. Although deeds of arrangement entered into under the Deeds of Arrangement Act 1914 were intended to satisfy this particular need, that procedure is not entirely satisfactory since only the creditors who agree to the deed of arrangement are bound by its terms. The procedure under the 1914 Act has been little used and is not considered further in this book. Therefore, the Insolvency Act 1986 has introduced a new alternative method by which debtors can come to binding arrangements with their creditors.

8.2   Interim order

If a debtor in financial difficulties wishes to propose a composition or scheme of arrangement to his creditors, he may apply to the court, even if a petition for his bankruptcy has already been presented, for an interim order to be made. However, if a bankruptcy petition which the debtor himself presented is pending, no application for an interim order can be made by the debtor if the court has already appointed a qualified insolvency practitioner to report on the debtor's affairs (although the court may, of its own volition, make the order). The application can also be made if the debtor wishes to appoint a nominee to act as trustee or otherwise supervise the implementation of the scheme. However, in this case the court will only entertain the application if the nominee is a qualified insolvency practitioner who is willing to act on the debtor's proposals. Once the application for the interim order has been made, the court has power to stay any action, execution or other legal process against the debtor and his estate.

The purpose of the interim order is to protect the debtor's property and the court will make the order if it will assist the consideration and implementation of the debtor's proposals. However, no order can be made unless the court is satisfied first that the debtor genuinely intends to make a proposal for a composition with his creditors and secondly that the debtor could have petitioned for his own bankruptcy (or was an undischarged bankrupt, as appropriate). Furthermore, no order will be made if the debtor has made an application for an interim order within the 12 months preceding the present application.

Once the interim order is made, no bankruptcy petition can be presented against the debtor and no other proceedings, execution or legal process can, without the leave of the court, be commenced or prosecuted against the debtor or his assets.

The interim order is relatively short-lived since it will cease to have effect at the end of the period of 14 days beginning with the day after the order was made, although the court has power to extend the period.

While the voluntary arrangement may be used as a way of avoiding bankruptcy, it can also be used where a bankruptcy order has already been made, in which case the application is made by the trustee in bankruptcy or official receiver.

8.3 Procedure following the making of the interim order

After the order has been made (and before it ceases to have effect), the debtor must provide the nominee (that is to say, the proposed 'trustee' of the arrangement) with a statement giving details of the proposed composition or scheme. He must also give a statement of his affairs, which will give details of his assets and liabilities. Failure to do so may result in the interim order being discharged.

The purpose of providing this information to the nominee is to enable him to consider the merits of the debtor's proposals and to enable him to prepare a report to the court stating whether the proposals should be put to a meeting of the debtor's creditors. If the nominee cannot reach a conclusion before the expiry of the period during which the interim order has effect, that period can be extended by the court.

If, having considered the debtor's proposals and statement of affairs, the nominee considers a meeting of creditors should be held, the report to the court will state the date, time and place for the meeting. In this case, the court has power to extend the period of effectiveness of the interim order to enable the creditors to meet and consider the proposals before the order expires.

If the nominee decides that a meeting should not be called and the court agrees, the interim order may be discharged.

Should the nominee fail to deliver the report to the court before the interim order expires, the debtor can apply to the court to have the order renewed or extended and the debtor may also apply to have the nominee replaced.

8.4 Consideration of the debtor's proposals

If the nominee has submitted a report to the court recommending that a creditor's meeting be called to consider the debtor's proposals, subject to any directions made by the court, the nominee gives notice of the meeting (at the date, time and place specified in his report to the court) to all creditors of whom he is aware. The term 'creditors' in relation to an undischarged bankrupt includes all persons who are creditors under the original bankruptcy as well as persons who would be creditors if the bankruptcy had commenced on the day the notice was given.

At the meeting the proposals will be considered and the proposals may be approved as proposed or with any changes thought appropriate. However, any changes must be approved by the debtor and no proposal or change can be accepted which will affect the existing rights of any secured creditor to enforce his security or of any preferential creditor to enjoy the benefit of prior payment unless the creditor in question agrees. The decision of the meeting must be reported to the court and if the decision is that the proposals are rejected, the interim order may be discharged.

8.5 Effect of accepting the proposal

Once the proposal is accepted by the creditors (whether in its original form or with changes), the composition or scheme takes effect as if the debtor had made it at the meeting. Once approved, all persons who had notice of the meeting and who were entitled to vote at the meeting (irrespective of whether they did so vote) are bound by the composition or scheme as if they were parties to it.

In cases where the debtor is an undischarged bankrupt the court may:

(a)   Annul the original bankruptcy order (but such a step cannot be taken until after the period during which challenges may be made — see paragraph 8.6 below — has expired); and/or

(b)   Give whatever directions it considers appropriate for the conduct of the bankruptcy and the administration of the bankrupt's estate to facilitate the implementation of the composition or scheme.

Subject to any challenges within the 28-day period referred to in paragraph 8.6 below, once the proposal has been accepted, any interim order in force ceases to have effect and any bankruptcy petition which was stayed by the interim order is deemed to have been dismissed (subject to a court order to the contrary).

8.6   Challenging the decision of the creditors' meeting

Once the creditors' meeting has reported its decision to the court, at any time during the 28 days commencing with the day the report is made to the court, that decision may be challenged by:

(a)   The debtor.
(b)   Any person who was entitled to vote at the meeting.
(c)   The nominee (or his replacement).

The grounds of challenge are limited to the following:

(a)   That the composition or scheme accepted by the meeting unfairly prejudices the interests of a creditor; and/or
(b)   That there was a material irregularity at, or in relation to, the meeting.

If the court confirms the challenge, the approval of the meeting may be revoked or suspended. Alternatively, the court may order a further meeting to be held to consider any revised proposal or (if the challenge is based on 'material irregularity' in relation to the meeting) order that the meeting be held again to reconsider the proposal.

Having ordered a further meeting to be held, the court can extend or renew the interim order. However, if the court is satisfied that no revised proposal will be submitted by the debtor, the order to hold a further meeting will be revoked and the approval given at the original meeting will be revoked or suspended.

8.7   Supervision of the composition or scheme

Once approved, the scheme or composition will be supervised by the nominee (or his replacement). In case of need, the supervisor can seek directions from the court on particular matters arising in respect of the composition or scheme. The court also has power to add to or replace existing supervisors as well as power to give directions to the supervisor or make any other order it thinks appropriate.

Finally, an application can be made to the court by the debtor, any creditor or any other person dissatisfied with the activities of the supervisor to confirm, reverse, or modify any act or decision of the supervisor.

Index